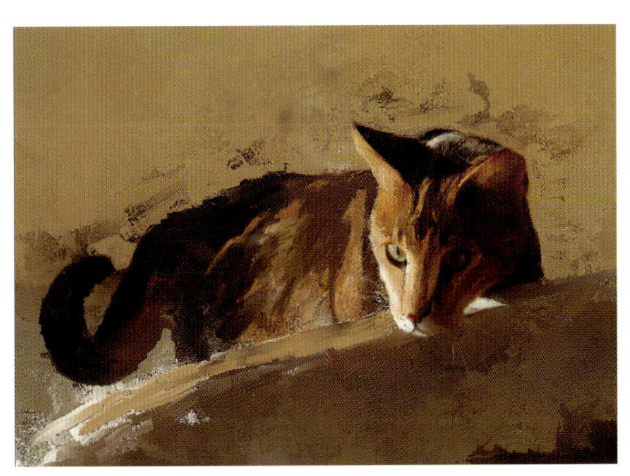

KAREN SPERLING'S PAINTING FOR PHOTOGRAPHERS

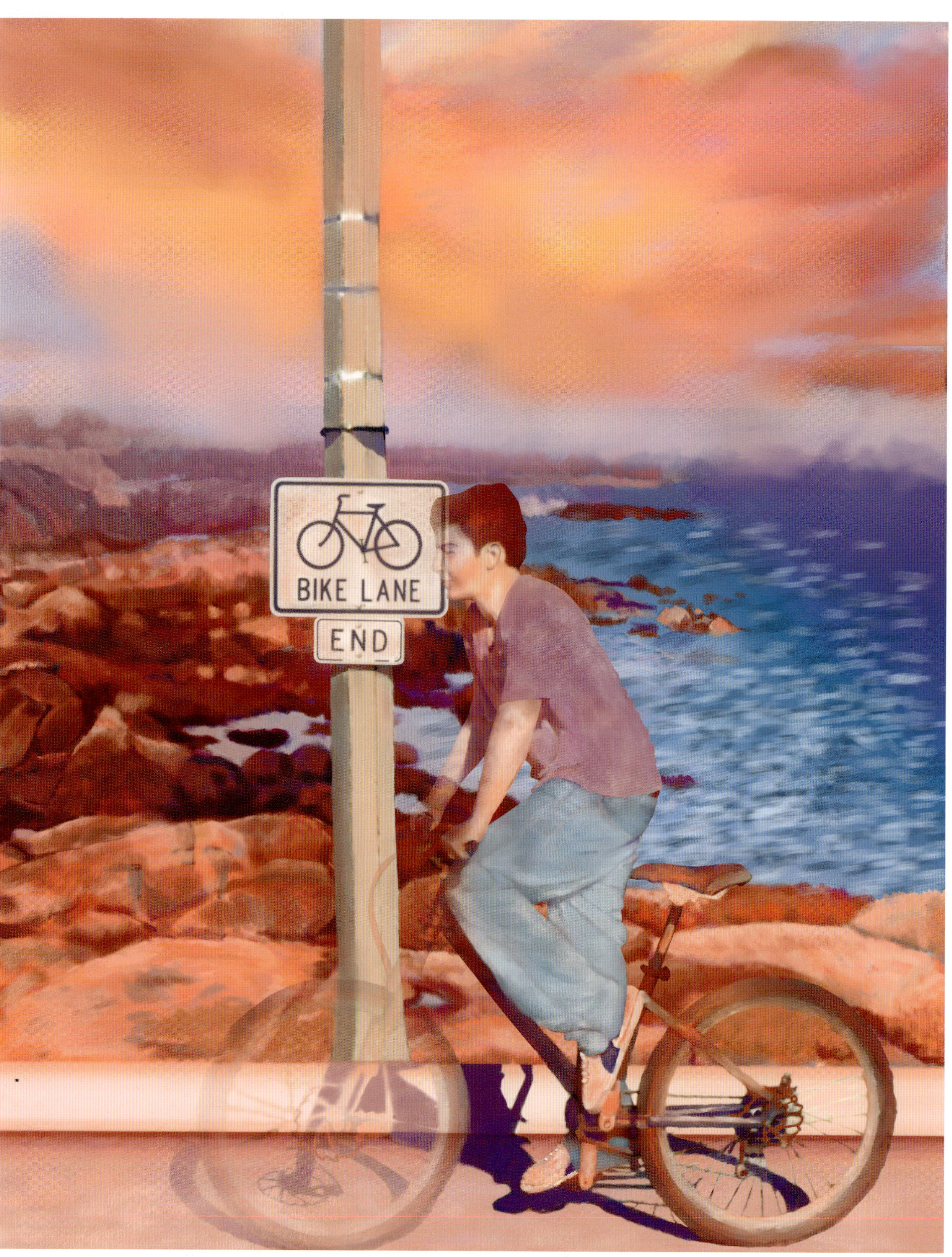
BIKE LANE
END

Karen Sperling's
Painting for Photographers

Steps and Art Lessons for Painting Photos in Corel Painter and Adobe Photoshop

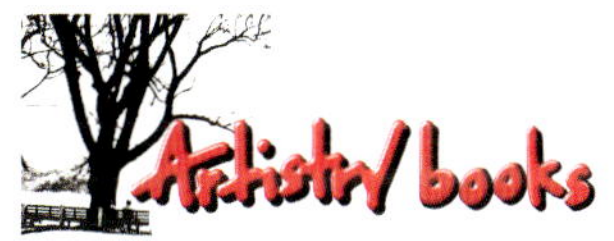

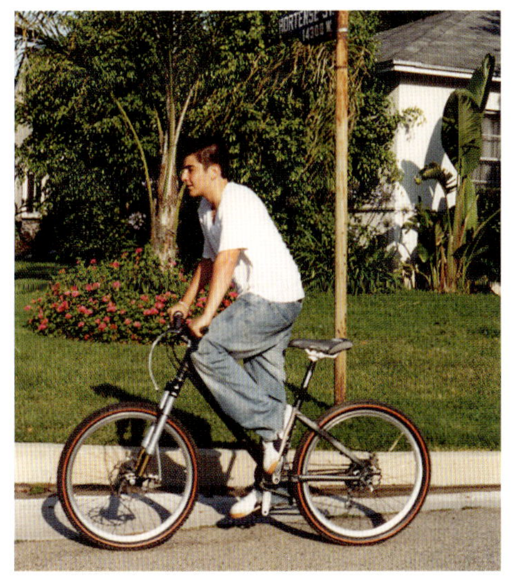

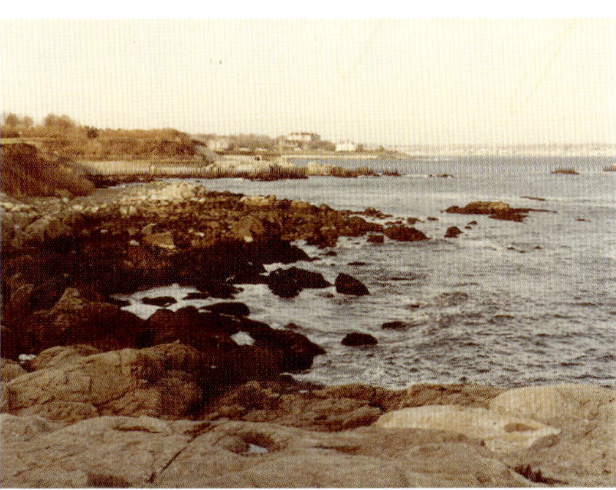

Bike Lane Ends

Painting and photos by Karen Sperling, covered in the December 2005 issue of Artistry Tips and Tricks http://www.artistrymag.com.

ACKNOWLEDGEMENTS
Thanks to all the readers and students of the Artistry tutorials and Artistry Painting for Photographers Retreats for their faith and support. *Painting for Photographers* is dedicated to them.
Special thanks to Rob McDonald at Corel, Allan Chasanoff, Mike Frey, Rhonda Rosburg and Stanley Zabar for their kind support.
Thanks to Steve Szoczei and Kelly O'Dwyer-Manuel at Corel; Vishal Khandpur and Bryan O'Neil Hughes at Adobe; and Douglas Little at Wacom for all their help.
Thanks to Mark Simonson, who designed the Mostra typeface; to Fujifilm for the use of the FinePix S3 Pro digital SLR; and to Alkit for the use of the Nikon 24-120mm lens.
Thanks to the photographers who contributed their photos:
Evan Agostini, page 72;
Kirk Allemand, page 32;
Katherine Beach, page 30;
Alfred Burgess, pages 34, 38;
Hernan Campero, page 24;
Phillip Stewart Charis, page 42;
David Derex, pages 36, 54;
Terri Gold, page 24;
Nancy Goodman, page 39;
Jackie Hicks, page 58;
Kevin Kubota, page 28;
Michelle Lamberth, page 68;
Anita Morrison, page 37;
Raymond Moy, M.D., pages 23, 26;
Barbara Okun, page 27;
Ken Partington, page 86;
Ellen Roije-Pauwels, page 108;
Rhonda Rosburg, page 26;
Susan Sexton, page 107;
Karen Sperling, pages 5, 6, 7, 10, 11,12, 13, 15, 17, 24, 25, 28, 29, 30, 34, 35, 36, 38, 50, 64, 81, 82, 86, 90, 94, 98, 102, 112, 114, 116, 118, 119, 120, 121, 122, 123, 124;
Renata Spiazzi, page 107;
Frank Stewart, page 32;
Terrie Strick, pages 17, 31;
Scott Stulberg, pages 9, 46;
Felicia Tausig, page 60;
Mary Wynn-Ball, page 41;
Zarek, page 76.

All paintings are by Karen Sperling.

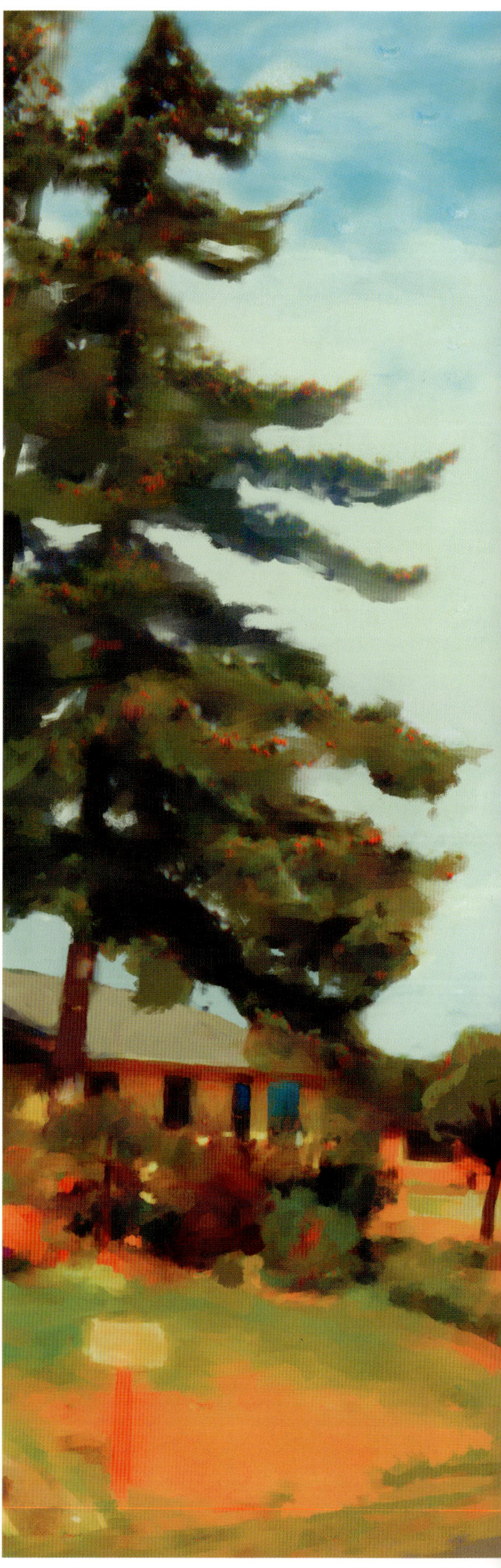

First published in 2009 by
Artistry Books
PO Box 57516
Sherman Oaks, CA 91413
http://www.artistrymag.com

Sperling, Karen
Karen Sperling's Painting for Photographers: Steps and art lessons for painting photos in Corel Painter and Adobe Photoshop
ISBN-10 0-9818163-0-4
ISBN-13 978-0-9818163-0-2
I. Art. 2. Photography.

Author, Designer, Editor and Illustrator: Karen Sperling

First Printing, 2009

Printed in Korea by asianprinting.com

CONTENTS

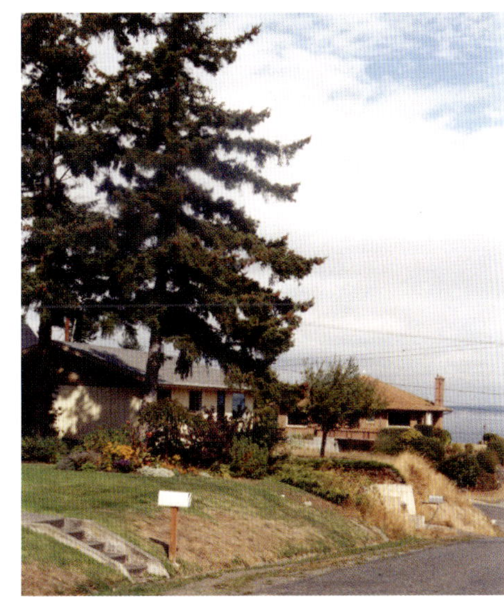

Landscape Painting
Painting by Karen Sperling from her photo, featured in the April 2007 issue of Artistry Tips and Tricks http://www.artistrymag.com/.

INTRODUCTION

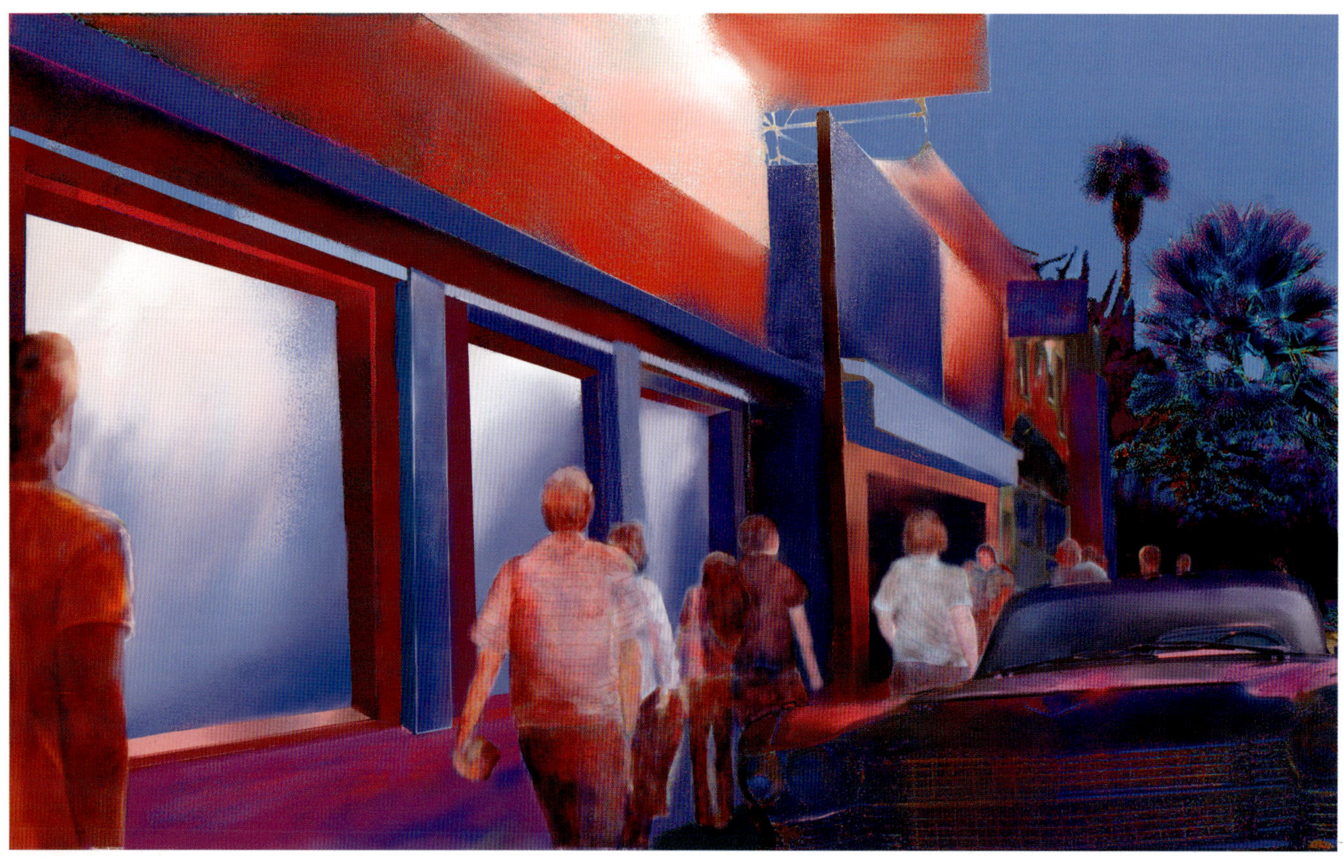

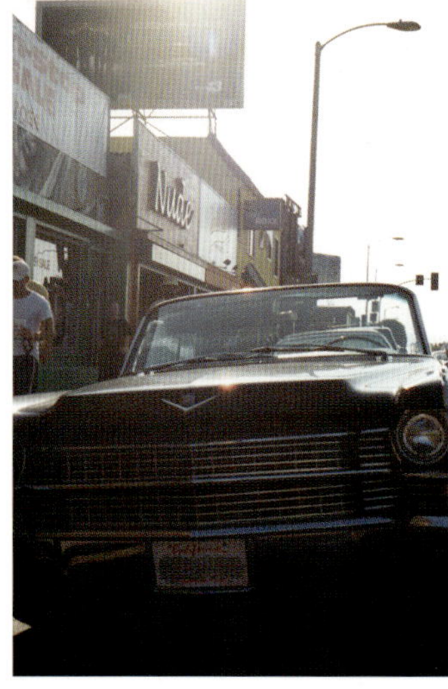

I was listening in the car to an audio CD of the book, ***Success Through a Positive Mental Attitude***, by Napoleon Hill and W. Clement Stone, when an amazing thing happened.

I heard these words: "If you think you can do something, you probably can."

Incredible! I have said that in my Artistry Painting for Photographers Retreats to encourage photographers who think they can paint to go for it!

And there were my words, coming from Napoleon Hill, who got the skinny on success from Andrew Carnegie.

So I guess you can believe me when I tell you that if you think you can paint photos, you probably can!

Of course, I already knew my words were true because I've done it.

I've gone from never finishing paintings to exhibiting my art in a gallery in New York's prestigious Chelsea section!

All because I figured I could.

So here it is: If you think you can create paintings from your photos, you probably can!

Many photographers believe that either you're an artist, or you're not.

This book dispels that myth.

If you're a photographer, you have a certain visual sense that led to your interest in photography.

Add to that the theories that artists learn in art school, and the knowledge of how to use Corel Painter and Adobe Photoshop, and voilá—you'll be painting your photos sooner than you can say Toulouse-Lautrec!

Sort of.

There is one other ingredient for turning your photos into paintings using Corel Painter and Adobe Photoshop: Practice.

And the practice isn't what you think.

You won't be trying to get better at drawing a straight line.

The practice will be in terms of making decisions about what to paint like choosing what to keep from the photo and what to leave out. These decisions are based on the art concepts that you will learn in this book.

I know that you can paint your photos in Painter and Photoshop, even if you've never painted before, because I see the photographers in my Artistry Painting for Photographers Retreats painting after three days in my class.

And in *Painting for Photographers*, you'll find information similar to that offered during my Artistry Retreats.

I also know the tips and techniques in this book work because I use them for my own art.

Though I painted as a child, and my mother was an artist, my main career has always been as a journalist, which is how I got to write the first several Painter manuals, three Painter books before this one and two Painter newsletters.

It's only in recent years that I've been painting, and if I can do it, you can do it! On these pages you see my first painting from photos in Painter—I think they make a very good illustration for encouraging you to try to paint your photos!

A word about this book's structure…

The book is set up to first give you an introduction to art concepts that you need to know to paint photos.

Aimed at photographers who didn't take art classes, these art lessons will help you to know what you want to paint.

Painting is 90% thought, 10% execution. Knowing what you're trying to do is more important than knowing how to do it.

Of course, computer know-how does play a part, and that's what's covered next, information about Corel Painter, Adobe Photoshop and Wacom.

Next, you'll find step-by-step instructions for painting portraits, landscapes and pets, in various styles, including oils, watercolors and pastels.

The book's final section covers painting on the canvas after the artwork is printed, including how to apply a first coat, and painting with acrylics and oils.

Keep in mind as you paint that you will get better the more you do it.

Also remember that everything you paint is an interim step and the more you work on the painting the better it will get.

As you paint, refer to the art lessons section of *Painting for Photographers*, and use the art concepts to guide you to help you figure out what to paint.

Just remember: If you think you can turn your photos into paintings, you probably can!

Tribute

The painting on the opposite page was created on September 11, 2001 with a red, white and blue color scheme in honor of those who lost their lives in the 9/11 World Trade Center tragedy. Photos and painting by Karen Sperling, featured in the Painting for Photographers tutorials http://www.artistrymag.com/.

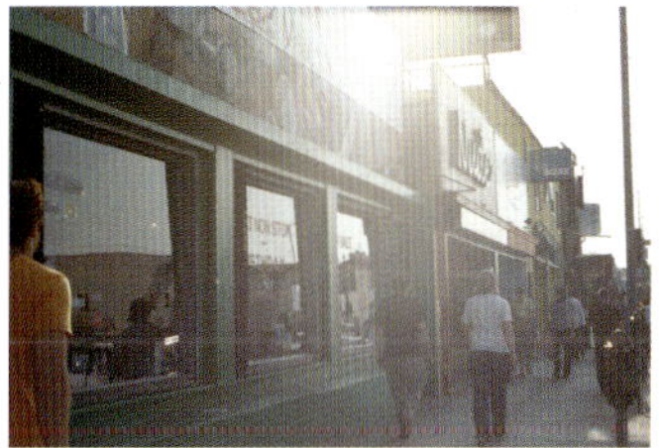

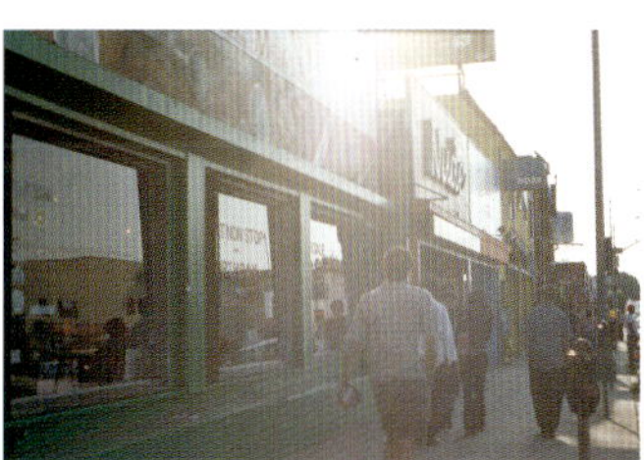

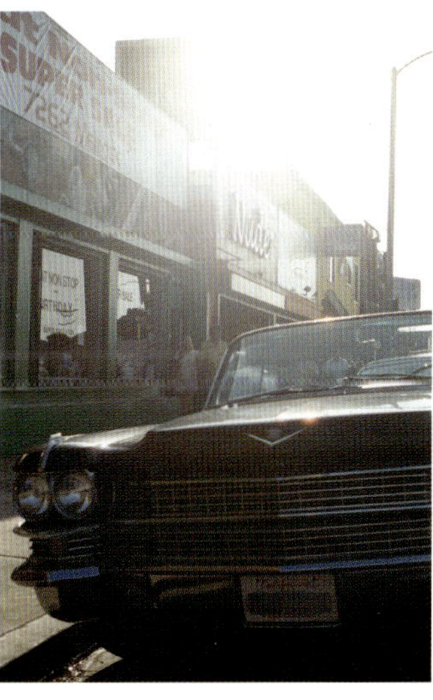

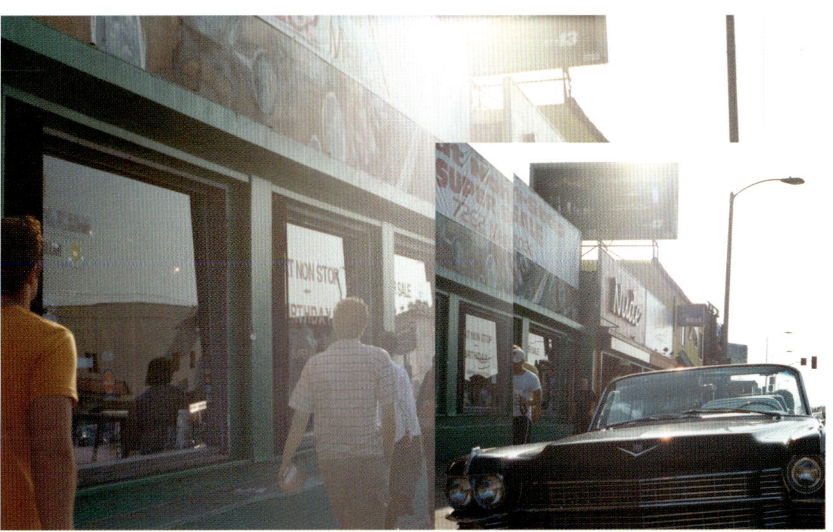

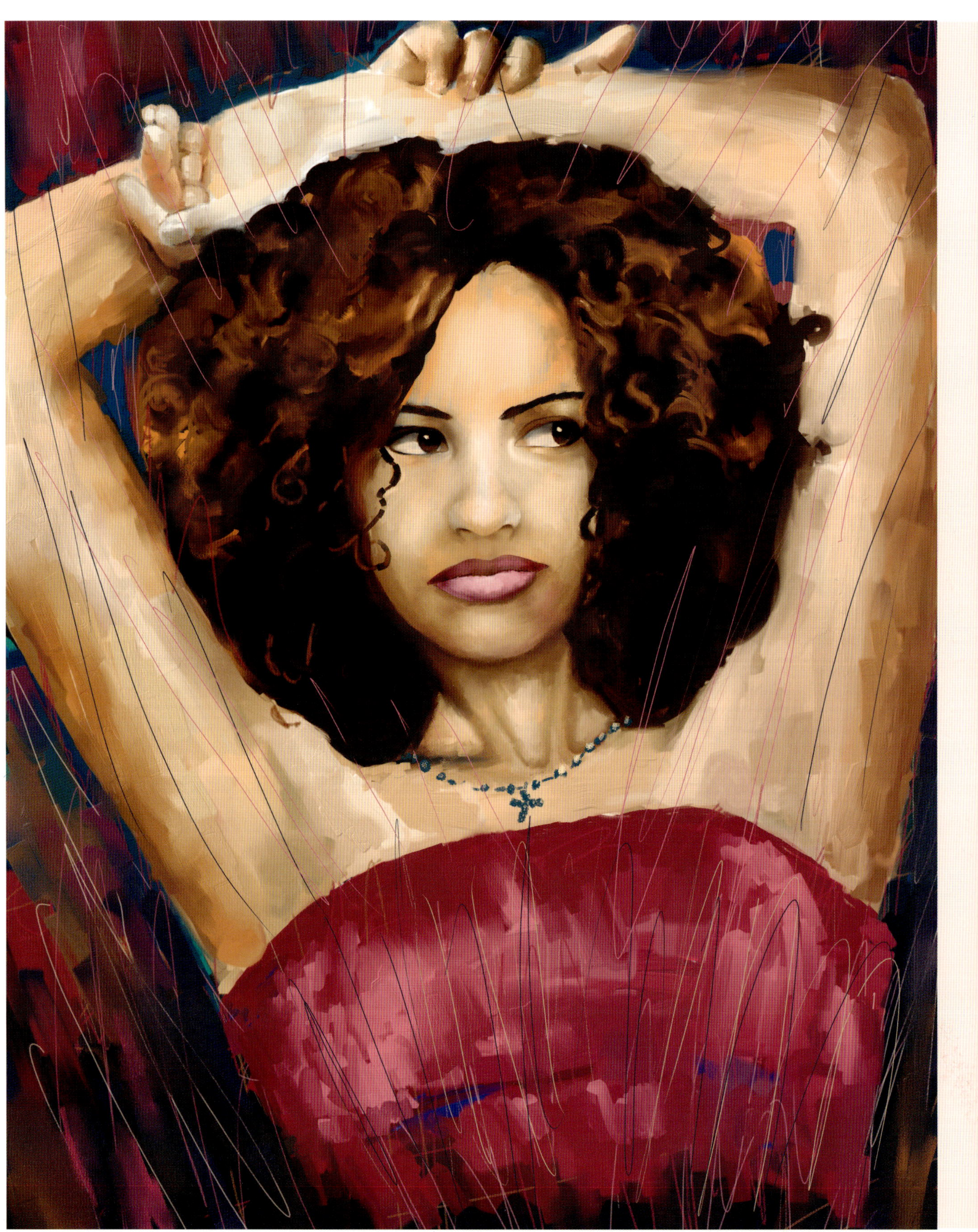

1
ART LESSONS

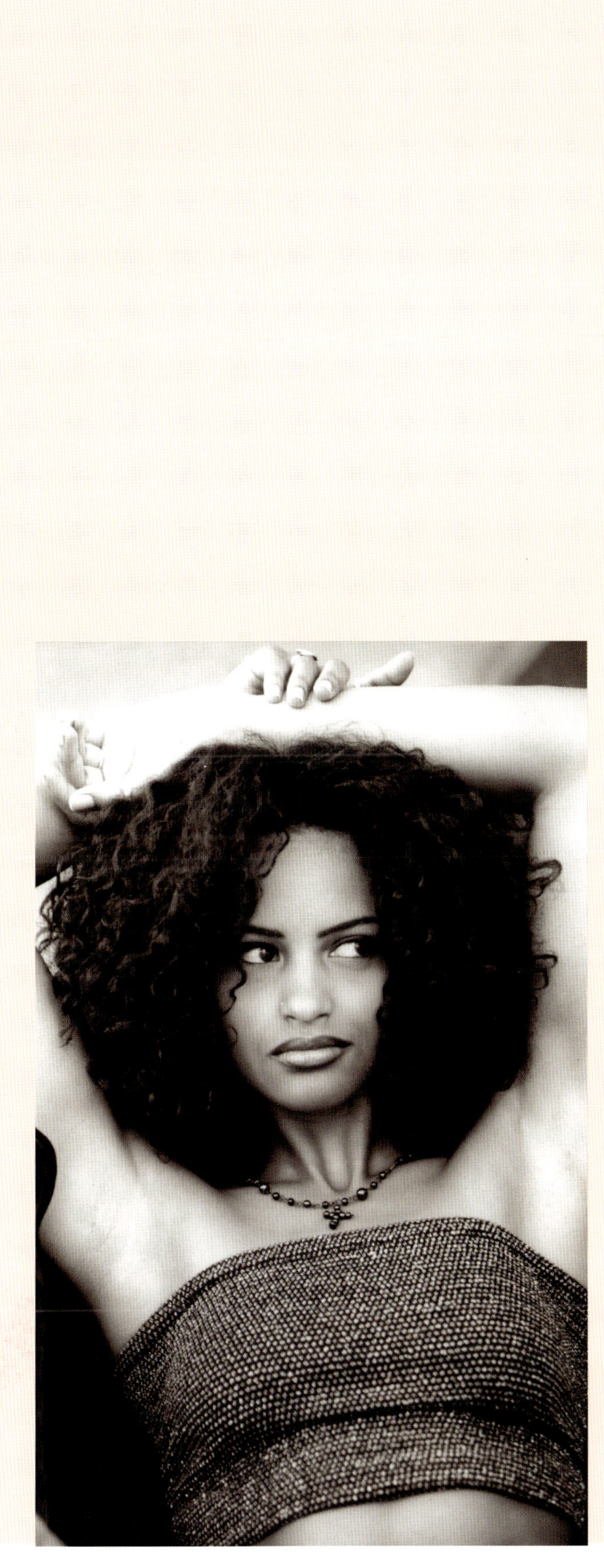

More often than not, when you try to turn a photo into a painting in Corel Painter or in Adobe Photoshop, it seems to be missing something. You can't quite put your finger on it, but there's something not quite right.

What's missing are the ingredients that make the photo a painting and not a photo with brush strokes.

And those ingredients have to do with traditional art concepts.

In this section on art lessons, you will learn the art concepts that you need to know to turn your photos into paintings in Painter and Photoshop, including how to tell if a photo is a good candidate to be transformed into a painting, how to choose colors and how to determine tones.

Knowing these art concepts will help you both when you paint in Painter and Photoshop and also when you add acrylics and oils to your printed artwork on canvas.

Heidi

Painting (opposite page) by Karen Sperling from a photo (this page) by Scott Stulberg, featured in the January 2005 issue of Artistry Tips and Tricks http://www.artistrymag.com/.

CHOOSING THE PHOTO

The first step in painting a photo in Corel Painter or in Adobe Photoshop is to determine whether the photo is a good candidate to be turned into a work of art.

The main ingredient that makes a photo a good candidate to be turned into a painting is if it has strong areas of contrast between highlights and shadows.

That's because when you paint, you're painting areas of light and dark, not objects like eyes, hair and trees.

You now know how to paint portraits, landscapes, pets—anything—because in every case, all you're doing is painting areas of light and dark.

Put another way, the better the contrasts are in the photo, the better the painting will be.

Other considerations go into painting, like composition and colors, but those characteristics are easy to adjust in Painter or in Photoshop.

It's not as easy to add highlights and shadows that aren't there in the original photo.

You can adjust highlights, shadows and contrast in the software, but you won't get as good a result as choosing a photo with good contrast to begin with.

A perfect example is David Derex's photo on page 54.

The photo's interesting shadows made the painting interesting, and you couldn't have added those shadows if they weren't in the photo to begin with.

Early morning and late afternoon are the best times of day to shoot high-contrast photos outdoors.

High Contrast

PAINTING IN PAINTER AND PHOTOS TAKEN AT BUTTERFLY HOUSE, TOPANGA, CA, BY KAREN SPERLING.

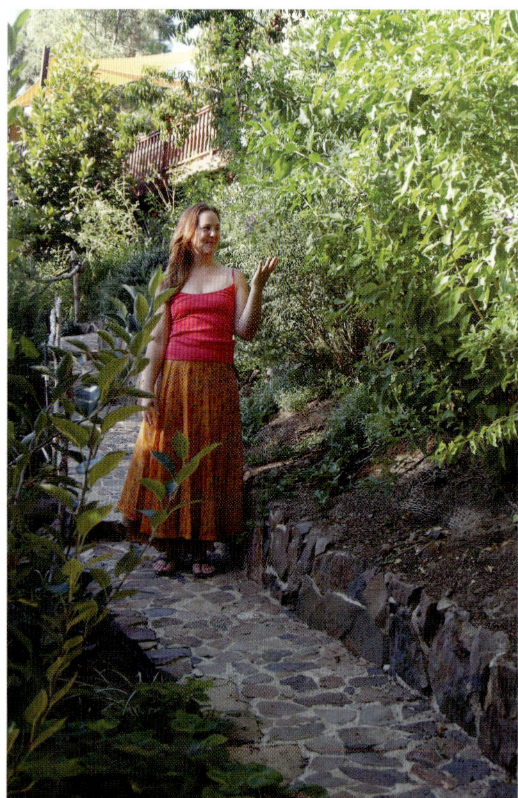

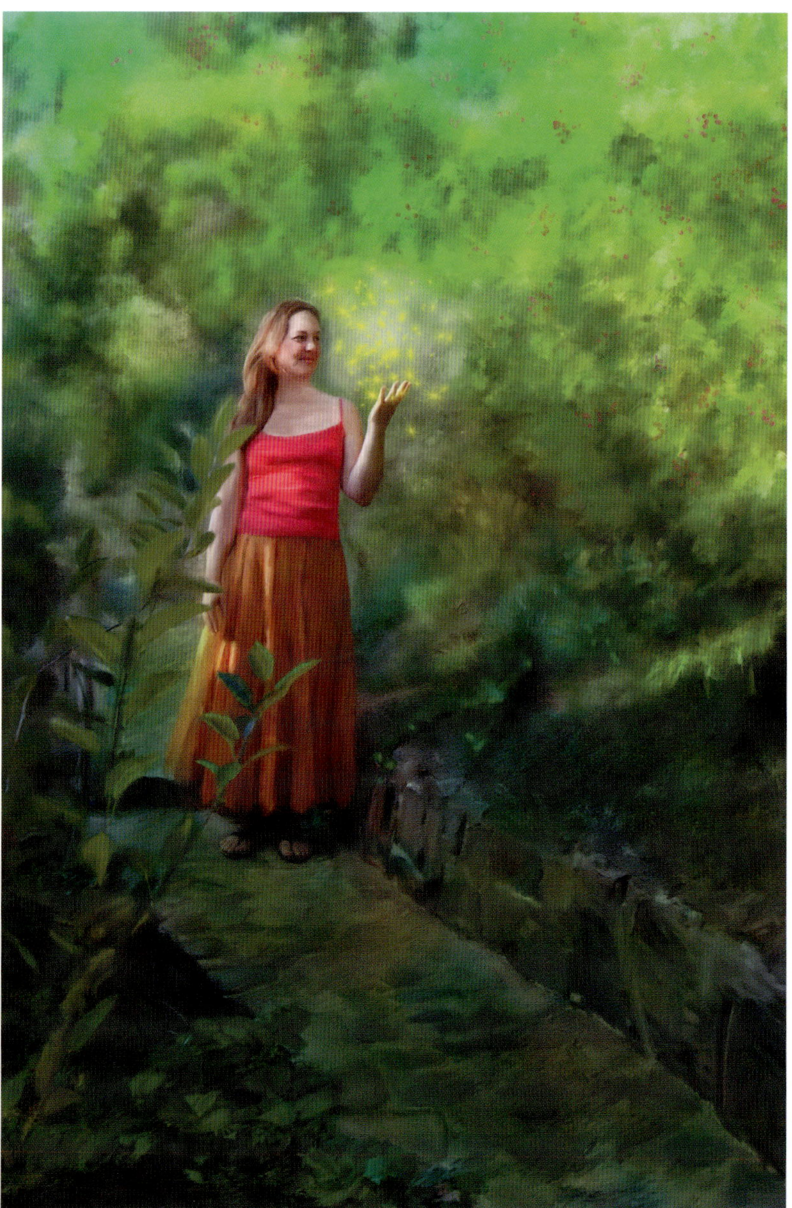

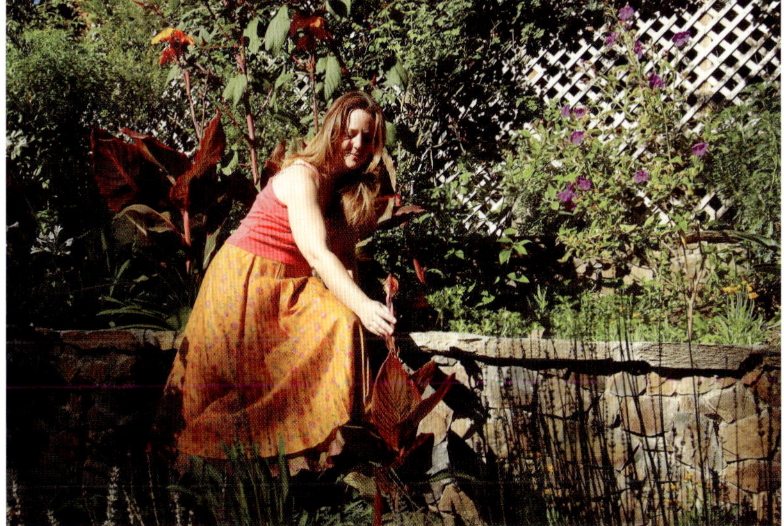
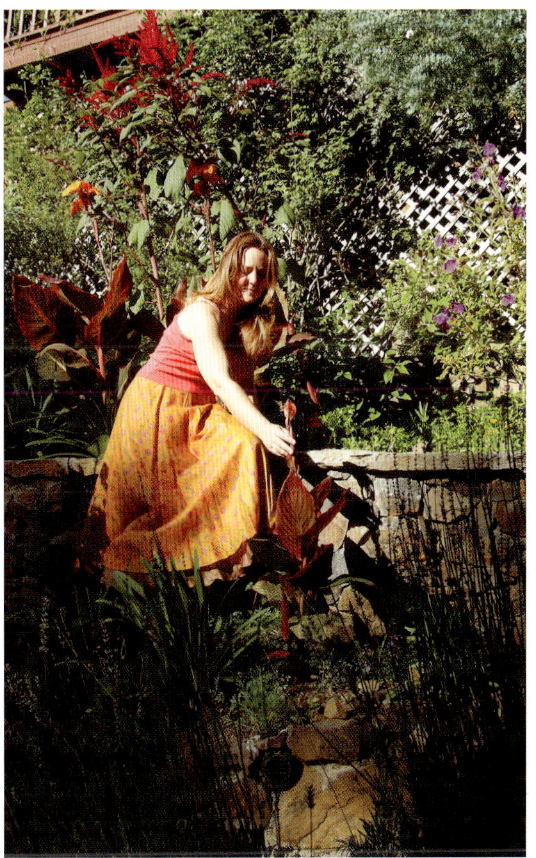
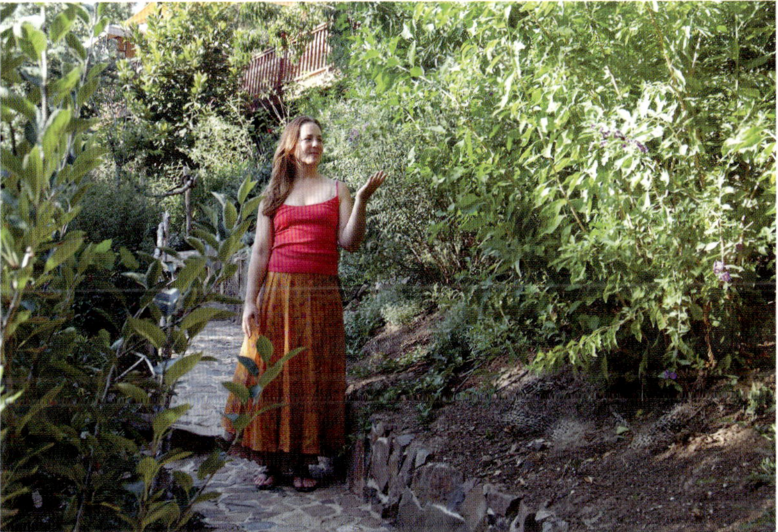

HOW TO CHOOSE

I took the photos on these pages close to sunset.

Though most looked great as photos, I chose the one I did to paint because it had a lot of contrast, and in the right places. The face in the photos I didn't choose had either too much contrast or too little.

In the chosen photo, the features were a bit in shadow with nice highlights on the side of the face and in the hair.

I chose the vertical version (opposite page), not the horizontal one (above), because painting more of the path and less foliage would result in a more interesting painting.

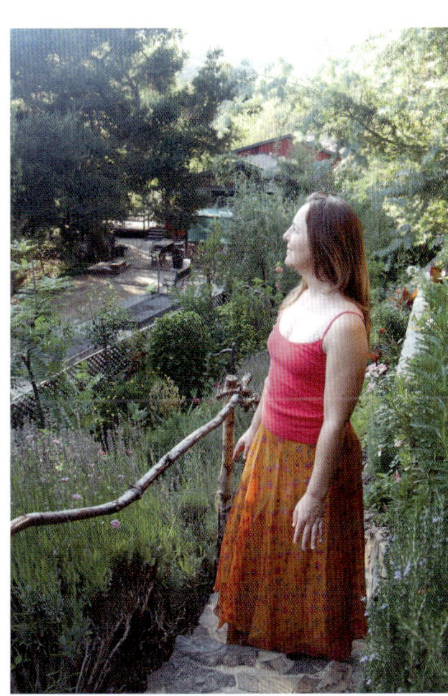
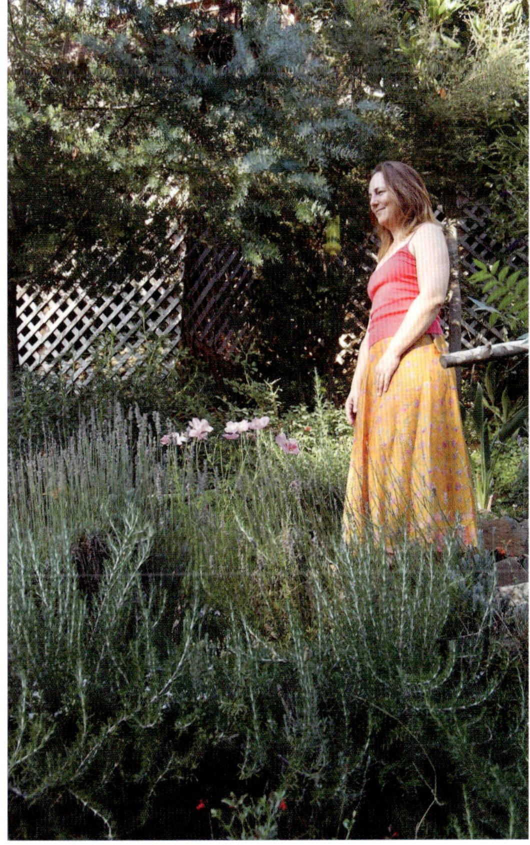

CHOOSING COLORS

Most people make the logical assumption that turning photos into paintings requires brush strokes.

However, just adding brush strokes won't make your photos look like paintings.

One of the key aspects of creating paintings is choosing a color scheme.

The reason is that the main difference between a photo and a painting is that a photo has random colors and a painting has a chosen color scheme.

Sometimes the photo's colors fit into a color scheme, in which case it's OK to use the photo's colors, as you're about to see.

CHOOSING A COLOR SCHEME

Color theory is a vast topic, and there are many ways to choose colors with which to paint.

I've found two color schemes that work well, and I describe both below.

I decide which one to use based on what I see in the photo.

Sometimes the photo's colors fall into one of these color schemes, in which case, I use the photo's colors.

When they don't, I paint with my own colors, based on my color scheme.

COLOR COMPLEMENTS

One method I use all the time to choose a color scheme is to use complementary colors, or colors opposite each other on the color wheel (above, right). To decide which complementary colors to use, I look at my photograph.

For instance, I took the photograph below in Newport, RI.

I liked it because it had good composition, but the colors in the photo wouldn't have worked in the painting—they were dark and unrelated.

Therefore, to choose a color scheme, I looked at the photo, and saw mostly sky and water, both of which are usually blue.

So I had my first color—blue.

I looked at the color wheel and saw that the opposite of blue, or complement, is orange, so I had my second color.

When you choose colors, you are choosing all the tones within a color.

By choosing blue and orange as the color scheme, I was also choosing all the shades of blue, including light and dark blue, and all the shades of orange, including cream and brown.

As you see below, I painted the water, sky, shore and mountains in tones of blue, and the houses, cliffs and dock in orange tones.

In general, if you add another color, adding its complement will improve your painting.

Lady Agnew by John Singer Sargent (opposite page) is an example of two colors and two complements.

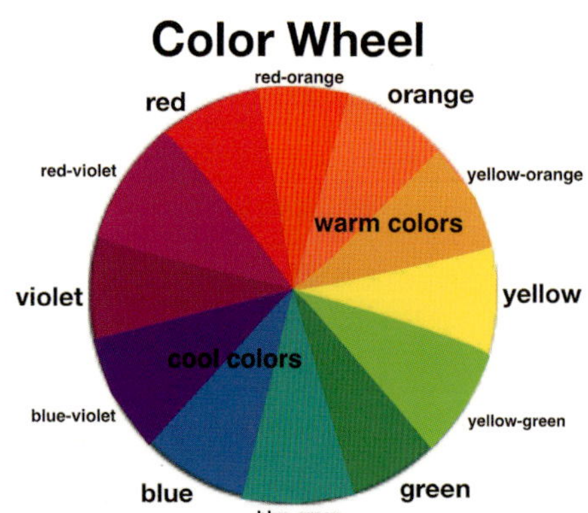

Sargent painted Lady Agnew with yellow and orange and their complements—violet and blue.

The face has yellow and orange, and all the other elements are the complements or repeats of the face colors.

The dress is violet, the complement

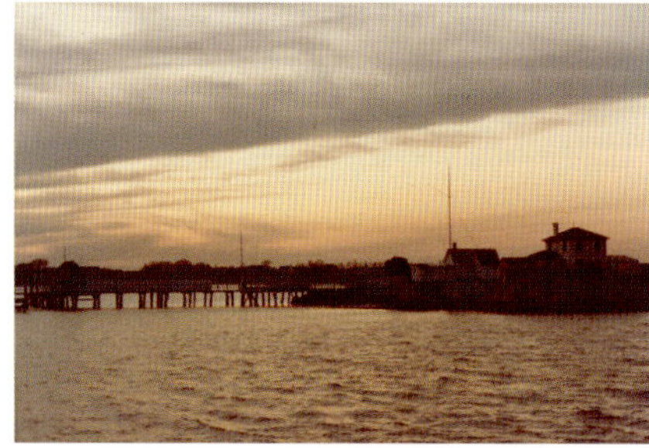

Complementary Colors
PHOTO AND PAINTING BY KAREN SPERLING.

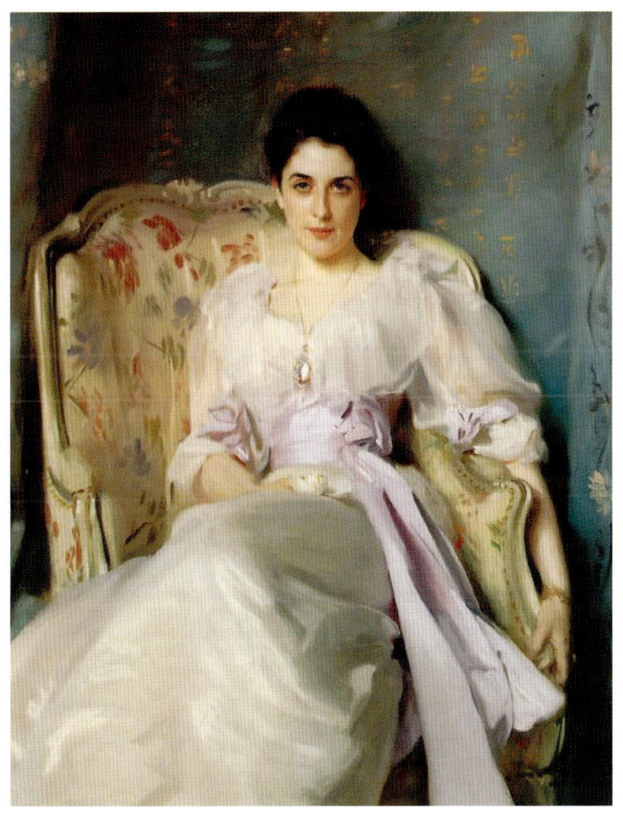

of yellow, the chair is yellow, the complement of the dress, and a repeat of the face. The background is blue, the complement of orange in the face and repeated in the chair. The yellow is repeated in the background.

Adjacent Colors

My other favorite way to choose colors is to use an adjacent color scheme, where you use colors adjacent, or next to each other, on the color wheel.

Below is an example of a painting with an adjacent color scheme.

If you compare it with the color wheel, you'll see that it has the colors starting with red-orange and going clockwise through orange, yellow-orange, yellow, yellow-green, green and blue-green.

I chose these colors based on the photo.

I saw that it had a blue-green sky, green grass and a tree, which could be brown, a shade of red-orange.

I looked at my color wheel and decided I could find a way to incorporate all the colors on the color wheel in between red-orange and blue-green.

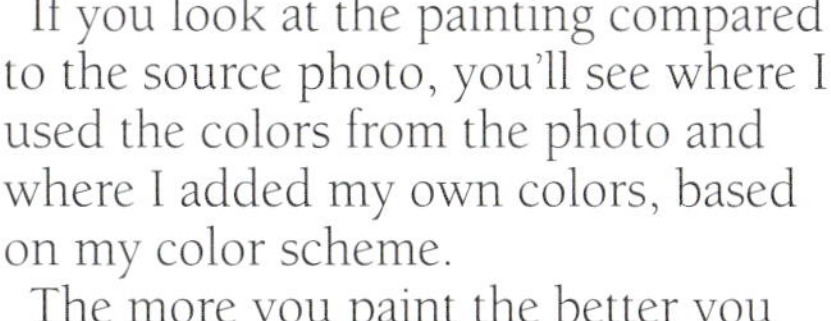

If you look at the painting compared to the source photo, you'll see where I used the colors from the photo and where I added my own colors, based on my color scheme.

The more you paint the better you will get at choosing colors. Just keep your color scheme and the photo's contents in mind, and choosing colors will get easier.

Color Harmony

Another idea to keep in mind when choosing colors is color harmony, where colors are repeated in the foreground and in the background.

Notice in all the paintings on these two pages that the colors are repeated throughout the artwork.

In the case of the Newport painting, the orange of the buildings is repeated in the sky and in the water.

In the Sargent portrait, the yellow and orange in the face are repeated on the chair and in the background.

And in the landscape on this page, the yellow and orange are repeated in the tree and on the ground.

One way to create color harmony is to use a color's complement in the shadows the way Sargent shaded the background in his portrait with orange, the complement of blue.

Aerial Perspective

To create the illusion of distance in paintings, artists use aerial perspective, the term for making the colors in the background a little bluer and less saturated than the colors in the foreground, which are brighter and more saturated.

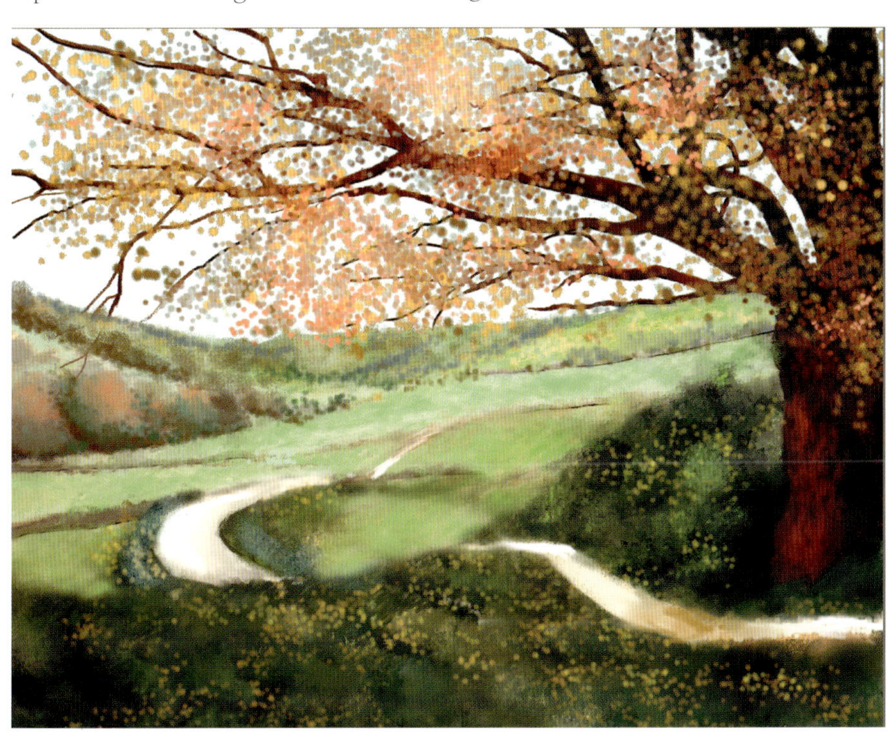

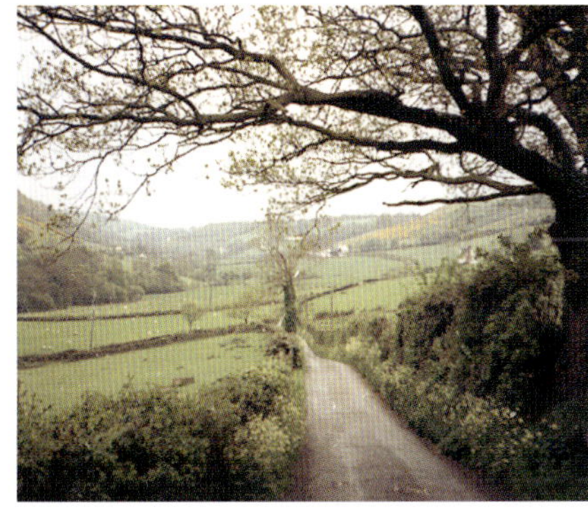

Adjacent Colors

Photo and painting by Karen Sperling.

TONES AND FOCAL POINTS

You now know that photos with strong contrasts of light and dark tones make the best candidates to be turned into paintings.

You also now know how to choose colors.

Contrast, tones and colors are actually related concepts because all colors have tones.

When you choose colors, you also choose tones.

Just like you can sometimes use the colors from the photo, you can also sometimes use the photo's tones. And you can also choose your own tones, just like you can choose your own colors.

This chapter covers ways in which to work with tones.

UNDERSTANDING TONES

All colors have tones and together the tones are your image's contrasts.

The fewer colors and the more tones your paintings have, the more dramatic they will be.

From now on, think of the subject of the painting, also known as the focal point, in terms of tones instead of objects like people or houses.

Thus, the definition of the subject, or focal point, is: The area of greatest contrast between light and dark.

As a result, to make something the subject, or focal point, like a person, make it the area of greatest contrast between light and dark.

The formal term for the contrast of light and dark tones in a painting is chiaroscuro.

It's the idea behind all the famous paintings through time by the masters, going back as far as Leonardo da Vinci, and including Caravaggio, Rembrandt, Rubens, Georges de La Tour, Velázquez, and anyone else whose portraits and landscapes have stark contrasts of light and dark.

In the examples on this page, you can see how the artists used chiaroscuro and limited colors to add drama to their artwork.

You can also see how they made the figures the subject of their portraits by making them the focal point, or area of greatest contrast between light and dark.

You can apply this theory pretty easily. Next time you create a portrait, if the figure is light, make the background dark, if the figure is dark, make the background light—it's that simple! Landscapes have focal points, too—see opposite page.

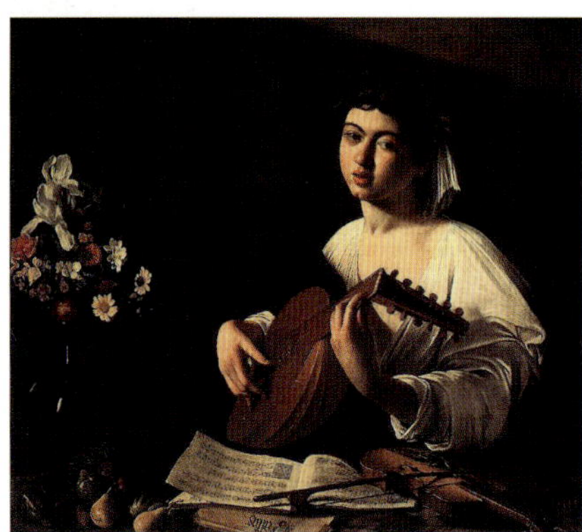

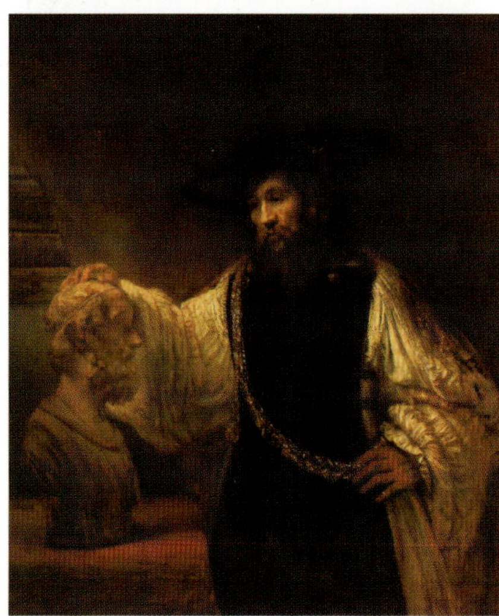

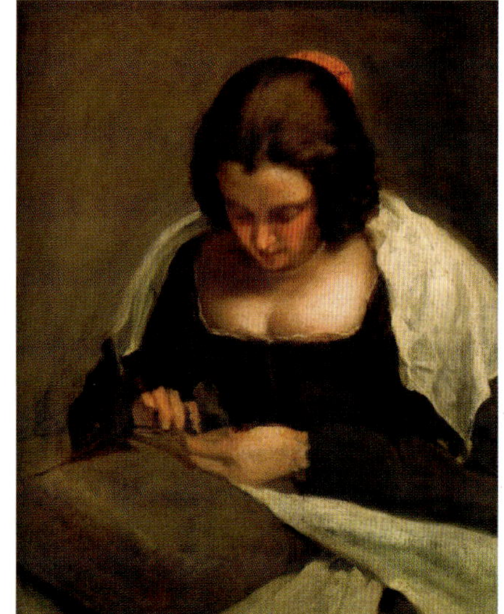

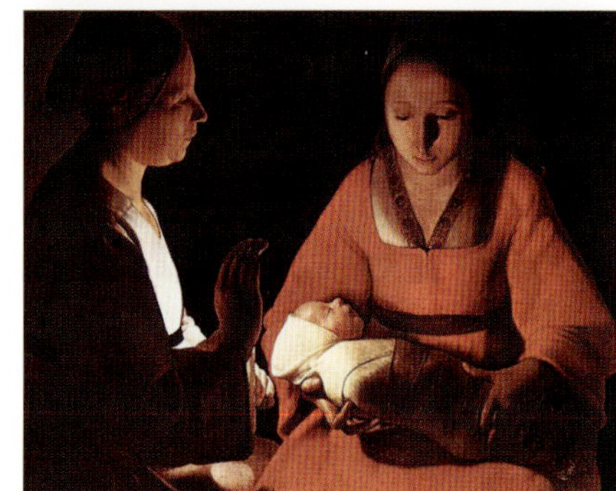

Chiaroscuro

Examples of chiaroscuro, or contrast of lights and darks, are seen in the paintings of Michelangelo Merisi da Caravaggio, Diego Rodríguez de Silva y Velázquez (top row); Rembrandt Harmenszoon van Rijn, Georges de La Tour and Peter Paul Rubens (bottom row).

Editing Tones

As you saw in the first chapter, it's better to paint photos with good areas of contrast between light and dark.

However, even the photos with great contrast don't always have the contrast in the right places.

This is especially true of focal points, which don't always appear where you want them to be.

The next chapter covers where to position focal points.

For now, let's look at how you can recognize and edit focal points.

For instance, I decided to paint the photo I took in Manhattan Beach, CA, that you see at right because it had good contrast.

To see the range of tones more clearly, including the focal point, shut off the colors.

In Painter, choose Effects: Tonal Control: Adjust Colors and move the Saturation slider all the way to the left.

In Photoshop, one way is to choose Image: Adjustments: Hue/Saturation and move the Saturation slider all the way to the left.

With the colors turned off, it's easier to see the photo's tones.

In the top row at right next to the Manhattan Beach photo is the photo after I applied Adjust Colors in Painter.

If you look at the photo without color, you see that the focal point, or area of greatest contrast between light and dark, is the trees.

However, I wanted the house to be the focal point.

In the second row at right is the painting.

I painted using an adjacent color scheme, discussed in the previous chapter on choosing colors.

Next to the painting, you see it with the colors turned off using Adjust Colors again in Painter.

Notice the difference in tones between the top and bottom black-and-white images.

In the bottom picture, the house is now the painting's focal point, or area of greatest contrast between light and dark, and not the trees, as in the image above it.

Once you figure out what you want your focal point to be, actually creating it is relatively easy.

To make the house the focal point, choose Edit: Undo to restore the colors, then lighten the house in Painter by painting with the Photo's Dodge variant and darken the foliage, sky and water around the house with the Photo's Burn variant.

Selecting brushes in Painter is discussed in more detail in the next section about painting tools.

But for now, it's enough for you to know that you can edit the tones in your paintings to create the focal point by using Dodge and Burn.

While painting, turn off the colors to see how the tones are shaping up using Adjust Colors, then choose Edit: Undo to restore the colors.

Making the house the focal point—and using a chosen color scheme—made the painting a painting and not just a photo with brush strokes.

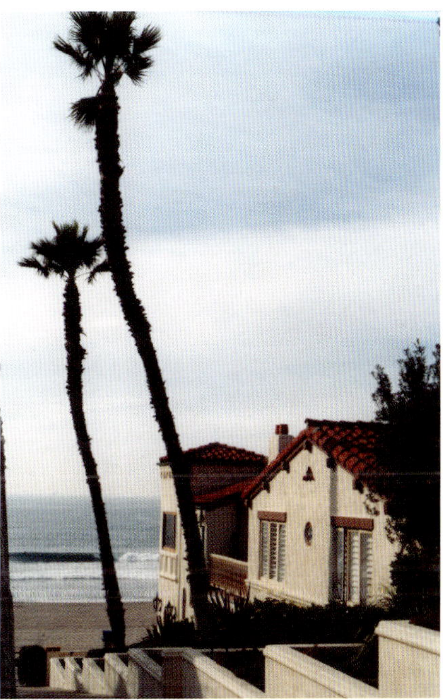

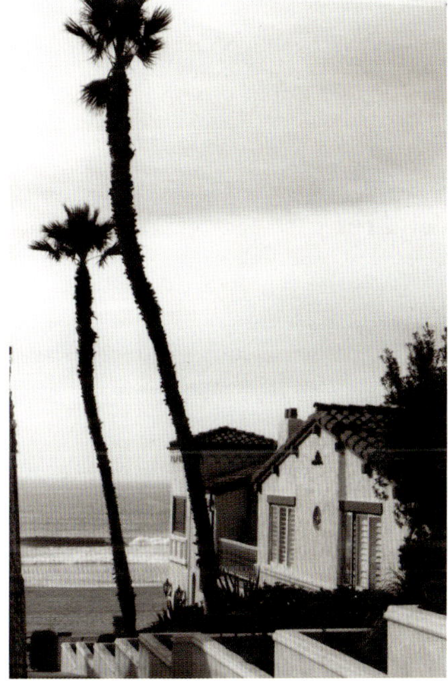

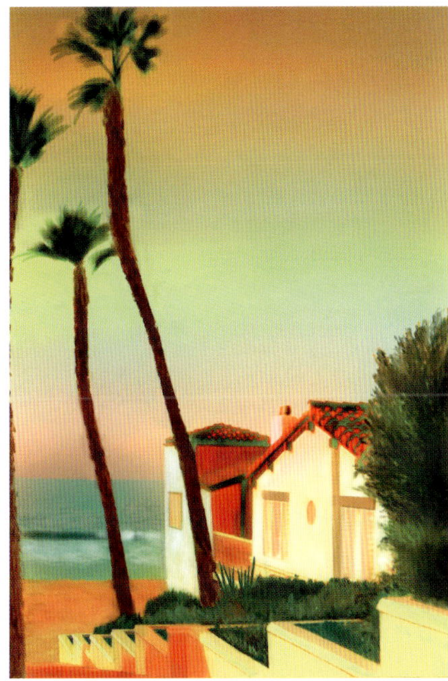

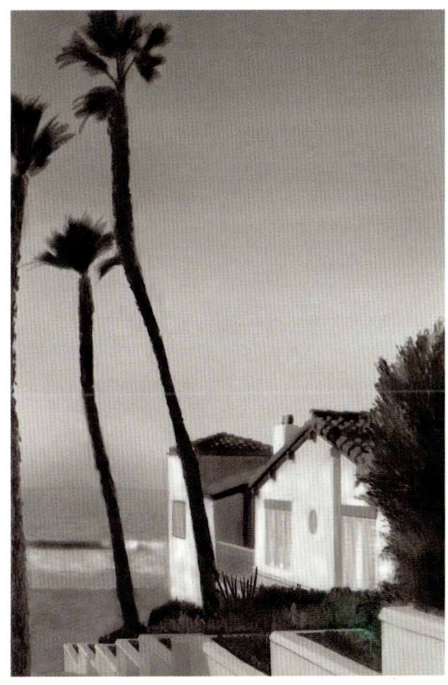

Focal Points

Photo and painting by Karen Sperling.

COMPOSITION

In the previous chapter, you learned about focal points and how to edit them.

In this chapter containing composition rules, you'll find out where to place focal points.

Of course, rules are made to be broken, but it's good to know what the rules are that you are breaking.

It seems that composition rules are the ones that people flout most often—or maybe they don't know them?

In any case, here's information about where to place focal points and some other composition guidelines to keep in mind, both when you're taking the photo and also when you're painting the artwork.

RULE OF THIRDS

The rule of thirds is a guideline for setting up your photo or painting's composition or layout.

When you follow the rule, you think of the image as divided in thirds and you put your subject/focal point—i.e., area of greatest contrast between light and dark—near the intersection of imaginary folds, marked by the blue circles in the images at right.

This rule is frequently broken. You'll often see portraits where the subject is right in the middle of the image.

But if you move the subject over, with the face having the greatest contrast and falling near the upper left- or right-hand circle, for instance, the portrait will be stronger.

A random sampling of Monet paintings reveals that Monet followed the rule of thirds in most of his art.

Notice that in all the paintings by Monet on this page, the focal point, or area of greatest contrast between light and dark, falls near the imaginary intersection of the paper folds.

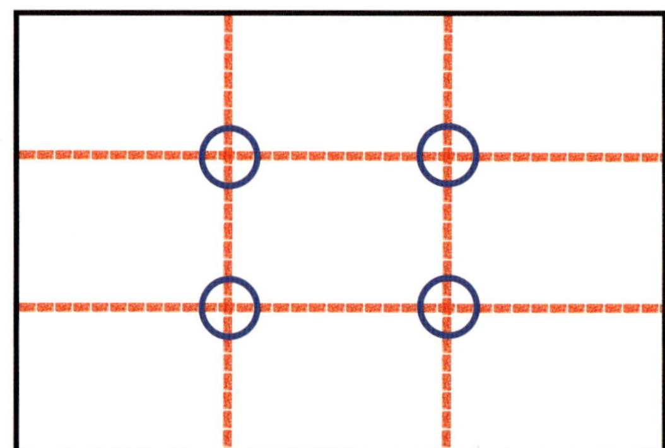

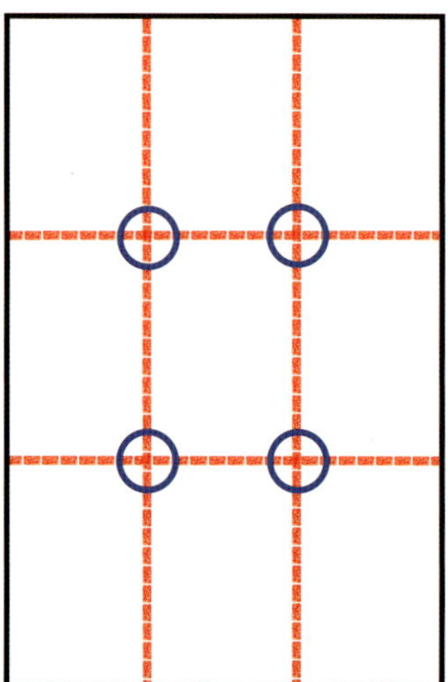

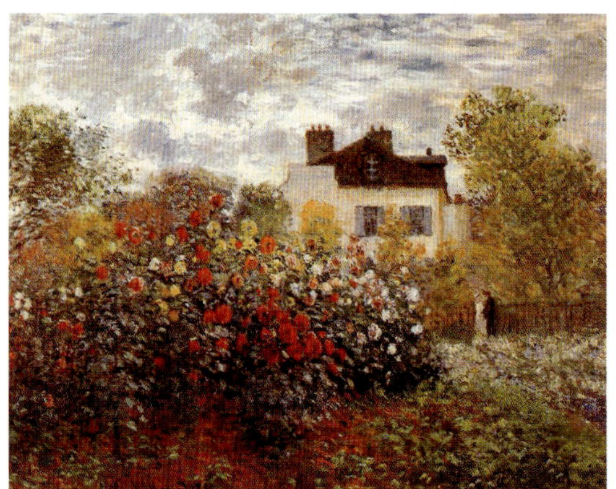

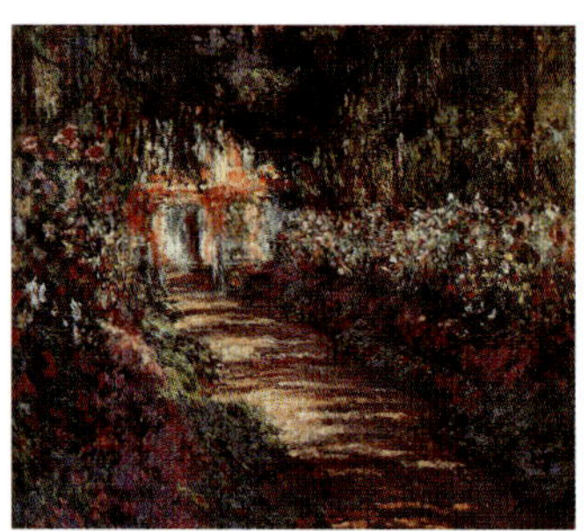

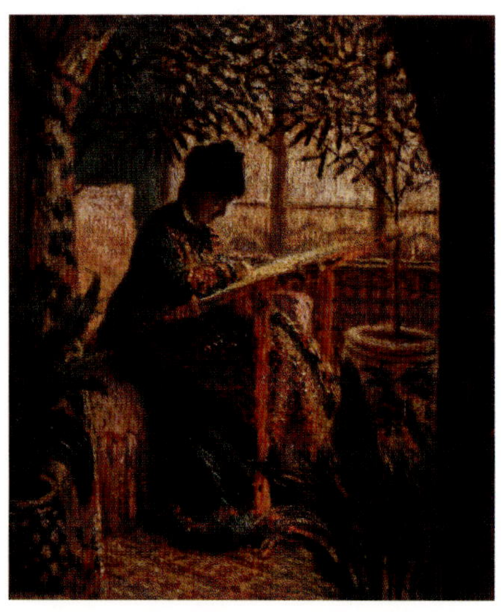

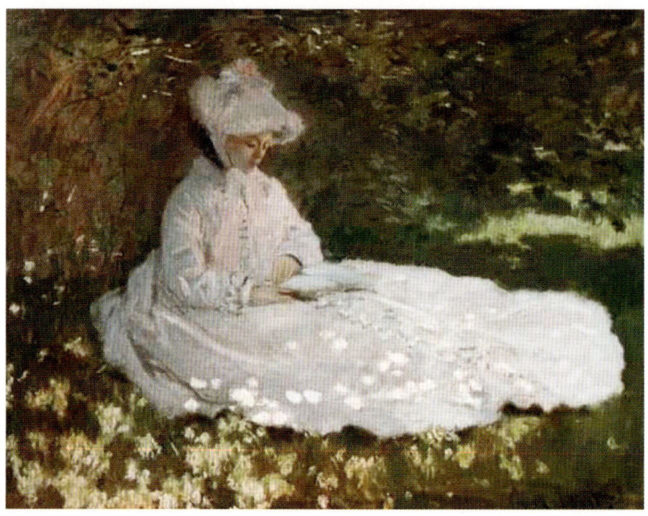

Rule of Thirds

Examples of Monet paintings where the subject/focal point—area of greatest contrast between light and dark— is near the intersection of paper folded in thirds, represented by the blue circles in the above images. In the top row of paintings, it's the buildings; in the bottom row, it's the women's faces.

ELIMINATE DETAILS

One of the differences between a photo and a painting is that a painting has less detail.

If a detail doesn't add to our understanding of what we're looking at, then it can be eliminated.

Instead of painting all the details that you see in the photo, paint the areas of highlights, midtones and shadows.

I think being an artist is less about learning the skill to draw a straight line and more about getting better at making the decisions about what to leave out and what to keep.

Photographers have a hard time with this concept, sometimes.

They want to include all the details, in addition to keeping the colors and the composition.

If that's the case, then don't paint the photo!

But if you want a photo to look like a painting, then eliminate details. Below and at right are examples in portraits and landscapes.

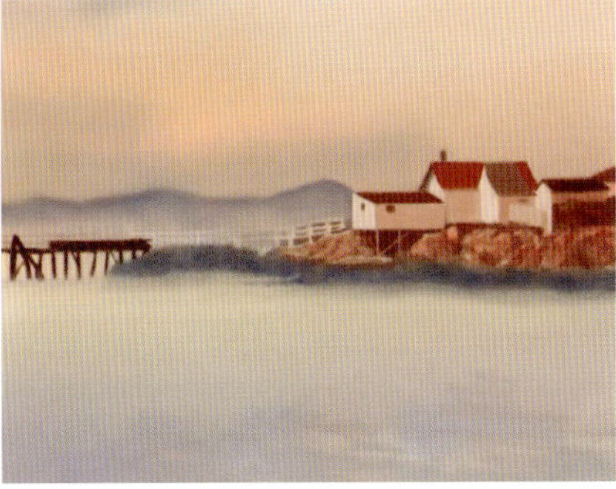

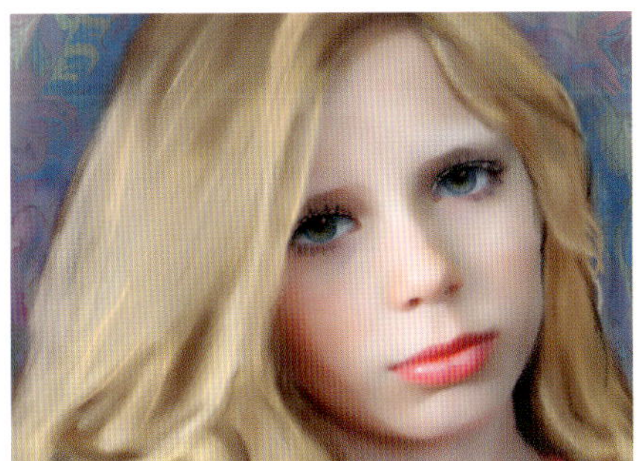

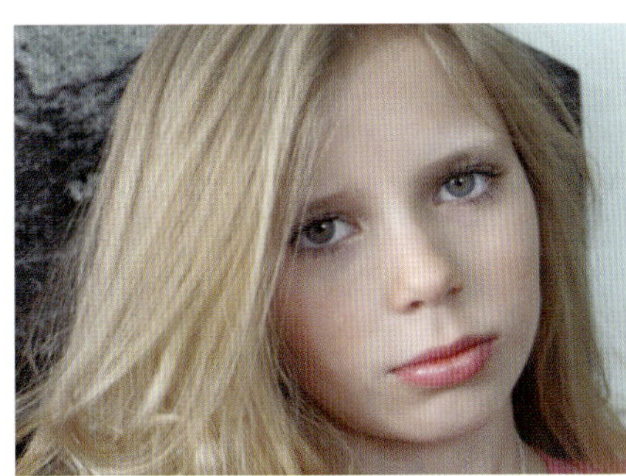

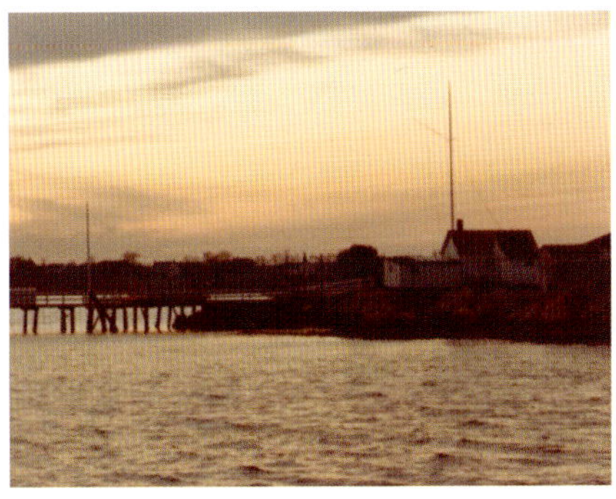

ELIMINATING DETAILS IN PORTRAITS

I blended out details in the skin, lips, eyes and hair in Terrie Strick's photo of her daughter, Haley. Then I painted back some suggestions of the details. The step-by-step tutorials in the Portraits section will show you the various techniques for eliminating details in Painter and in Photoshop.

ELIMINATING DETAILS IN LANDSCAPES

In the photo I took in Newport, RI (above), the background had a lot of details, including trees and buildings. In the painting I did (top), I eliminated the details in the background by painting a suggestion of mountains.

LEADING THE EYE IN

You want to lead the eye into your composition, not out of it.

In the photos I took at right, the ladies on the path in the left-hand photo are walking off the image.

The right-hand photo has the ladies on the path walking into the image, which is an improvement.

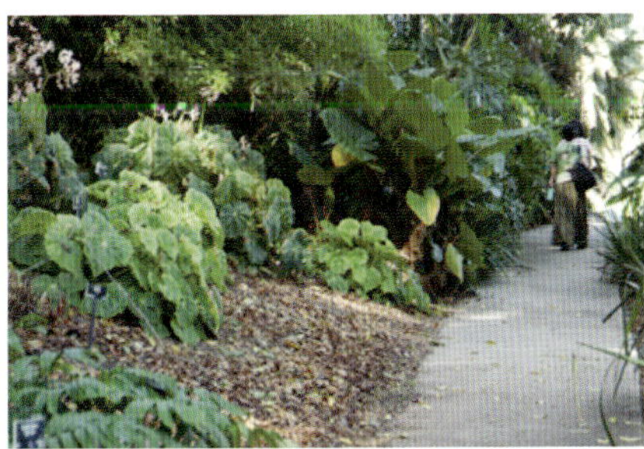

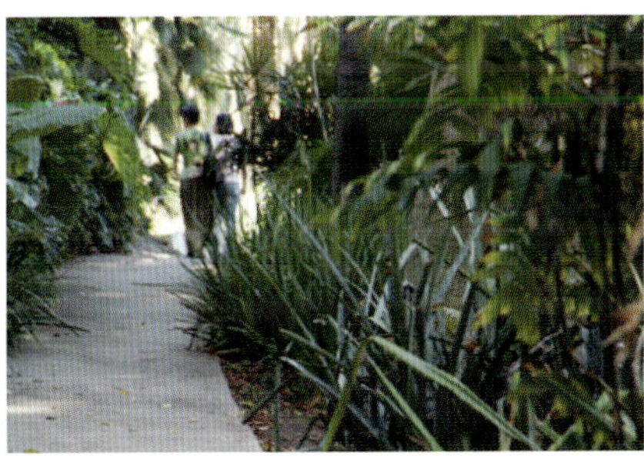

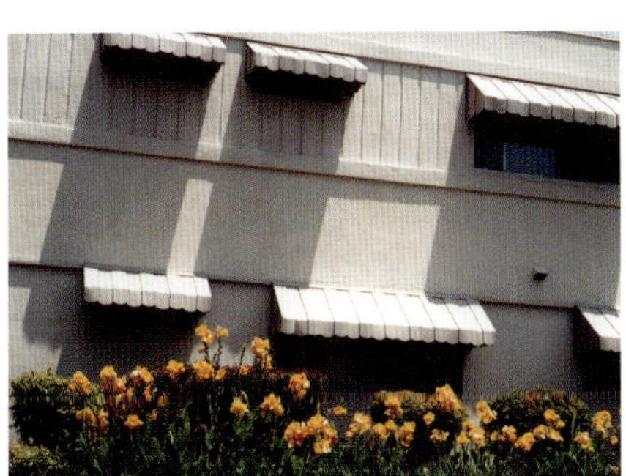

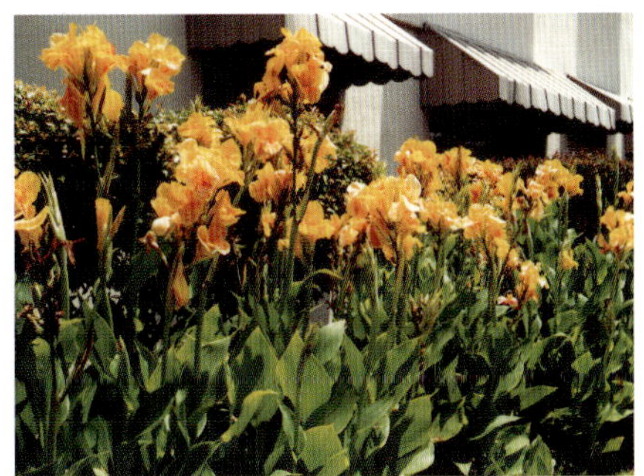

A DIFFERENT ANGLE

Take photos at an angle to create diagonal lines (photo above, right), which are more interesting than horizontal lines that you get when you shoot straight on (photo above, left). I took these photos in the same place, but the one on the right is so much more interesting.

Also, shoot from above or below at an angle, like the photo on the right.

ELEMENTS TOUCHING

Image elements should be together, like in the photo I took of Rossi Music below, right, and not apart, like in the photo I took below, left.

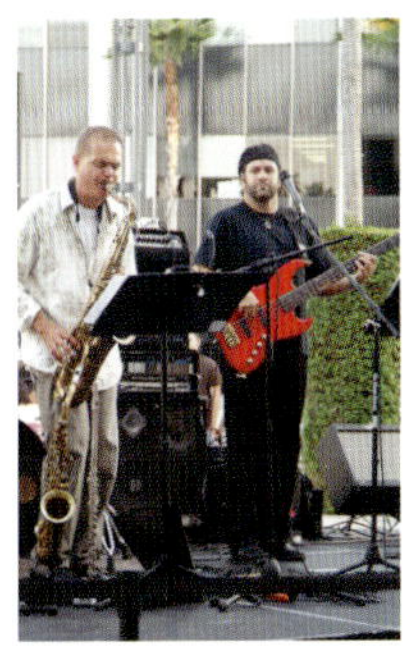

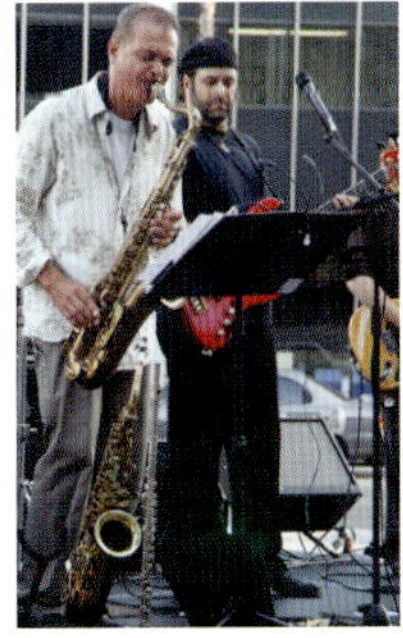

BODY PARTS

Artists paint features in a portrait based on some generally accepted rules or guidelines.

As previously stated, rules are made to be broken, but it's good to know what the rules are that you're breaking.

On these pages are the guidelines that artists use to represent eyes, noses, lips and hair in their paintings.

You can add these visual notations to make your paintings more painterly even if you don't see them in your source photos.

With time and practice, you'll feel better about venturing away from the source photo and using art concepts instead to guide you as you paint.

EYES

There are a few art concepts to keep in mind when painting eyes.

The main idea is that the eyes are spheres, and how you paint them is based on representing those spheres in relation to the light source.

For instance, paint the catchlight at the top of the sphere touching part of the iris and part of the pupil, as you see in the images at right.

Paint the catchlight on the left if the light is coming from the upper left, and on the right if the light source appears from the upper right.

Paint the top of the eye a little darker than the bottom of the eye, the theory being that the top of the eye is in shadow cast by the eyebrow.

Make the sides of the eye even darker to convey that the eyeball sphere gets darker as it recedes into the eye socket.

Paint some color over the corners of the eyes, a great example of how you eliminate detail.

We know we're looking at eyes without the details in the corners, so just suggest those areas with some dark color.

Apply the art concept of eliminating detail when you paint eyebrows and eyelashes, too.

Paint broad areas of light and dark based on what you see in the photo, then add suggestions of individual hair strands.

The section on painting portraits includes all the brushes to use.

Refer to the guidelines on this page to help you to decide what to paint.

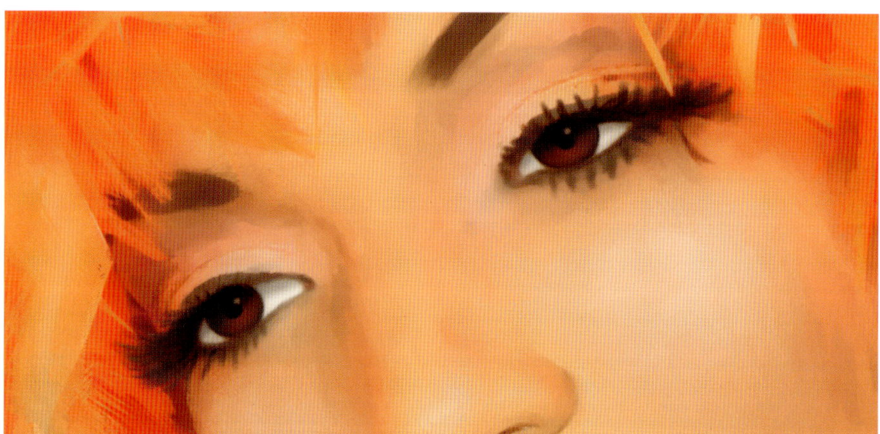

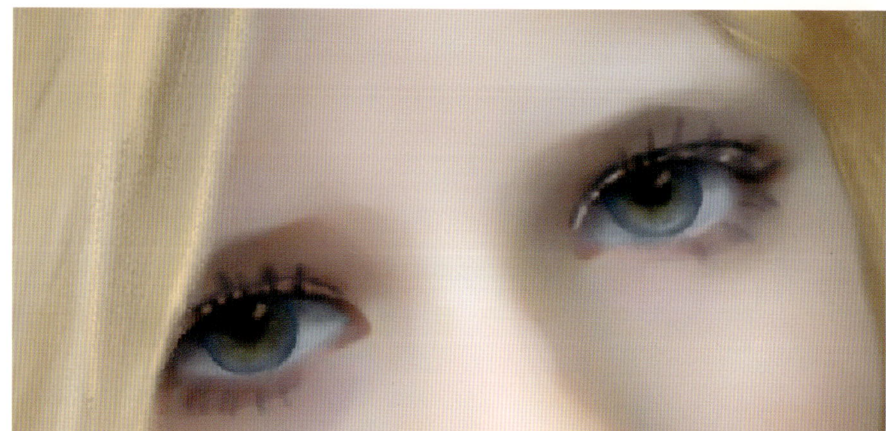

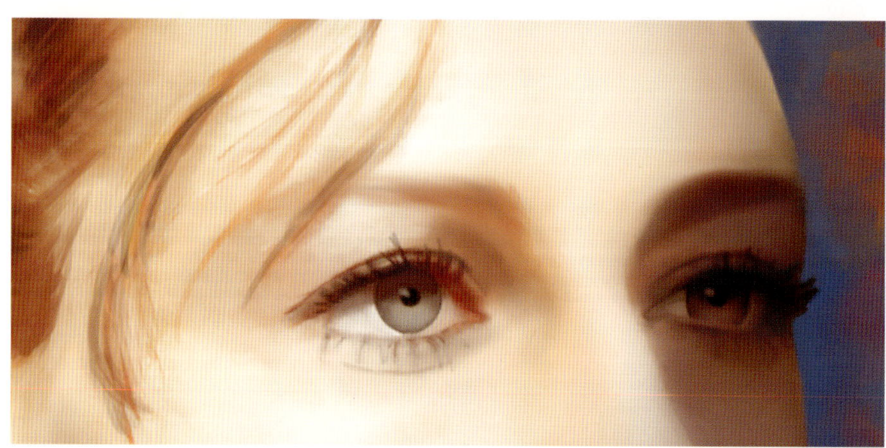

Eyes

Paintings by Karen Sperling from photos by Jackie Hicks (top); Terry Strick (middle) and David Derex (bottom).

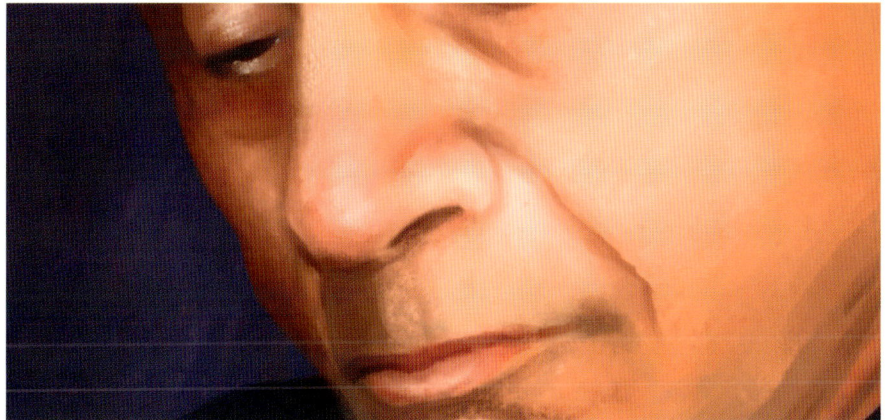

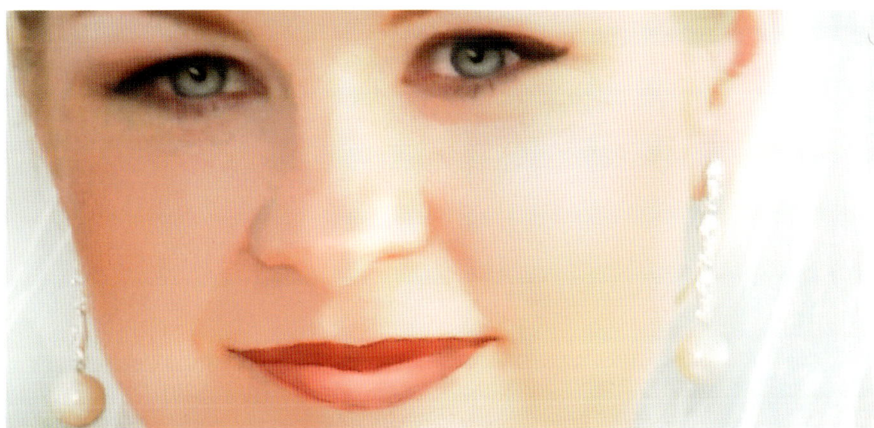

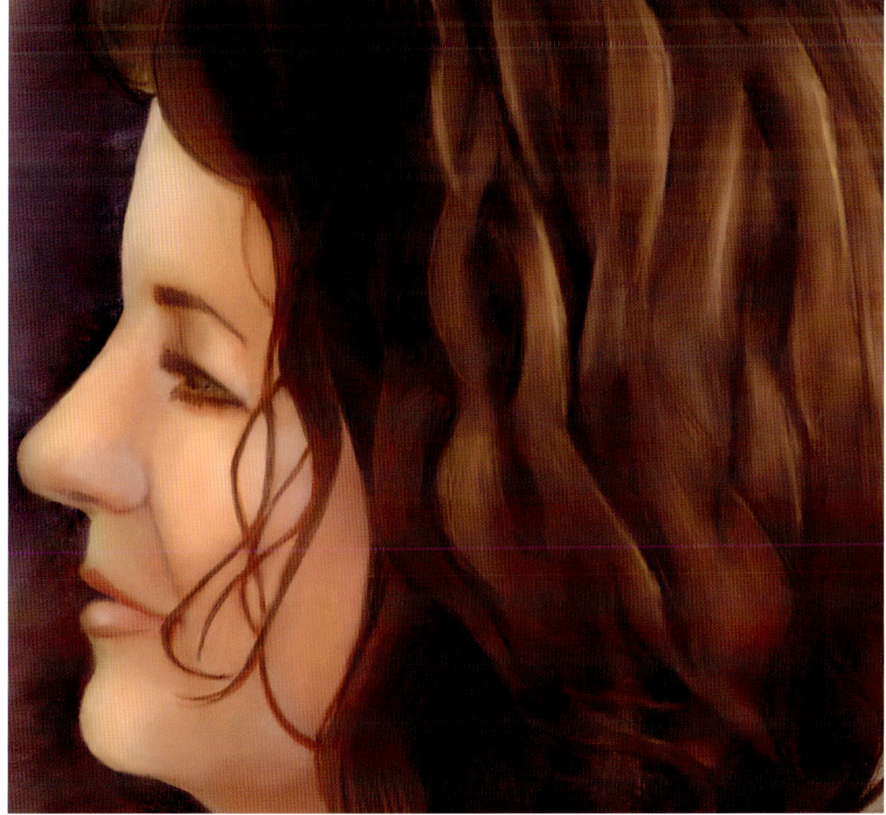

NOSES

As with eyes, when painting noses, the idea is to paint areas of light and dark based on the light source.

The light hits the bridge of the nose, so paint in a highlight even if you don't see one in the photo.

The darkest area of the nose is below the tip because the nose casts a shadow on the area above the lip. Paint in a shadow there even if you don't see one in the photo.

The rest of the nose is various midtones, and you can use the photo as your guide to paint these tones.

LIPS

Based on the light source, paint the upper lip darker than the lower lip, the idea being that the upper lip is in shadow and the light hits the lower lip. Add a highlight on the lower lip to show the light hitting it even if there isn't a highlight there in the photo.

HAIR

People always ask me what brush to use to paint hair because they think there's a special way to paint all the strands.

But now that you know you're painting areas of light and dark, not objects, and that you're eliminating details that are in the photo, you know that you're not painting individual strands of hair.

To paint hair, paint areas of light and dark, using the photo as your guide. Then add a few strands to suggest hair when you're done.

APPLYING THE CONCEPTS

Use these art concepts to guide you both when you paint portraits digitally and when you paint on the canvas after it's printed.

In both cases, you're painting areas of light and dark, and you can do so with either digital paint or traditional oils and acrylics.

Noses, Lips and Hair

Paintings by Karen Sperling from photos by her (top and bottom) and Michelle Lamberth (middle).

ART EXAMPLES

I use traditional art for reference all the time.

If I'm uncertain how to paint something, I do a google.com search and see how other artists have handled the same aspect of their paintings.

On these pages are some of the artists whose work influenced the paintings in this book.

Knowing great art is the best way to create your own. Go to galleries and museums, or look at books and web sites to build your art knowledge. Then use this knowledge when figuring out what to paint in your photos.

EDWARD HOPPER

Edward Hopper's paintings have several things in common.

These include:

1. The use of a limited color palette, in many cases, an adjacent color scheme (see page 13);
2. Simple, realistic subjects;
3. A sense of solitude;
4. Stark contrasts between lights and darks.

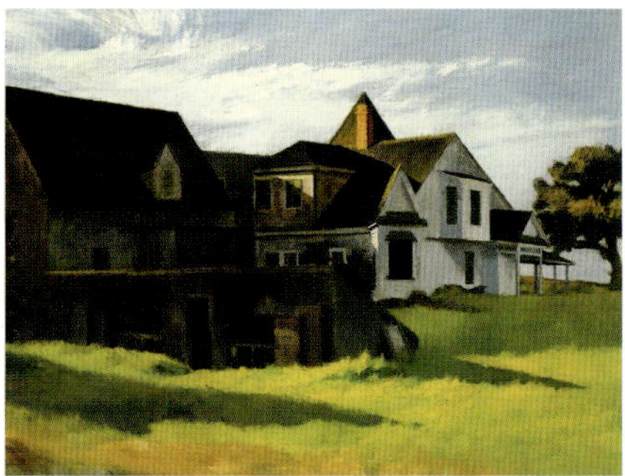

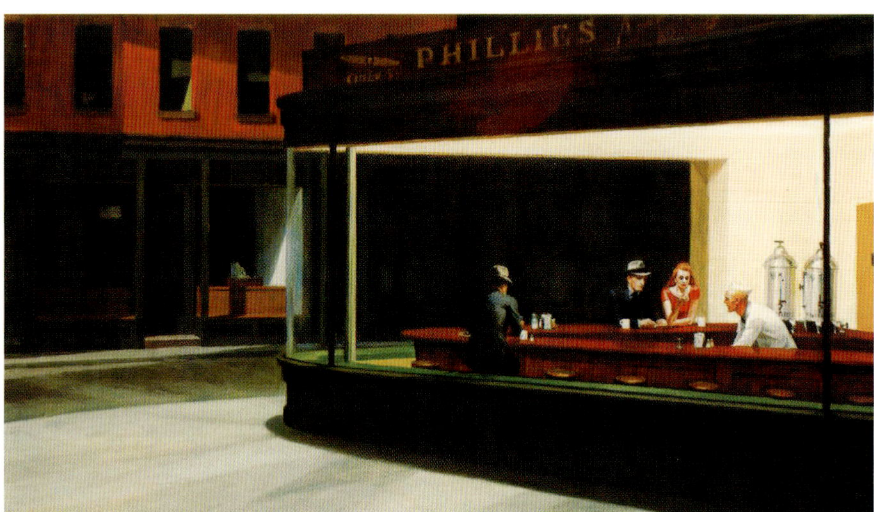

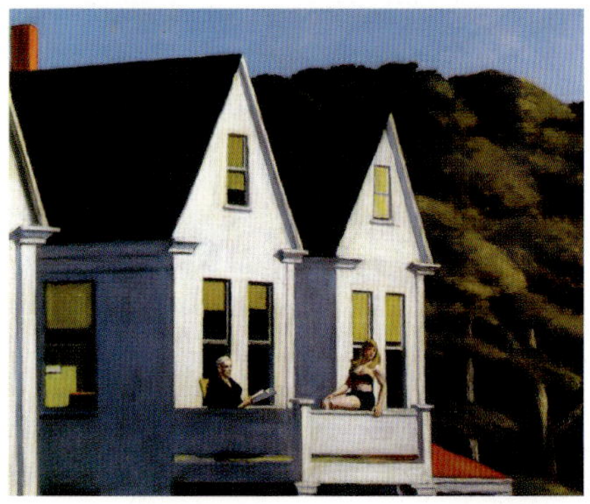

ENGLISH LANDSCAPES

Paintings by English watercolor landscape artists have a limited color scheme and high contrast in dramatic skies with clouds.

Each has a subject, or focal point, or an area of greatest contrast between light and dark that's very clearly seen.

This subject is a building, a mountain or even a horizon line.

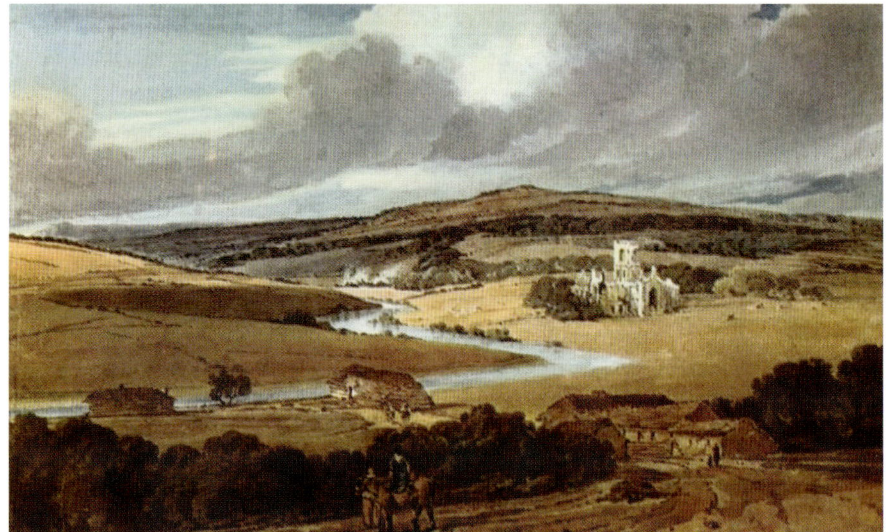

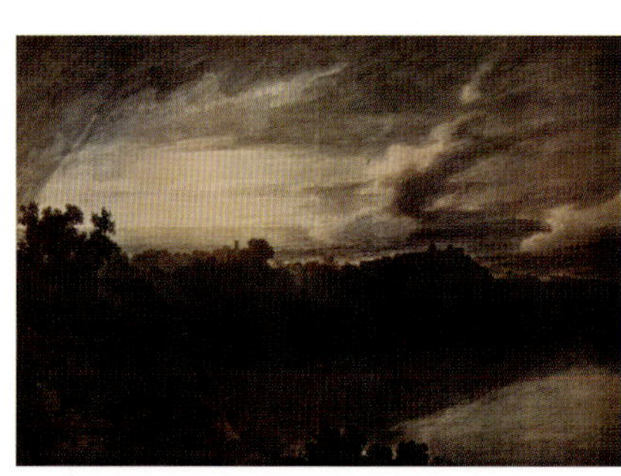

Landscapes

Paintings by Edward Hopper (top) and English landscape artists John Robert Cozens (left) and Thomas Girtin (above).

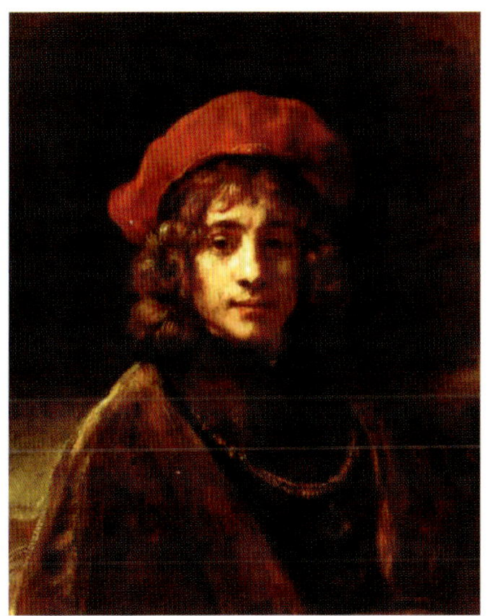

↓ RENOIR

Pierre-Auguste Renoir's paintings have a limited color scheme; ornate, detailed backgrounds; and a lot of detail in the clothing.

The dresses, though clearly white, have colors in the shadows.

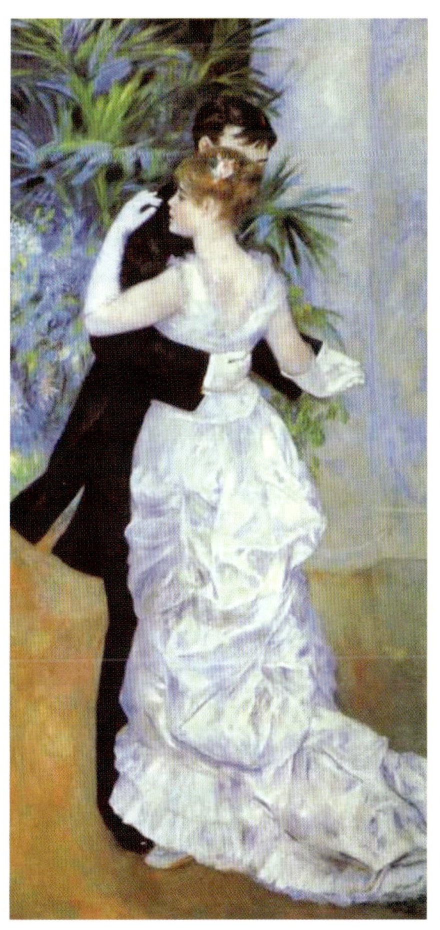

← REMBRANDT

Rembrandt Harmenszoon van Rijn's portraits have stark contrasts. The faces are very light and the backgrounds are very dark, and within the faces are distinct highlights and shadows. The clothes also have distinct highlights and shadows as well.

Rembrandt used a limited color palette. The colors are mostly reds, yellows, browns and greens, and he frequently used dark outlines.

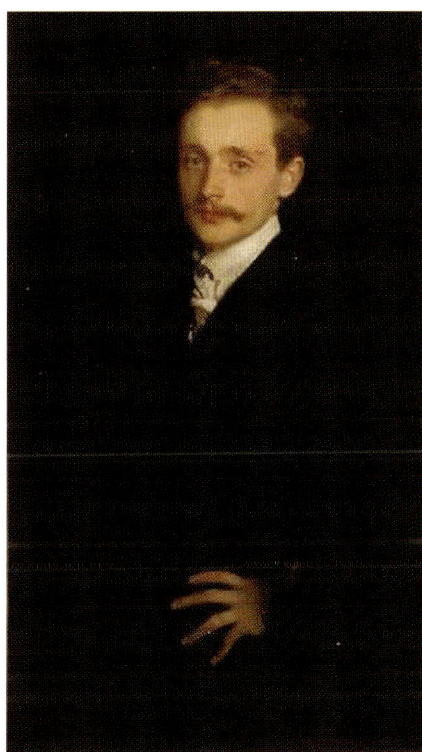

↑ JOHN SINGER SARGENT

In many cases, Sargent painted faces lighter than the backgrounds, and the backgrounds are mostly either the same color as the clothes or a darker value of the color of the faces. In most cases, he painted a plain background with brush strokes.

Many of his paintings have limited color schemes of just two colors and all the saturations and values within the chosen colors.

He painted distinct areas of light and dark in the faces.

The highlights and shadows have visible brush strokes.

Hair is broad areas of color with suggestions of individual strands.

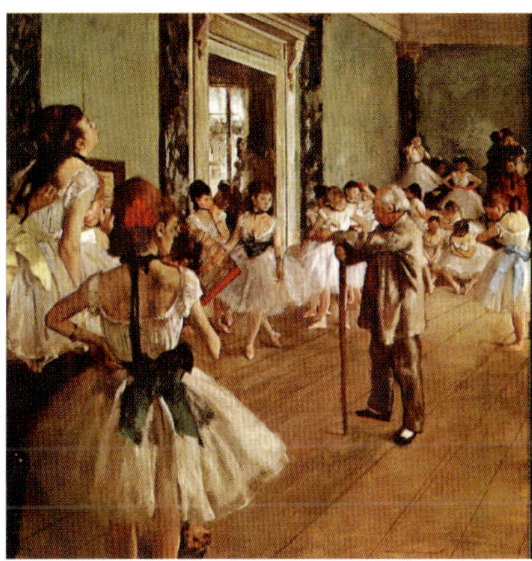

↑ DEGAS

Edgar Degas painted with limited color palettes with strong contrasts between areas of light and dark.

His dancers have interesting poses seen from above or from an angle.

Seen mostly in groups, the dancers are usually touching, which is better composition than showing them apart from each other.

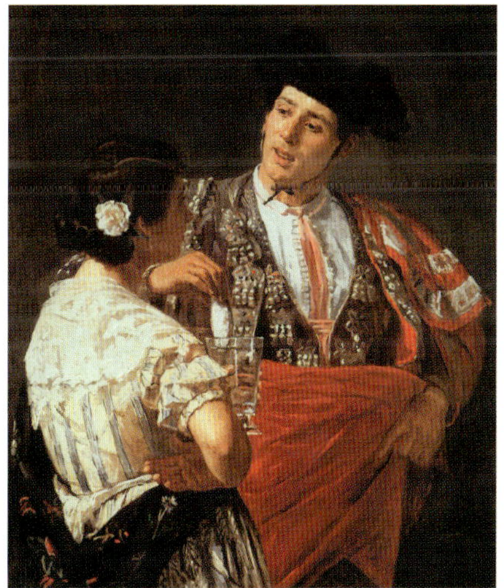

↑ MARY CASSATT

Mary Cassatt was an American painter who lived and worked in France and who was a contemporary of Degas, Manet, Cézanne, Renoir and Morisot. Cassatt captured subjects in the middle of activities including talking, sipping tea and bathing children.

In most of Mary Cassatt's paintings, two or more people are touching or interacting in some way so that the viewer is witnessing personal moments between the subjects.

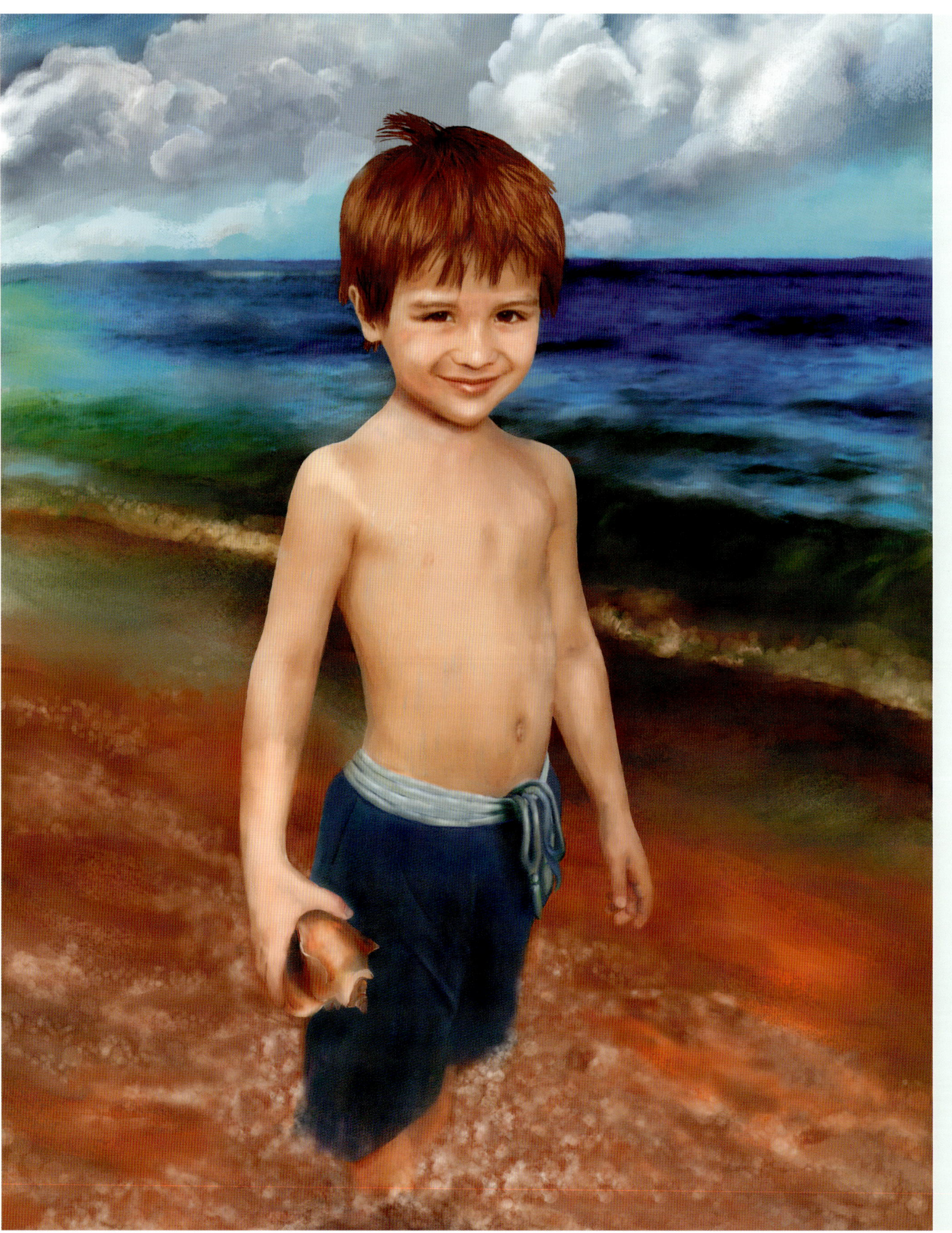

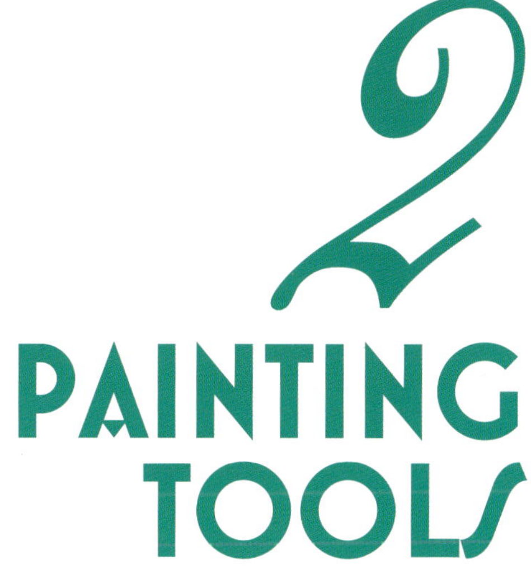

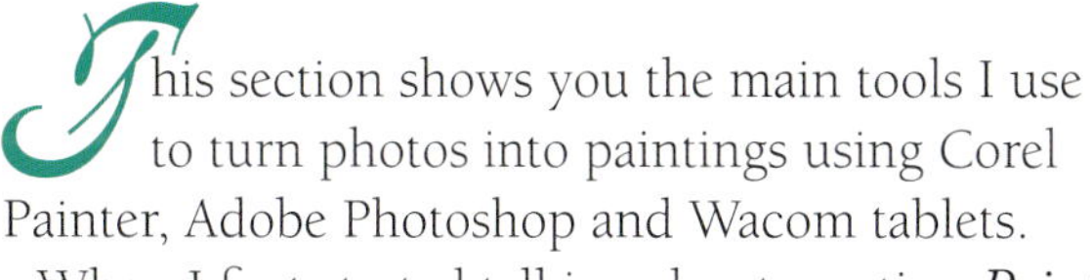

2 PAINTING TOOLS

This section shows you the main tools I use to turn photos into paintings using Corel Painter, Adobe Photoshop and Wacom tablets.

When I first started talking about creating *Painting for Photographers*, people told me that they didn't want another book with more software and hardware tools than they'll ever use.

Everyone said to keep it simple and to just show them the software and hardware they need for turning photos into paintings.

And that's what I've done in *Painting for Photographers*!

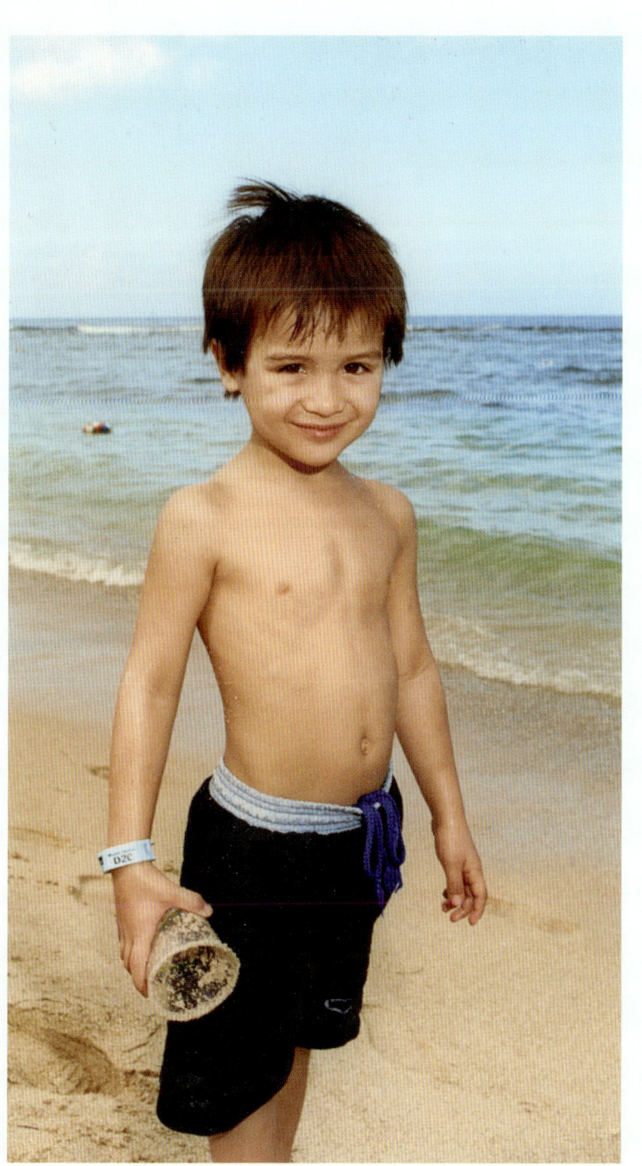

Portrait

Painting (opposite page) by Karen Sperling from a photo by Raymond Moy, M.D. (this page), featured in the July 2005 issue of Artistry Tips and Tricks. http://www.artistrymag.com/

CoREL PAINTER BRUSHES

You have arrived at the most important part of Painter, the brushes.

Painter has always offered brushes unlike those found in any other software program, and now, close to 20 years after Painter's debut, it's still true.

In this chapter, you'll learn the basics for selecting brushes and customizing them.

In addition, you'll discover tips for getting the most out of two handy painting tools, namely Auto-Painting and custom palettes.

The tutorial chapters later in the book also discuss these painting features, and this chapter serves as a quick reference for using Painter's brushes.

BRUSH SELECTOR

All the mark-making tools in Painter, from Oils to Pencils, are called brushes, regardless of whether their real-life counterparts are indeed brushes.

They live in the Brush Categories icon in the Brush Selector.

To select a brush:

1. Click the Brush Categories icon in the Brush Selector. A drop-down menu appears.
2. Click on the desired brush's icon.

Variants are the variations within a Brush Category, like the Square Chalk variant of the Chalk, pictured below.

To select a variant:

1. Click the Variants icon in the Brush Selector. A drop-down menu appears.
2. Choose a variant in the menu.

Now you can paint!

PROPERTY BAR

The Property Bar has the settings you'll use most often to customize your brushes.

Some brushes have different settings, but here are the most common ones.

Size: Brush stroke width. Lower for thinner strokes, raise for wider ones.

Opacity: Brush stroke transparency. Lower for more transparent strokes, raise for opaque ones.

Grain: Brush stroke texture. Lower for more texture (yes, it's counterintuitive), raise for less texture.

Resat: Amount of color.

Bleed: Amount colors bleed together.

Resat and Bleed work together. Lower Resat to 0% and raise Bleed to 49% and you have a blender brush.

Jitter: Randomness of dabs within brush strokes. Raise jitter for multiple dabs in a stroke. Useful for textures.

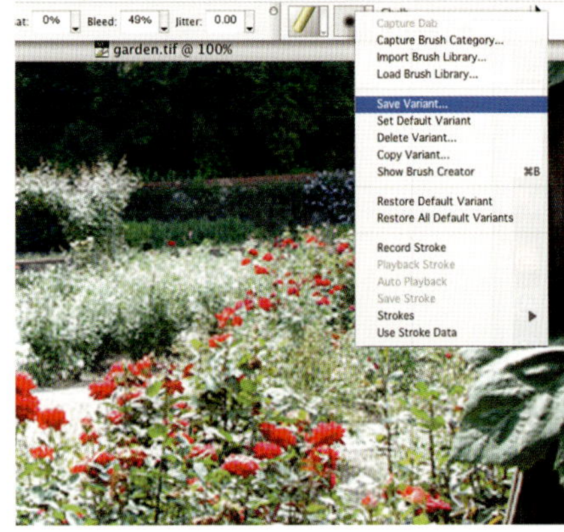

SAVE NEW SETTINGS AS A VARIANT

To save brush adjustments, create a new variant. Here's how:

1. Click the triangle in the Brush Selector.
2. Choose Save Variant. The Save Variant dialog box appears.
3. Type a name for the new variant.
4. Click OK. Your new custom variant is listed in the Variants menu (click the Variants icon to see it).

To restore a variant's initial settings:

1. Click the triangle in the Brush Selector.
2. Choose Restore Default Variant. The variant's original settings are restored.

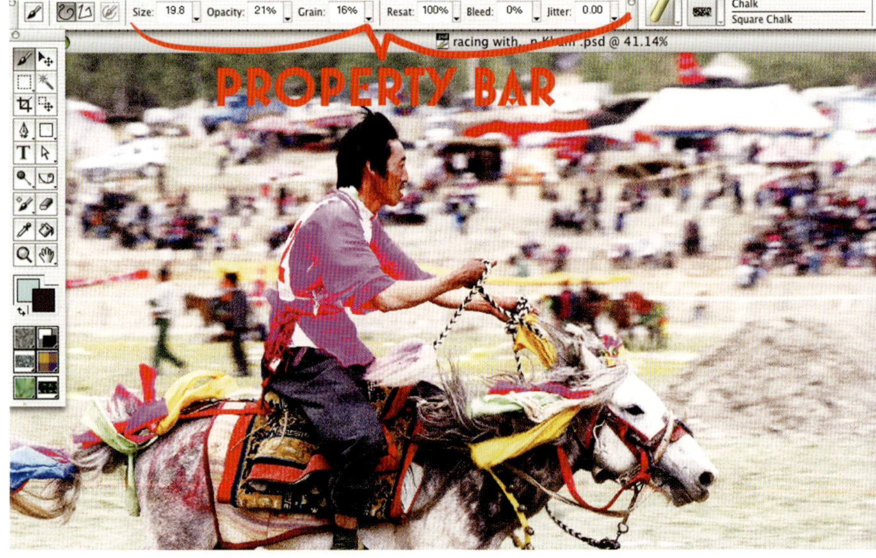

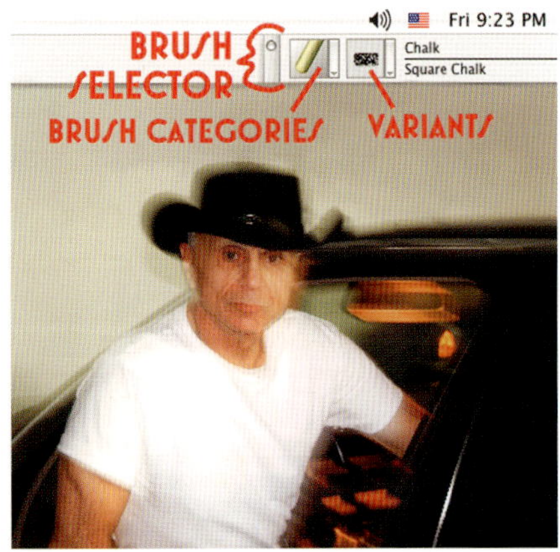

Locating Painter's Brushes

PHOTOS BY TERRI GOLD (LEFT), HERNAN CAMPERO (TOP) AND KAREN SPERLING (ABOVE).

AUTO-PAINTING

Auto-Painting is a great way to paint brush strokes quickly.

You can use the supplied strokes or create your own.

After you File: Open a photo, choose File: Clone (cloning is explained on the next page). Next, set up a brush:

1. Open the Auto-Painting palette (Window: Show Auto-Painting).
2. Choose a brush: The Artists' Sargent Brush and Impressionist variants work well.
3. Click the rubber stamp in the Colors palette.
4. Choose a stroke in the Stroke menu in the Auto-Painting palette.
5. Click the arrow in the Auto-Painting palette to run the strokes. Run them until you have large areas of brush strokes.
6. Click the red button in the palette or anywhere in the image to stop the strokes.

When the boxes beneath Randomness are checked, the strokes are haphazard/random.

I think you get a better result when you control the brush strokes by deselecting the Randomness boxes and adjusting the sliders.

The ones I use most often are the Rotation slider, which determines stroke direction; the Length slider, which decides how long they are; and the Brush Size slider, which controls their width as a percentage of the setting in the Property Bar's Size slider.

To slowly build up a painterly look, choose a setting for the sliders, run Auto-Painting, stop, adjust the sliders again, run Auto-Painting some more, keep repeating till you get the look you like.

You can personalize Auto-Painting by painting with your own, custom-made stroke in the Stroke menu.

To create a custom stroke:

1. Click the triangle in the Brush Selector.
2. In the drop down menu, chose Record Stroke.
3. Paint a short stroke.
4. Choose Save Stroke in the same menu and type a name for the stroke in the dialog box that appears. Click OK.
5. Choose this new stroke in the Stroke drop-down menu in the Auto-Painting palette and run Auto-Painting.

CUSTOM PALETTES

Use custom palettes to access your frequently used brushes.

To create a custom palette:

1. Click on a brush or on a variant in the Brush Selector and drag to the middle of the image. You'll see a little square.
2. Let go. The square becomes a custom palette.
3. To add a brush, choose it in the Brush Selector and drag it onto the new custom palette.
4. To move a brush within a custom palette, press shift and click and drag on its icon.
5. To delete a brush, press shift and click and drag it off the custom palette.

To name the custom palette:

1. Choose Window menu: Custom Palette: Organizer. The Custom Palette Organizer dialog appears.
2. Click on the new palette in the list. Click Rename.
3. Type in a name for the custom palette. What I do is type in the first name and hit the space bar a few times then I type the second name, etc. This way, each variant's name appears above its icon in the custom palette, as you see in the photo below.
4. Click OK, then click Done.

The names you typed now appear in the custom palette.

To delete a custom palette:

1. Choose Window menu: Custom Palette: Organizer. The Custom Palette Organizer dialog appears.
2. Click on the palette you wish to eliminate in the list. Click Delete.

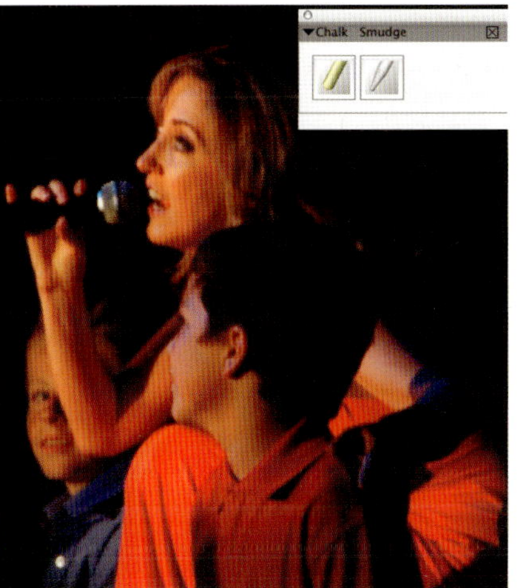

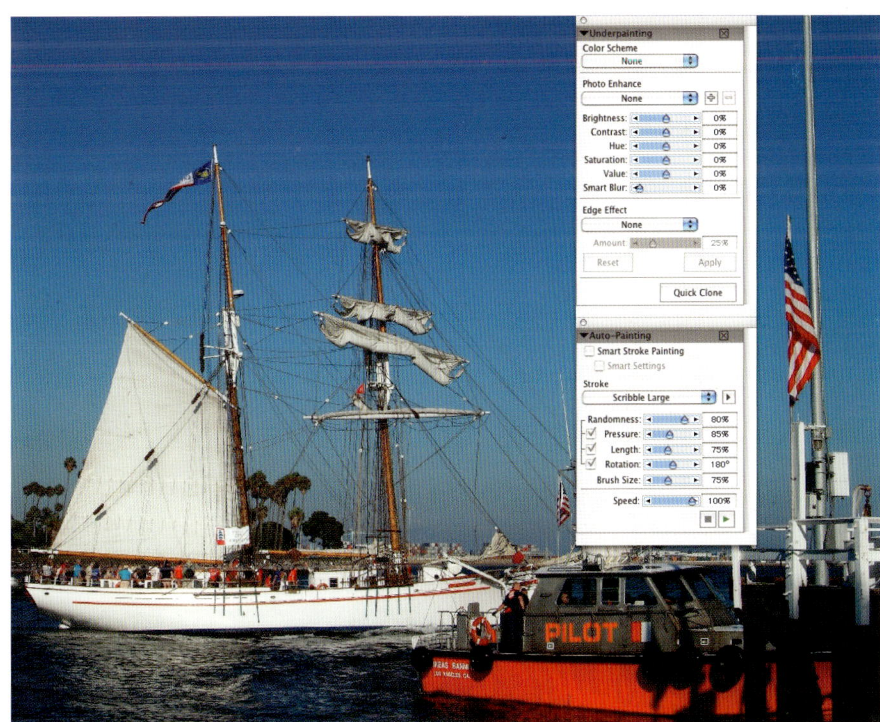

Using Painter's Brushes

Photo of Laura Pursell (top) and San Pedro, CA ships by Karen Sperling.

Corel Painter Tools

Artists have used photos for reference probably since photos were invented, from the fine artist, who "eyeballs" a photo attached to his or her easel, to the commercial artist, who projects photos on paper or canvas and paints by "tracing" the projection.

Painting from photos, then, isn't new, and Painter offers several tools to help you in the process.

This chapter shows tools that you will use most often when painting from photos. You'll also see how to create custom brushes, which are useful for painting backgrounds and softening the figure's sharp, photographic edges.

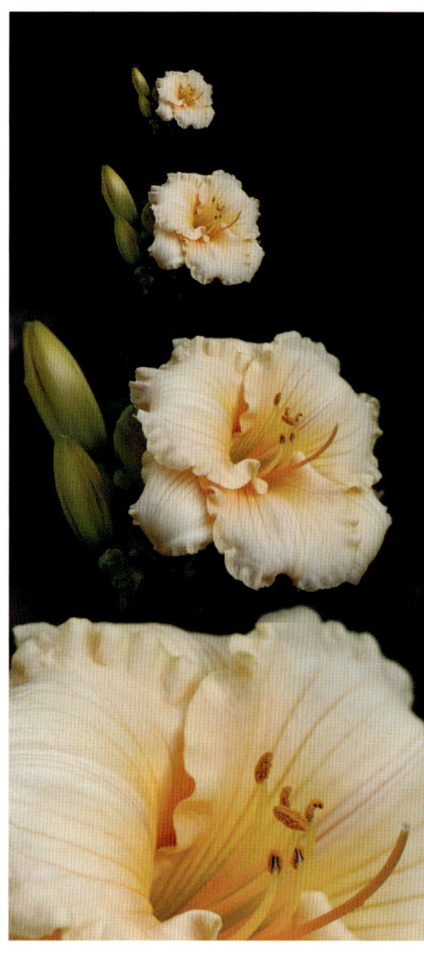

Clones

The word "clone" is thrown around a lot in Painter.

After you use the software for awhile, you get used to all the different clone references, but when you're starting out, they may not be clear.

Here's what's going on: The word clone is used in Painter as both a noun and as a verb.

Used as a noun, think of a clone as a painting.

As a verb, clone in Painter means to paint from a source, usually a photo. Easy, right?

Establishing a Clone Source

When you paint, or clone, from a photo, you have to establish the photo as the clone source.

Here are the three ways to set up the photo as a clone source:

- File: Clone

With a photo open, choose File: Clone. Now the clone is the painting, and the photo is the clone source.

- Option/alt and click

To paint within one image or between different-sized images, choose a Cloners' variant, press option, Mac; alt, Windows, click to establish the clone source and paint.

- File menu: Clone Source

Use this method to reconnect a clone source and clone that are the same size (usually a clone that you created when you chose File: Clone). Here's how:

1. Open both the source image and the clone image.
2. With the clone as the active window, select File menu: Clone Source and select the source image (as you see in the image below). The clone source is now set up.

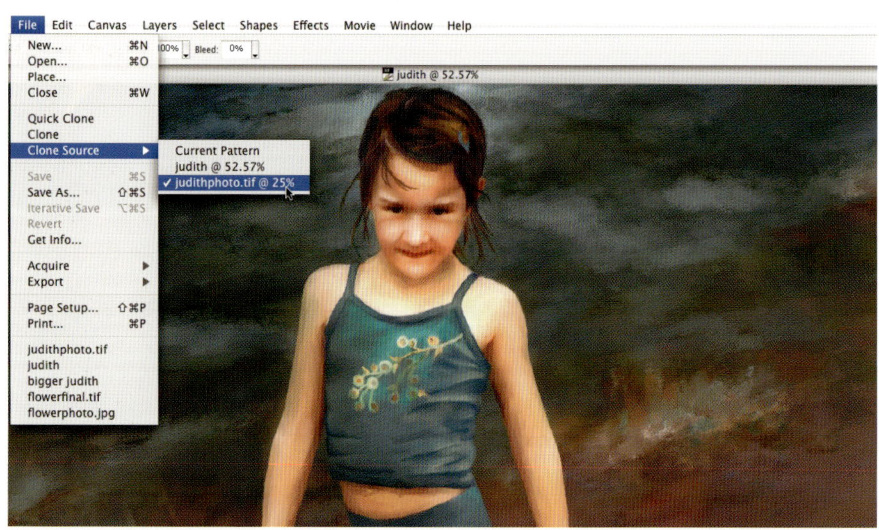

xScale 2P Variant

An exception to using option/alt and clicking to establish a clone source is when you use the Cloners' xScale 2P variant, which scales as you clone.

You establish your source and destination with two clicks instead of one.

1. Press option, Mac; alt, Windows, then click a point at the top and bottom of what you want to copy.
2. In the same image, or in a different one, press shift+option on Mac; shift+alt on Windows and click a point at the top and bottom of where you want to paint.
3. Paint. The source comes in resized.

Cloning

Painting (left) by Karen Sperling from a photo by Raymond Moy, M.D.; photo (above) by Rhonda Rosburg.

TRACING PAPER

Tracing Paper is another one of those useful Painter tools that's easy to use once you get the hang of it.

Turning Tracing Paper on lets you see your photo in your painting while you paint it.

You might think at first that it looks like the photo is part of the painting. It isn't.

When Tracing Paper is turned on, you see a 50% non-printing ghost of the photo.

When Tracing Paper is off, you just see your painting/clone without the photo.

Meanwhile, when you paint with Tracing Paper turned on, you see your brush strokes on 50% opacity.

So you don't want to paint the whole painting with Tracing Paper turned on and then shut it off at the end because the result will be far different than it appeared with Tracing Paper turned on.

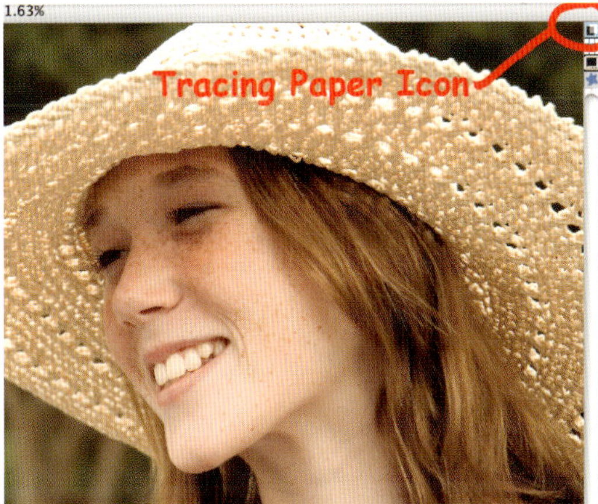

The way to work with Tracing Paper is to turn it on, paint some strokes, turn it off, view your progress, turn it on, paint some more strokes, etc.

To turn on Tracing Paper:

1. Open a photo.
2. Choose file: Clone. A clone of the original photo appears.
3. Select: All (command+a, Mac; ctrl+a, Windows).
4. Press delete, Mac; backspace Windows. The image clears.
5. Choose Canvas: Tracing Paper (command+t, Mac; ctrl+t, Windows, or click the Tracing Paper icon in the image window's top, right-hand corner). Tracing Paper appears.
6. To change Tracing Paper's opacity, click and hold on the Tracing Paper icon and choose an opacity setting. The default is 50%.

You clear the image to paint from scratch. To add brush strokes to the photo, create the clone, but don't select and delete. However, you won't see the Tracing Paper till you have painted in the clone.

If you have layers or selections in the photo, you'll lose them if you clone, so set up Tracing Paper this way:

1. With the photo open, choose File: Save As and name the new file.
2. Keep the new file open and open the previous photo.
3. Attach the images (see the instructions on the previous page under File Menu: Clone Source).
4. Turn on Tracing Paper (see number 5 above). Tracing paper is on and you also have your layers and selections to work with.

CUSTOMIZING BRUSHES

A great way to create your own, unique look and to add texture to your brush strokes is to create your own custom tip, which creates the brush stroke's silhouette. The Artists' Impressionist variant is an example of a brush with a custom tip.

You can create "abstract" tips for general textures, or you can create "realistic" ones, like leaves.

To create a custom tip:

First create a new variant:

1. Choose a brush and a variant. The variants that work particularly well are the Artists' Impressionist and the Sponges' Smeary Wet Sponge.
2. Choose Brush Selector icon: Save Variant. The Save Variant dialog appears.
3. Type in your new variant's name. Click OK.
4. Choose the new variant in the Variants pop-up menu.

You now have a new variant that has

Customizing

Photo (top) by Barbara Okun; painting (above) by Karen Sperling.

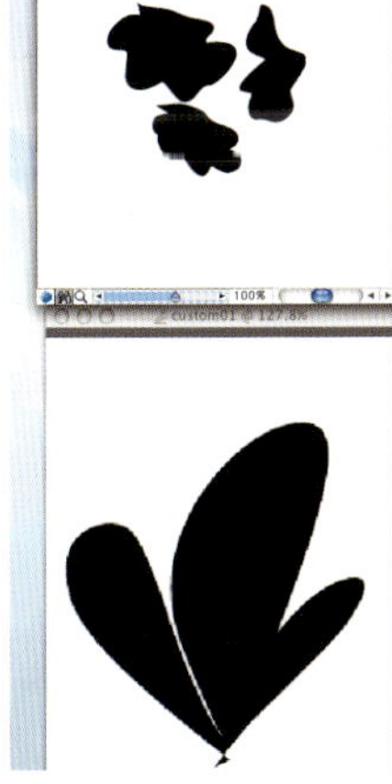

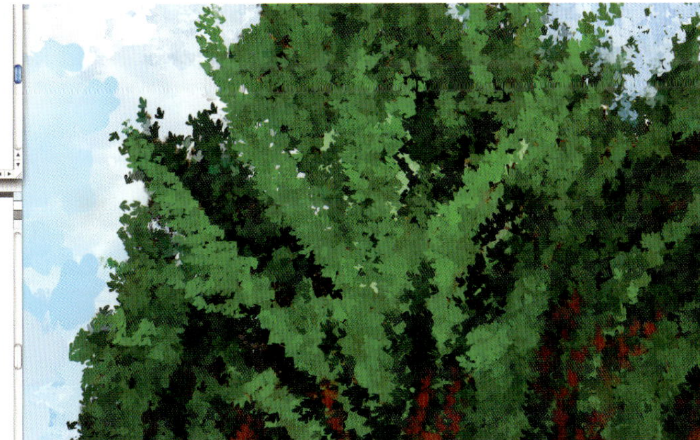

the same properties as the original brush variant.

Next, create a new brush tip for the new variant (see the examples above).

1. Start a new image (File: New).
2. Choose black in the Colors palette.
3. Create selections with the lasso from the toolbox and fill with black (Effects: Fill) to get the tips above, or paint tips with the Impressionist brush for painterly results.
4. Draw a selection around the new tip with the rectangle tool from the toolbox.
5. Choose the Brush Selector menu icon (the little arrow all the way to the right): Capture Dab, which adds the new tip to the variant.

Save the variant one more time.

1. Choose Brush Selector icon: Save Variant.
2. In the Save Variant dialog, click OK. A prompt asks if you want to replace the variant. Click Yes.
3. Choose Select menu: None (command+d) to deselect the selection.
4. Paint with your new variant.

COLOR IN PAINTER

You've seen how to choose a color scheme and how colors are related to tones.

This chapter has the basics for applying color in Painter, from choosing colors to paint with to adding colors in an automated way.

You'll use color in Painter not just to paint brush strokes, but also to create an underpainting, which, in art terms, is the first coat of paint applied to the canvas or paper.

An underpainting unifies the painting's colors and it speeds up the painting process by filling broad areas with color.

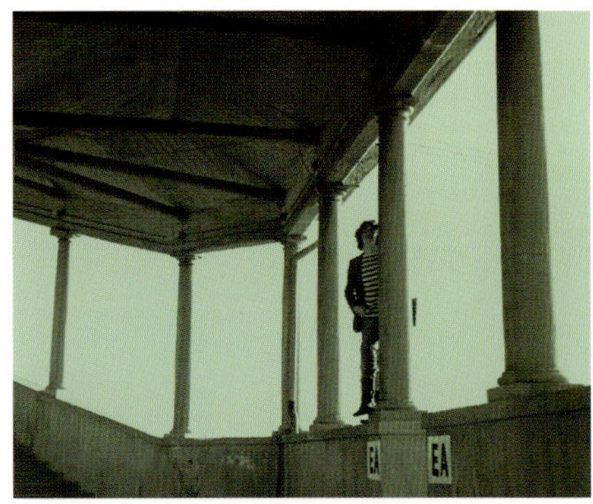

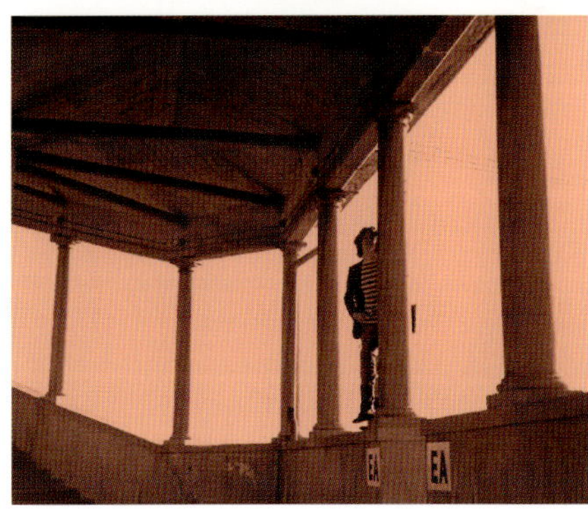

COLORS PALETTE

The main way to choose colors in Painter is to select them in the Colors palette, found in the Window menu under Color Palettes.

The Colors palette is pretty easy to use, once you get used to it.

The circle is called the hue ring, and you choose a color family in it.

The triangle shows saturation from left to right, with the least saturated color, gray, all the way to the left, and the most saturated color to the right.

The triangle from top to bottom represents values or tones, with the top being the lightest, or white, and the bottom being the darkest, or black.

Most brushes won't paint the color chosen in the rear color square, so make sure the front square is chosen by clicking on it before painting.

MORE COLOR OPTIONS

In addition to using the Colors palette, choose colors by:

- Using Cloners variants, which paint the clone source's colors (see page 26 for ways to establish a clone source).
- Clicking the rubber stamp in the Colors palette, which turns any non-Cloners brush into a cloner that uses the clone source's colors. Setting a clone source allows you to pick up all the source's colors when painting.
- Pressing option, Mac; alt, Windows and clicking on the desired color with a non-Cloners variant chosen, which is a shortcut to the eye dropper tool. This lifts the clicked color from within the image or from another image.

Here it is in a nutshell: For non-Cloners brushes, pressing option/alt and clicking picks up a single color. For Cloners or non-Cloners with the rubber stamp selected, pressing option/alt and clicking sets a clone source for you to pick up all colors.

LAYERS

Painter's layers can be helpful for creating a color scheme (see page 30 for more information about layers).

1. With a photo open, choose Layers menu: New Layer.
2. Uncheck Preserve Transparency in the Layers palette (found in the Window menu).
3. Choose a color and choose Effects: Fill, click OK.
4. Choose Color in the Layers palette. The chosen color now tints the photo and you have a selected color scheme (see above images).

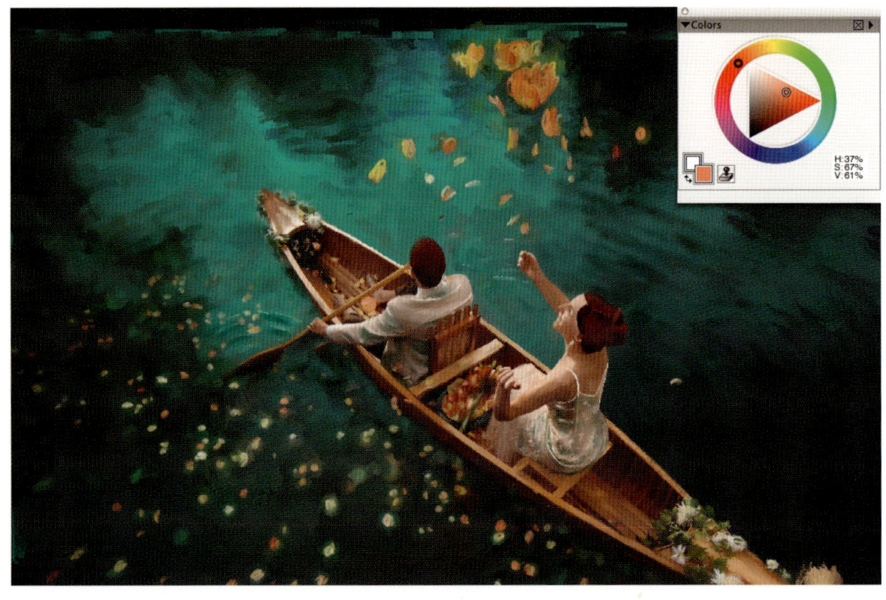

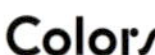

Colors

PAINTING (LEFT) BY KAREN SPERLING FROM A PHOTO BY KEVIN KUBOTA; PHOTOS (ABOVE) BY KAREN SPERLING.

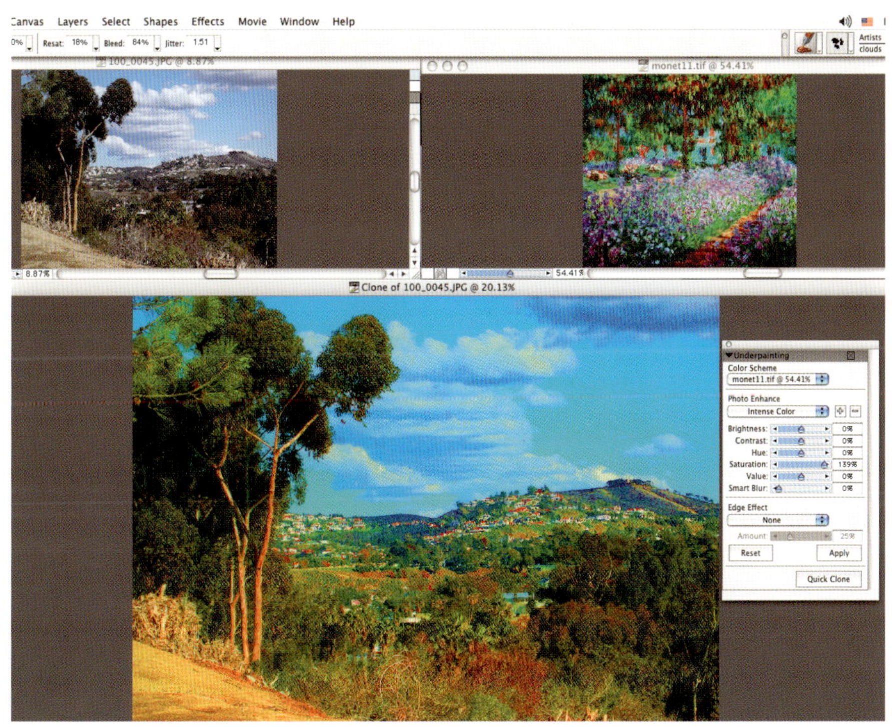

USING COLOR SCHEMES

Edit your photo's color scheme using the Underpainting's Color Scheme menu, which applies another image's color scheme based on areas of light and dark (luminance).

Get paintings from the internet or scan them from books and use their color schemes in your art!

1. Choose Window: Underpainting palette.
2. Open the source image and destination image.
3. With the destination image as the active window, choose the source image—in this case, a Monet painting—in the Underpainting palette's Color Scheme menu.

The colors appear in the image.

In the Underpainting palette, choose Photo Enhance menu: High Contrast, click Apply, then choose Intense Color to intensify the effect.

GRADIENTS

Use Painter's Gradients and Color Schemes to create underpaintings.

Here's how you create a gradient:

1. Choose the Colors palette in Window menu: Color Palettes and the Gradients palette in Window menu: Library Palettes.
2. Choose Two-Point in the gradients list at the top, right corner of the Gradients palette.
3. Choose a color in the Colors palette, then click on the rear square and choose a second color. Click on the front square again to make sure it's selected.

You now have a two-point gradient that you can see in the Gradients palette preview.

Click and drag on the red dot in the Gradients palette to reposition the gradient direction.

You can adjust the gradient to experiment with different colors.

Choose Gradients palette: menu icon (the little arrow in the upper right-hand corner): Edit Gradient. The Edit Gradient dialog box appears.

You can add colors from the Colors palette while the Edit Gradient dialog box is open.

To add a color to the gradient:

1. Click under the color bar in the Edit Gradient dialog, which adds a triangle.
2. Click a color in the Colors palette. You now have a new color in the gradient, and you see how it looks in the Gradients palette preview.

You can keep clicking new triangles and choosing colors for them in the Colors palette.

To change an existing triangle's color, click it, then choose a color in the Colors palette. Dragging the triangles in the Edit Gradient dialog changes the colors' ratios to one another. To delete a color, click on its triangle and press delete, Mac; backspace, Windows.

All changes appear in the Gradients palette preview.

When done, click OK to close the Edit Gradient dialog.

Now you can apply the gradient in one of these ways:

- Effects: Fill, click next to gradient.
- Choose Gradients palette: Menu icon: Express in Image. Click OK. The gradient appears in the image based on luminance, or areas of light and dark.
- Paint bucket. Click where you'd like the gradient to appear.

Gradients, Color Schemes

IMAGES ON THIS PAGE BY KAREN SPERLING.

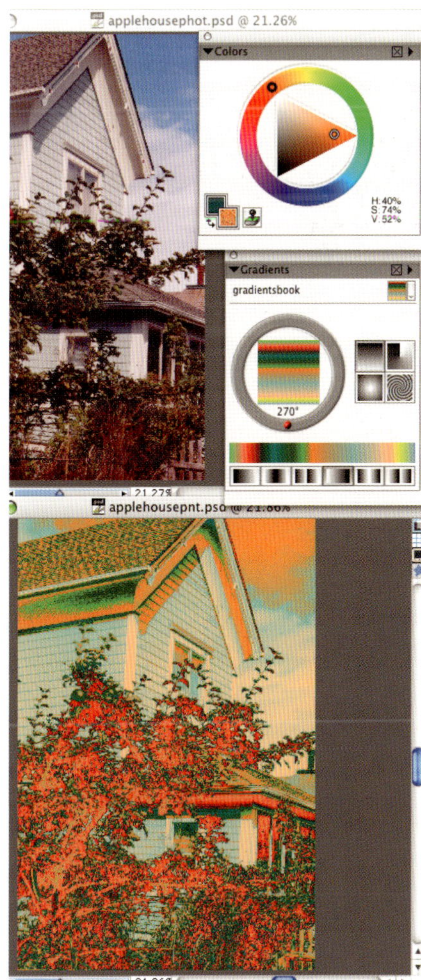

LAYERS IN PAINTER

I don't use layers a lot.

I'm in the habit of painting mostly on the canvas because doing so is the most similar to the way you paint in real life.

Layers do come in handy, though. I use them when I am painting a portrait—I'll put the figure in a layer and paint in the background.

I also use layers to composite the source photo/image.

Layers are great for creating image hose nozzles, discussed on page 32.

You usually create a layer from a selection.

I use Photoshop's Magnetic Lasso to select, which is described on page 36.

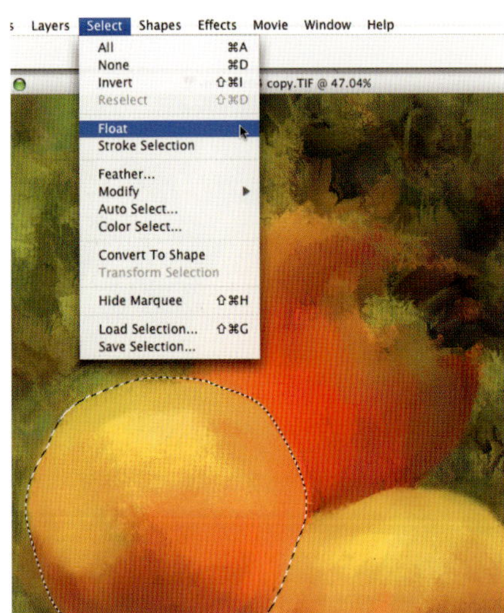

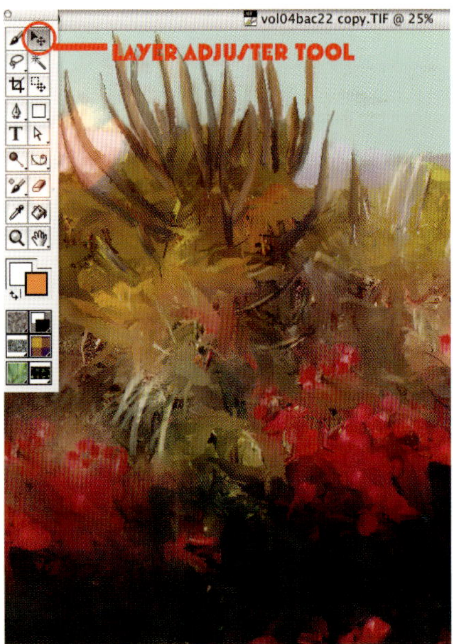

CREATING LAYERS

You can create a new layer as easily as choosing Layers menu: New Layer.

I usually make a layer from a selection of a subject like a person, a pet, a flower, etc.

You create a layer from a selection in several ways.

FLOAT

With a selection active, choose Select menu: Float. Hold option, Mac; alt, Windows to create a copy

CLICK

1. With a selection active, choose the Layer Adjuster tool, located next to the Brush in the toolbox (or type f to access it).
2. Click inside the selection. The selected area becomes a layer. Hold option, Mac; alt, Windows when you click to create a copy.

COPY/PASTE

1. With a selection active, choose Edit: Copy.
2. Choose Edit: Paste. It's now a layer.

CLICK AND DRAG

1. Click within a selection and drag it either within the same image or onto another image.
2. The selected area becomes a layer.

LAYER TOOL AND LIST

Layers are listed in the Layers palette, found in the Window menu.

Move layers in the image with the Layer Adjuster tool. Click Auto Select Layer in the Property Bar to select individual layers in the image without having to click them first in the Layers palette.

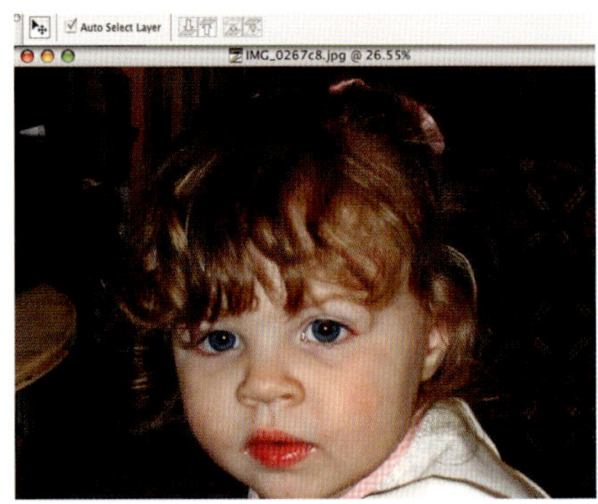

MAKING THE CANVAS A LAYER

In Painter, the Canvas isn't a layer. It's like the floor—it doesn't move.

You can place the contents of the Canvas into a layer. Here's how:

1. Click Canvas in the Layers palette.
2. Choose Select: All.
3. With the Layer Adjuster tool selected, click anywhere in the Canvas or choose Select menu: Float.

The Canvas contents are now a layer and the Canvas is white.

If you want a copy of the contents to remain in the Canvas, press option, Mac; alt, Windows when you click on the Canvas to make it a layer or when you choose Select: Float.

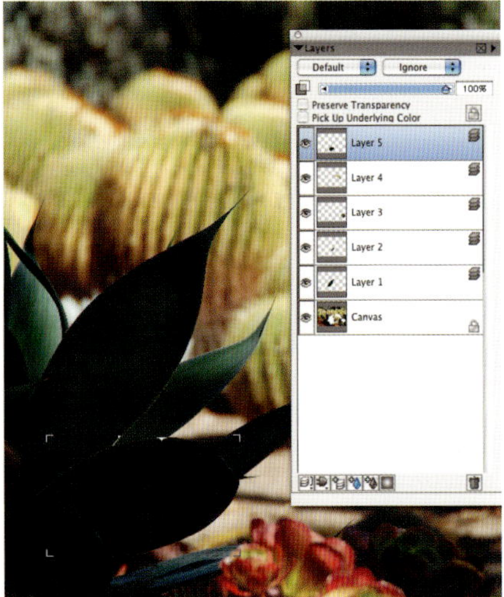

Layers

Top photo by Katherine Beach, other images by Karen Sperling.

PAINTING BEYOND A LAYER OBJECT

I use layers mostly for portraits.

I have the figure in a layer and the background is the Canvas.

The layer's edges are defined by the original selection used to create the layer.

Editing layer edges is useful for changing objects like hair, as you see in the images at right.

You can edit the layer's edge using Preserve Transparency and Layer Masks.

Preserve Transparency lets you paint beyond the layer's edge.

Try it yourself:

1. Select a layer, click Preserve Transparency in the Layers palette
2. Choose the Chalk's Sharp Chalk and paint in the layer. The brush strokes stay within the layer's edge.
3. Deselect Preserve Transparency and paint in the layer. Your brush strokes go past the visible edge.

When you paint past the edge, your strokes become the new edge.

1. Click Preserve Transparency again.
2. Paint on the edge. Your strokes now go on the new strokes, but not past them.

REDUCING THE LAYER OBJECT

You reduce the layer object's visible edge by painting in the layer mask. Use layer masks to create transparency within a layer, too.

1. With the layer chosen in the Layers palette, select Layers menu: Create Layer Mask. A new mask icon appears next to the layer icon in the Layers palette.
2. Click on this new mask icon. The icon is now outlined in black.
3. Paint in the layer mask in the image with the Airbrushes' Digital Airbrush with black chosen in the Colors palette. Adjusting the Opacity slider in the Property Bar produces varying levels of transparency, with 100% being opaque. Paint with white to restore color.

When done, choose Layers menu: Apply Layer Mask to merge the mask with the layer.

It's a good idea to apply the layer masks right away because they tend to corrupt easily, especially when you move the layers.

FLATTENING LAYERS

Choose Layers menu: Drop to flatten one layer at a time; choose Layers menu: Drop All to flatten all the layers simultaneously.

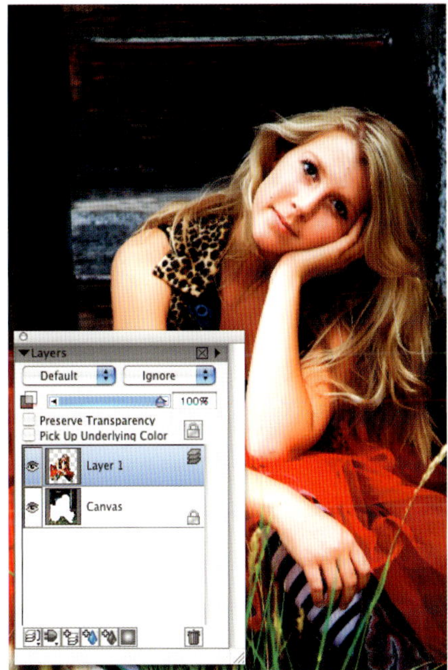

BEFORE PRESERVE TRANSPARENCY

The hair layer before it's painted. The girl is a layer and the background is in the Canvas.

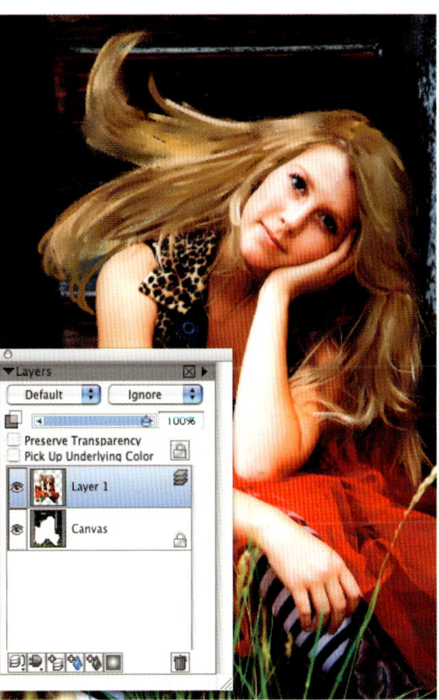

AFTER PRESERVE TRANSPARENCY

The hair after it's painted with the Sharp Chalk with Preserve Transparency deselected.

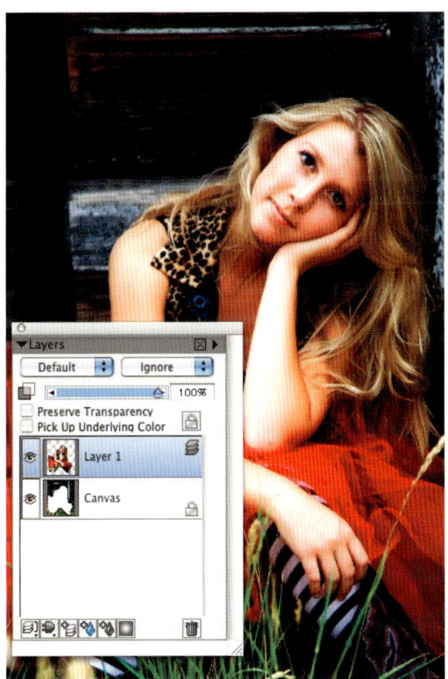

BEFORE LAYER MASK

The girl is a layer and the background is in the Canvas.

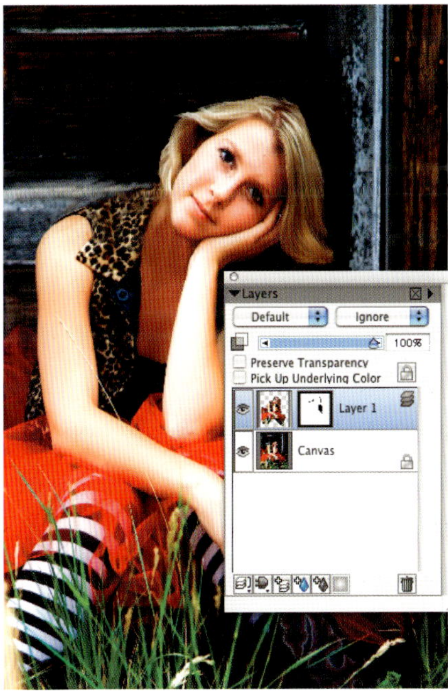

AFTER LAYER MASK

Painting in the layer mask using the Digital Airbrush trimmed the hair.

Layer Objects

PHOTO BY TERRIE STRICK, PAINTING ADDED BY KAREN SPERLING.

IMAGE HOSE/TEXTURES

One of the best things about Painter is that it offers many tools for you to create your own look and style rather than copy someone else's.

You saw on page 25 and page 27 how to create your own Auto-Painting strokes and custom brush tips.

In this chapter are instructions for creating your own image hose nozzles and paper textures.

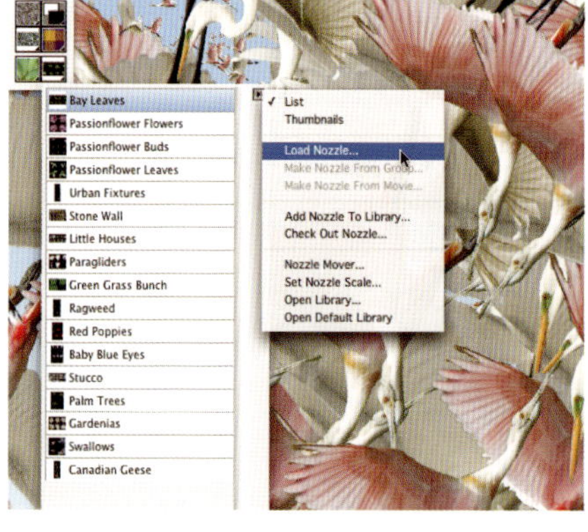

USING THE IMAGE HOSE

The image hose sprays multiple images from nozzles.

For instance, you can create an image hose nozzle of flowers and fill a background with them, which is what I did in the photo of the girl on the opposite page.

Here's how the Image Hose works.

1. Start a new image (File: New) or paint on an existing image. Choose Brush Selector: Image Hose.
2. Click the icon in the toolbox's lower right-hand corner. The Image Hose nozzles list appears.
3. Click on the various icons and paint in the image. The Image Hose sprays multiple images from the chosen nozzle.

The Image Hose variants with the word linear paint in lines; the ones with the word spray paint randomly.

Adjust element size using the Size slider in the Property Bar.

You can change nozzle element colors. For instance, in the image on the opposite page, I made the flowers in the background darker to appear further away:

1. Click on the rear square in the Colors palette. Choose a color, then click on the front square.
2. Move the Grain slider in the Property Bar to the left.
3. Paint with the Image Hose. The elements are the color you chose for the Colors palette's rear square. The more you move the Grain slider to the left, the truer the color will be to the one you selected; the more you move the slider to the right, the closer the color will be to the original nozzle-element color.

You can create your own nozzles.

1. Start a new image (File: New). Make it 7" x 5" at 300 dpi.
2. Open a photo or a painting. Select six elements one at a time with the lasso. For example, I selected flowers from the photo below for my image hose nozzle.
3. Click and drag each element into the new image with the Layer Adjuster tool with Auto Select Layer chosen in the Property Bar.
4. Click Canvas each time before you click and drag on a layer in the source image. If you don't see the layer in the destination image, double click it in the Layers palette and type 0 in the Top and Left fields, then click OK.

Next, save as a nozzle.

1. In the Layers palette, highlight all the layers by pressing shift and clicking on each one.
2. Choose Layers menu: Group.
3. Click the icon in the toolbox's lower right-hand corner. Click the triangle in the drop-down menu's upper right-hand corner. Choose Make Nozzle From Group. An image appears. This is your new image hose nozzle.
4. Choose File: Save As and save it in the RIFF format. Close the image.

Paint with your new nozzle.

1. With the Image Hose selected in the Brush Selector, in that same triangle in the toolbox, choose Load Nozzle (above image). Find your nozzle in the dialog and open it.
2. Start a new image and paint with the Image Hose. The Image Hose sprays your nozzle elements!

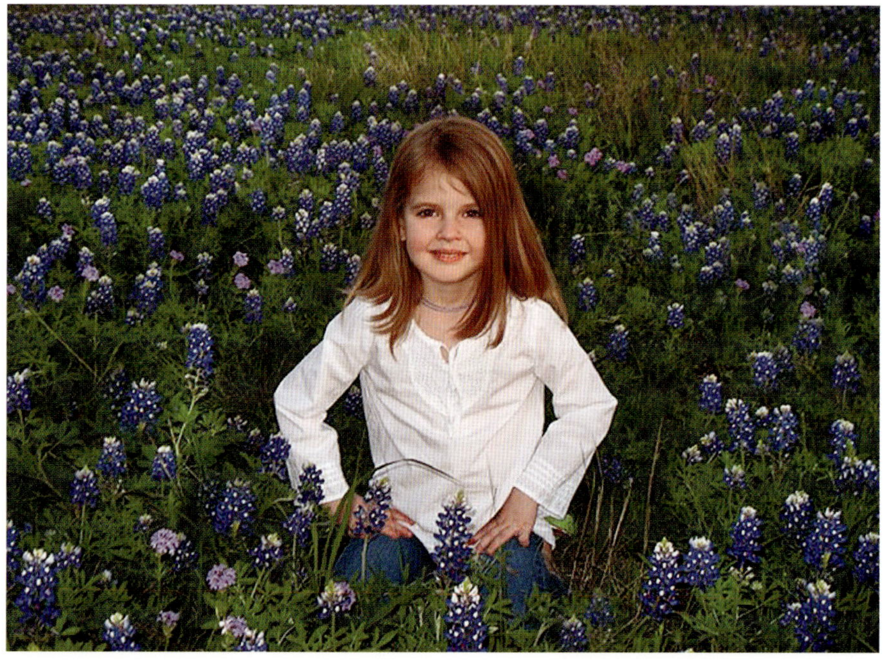

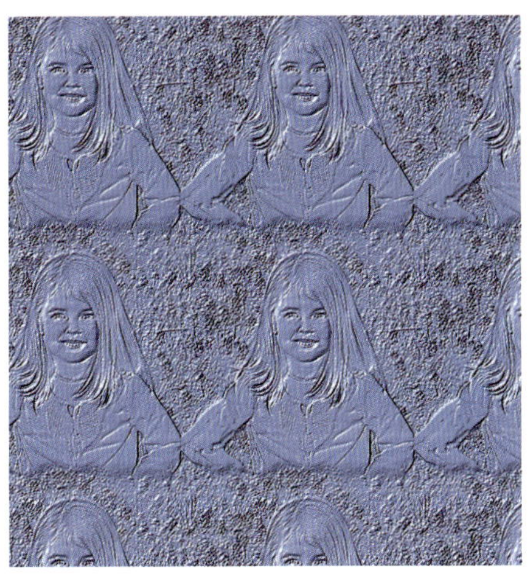

ADDING PAPER TEXTURE

Painter has powerful tools for adding paper texture either with paint brushes or with the Effects menu.

Brushes that interact with paper grain show the Grain slider in the Property Bar when selected.

To paint with paper texture, use a paper-sensitive brush like the Chalk's Square Chalk variant and choose a texture in the first icon in the group of icons at the bottom of the toolbox.

You can choose as many different textures as you like.

In addition to painting with paper texture, you can also add paper texture, either to the entire image, within a selection or on a layer, by choosing Effects: Surface Control: Apply Surface Texture. Choose Paper in the Using menu to apply the chosen texture, or choose Image Luminance, which adds texture based on the image's light and dark areas. Using Image Luminance adds depth and texture to individual brush strokes.

When you see paintings from photos with a little bit of texture, like the portrait on page 40, you're probably looking at an example of Apply Surface Texture using Image Luminance.

EDITING TEXTURE

Change the scale of the chosen paper texture in the Window menu: Library Palettes: Papers palette by moving the top slider.

Adjust the amount of texture in your brush strokes using the Grain slider in the Property Bar.

Move the Grain slider to the left to show more texture; move the slider to the right for less texture.

This is counterintuitive, but in the very early versions of Painter, the Grain slider was called the Penetration slider. So moving it to the left meant the color penetrated the paper grain less, revealing more texture. Moving the slider to the right meant the color was penetrating the paper more, hiding more paper color. So the slider affects not paper texture, but how color mixes with paper texture.

The Digital Watercolor brushes work differently from the other brushes. Moving the Grain slider all the way to the left shuts off paper texture—the opposite of all other brushes.

CREATING TEXTURE

You can create paper textures from brush strokes, original art, photos, recognizable shapes, abstract designs, gradations, scanned textures—anything—and save them in the Papers palette.

For the texture at left, I cropped the photo, below.

Here are the steps:

1. Crop the photo to what you want to appear as the paper texture: With Painter's Crop tool in the toolbox, select the desired area, then click inside the selection to crop.
2. In the Patterns palette (it's in the Window menu under Library Palettes) choose menu icon (the little arrow all the way to the right): Define Pattern, which makes the image wrap around.
3. Press shift and spacebar and click and drag in the image—you can check the paper's repeating pattern, including any obvious seams.
4. Paint over seams with the Cloners' Soft Cloner—press option/alt and click on the area next to the seam and paint on the seam to hide it. Check the seams again, blend more of them out, repeat.
5. When done, choose Select: All.
6. In the menu icon in the Papers palette choose Capture Paper. The Save Paper dialog box appears. Type a name and click OK. Your new paper texture now appears as an icon in the list of paper textures both in the Papers palette and in the paper icon in the toolbox.

Now you can paint with this texture with a paper-sensitive brush, or apply it with the Effects menu. For my image at the top of this page, I started a new image, filled with a color (Effects: Fill) then used Effects: Surface Control: Apply Surface Texture using Paper.

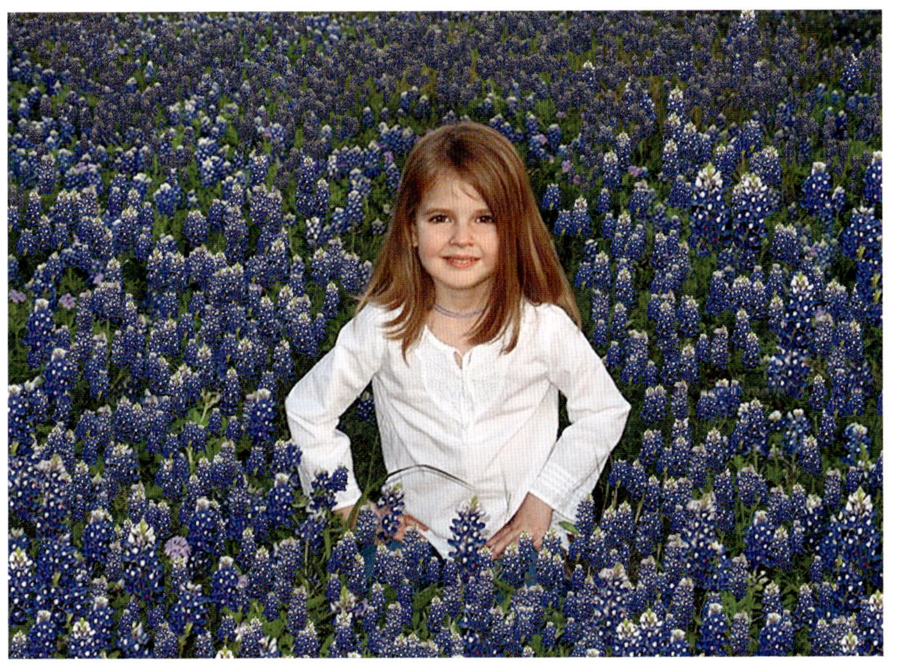

Image Hose

PAINTINGS BY KAREN SPERLING FROM PHOTOS BY FRANK STEWART (LEFT) AND KIRK ALLEMAND (TOP, OPPOSITE PAGE).

ADOBE PHOTOSHOP BRUSHES

One of the questions I hear most frequently is, "What's the difference between Photoshop and Painter?"

The answer used to be simple: Photoshop's metaphor was a photographer's darkroom; Painter's was an artist's atelier.

Those distinctions aren't quite true anymore because Photoshop's brushes are more powerful today than ever before.

Interestingly, the contrast between the two applications nowadays is in the different effects achieved with each program's brushes.

I find it's easier to paint brush strokes with texture and variety in Painter, while you can more easily create bold, smooth, maybe even slicker brush strokes in Photoshop.

You can adjust controls in both programs to get just about any effect you want, but I'm interested in what each program does best without the user having to jump through software hoops to get good results.

In these chapters, I go over some of the Photoshop brushes and features that I use most often.

You'll also find Photoshop instructions in the tutorials section.

This book has more Painter tutorials because Painter offers a broader assortment of brushes.

However, Photoshop's brushes provide additional creative possibilities!

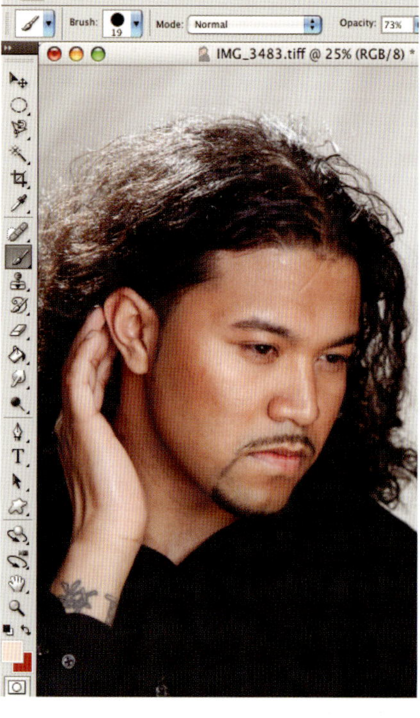

BRUSH AND SMUDGE

I paint in Photoshop the way I paint in Painter, that is, I paint color, then blend it, then paint some more, then blend some more, building up the painting based on the lights and darks in the photo.

Photoshop's two main painting tools for me, then, are the Brush and the Smudge, found in the Tools panel.

You choose variations of the Brush and Smudge tools in the Brush Preset picker in the options bar.

After you select a preset, press return, Mac; enter, Windows to hide the Brush Preset picker.

You can also choose brush presets from the Brushes panel, accessed in the Window menu.

I like to leave the Brushes panel open because it's easier to quickly access brush presets there than in the Brush Preset picker, which you open and then close each time you choose another brush preset.

Whether you use the Brush Preset picker or the Brushes panel, choose Text Only in the drop down menu (in the little triangle) to see the brush presets' names, which makes selecting them easier.

In both locations, the Master Diameter slider controls brush stroke width. Move the slider to the left for more narrow strokes and to the right for wider ones.

Hardness in the Brush Preset picker

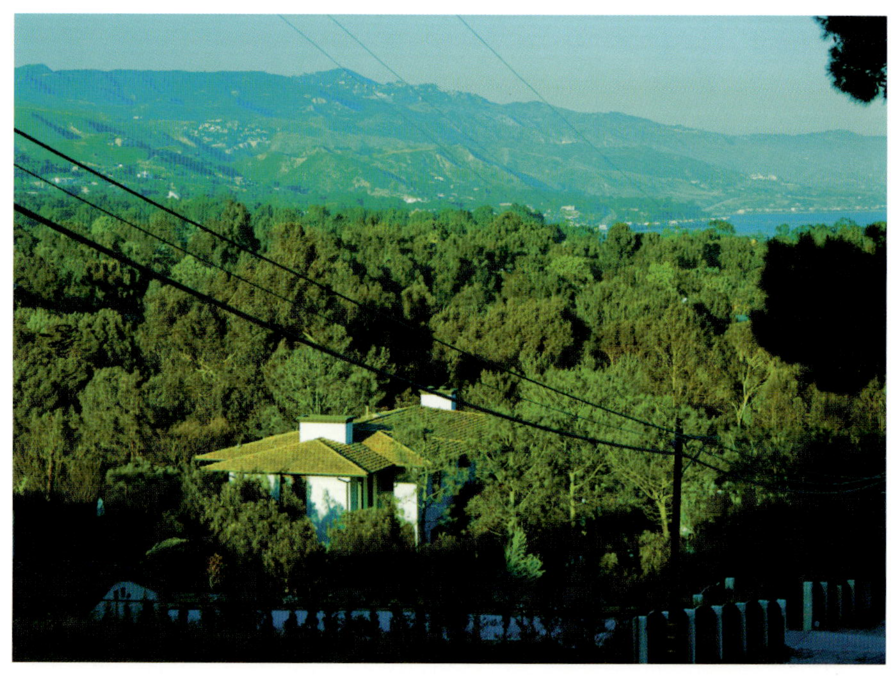

Photoshop Brushes

Photos by Alfred Burgess (top) and Karen Sperling (right and opposite).

refers to stroke edge.

Moving the slider to the right produces an aliased, or hard-edged stroke. Moving the slider to the left creates anti-aliased, or soft-edged strokes.

Opacity in the options bar controls stroke transparency. The lower the setting, the more transparent the stroke will be. The higher the setting, the more opaque it will be.

I generally paint broad areas with the Brush tool and a soft-edged preset like the Soft Round, the Airbrush Soft Round or the Airbrush Dual Brush Soft Round, and details with a hard-edged preset like Hard Round.

To blend the strokes, choose the Smudge tool and the Charcoal Large Smear preset, which blends with texture. To blend with less texture, use a Chalk preset on a low Master Diameter setting.

When you use the Smudge tool, if you're painting on layers, click Sample All Layers in the options bar to blend using color data from all visible layers. If you don't select it, the Smudge tool uses only the active layer's colors.

For rougher areas, like hair, paint with the Brush tool and the Spatter or the Rough Round Bristle presets and blend with the Smudge tool with the Oil Medium Wet Flow preset.

Artists frequently paint outlines to add definition to objects like clothing and buildings. Paint with a Spatter brush on various opacity levels to create outlines.

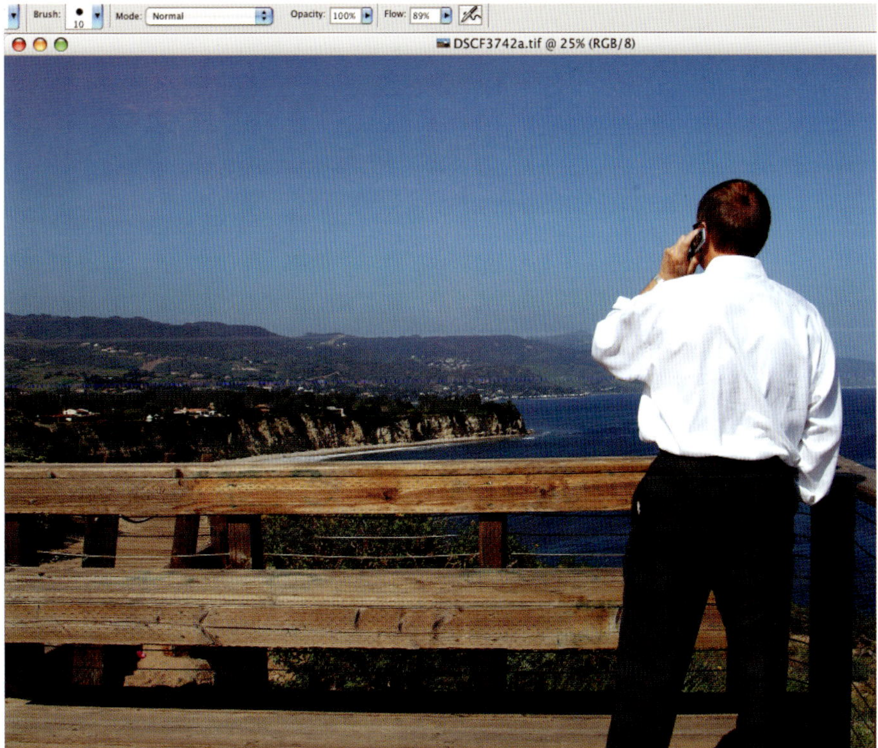

CUSTOM BRUSH PRESETS

Use textured presets like the Scattered Leaves for backgrounds—see page 54 for an example.

You can also create your own presets. Here's how:

1. Using any selection tool, select the image area you want to use as a custom preset.
2. To create a brush with sharp edges, set Feather in the options bar to zero pixels. To create a brush with soft edges, increase the Feather setting.
3. Choose Edit: Define Brush Preset. The Brush Name dialog appears.
4. Type in a name for the preset, click OK.

Choose the brush tool and your new preset and paint—instant texture!

SPOT HEALING BRUSH

You read in the art lessons chapters that one of the differences between a painting and a photo is that a painting has less detail (see page 17).

Using Photoshop's Spot Healing Brush tool is a great way to eliminate details like telephone lines, as you see on the previous page and this one in these photos I took in Malibu.

The Spot Healing Brush tool can't be any easier to use, you just scribble on the spot you want to remove and poof, it's gone. It works better on a pattern like trees than on flat color.

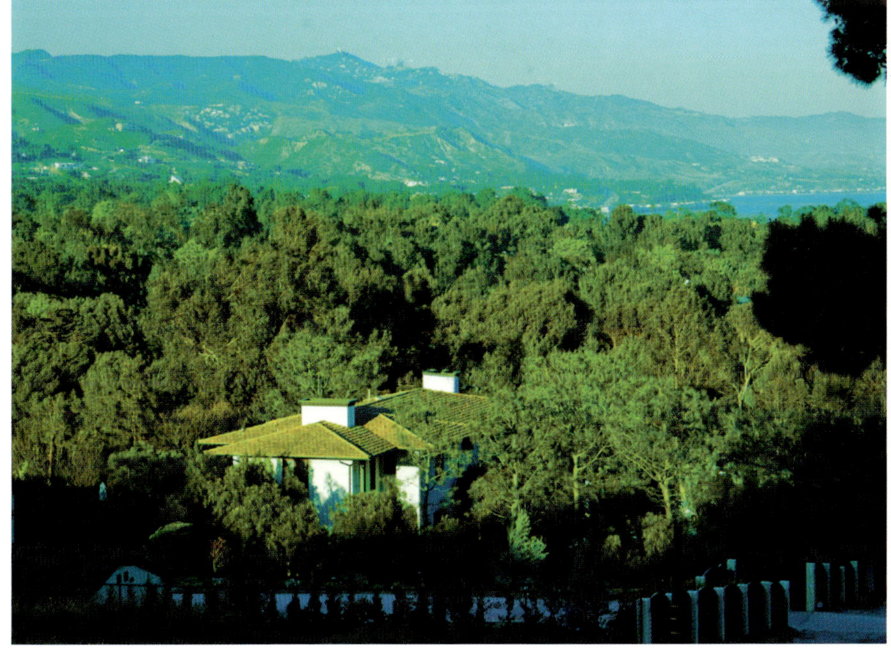

ADOBE PHOTOSHOP TOOLS

This chapter covers the Photoshop tools that I use the most often when turning photos into paintings.

I've been using Painter longer, so I do a lot of things there that experienced Photoshop users might do in Photoshop.

If you are used to working in Photoshop, use all the tools that you know how to use. These pages aren't trying to imply that these are the only Photoshop tools there are, they're just the ones I use.

If you're like me and know Painter better, these are the main Photoshop features you need to know for painting photos.

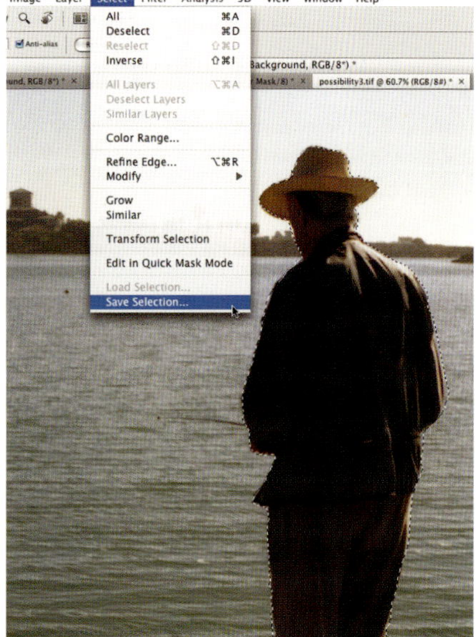

MAGNETIC LASSO

The Photoshop tool that I use the most often is the Magnetic Lasso, found in the Tools panel by clicking and holding on the Lasso tool.

I use the Magnetic Lasso for selecting everything from figures for portraits to image objects for creating image hose nozzles in Painter.

Here's how the Magnetic Lasso tool 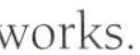 works.

1. Click a starting point.
2. Move the cursor along the edge of the area you want to select.
3. Click a point every inch or two as you go along the edge of the figure, or whatever you're selecting. The line acts as a magnet and sticks to the areas between the clicks.
4. If you click in the wrong spot, press delete, Mac; backspace, Windows to go back.
5. If the selection gets hopelessly jumbled, press return, Mac; enter, Windows, which completes the selection. Press command+d, Mac; ctrl+d, Windows to deselect the selection. Start over again.
6. Keep going till you get to the starting point and click your last point on the first one, or press return/ enter, which results in a selection marquee.

Once you have the selection marquee, you can edit it with the Lasso. To reduce the selection, hold down option, Mac; alt, Windows and draw a circle with the Lasso where you want to reduce the selection. The no. 1 circle in the image at left shows you the direction in which you would drag the circle to reduce the selection. To add to the selection, hold down the shift key and draw a circle with the Lasso around the section where you want the selection to extend to. The no. 2 circle shows you where you would draw the circle.

Once you have your selection the way you want it, choose Select menu:

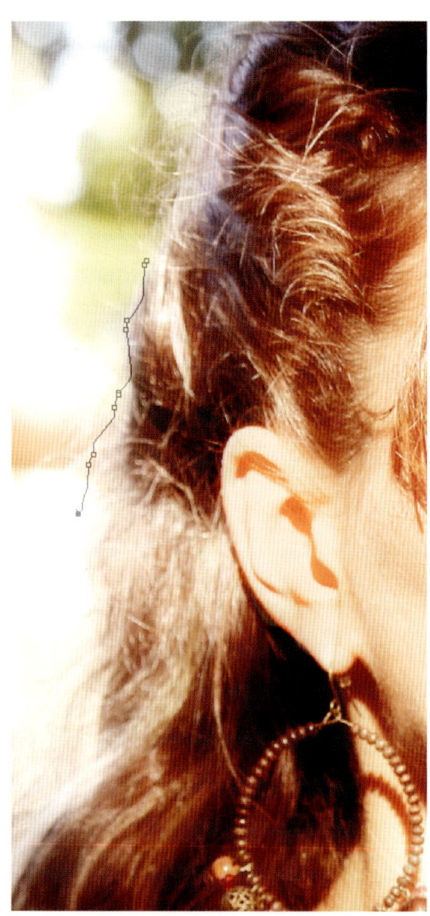

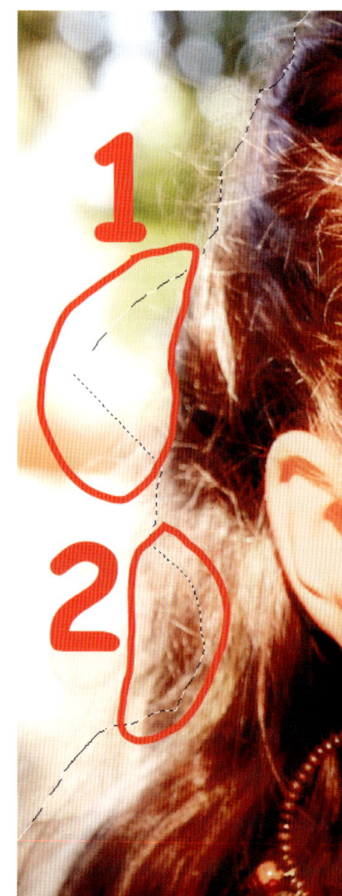

Selecting

Photos by Karen Sperling (top) and David Derex (left).

Save Selection. The Save Selection dialog box appears. Type in a name for the selection and click OK. Save the file in the Photoshop .psd file format.

This selection is then available here in Photoshop by choosing Select menu: Load Selection.

You can also use the selection in Painter by opening the image in Painter and choosing Select menu: Load Selection.

SMART BLUR

I use Smart Blur sometimes to blend out details before I start painting.

1. Choose Filter: Blur: Smart Blur. The Smart Blur dialog box appears.
2. Choose a Radius setting of 25.6 and a Threshold setting of 41.9. Click OK. The image is now slightly blended.

LAYERS

Command+j, Mac; ctrl+j, Windows makes a layer copy. If you select an area first, then you get a layer copy of just the area within the selection, like a figure, for example.

ADDING TO THE LAYER

I edit figure layers in Photoshop the way I edit them in Painter, painting into and beyond the layer edge.

To paint past the layer:

1. Click the x next to Lock: in the Layers palette to deselect it.
2. With the layer selected, paint—in the second image in the top row at right, I used the Clone Stamp to extend the hair (press option, Mac; alt, Windows and click on the source and paint in the destination—in this case, I pressed option/alt and clicked on one part of the hair and painted in another). The painted area extends past the layer, but it's still part of the layer.
3. Click the x in the Layers palette. Now the brush strokes stay within the visible layer, including the new brush strokes that you just painted.

When you paint past the edge, your strokes become the new edge.

Photoshop Layers

Paintings by Karen Sperling from a photo by Anita Morrison.

I lightened the hair by painting with a Soft Round with Soft Light chosen in the Mode menu in the options bar. The brush strokes remained within the new edge (second row, first image).

REDUCING THE LAYER

Layer masks work pretty much the same in Painter and in Photoshop.

I use the mask in both to reduce the layer's edges. In Photoshop:

1. With the layer chosen in the Layers palette, click the Add Layer Mask icon (the circle in the square). An icon appears next to the layer icon.
2. With the Brush tool and a Soft Round preset selected, and Normal chosen in the Mode menu, paint with black to reduce the layer. I reduced the size of the hair (second image, second row, below).

If you paint out too much, choose white in the Color panel and paint back what you took out.

When you're done painting in the layer mask, choose Layer menu: Layer Mask: Apply. The mask is now merged with the layer and the layer's edge is reduced.

COLORS

Use the Color panel accessed in the Window menu to choose colors.

Choose HSB (Hue, Saturation and Brightness) Sliders in the menu icon.

This way, you choose the main color family in the H slider and then you can play around with the various values and saturations in the other two sliders, and the Color panel stays open the whole time.

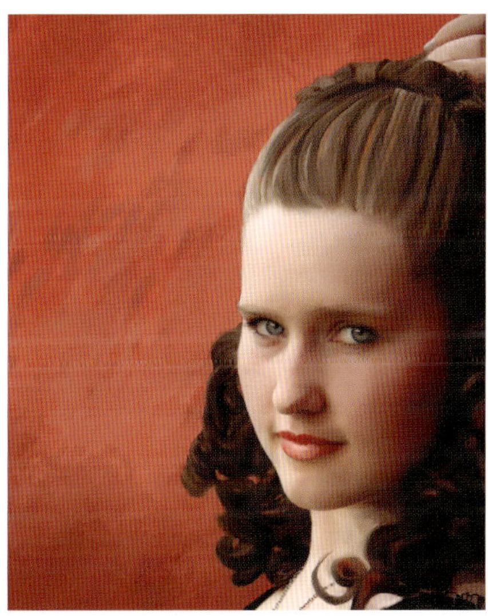

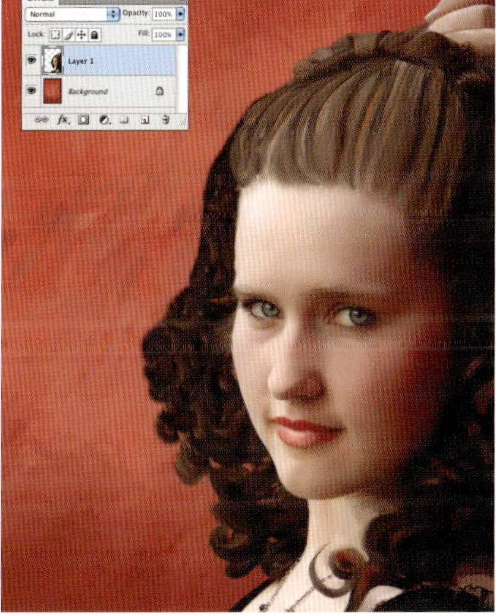

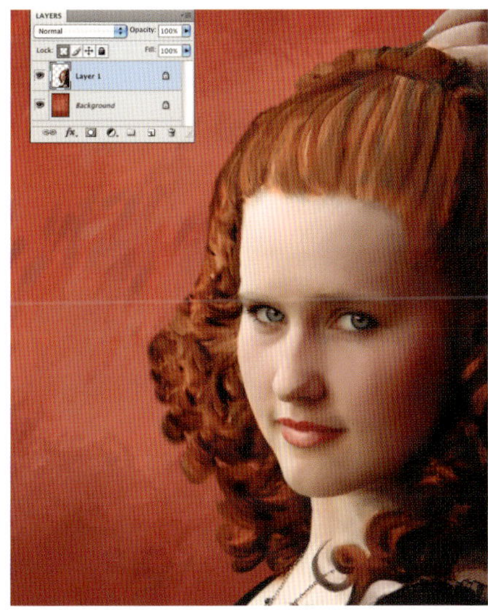

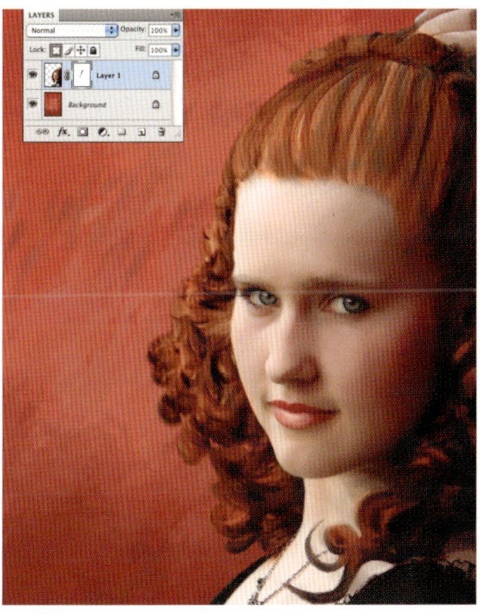

WACOM TABLETS/SHORTCUTS

I've been using Wacom tablets since I demonstrated the first version of Painter when it debuted at the August 1991 Boston Macworld at the Wacom booth, which Painter shared.

Wacom (pronounced WAH-come, not way-calm) tablets and pen displays allow you to edit pixels by painting with a stylus with a hand motion similar to that of painting or drawing with traditional brushes.

If you've never heard of Wacom, take a look at wacom.com.

If you don't use a Wacom tablet, go get one.

Painting in Painter and in Photoshop is greatly enhanced when you do it with a stylus. Tablet companies come and go, but Wacom is the standard.

This chapter covers how I use Wacom tablets.

The wacom.com site has a lot of good information for using Wacom tablets, and offers updated drivers—it's always a good idea to update the drivers to keep things running smoothly. Visit the web site for details.

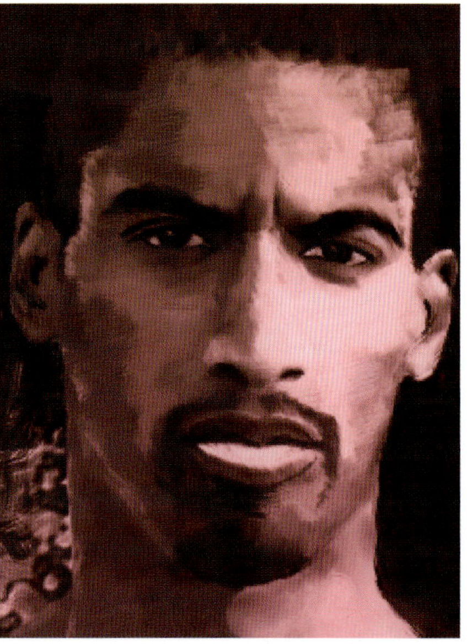

Wacom tablets come in two varieties: The Intuos-type devices, where you paint on a tablet and the information appears on your computer monitor; and the Cintiq version, where you paint directly on a computer screen.

I have always used a medium-sized Intuos-style tablet in its various incarnations, the latest being an Intuos4.

I also have a Cintiq, which I use as my main monitor for my desktop Mac. I have an LG monitor as my second monitor. The Cintiq, which you can calibrate for printing, has the image I'm working on, and the LG has all the Painter/Photoshop palettes.

PRESSING BUTTONS

The Intuos and the Cintiq have buttons that people like to customize for frequently used shortcuts and tools.

I like to use the buttons on the default settings, which I find work great, a compliment to Wacom!

You might prefer to set up the buttons to coordinate with shortcuts different from those offered in the default settings, and it's very easy to adjust these controls to fit your unique working style.

Painting with Wacom Tablets

Photo by Karen Sperling (right). Painting by Karen Sperling from a photo by Alfred Burgess (top). Painting by Karen Sperling from a photo by Nancy Goodman (opposite page).

Wacom tablets also offer a touchstrip for adjusting brush stroke size, or it can control image zooming.

I use the keyboard to edit brush size.

Photoshop CS4's brush resize shortcut is control+option+click and drag, Mac; alt+click the button on the stylus (i.e., right click)+click and drag, Windows.

In Painter, the resize shortcut is option+command+click and drag, Mac; alt+ctrl+click and drag, Windows.

For image zooming, I use the navigator in Photoshop and the zoom slider at the bottom, left-hand side of the image window in Painter.

SENSITIVITY: PAINTER

In Painter, you can set the stylus sensitivity in Preferences: Brush Tracking (image below).

Holding the stylus, click and drag a stroke across the Scratch Pad area.

If you want to make strokes using a light touch, then drag lightly across the Scratch Pad area. If you tend to have a heavy touch, drag more heavily. Click OK. The stylus is now more responsive to your personal touch.

PAINTER PRESSURE

You can set up the stylus to control brush stroke characteristics like size and opacity based on pressure.

In Painter, the settings are in Window: Brush Controls: Expression menu in each of the listed palettes.

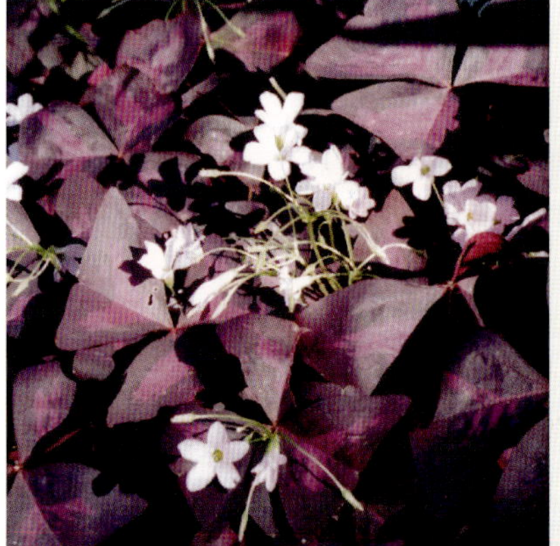

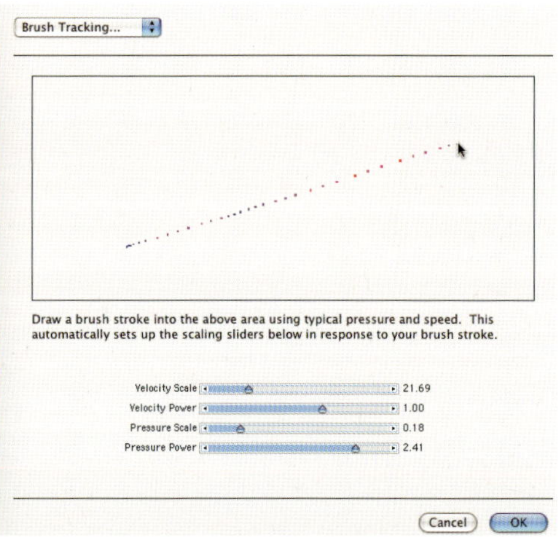

For instance, paint with the Airbrushes' Digital Airbrush. The stroke is one width no matter how you press down on the stylus.

In Window menu: Brush Controls: Size, choose Pressure in the Expression menu and move the Min Size slider to the left. Now, painting with light pressure produces narrow brush strokes; painting with heavy pressure gives you wide strokes.

Painter 11's variants with the word Real in their names take special advantage of the Wacom stylus.

Choose the Pencils' Real 2B Pencil, for instance. Hold the stylus perpendicular to the tablet as you draw and you get a thin line, like under the lip in the portrait on the opposite page. If you draw with the stylus tilted slightly you can shade as if you were tilting an actual pencil, like on the forehead on the opposite page.

PHOTOSHOP PRESSURE

In Photoshop, I painted the flower on this page without changing brush size. All I did was set up the brush so that pressing lightly on the stylus gave me a thin stroke and pressing heavily gave me a thick one.

The first image in the top row is the photo, the one next to it shows you the early brush strokes and the settings—I used a Hard Round brush and chose Pen Pressure in the Control menu in Shape Dynamics (see below).

Pressing lightly on the stylus, I painted short, thin strokes to create texture and long, thin outlines to establish lights and darks. I lowered the opacity in the options bar, pressed heavily on the stylus and painted the wide areas of color.

In the second row, the first image is a little further along in the process. I made the area in the image's lower right-hand corner yellow-orange, the color complement of the blue-violet in the flower and I painted where I saw lights and darks in the photo.

The image next to it is the final painting. I added yellow-orange in the flower and blue-violet in the background for color harmony.

I blended colors by adding strokes on 30% opacity. The more you paint, the more they blend.

HIDE THE CURSOR

If you're using the Cintiq, in Painter, choose Preferences: General: Single pixel, which pretty much hides the cursor while you paint (you still see a tiny circle).

I use the Intuos for painting large areas and the Cintiq for painting details. You don't need both, but if you have both, painting is great fun!

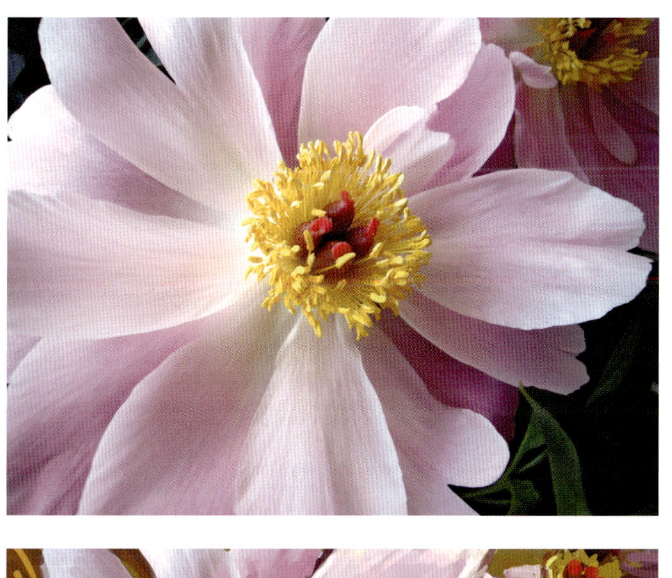

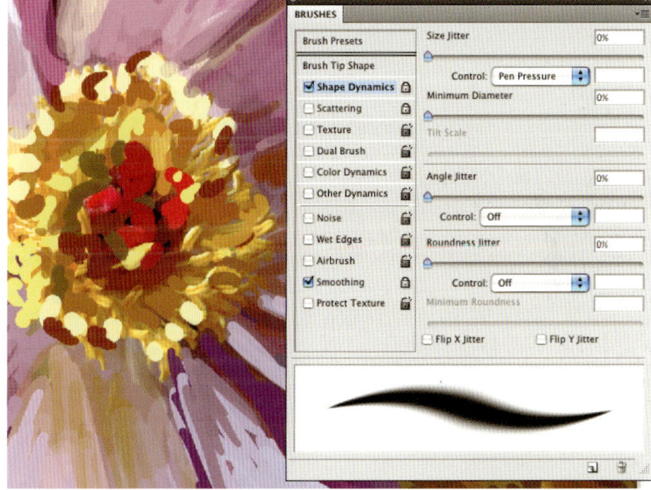

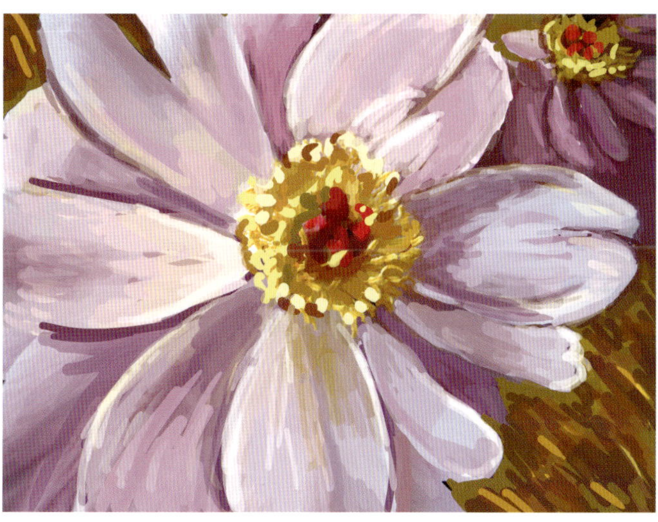

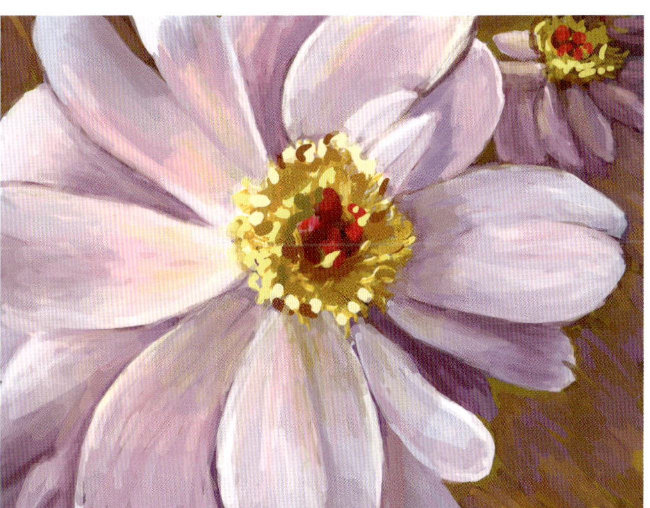

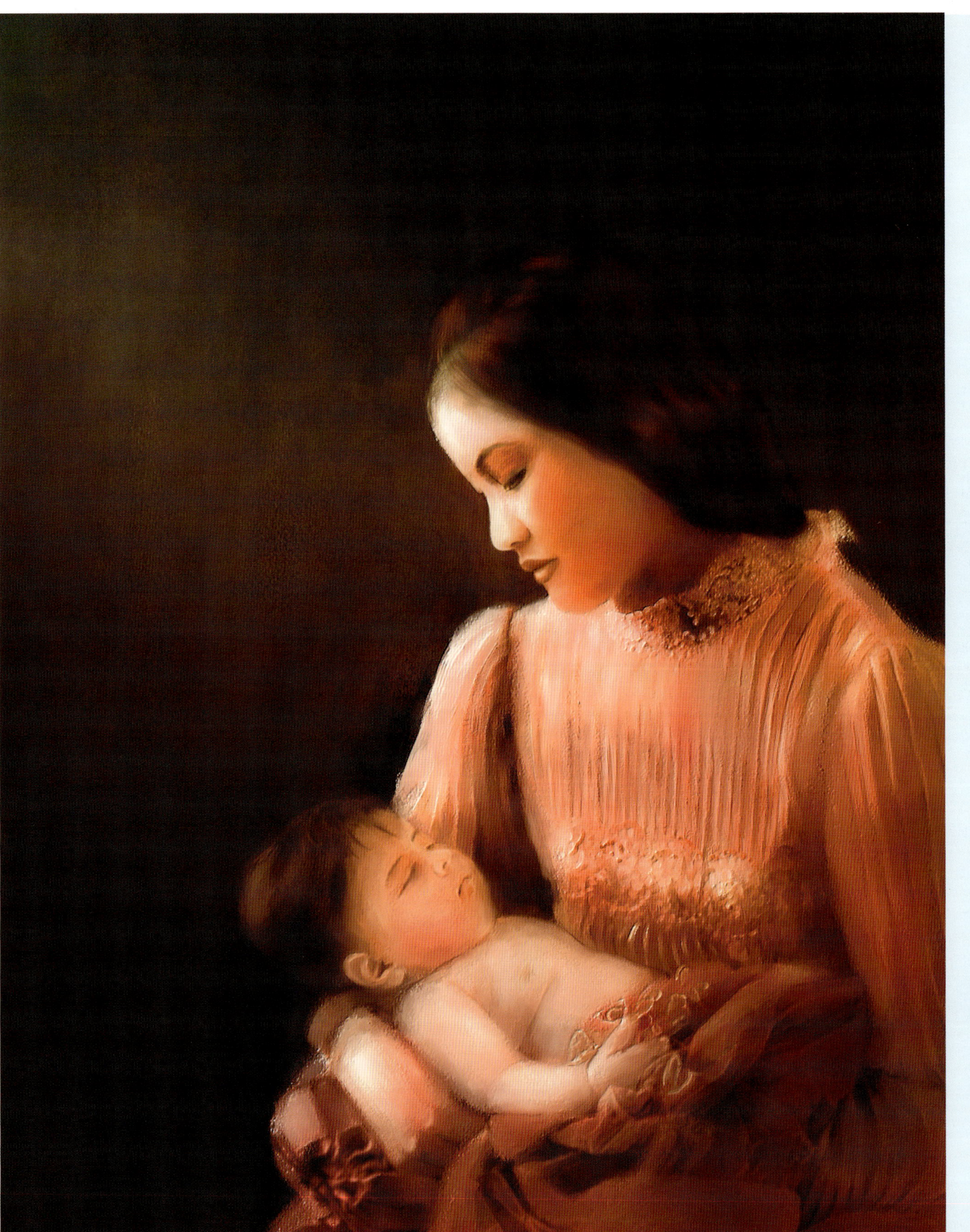

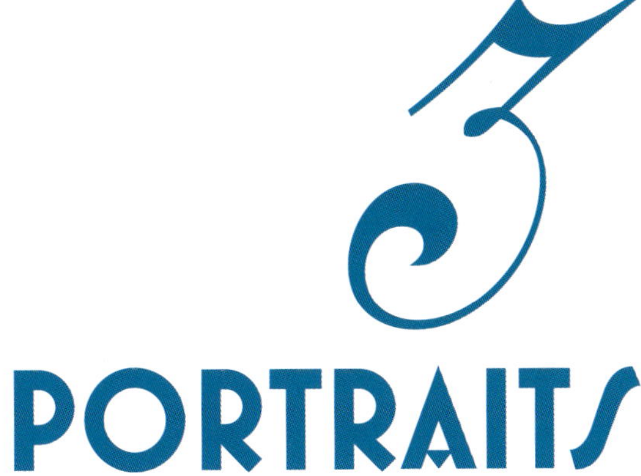

PORTRAITS

Painting portraits tops most peoples' lists for what they'd like to do with photos in Corel Painter and in Adobe Photoshop.

In this section, you'll apply the art theories you learned in Section 1 and the painting tools you discovered in Section 2 to painting portraits in Painter and in Photoshop.

By the way, use 300 dpi as your standard resolution for files that you output to paper or canvas, including portraits, landscapes, pets and any other paintings that you do.

Using 300 dpi, the dimensions are the actual size, i.e., if you create a file at 8" x 10" at 300 dpi, it will print out at 8" x 10".

To paint from photos, make sure the source photo is the desired dimensions because the resulting painting is the same size as the source photo, usually—you may crop at the end, etc., but generally, the photo and the painting are the same size.

One other thing, if you get into really large output sizes, like 30" x 40", you can create the file half the size at 15" x 20" then resize up in Photoshop to 30" x 40" at the end.

Working at half the size will help things go more quickly.

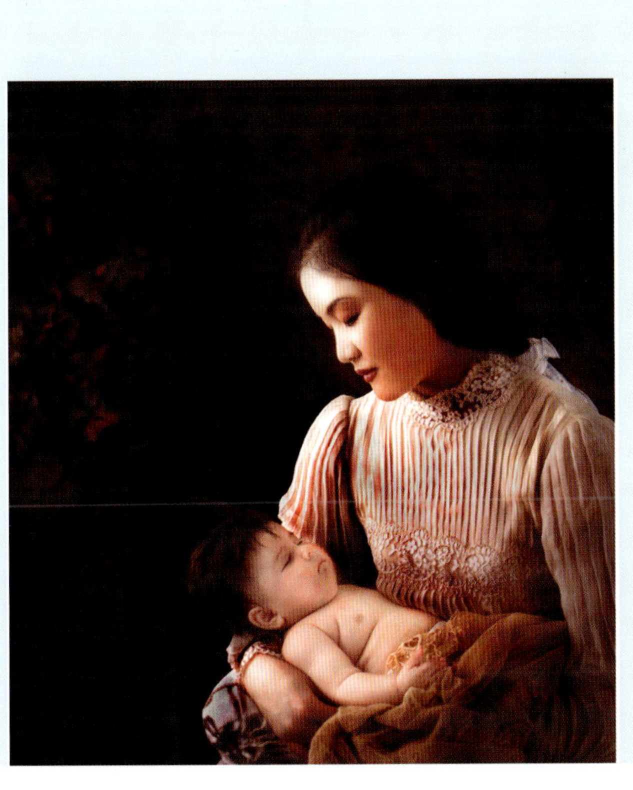

Portrait

Painting by Karen Sperling from a photo by Mary Wynn Ball, featured in the August 2005 issue of Artistry Tips and Tricks http://www.artistrymag.com/

OIL-PAINTED PORTRAITS

I used Painter to create this portrait in an oil-painted style from a photo by renowned photographer Phillip Stewart Charis.

When you paint portraits, whether it's in Painter or in Photoshop or with traditional paints, you paint tones rather than objects like hair and faces. Painting the tones will give you a painterly result and will insure that the person in the painting resembles the one in the photo.

What makes the final image more painterly than the photo is the use of the art concepts described starting on page 10—high contrast, unified colors and fewer details.

Start this painting by opening the photo in Photoshop. Choose Image: Duplicate and select the light part of the girl (head, shoulders, arms, etc.) with the Magnetic Lasso (see page 36 for instructions). Use Image: Adjustments: Levels to lighten the selected area to create a clear focal point, or area of greatest contrast between light and dark with the background—see page 14 for information about focal points.

Use Image: Adjustments: Color Balance to make the figure a little less yellow and a little more red to fit in better with the predominantly red color scheme.

Open the photo in Painter and choose File: Clone and File: Save As.

Choose the Window menu: Underpainting palette, set Smart Blur on 34% and click Apply. Smart Blur removes some of the detail, making the image more painterly. Save this version, choose File: Clone again, and name it.

As you proceed through the following steps, turn Tracing Paper on and off—see page 27 for instructions.

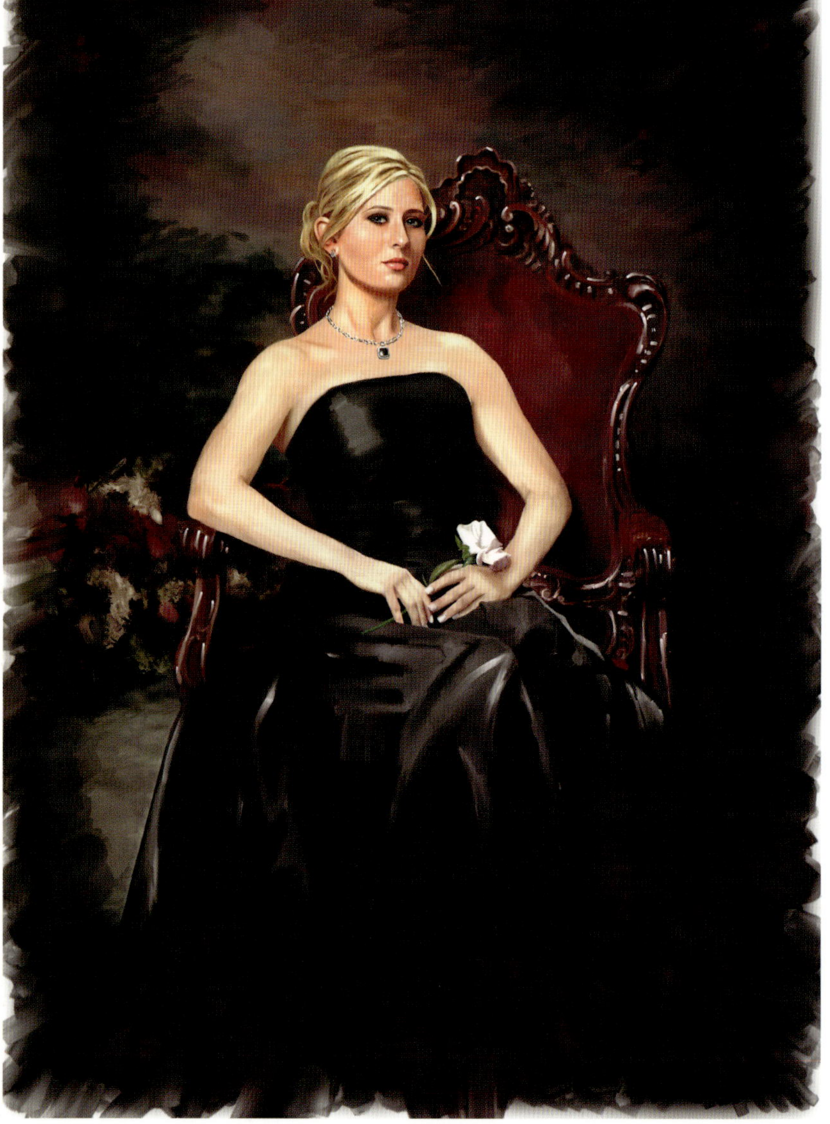

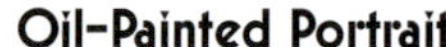

Oil-Painted Portrait

Painting by Karen Sperling from a photo by Phillip Stewart Charis.

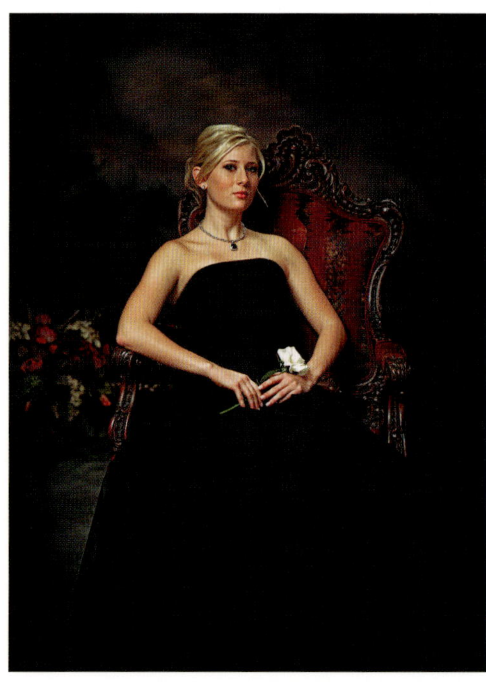

1 ADDING PAINT

Begin the painting using the RealBristle Brushes' Real Oils Short brush for bristly strokes, like on the jaw and in the hair; the Chalk's Square Chalk for textured strokes, like on the forehead; and the Chalk's Sharp Chalk for tonal strokes like under the lip and in the hair. Pick up color by pressing option, Mac; alt, Windows and clicking in the image, choose a lighter or darker tone in the Colors palette, and then paint.

Learning to paint isn't as much about acquiring painting dexterity as it is about getting good at observing tones and painting them. The more you paint, the better you get.

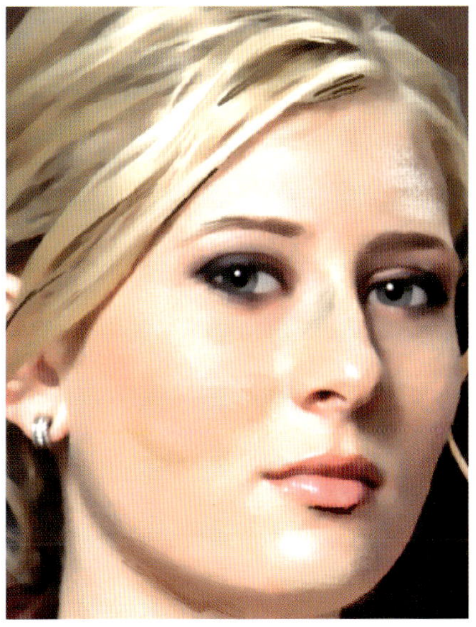

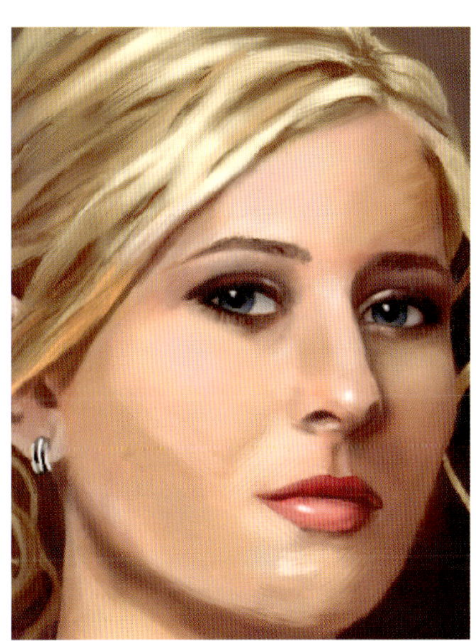

2 EYES

Paint the irises by blending with the Blenders' Just Add Water and lightening the bottoms a little with the Photo's Dodge.

Paint shadows at the tops of the eyes with the Digital Watercolors' New Simple Water on 2% opacity. See the art lessons on page 18 for details about painting eyes.

Painting with the RealBristle Brushes' Real Oils Short, continue adding tones and colors in the skin, then blending them back, building up the portrait based on the tones in the photo. Paint and lift and paint again to get color; paint without lifting and the strokes blend together.

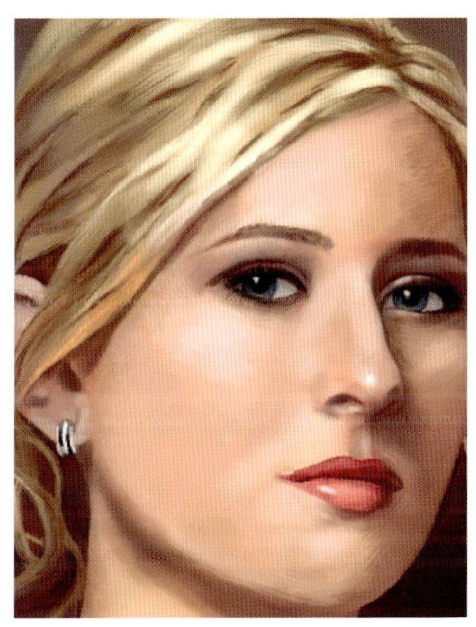

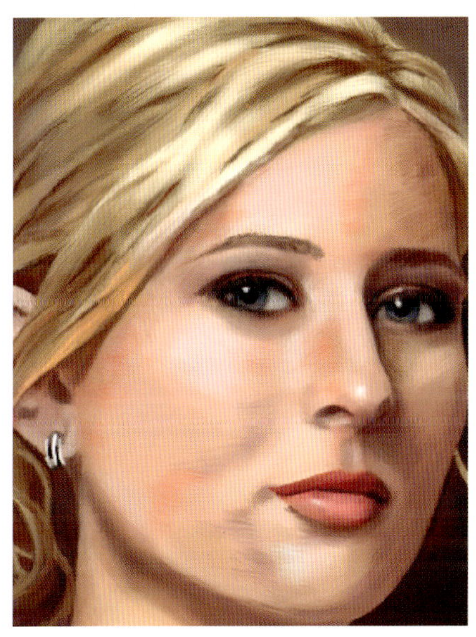

3 LIPS

Paint the lips by blending them with the Just Add Water, adding color with the Chalk's Sharp Chalk, blending some more with Just Add Water, then repeating. Follow the tones in the photo and also the art concept that the upper lip is darker than the lower lip (see page 19). Notice in all the images how the lips changed shape as I worked on tones. I was trying to get them to look like the photo and like a painting, too! In the photo on the far right in this row, I painted color on the entire face with the New Simple Water. I wanted to adjust the tones, but I didn't want to affect the brush strokes I had so far.

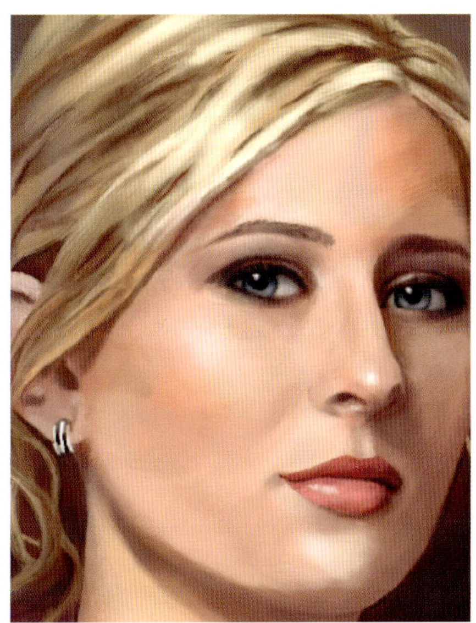

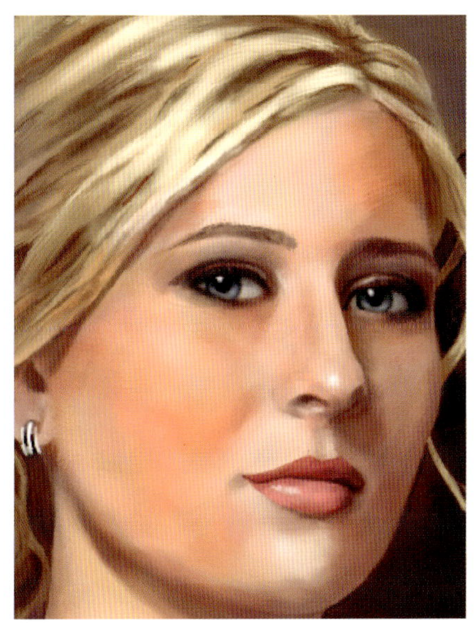

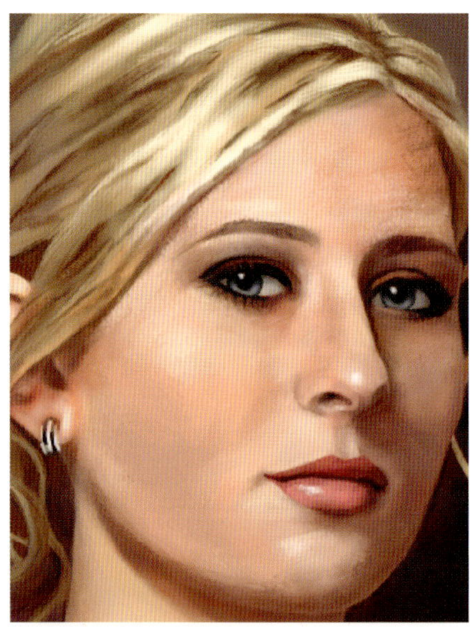

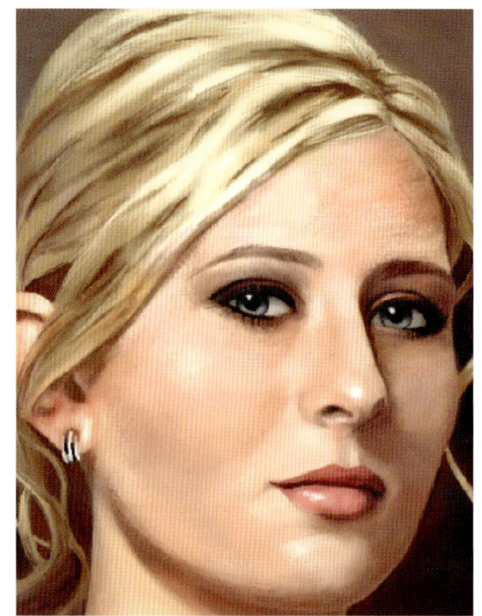

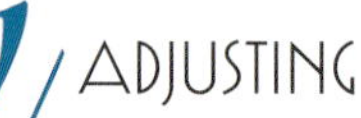

4 Adjusting

Choose Layers: Dry Digital Watercolor for other brushes to interact with the Digital Watercolor strokes. Paint light strokes with the Square Chalk, and blend with a blender variation of the Square Chalk.

See the steps on page 24 for turning brushes into blenders and saving as new variants.

Continue to paint with the previously mentioned brushes, painting more color here, lightening there, following the tones in the photo.

Add dark tones around the eyes and lips with the New Simple Water.

Adjust levels and color balance in Photoshop at the end of the painting.

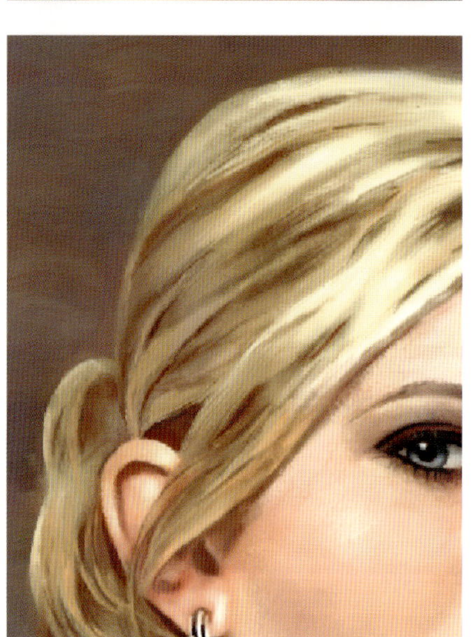

5 Hair

As you saw on page 19, paint hair using broad areas of light and dark, then add a few strands.

Paint areas with the Real Oils Short variant. Press option, Mac; alt, Windows and click on a light color in the photo and paint over it with a lighter version chosen in the Colors palette. Press option/alt and click on dark tones and paint with darker versions.

When you have broad areas of light and dark, paint a few individual strands with the Chalk's Sharp Chalk.

Paint over parts of the strands with the Real Oils Short to blend.

Roughen things up a bit by painting with the Square Chalk as a blender.

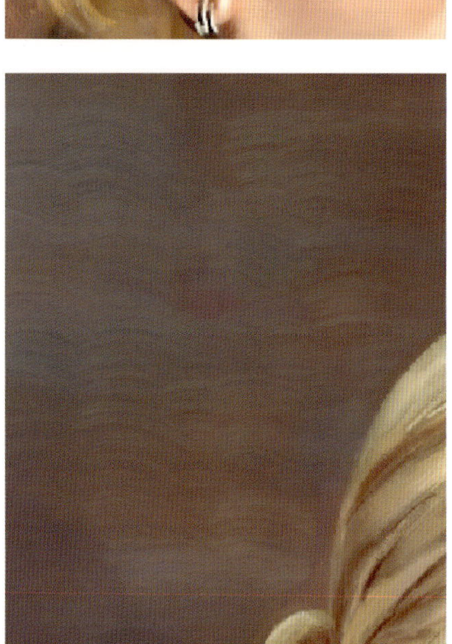

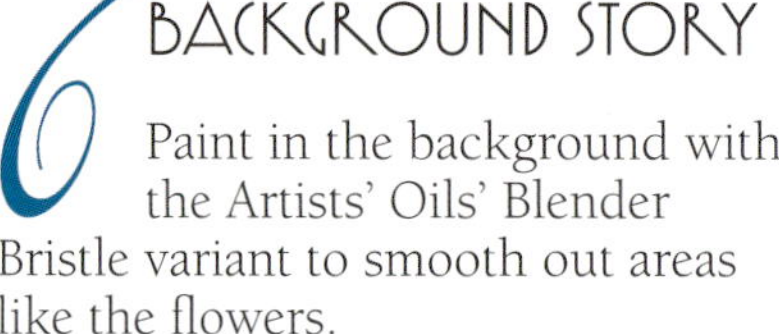

6 Background Story

Paint in the background with the Artists' Oils' Blender Bristle variant to smooth out areas like the flowers.

Add some brush strokes using the Window: Auto-Painting palette.

Select part of the background with the lasso, and with the Artists' Oils' Blender Bristle chosen, set up Auto-Painting on the following settings (deselect the check boxes, too):

Stroke: Fade In/Out
Pressure: 85%
Length: 33%
Rotation: 97°
Brush Size: 129%
Speed: 24%

Speed controls how fast the brush strokes appear—adjust to taste.

Click the arrow and let the brush strokes go for awhile, then click in the image to stop them.

This produces some nice horizontal strokes in the background.

Paint with the Cloners' Soft Cloner to fix edges.

For the brush strokes going around the image edge, first choose Window menu: Underpainting palette: Edge Effect: Jagged Vignette and lower the Amount slider.

Then, paint over the vignette with the Blender Bristle to create the brush strokes. Paint both with red and with black to add a little color and texture to the black.

7 JEWELRY/FLOWERS

Blend out the photographic jewelry with the Square Chalk as a blender.

Then use the Pens' Scratchboard Tool to paint the necklace and earrings back in. Paint white, black and gray where you see light, dark and medium tones in the photograph, using Tracing Paper as your guide.

Fix up the skin and flower by painting with the Artists' Oils' Blender Bristle and the RealBristle Brushes' Real Oils Short.

Add color to the highlights and shadows with the Chalk's Sharp Chalk, then blend with the Blender Bristle and Real Oils Short.

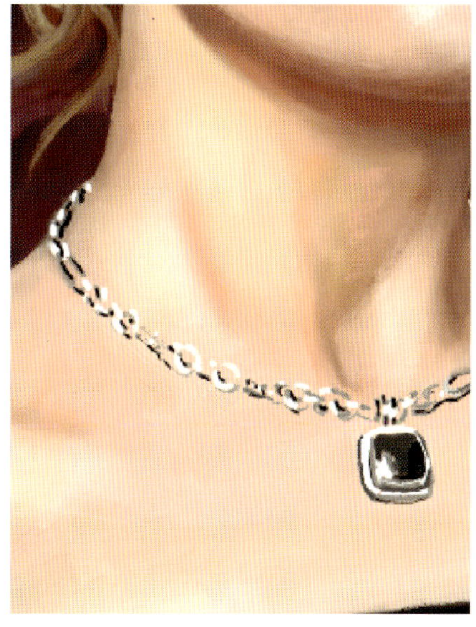

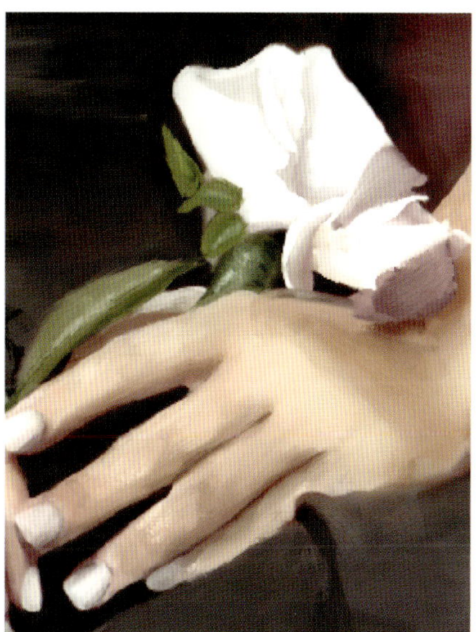

8 CHAIR

As you learned in the art lessons on page 17, one of the differences between a painting and a photo is that a painting has less detail than the photo.

For the chair, smooth out tones in the wood and in the upholstery using the Square Chalk as a blender, creating distinct areas of light and dark while blending out the details.

For instance, the top of the chair at right is a light tone, below it is a dark one and below that is a midtone. Paint out details within each tonal section, and create the edges defining each section. These edges are details that add to our understanding of the chair we are looking at, so leave them in.

After blending with the Square Chalk as a blender, paint back highlights, midtones and shadows using the Artists' Oils' Blender Bristle. Notice I didn't paint back all the scrolls in the wood or the pattern in the fabric—I just suggested them with tones.

To add the color full strength, paint and lift the stylus, then paint again.

To gradually fade the color as you paint, keep painting without lifting the stylus.

Paint with the Cloners' Soft Cloner to bring back some of the edges. The more you add your own strokes, the more painterly the image will look, so go easy on the Soft Cloner.

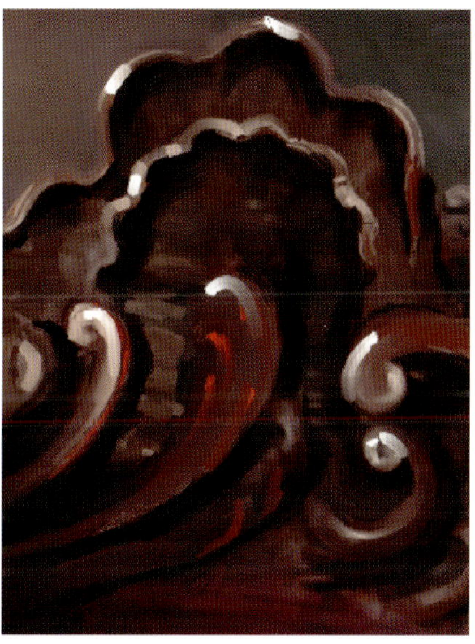

9 DRESS

Lighten the source image to see the folds in the dress better (Effects: Tonal Control: Adjust Colors, move the Value slider to the right).

Turning Tracing Paper on and off (click the icon in the image window's upper right-hand corner), paint the folds in the dress with the Artists' Oils' Blender Bristle, using different tones of the basic dress color based on the lights and darks in the source image.

To get the effect in the dress, you paint with the Artists' Oils' Blender Bristle in a sort of scribbling motion. As you paint, the brush runs out of color. So you have the full color, or in this case, white, where the highlight is on a fold, and then as you scribble and as the brush runs out of color, you paint into the shadows to create a blended effect.

When done, choose Edit: Undo in the source image to get the original tones back.

I rarely make a brush stroke that looks perfect.

The process is like I describe in this tutorial. You paint, then you blend, then you paint, then you blend again, continuing to build up paint based on the areas of light and dark in the photo. Eventually, you get a painting!

And that's how I painted a photo by Phillip Stewart Charis!

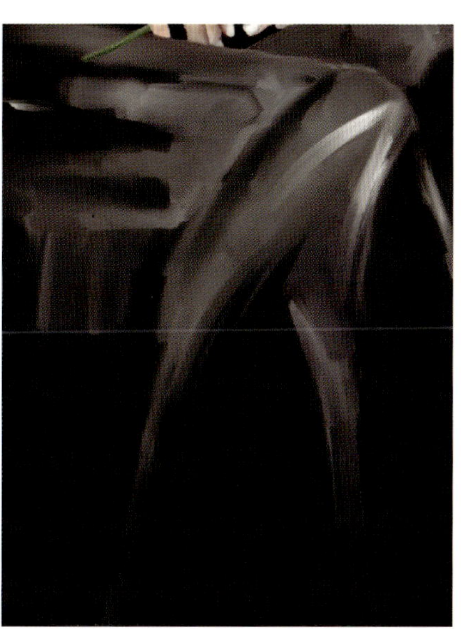

WATERCOLOR PORTRAITS

Watercolor Portrait
PAINTING BY KAREN SPERLING
FROM A PHOTO BY SCOTT STULBERG

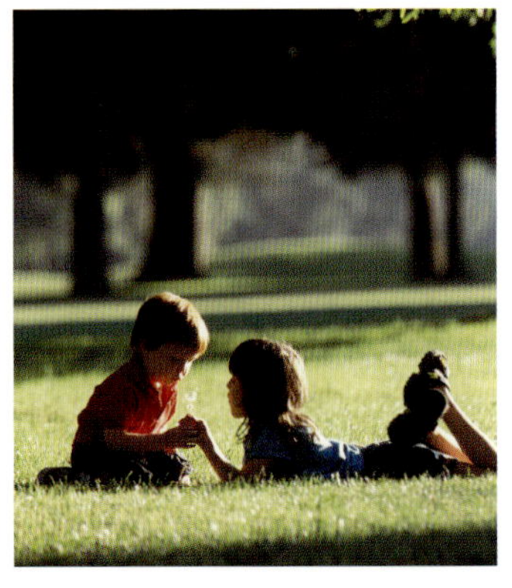

I painted this watercolor portrait in Painter from a photo by Scott Stulberg.

Scotty's photo was perfect for a watercolor painting because of its bold areas of light and dark.

In traditional watercolor, you let the unpainted paper serve as your lightest areas, or highlights. Therefore, I left the highlights unpainted to emulate the look of paper in a watercolor painting.

The photo's main colors, red and orange, and their complements, green and blue, were just right for a painting.

I cropped the photo in Painter. To do so, click the crop tool in the toolbox (or type c to access it quickly), click and drag to select the area you want to keep, then click within the selection to complete the crop. To paint, click on the brush in the toolbox (or type b).

Then turn on Tracing Paper.

1. Choose file: Clone.
2. Clear the clone (Select: All, press delete, Mac; backspace Windows).
3. Click the Tracing Paper icon in the image window's top, right-hand corner to turn on Tracing Paper. (Click it again to turn Tracing Paper off).

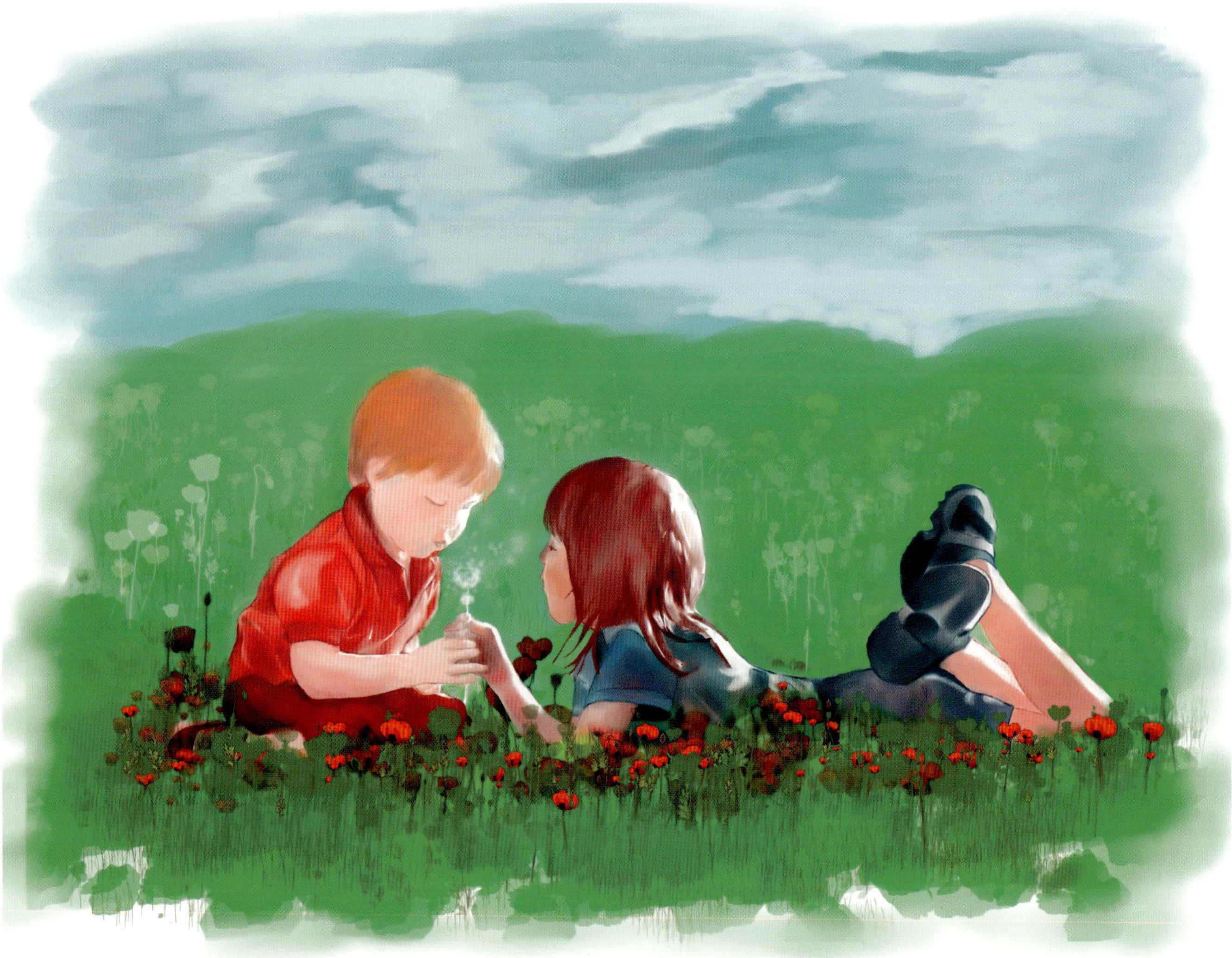

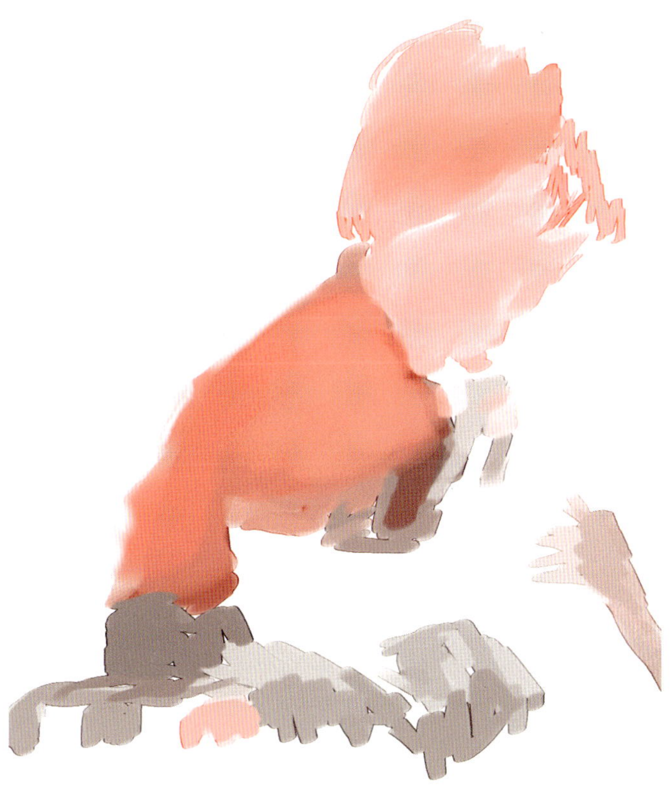

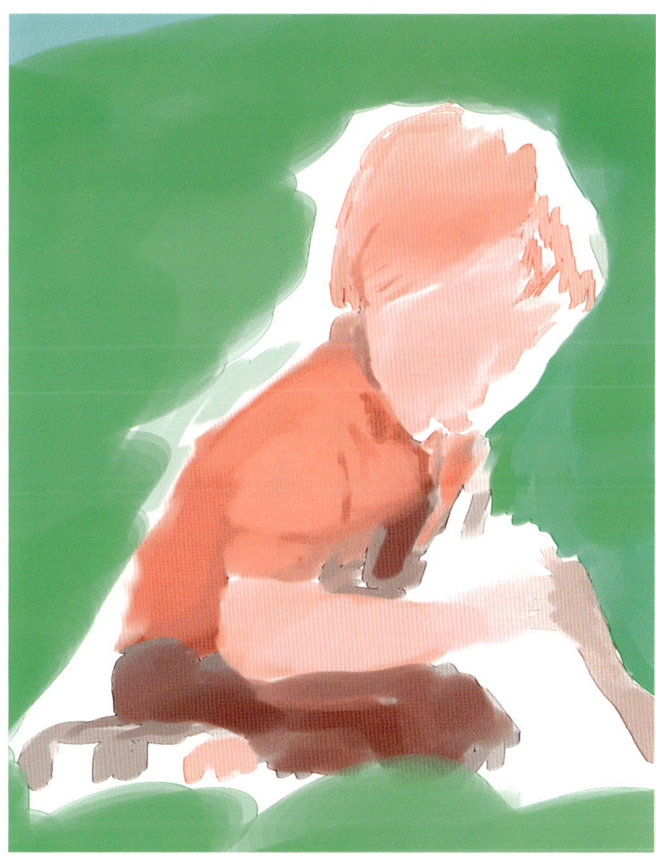

1 FIRST, THE BOY

Choose the Digital Watercolor's New Simple Water and make these adjustments:

Window menu: Brush Controls: General palette: Stroke Type: Rake. Brush Controls: Angle palette: Squeeze slider: 39%; Angle slider: 199°. Set Opacity on 20%, Grain on 0% and Wet Fringe on 50% in the Property Bar. Save the changes as a variant (see page 24 for steps).

In traditional watercolor, you paint the lightest tones first, then work your way up to the darker ones.

Choose a light value of red-orange in the Colors palette and begin to paint in the boy's hair. Shut off Tracing Paper to check your progress.

Turn Tracing Paper back on and continue to paint, using different-width strokes by adjusting the Size slider.

Scribble Digital Watercolor strokes to blend colors together. Also, if you start on a light area and drag you'll get a lighter color, start on a darker area and the brush stroke will be darker. Choose a lighter value for the boy's face and a darker value for his shirt in the Colors palette and keep painting. You're putting in washes of color, so it's OK if you don't have details at this point.

Meanwhile, the Wacom Intuos4 tablet produces more flexibility when painting Digital Watercolor strokes than I've ever seen with previous models.

Press lightly and paint: The brush strokes will blend, giving you true-to-life watercolor effects.

2 THEN, THE GIRL AND BACKGROUND

Continue to paint light strokes. Choose a blue-green and paint the girl's clothes.

You paint by building up all the areas of the painting at the same time. You don't, for example, paint the boy until he's completely done and then move onto the girl.

The idea is to build up the tones throughout the painting, and as you do so, details will emerge.

One of the many nice things about the Digital Watercolors is that you can easily fix strokes by simply painting over them while the strokes are still "wet." They remain wet until you dry them (Layers menu: Dry Digital Watercolor). They also stay wet if you save in Painter's native .rif (RIFF) format. You can't open .rif files in Photoshop, by the way.

Paint and lift and paint and lift to get strokes with edges; paint without lifting to get blended strokes.

Next start to fill in the background. Notice how the color next to the boy's head gave definition to the boy's profile even though I didn't put any color there. That's a traditional art technique called negative painting, where you paint around a space to create the space itself.

The secret to painting the green area next to the face as you see in the above image is to first paint a thin line around the silhouette and then fill in the color next to the line with a wider brush (use the Size slider to adjust brush stroke width, or use the shortcut option+command+click and drag, Mac; alt+ctrl+click and drag, Windows).

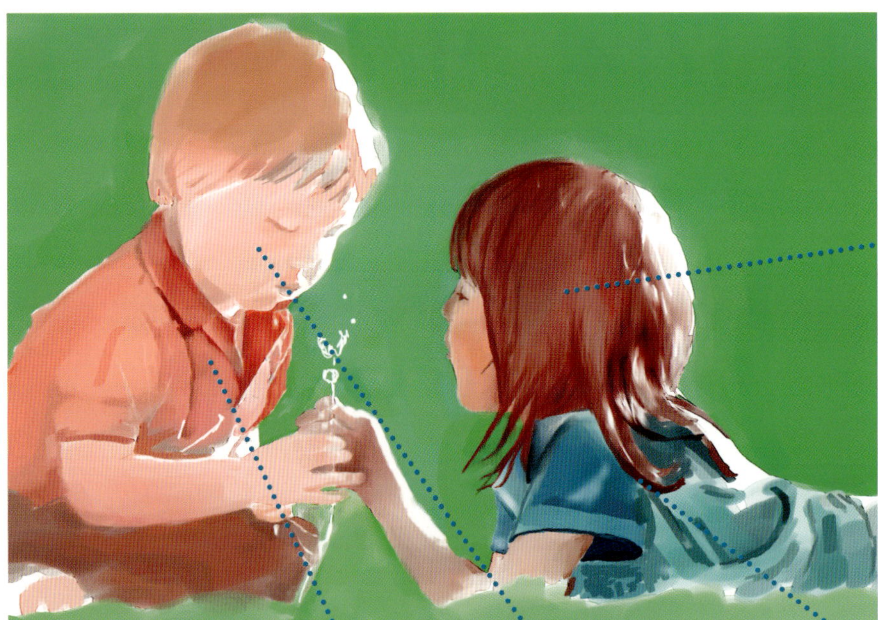

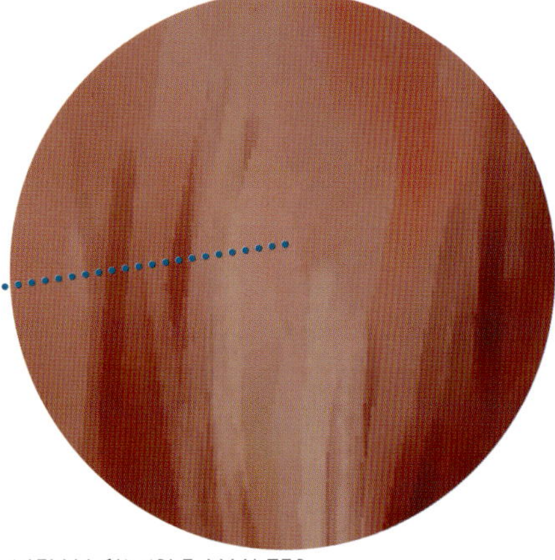

NEW SIMPLE WATER
With high size and low opacity settings, paint areas like hair, clothing and backgrounds.

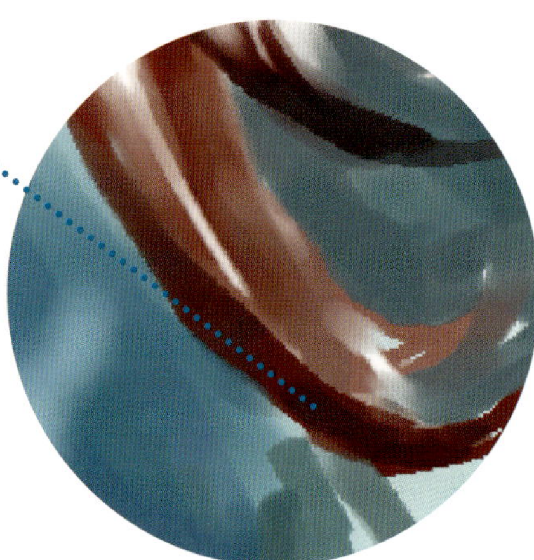

NEW SIMPLE WATER
With low size and high opacity settings, paint details like hair strands and clothing outlines.

3 ADDING DETAILS

Using the custom New Simple Water you created, raise the Size slider to paint wide strokes for broad areas like the clothing and background rather than a lot of narrow strokes.

Lower the Size slider to paint details like on the sleeves and the eyes.

Turn up the Grain slider a little for the clothing and hair.

Paint darker and lighter tones by adjusting the Opacity slider, using the photo's tones to guide you.

Paint with a lower opacity on the broader areas of color and a higher opacity on the details.

Use the Digital Watercolor's Wet Eraser on high size and low opacity settings to lighten tones.

I made the girl's face darker than the boy's to create dramatic areas of light and dark. I figured since the boy was facing the light, and the girl was facing away from it, that her face would be darker, even though it was hard to see that difference in the photo.

Sometimes you make decisions like that based on logic and not necessarily on what you see in the photo.

Paint highlights like on the boy's shirt with the Wet Eraser on low size and high opacity settings.

Paint with the New Simple Blender on a low opacity to blend some brush strokes. Don't blend too much—showing the brush strokes makes the image look more painterly.

To paint the girl's hair:

1. Paint broad color with wide (high Size slider) strokes using the custom New Simple Water.
2. Paint strands with narrow (low Size slider) strokes using the custom New Simple Water.
3. Blend with the New Simple Blender. Paint the line ends to blend them into the big areas of color. Leave the boy's hair less defined than the girl's because he's younger and his hair would be finer.

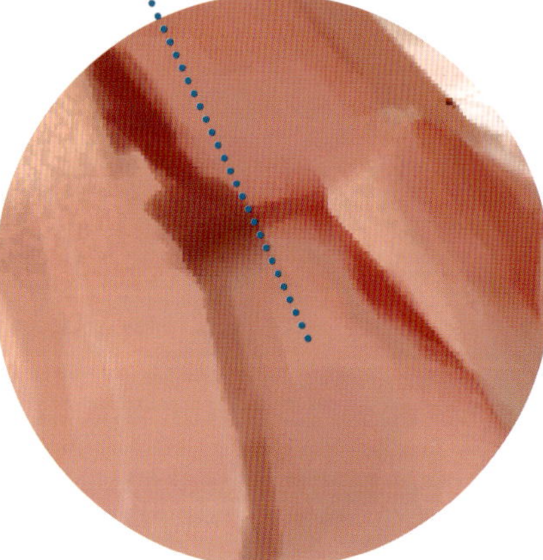

ROUND WATER BLENDER
With low opacity and wet fringe, and high size settings, paint to blend. Paint white highlights on the shirt with the Wet Eraser. Use the New Simple Blender to blend watercolor strokes like on the boy's shirt and on his arms.

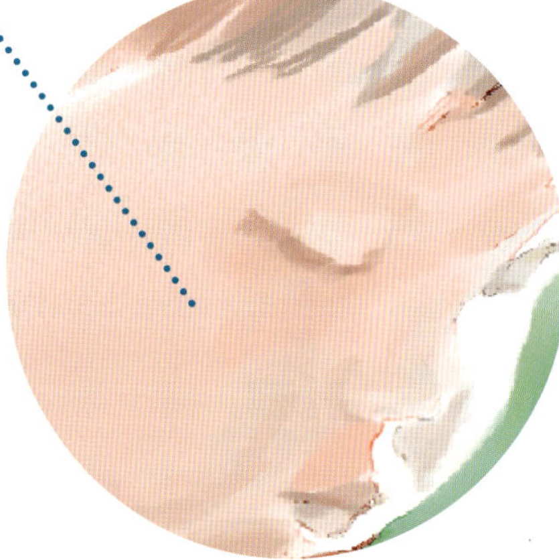

FACE TONES
Set the Grain slider higher for the clothing, hair and background; lower for the faces. Lighten tones with the Digital Watercolor's Wet Eraser with a low opacity.
Leave highlights white like the paper showing through in traditional watercolor paintings.

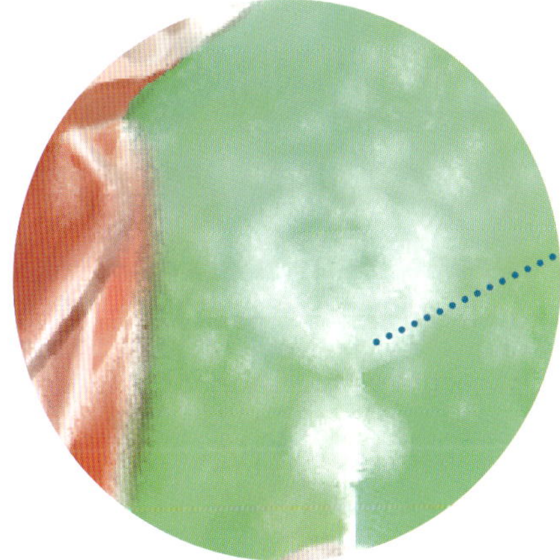

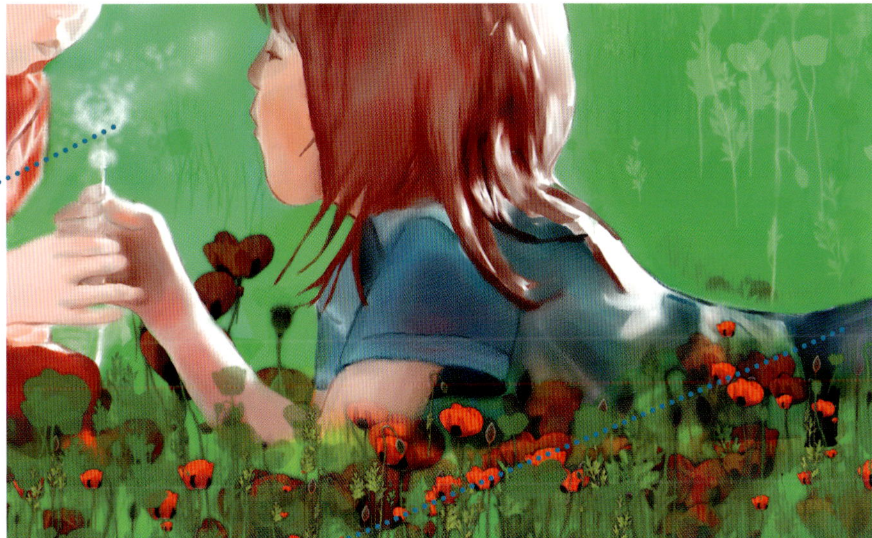

DIGITAL WATERCOLOR'S SALT
To paint the dandelions, use the Digital Watercolor's Salt variant, which paints white into Digital Watercolor strokes before they're dried.

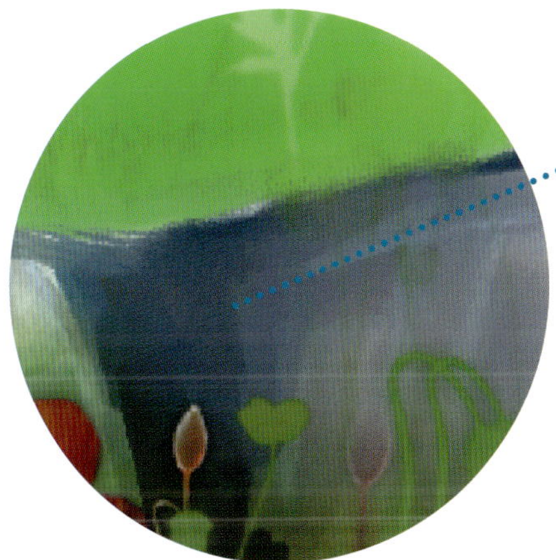

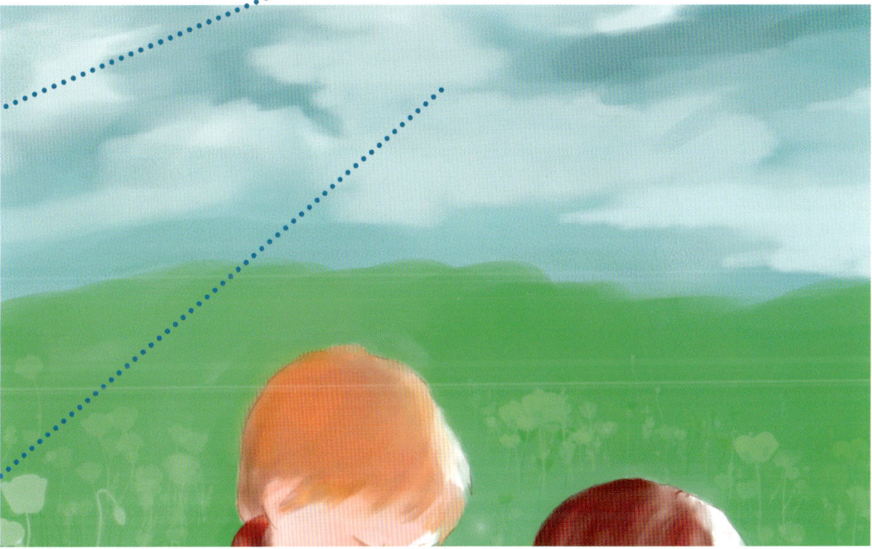

FINISHING TOUCHES
Use the Finer Mop Brush to paint large areas with diffused, textured strokes. Lower the Diffusion slider in the Property Bar for less diffusion and more bristles in the strokes. Lower opacity and press lightly on the stylus for more subtle strokes.

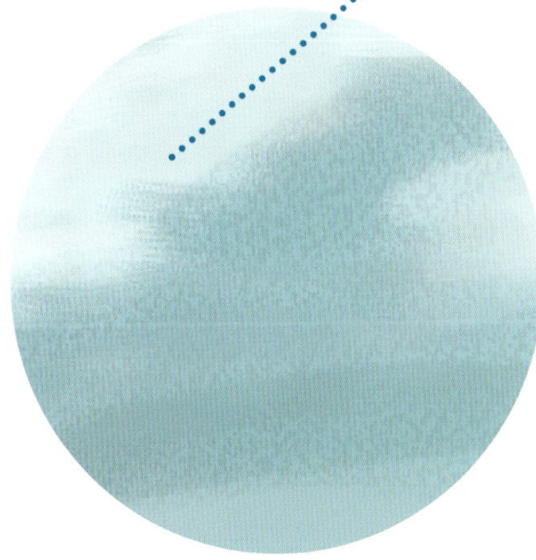

CLOUDS
Use the Wet Eraser on wet watercolor to create clouds. Blend with the Pure Water Bristle.

4 FINISHING UP

Keep painting where you see lights and darks in the photo. It's an editing process, mostly. You paint, then you fix what you painted, either by lightening or darkening tones, or by blending.

Paint details with the Fine Tip Water with a low Size slider setting. Blend the lines a little, and add bristles to them by painting over part of them with the Pure Water Bristle, which is also good for cleaning up outlines where there is too much diffusion.

At this point, dry all the Digital Watercolor Strokes.

You dry Digital Watercolor strokes either by choosing Layers: Dry Digital Watercolor or by saving in any file format other than Painter's native .rif format and closing the file.

Paint new Digital Watercolor strokes over dried areas to darken tones and to create edges where the newly painted strokes and the previously dried colors meet.

Next, paint with Image Hose variants with the word linear in them. Use the Red Poppies and the Green Grass Bunch nozzles.

See page 32 for information about painting with the Image Hose.

Blend the Image Hose strokes so that they don't look pasted on by painting with the Blenders' Smudge to blend with texture and the Just Add Water variant to blend without texture.

PASTEL PORTRAITS

I used Painter to create this pastel drawing of a couple on their wedding day, which I photographed.

I drew with the Chalk's Square Chalk and blended with the Blenders' Smudge. I didn't blend that much—I left the Chalk strokes to make the image look like a pastel drawing. For details I used the Chalk's Sharp Chalk.

I used some shortcuts to make the drawing go faster, as you're about to see in the next few pages.

I decided that the photo was a good candidate to be turned into a painting because it had two of the characteristics described in the art chapters starting on page 10: It had good contrast and the people were touching.

After that, I looked at the photo to decide on a color scheme, discussed on pages 12-13.

You saw in the previous two chapters about oil painting and watercolors that I pretty much used the colors that were in the photos.

However, the colors in this chapter's photo didn't lend themselves to being painted.

I looked at the photo and at the color wheel on page 12 to come up with a color scheme.

The bride's dress and the skin tones were all in the peach family, so I chose red-orange, which is a shade of peach, as my first color, which meant blue-green, the color opposite red-orange on the color wheel, or its complement, would be my second color. I thought blue-green would work well for the dark areas like the groom's dark jacket.

When you choose a color scheme, you use all the values within the color, so deciding to use red-orange meant I could use peach, orange and brown, all different values of red-orange, and light, medium and dark versions of blue-green.

Now that I had decided on a color scheme, I chose File: Clone to make a copy of the photo, and closed the photo to save it intact. I made the color changes on the next page on this clone, which would now be the source image.

That's what you should have open on your monitor, a clone of your photo, which you're about to edit.

Pastel Portrait

Painting and photo by Karen Sperling.

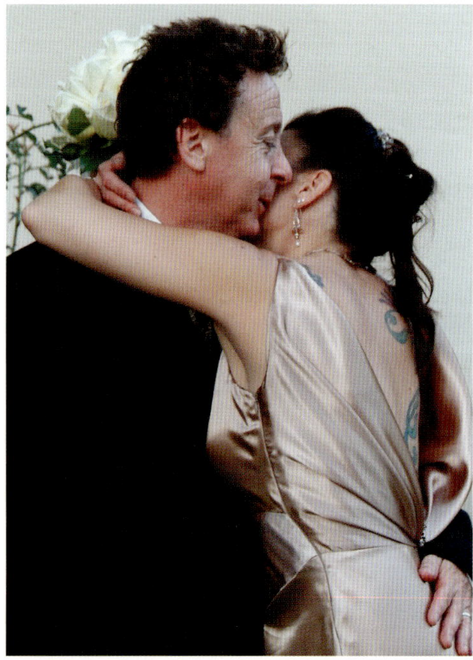

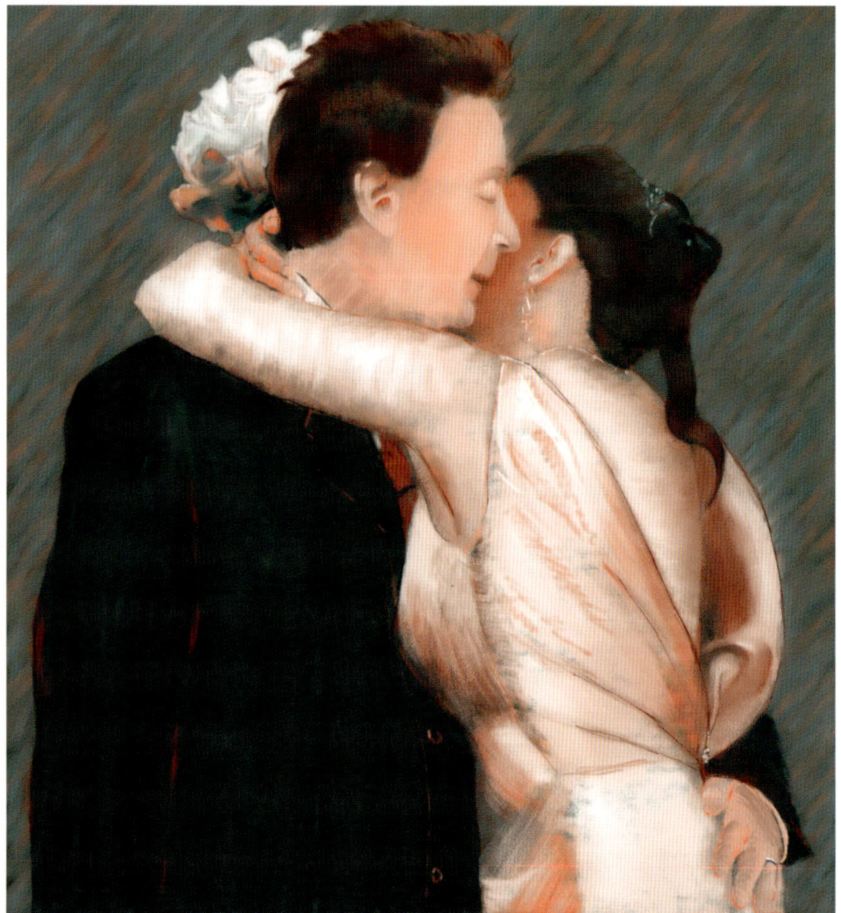

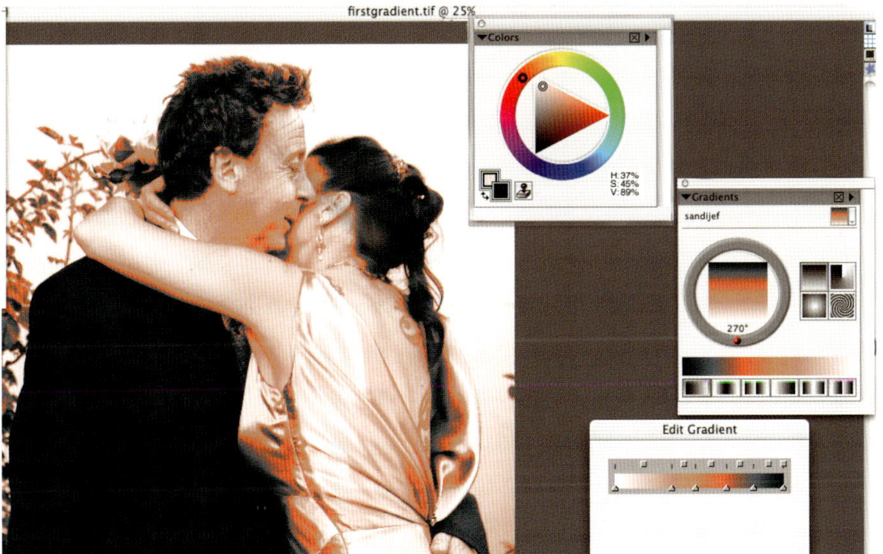

1 COLOR SCHEME

Edit the photo so that it has the red-orange/blue-green color scheme.

This edited photo is the new source image so that you can clone the colors from it into the drawing later.

To edit the colors, create a gradient and then use Express in Image.

The steps for doing so are on page 29 in the Color in Painter chapter.

At left is the gradient that I created to get the color scheme that you see in the image.

This image is now the new source image.

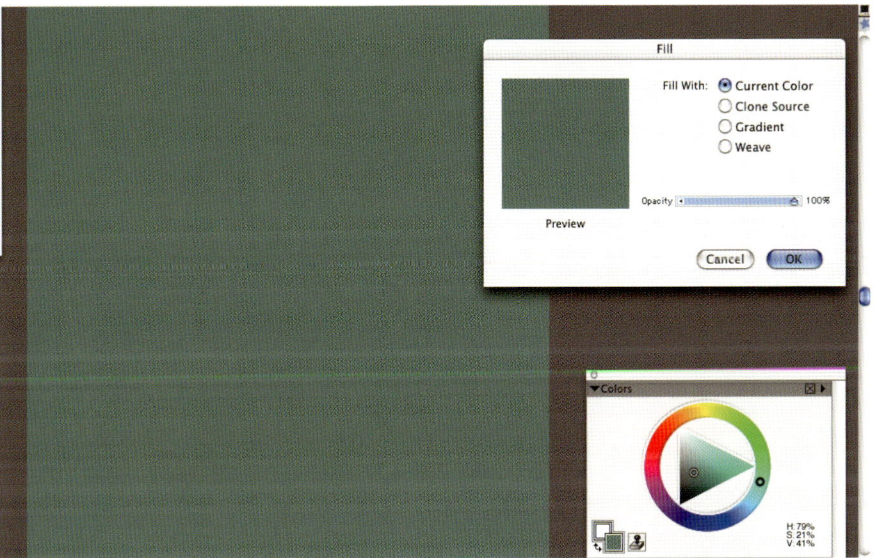

2 PAPER COLOR

Pastel artists draw on paper that is a midtone of their drawing's colors for two reasons:

- Create color harmony because the paper's color shows through parts of the final drawing;
- It's a shortcut—by starting with colored paper instead of white, it saves brush strokes.

Fill with a color to reproduce the effect of using colored paper.

First, choose File: Clone and File: Save As. This new image is the painting. Next, choose a medium blue-green in the Colors palette and Effects: Fill using Current Color. The image is now blue-green.

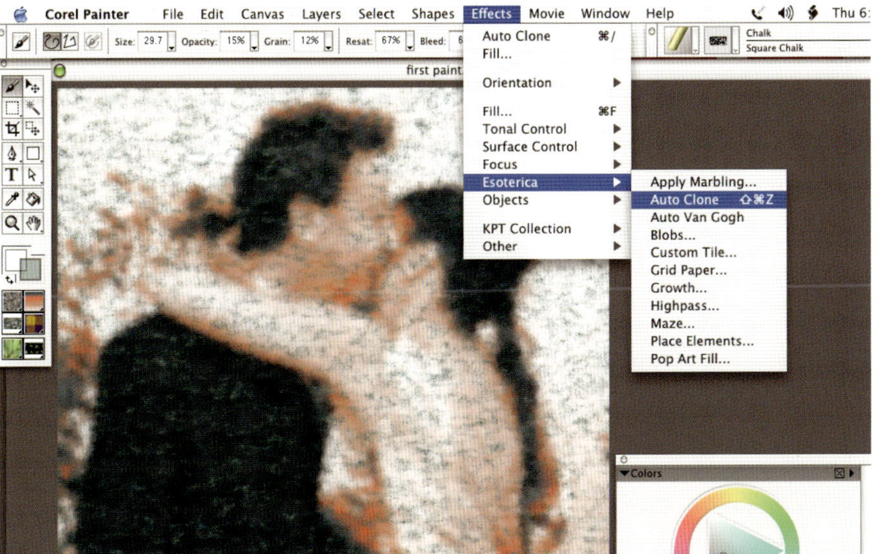

3 AUTO CLONE

Next create an underpainting using Auto Clone. Choose the Chalk's Square Chalk variant and lower the Opacity slider to get transparent strokes to build up the effect gradually. Also, lower the Size slider.

To clone the colors from the previous image, click the rubber stamp in the Colors palette.

Choose Effects: Esoterica: Auto Clone. Chalk strokes appear, lightly bringing in the photo as a pastel.

To stop the cloning, click anywhere in the image.

Deselect the rubber stamp in the Colors palette.

4 CLONING AROUND

Next, clone in some details from the source image.

Choose Canvas: Tracing Paper to show the source image, and with the Cloners' Soft Cloner, paint a little in the faces and hair.

At this stage, you're just bringing in some of the details (see image at right) from the source image, not the whole thing.

Move the slider in the image window's lower left-hand corner to zoom up on the image.

Press the spacebar and click and drag in the image to locate the spot you want to paint.

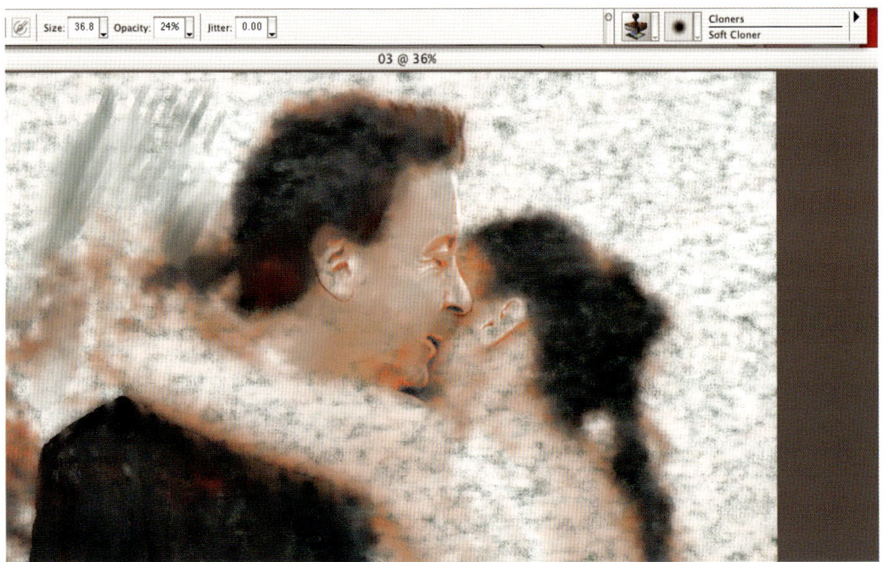

5 IT'S GETTING DARKER

Make the background darker to contrast with the figures.

Select with the Magnetic Lasso tool in Photoshop, reopen the file in Painter and load the selection.

For instructions how, see page 36 in the Photoshop Tools chapter.

Next, in Painter, reattach the painting image and the source image. See page 26 for instructions.

Choose blue-green in the Colors palette, and Effects: Surface Control: Color Overlay. Choose Image Luminance in the Using menu, keep Dye Concentration selected and move the Opacity slider to 40%. Click OK. The background is now darker.

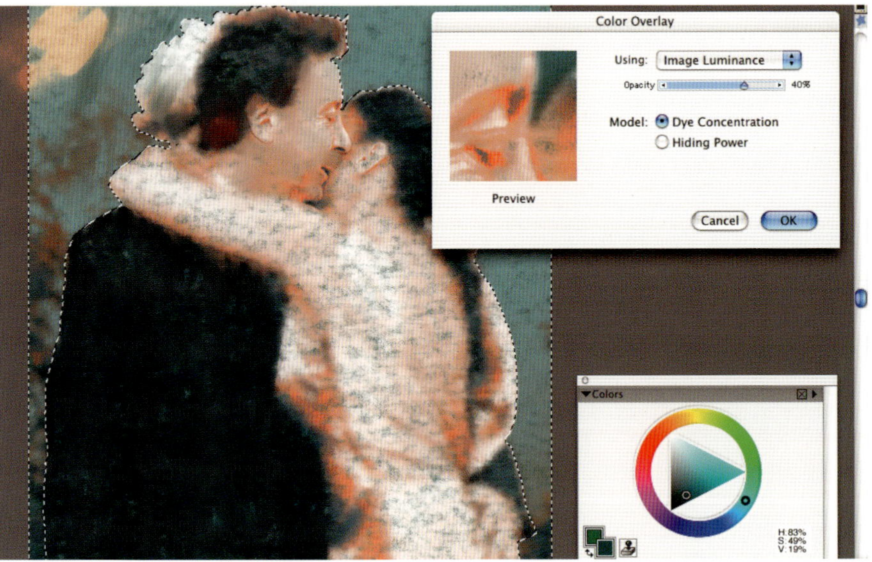

6 A NEW SLANT

With the Chalk's Square Chalk selected, choose Record Stroke in the Brush Selector popup menu. Choose a dark blue-green and draw a short, slanted stroke. Choose Auto Playback in the Brush Selector popup menu, and the stroke appears repeatedly (see image at right). Click in the image to stop the strokes. Choose peach—a tone of red-orange—and choose Auto Playback again, then stop. Blend the strokes by lowering Resat, raising Bleed and choosing Auto Playback again. Raise Resat and lower Bleed, choose another color and choose Auto Playback again. Repeat till you're happy with the result.

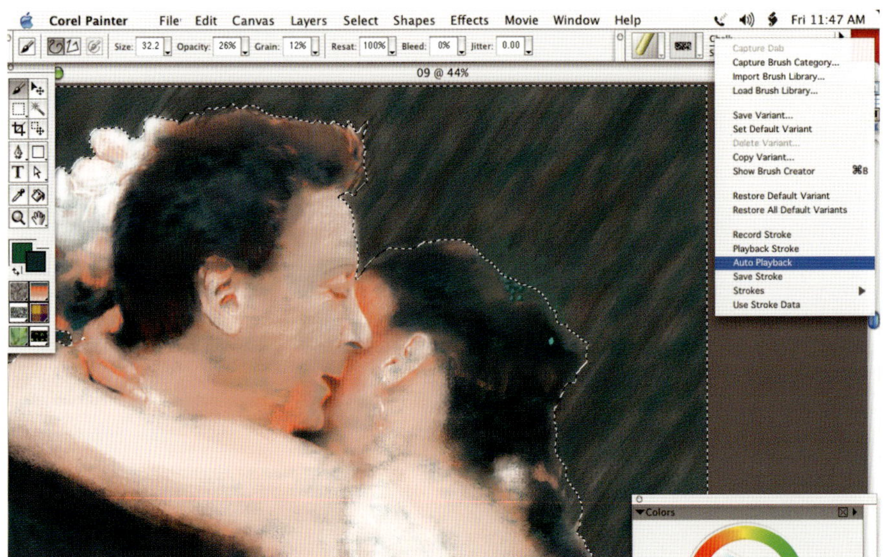

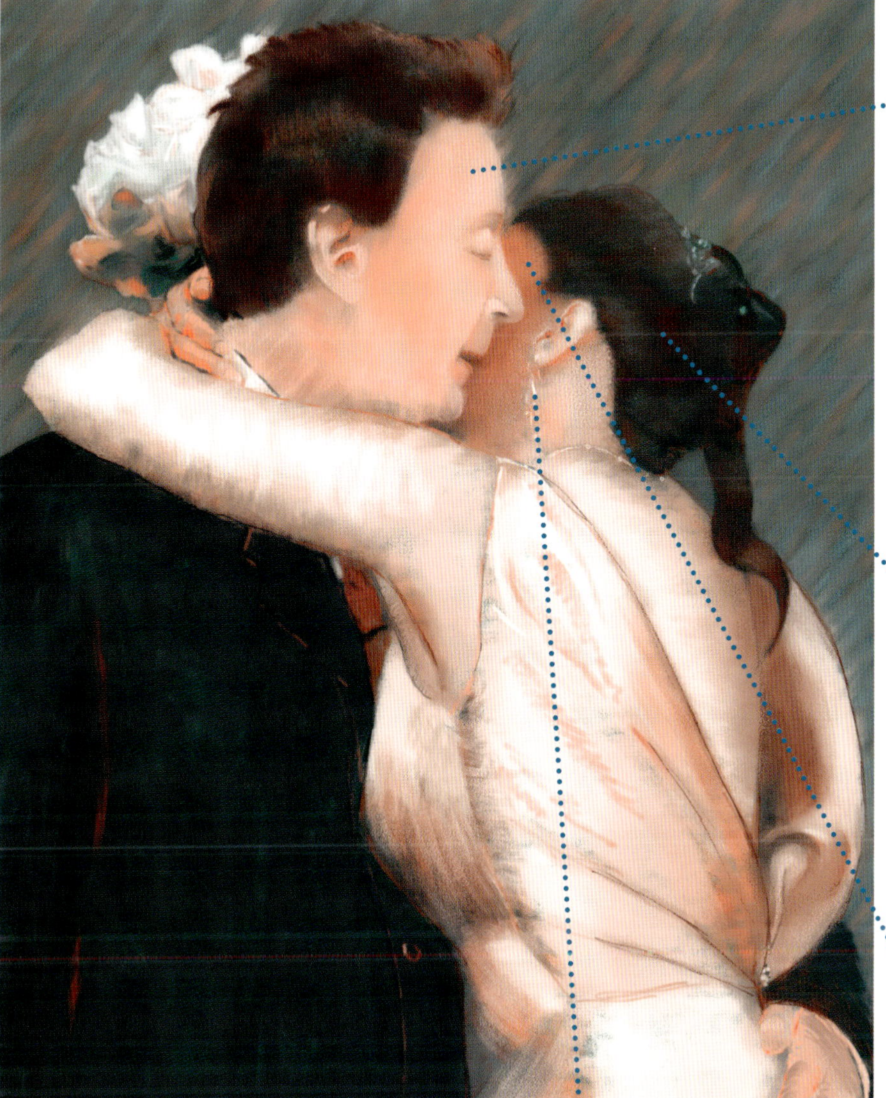

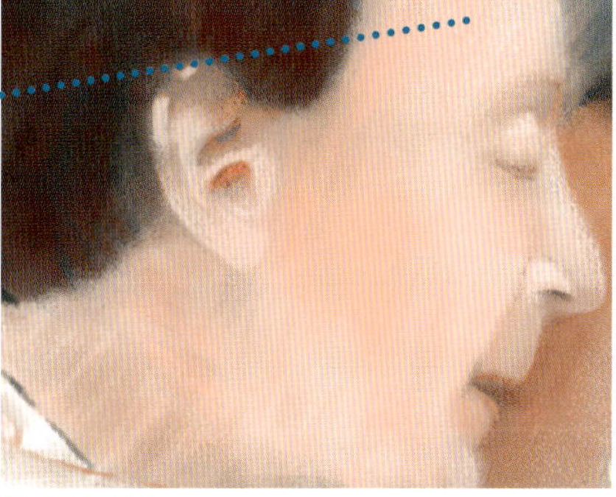

BLENDING

Blend more with the Smudge on the faces and in the hair than on the clothing and in the background.

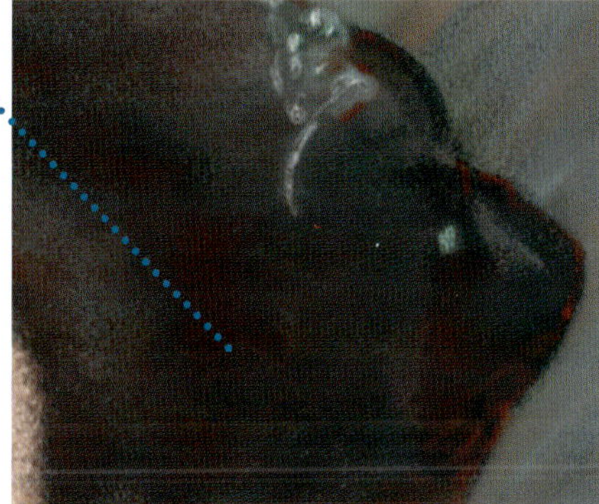

HAIR

Leave the blue-green tone in the hair because it adds to color harmony, where colors repeat throughout the painting. Add brown with the Square Chalk on low opacity and high size settings, providing color and texture to the hair. Draw a few lines with the Chalk's Sharp Chalk to suggest hair strands.

7 READY, SET, DRAW!

Deselect the background (command+d, Mac; ctrl+d, Windows) and use the Square Chalk to draw light and dark strokes going in one direction to indicate tones like on the bride's arm, for instance.

Draw edges between tones like on the back of the bride's dress, for example, using the Chalk's Sharp Chalk.

Blend a little with the Blenders' Smudge, but not too much—you want the strokes to look like pastels.

Slowly build up these strokes. Turn Canvas: Tracing Paper on and off to see the highlights and shadows in the source image and add them in the drawing.

Keep painting a little, blending a little, and repeating, till you're done!

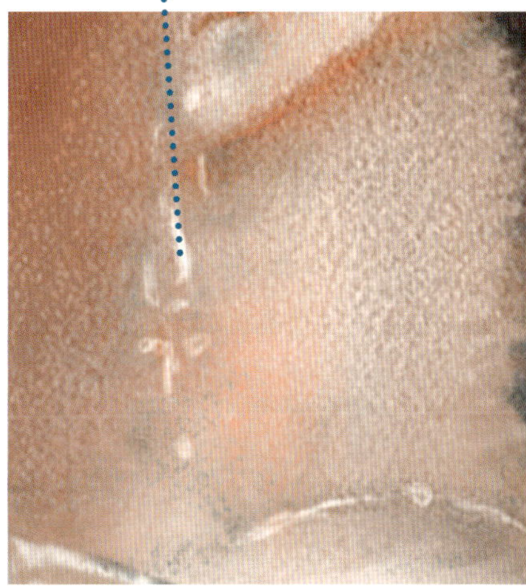

JEWELRY

Paint the bride's jewelry and hair ornament with the Photo's Dodge. Lower the Size slider and with Tracing Paper turned on, draw where you see the jewelry in the photo.

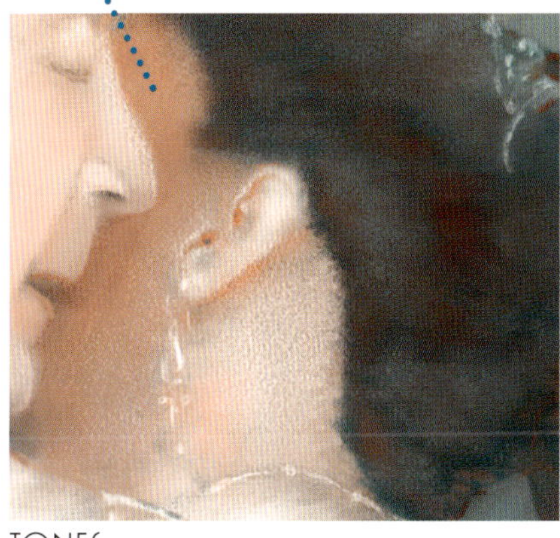

TONES

Make the bride darker because she is in shadow and because doing so creates good contrast with the light groom, adding drama in the drawing. Darken the bride by painting with the Photo's Burn variant on high size and low opacity. Add some texture to the bride by painting with the Photo's Add Grain variant.

AIRBRUSHED PORTRAITS

Photoshop's brushes lend themselves to a "slick," airbrushed look in contrast to Painter's brushes, which I find are better for painting subtle, textured strokes.

I enjoyed using Photoshop to paint David Derex's photo, which was a good candidate to be turned into a painting because of the strong contrasts created by interesting highlights and shadows.

David's photo is a perfect example of how a source image with strong contrast makes the best painting.

Notice how much more interesting the torso is with the shadow patterns than if it had been just one tone throughout.

Even the most experienced artist would have a difficult time creating those shadows if they weren't there in the source photo for reference.

Set up the photo to paint in Photoshop.

1. Open the photo in Photoshop and chose Image: Duplicate.
2. Save and name the duplicate (File: Save As). Close the original to have it intact.
3. Select the figure with the Magnetic Lasso tool (see page 36 for instructions).
4. Make the selection a layer (command+j, Mac; ctrl+j, Windows).
5. Apply Filter: Blur: Smart Blur, making the figure less detailed and more painterly.

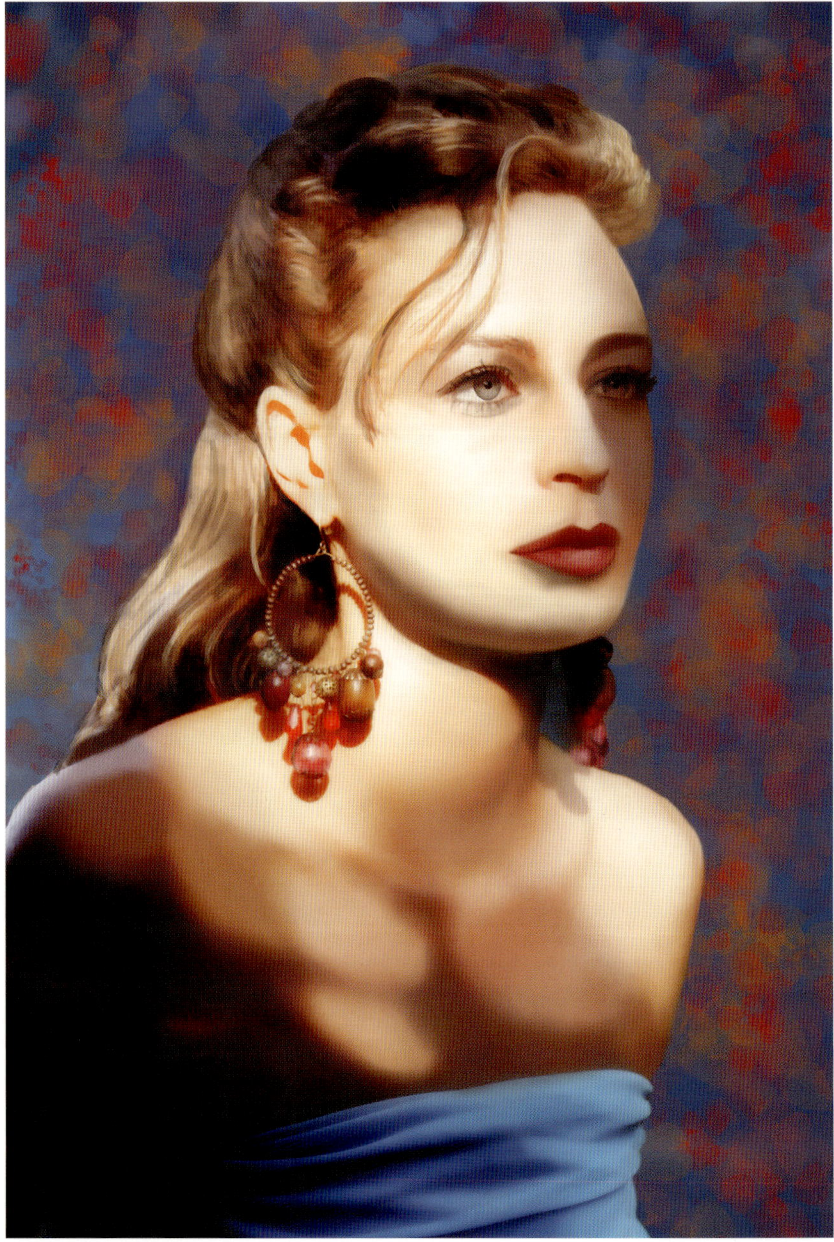

Airbrushed Portrait

Painting by Karen Sperling from a photo by David Derex.

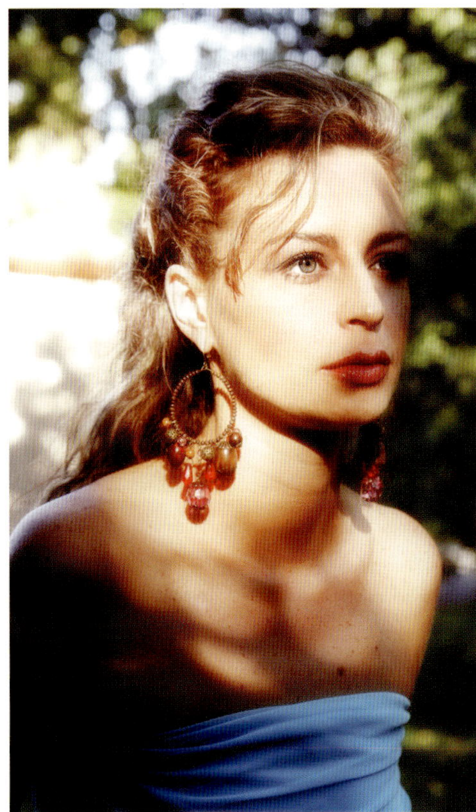

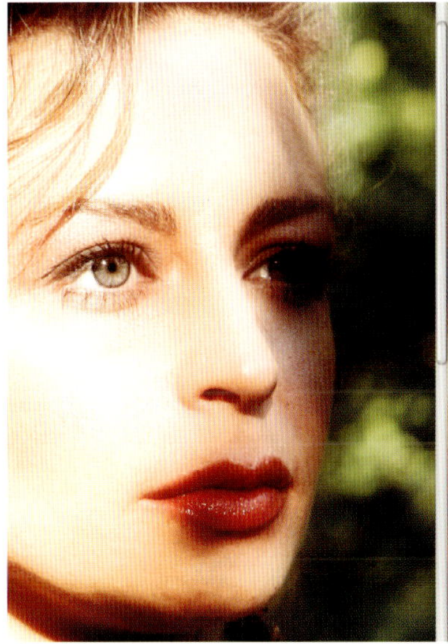

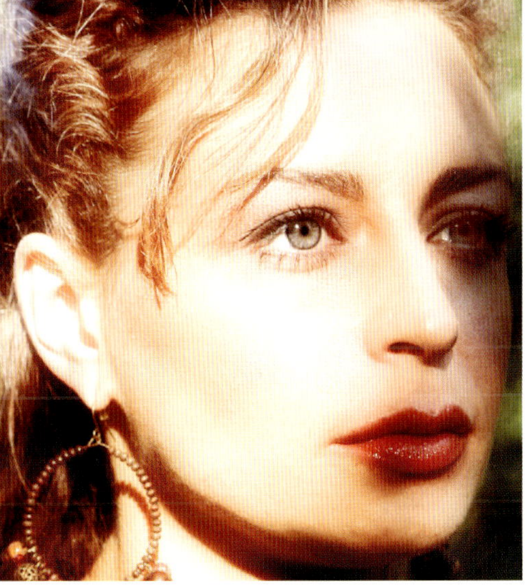

1 Light Adjustment

The girl's left eye was in too much shadow, which would have been difficult to paint.

Choose the Dodge tool in the Tools panel and select Shadows in the Range menu in the options bar.

Paint in the girl's left eye just enough to make out details so that you can see them to paint them (see before and after images at left).

Paint a dark outline around the irises with the Brush tool and a Hard Round preset on 53% opacity. Press option, Mac; alt, Windows and click on the eyelashes to pick up their color and paint the iris outlines.

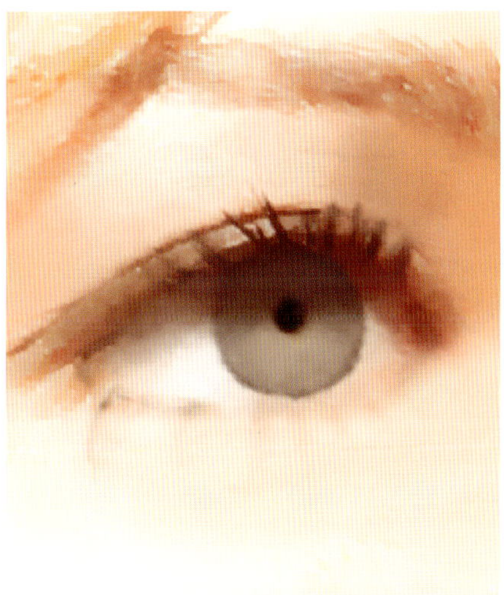

2 Eye for an Eye

Use a Soft Round preset on a Master Diameter of 21 pixels and Opacity on 25% to paint the irises. Press option/alt and click on the iris to get the color and then paint one shade of it in the lower part of the iris and a darker version on the top to show a shadow cast by the brow. See page 37 for information about choosing colors and page 18 for art theories for painting faces.

Blend with the Smudge tool with the Charcoal Large Smear preset selected. Set Master Diameter on 8 pixels, Strength on 23% and select Sample All Layers in the options bar to smudge using color data from visible layers.

Click the eye next to the layer in the Layers panel on and off to make sure the edges in the painting line up with the edges in the photo.

Paint the eyelashes and pupils with the Brush tool and a Hard Round preset. With a Soft Round preset chosen, paint the catchlights, raise the Master Diameter a bit and paint the areas around the eyes and add shading at the top of the whites of the eyes.

Paint based on the tones in the photo, using lighter and darker versions of the photo's tones to add contrast.

Using a low opacity, you overlap strokes and gradually build up paint.

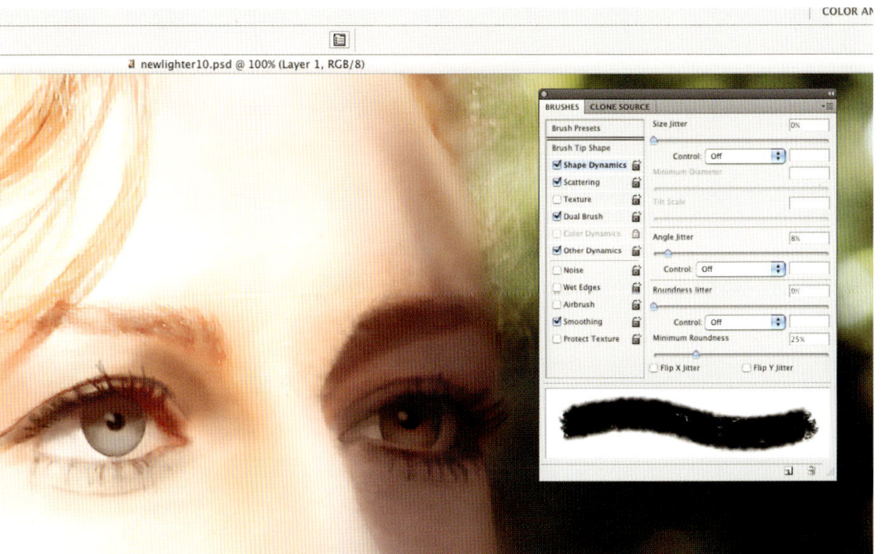

3 Less Jittery

Paint with the Dodge tool at the bottom of the irises.

Use the Burn tool on the girl's left eye to depict that it is in shadow.

Blend in places with the Smudge tool and Charcoal Large Smear preset.

Click the checked options in the left-hand column in the Brushes panel to reveal more options on the right (see image at left).

Lower sliders with the word jitter to reduce randomness so that the Smudge strokes are more even.

Just lower the sliders a tad. The Smudge strokes are nice with a little jitter, or randomness.

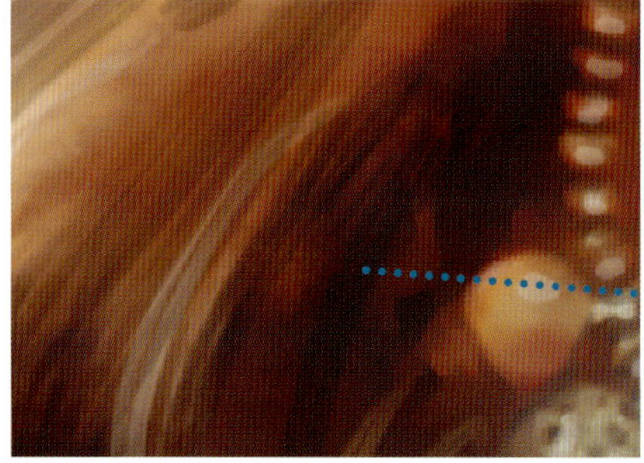

HAIR RAISING

Blend with the Smudge tool and the Oil Medium Wet Flow preset with Strength on 76%. Blend to create areas of light and dark. Next, paint some strands with the Brush tool on 60% opacity and the Rough Round Bristle preset selected. Press option/alt and click on a color in the hair to pick it up and either paint with it or choose a lighter/darker tone to emphasize highlights/shadows.
Then, with the Smudge tool, blend at the ends and edges of strokes to make them look more like they're part of the hair and not pasted on. This is a back-and-forth process.
Paint some strokes, blend, paint, blend—keep going till you are happy with the result.

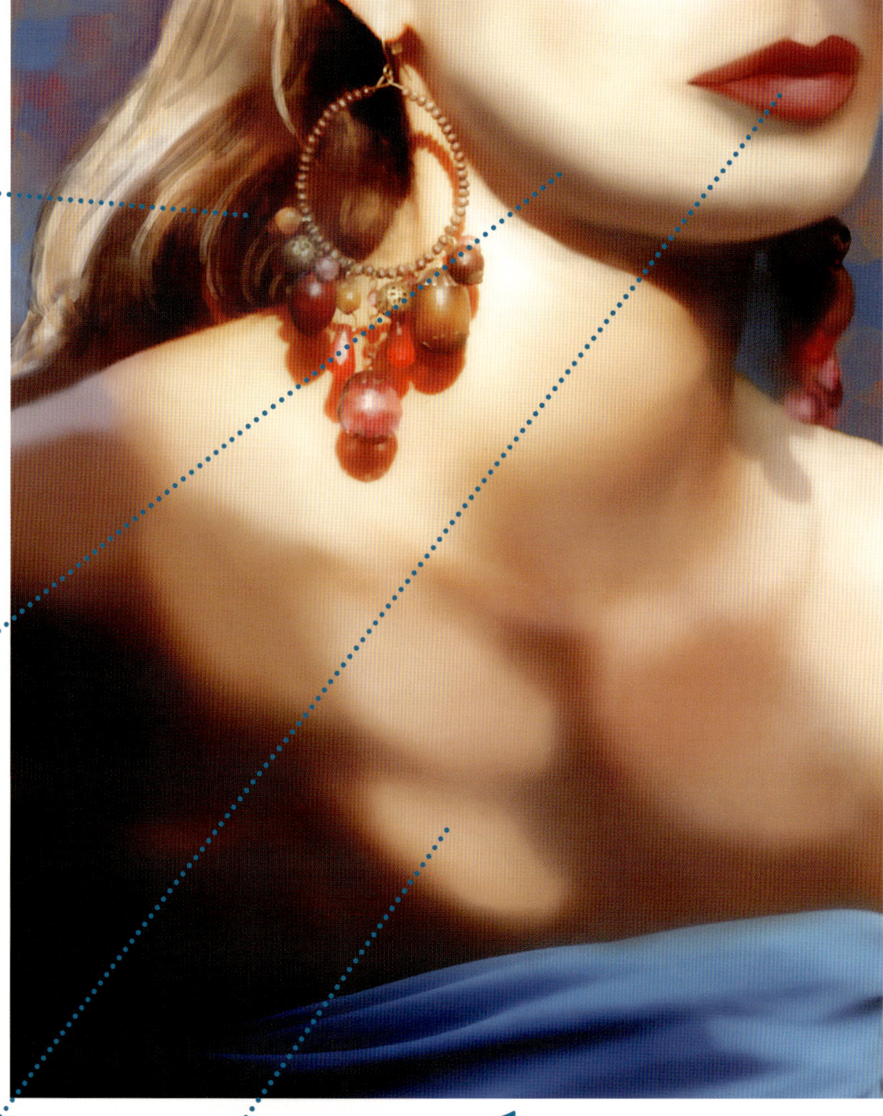

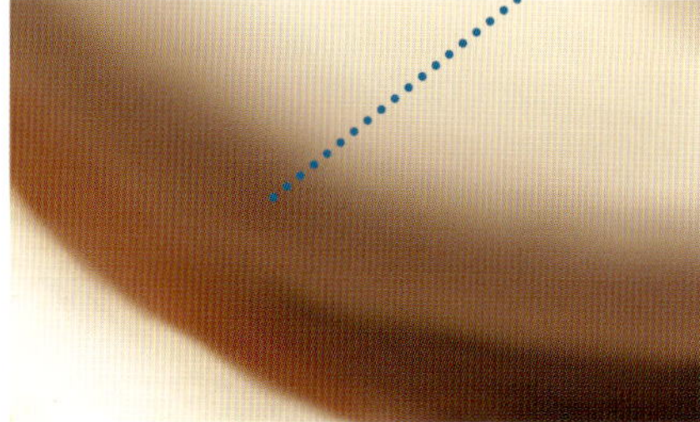

JAW

Paint some shadow on the jaw line and below the lips with the Brush tool and a Soft Round preset on 30% opacity. Layer brush strokes to build up the smooth transition between tones.

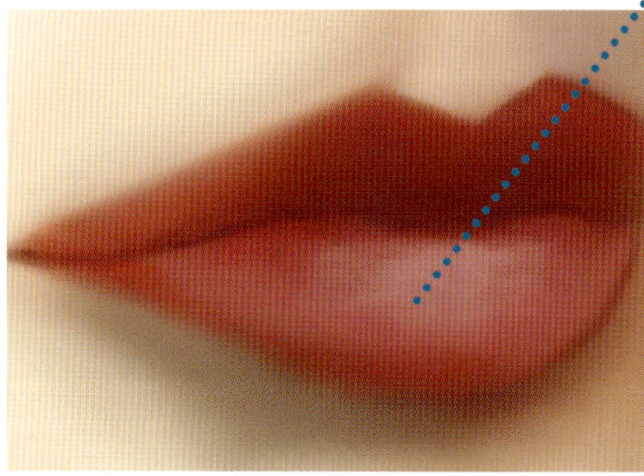

LIPS

Blend the lips with the Smudge tool and the Oil Medium Wet Flow preset with Strength on 76%. Add tones with the Brush tool and a Soft Round preset on 30% opacity. In general, when painting the lips, the idea is to make the upper lip darker than the lower lip even if that's not how it looks in the photo.
See page 19 for art concepts for painting lips.

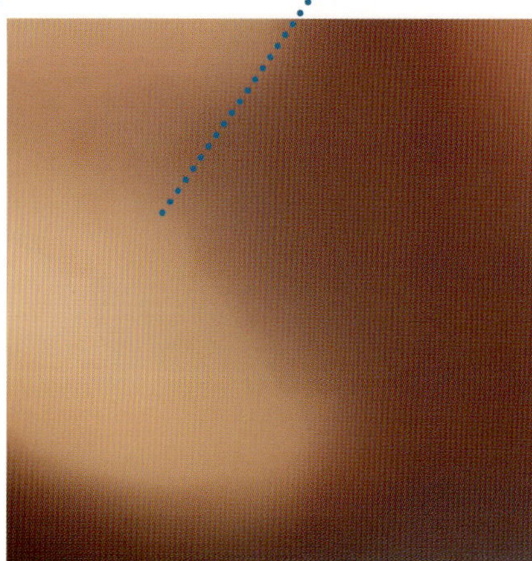

TORSO

Paint the areas of light, medium and dark tones with the Brush tool and a Soft Round preset on 30% opacity. Layer brush strokes to build up the smooth transition between tones.

4 HAIR-ETICAL

Paint the skin, lips and jewelry using the same tools.

Paint the jewelry and the light part of the face with the Brush tool and a Soft Round preset. Paint the edges of the jewelry with a Hard Round preset and use the Smudge tool to blend between the hard edges and the soft inner strokes.

Paint the dark tones darker and light tones lighter to create more drama.

One of the differences between a photo and a painting is that a painting has less detail, so to paint the hair, blend individual hair strands to create large areas of highlights, midtones and shadows, then suggest strands (see Hair Raising caption above, left).

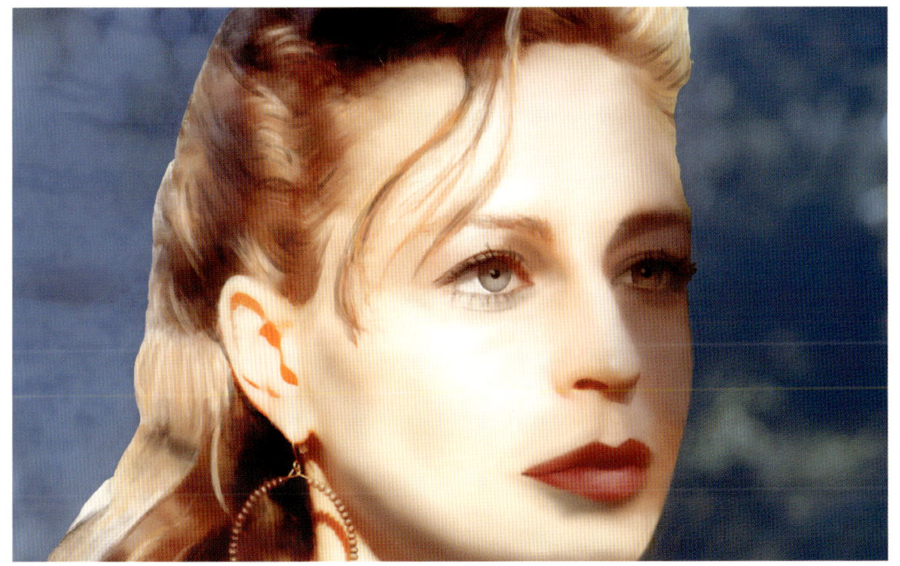

5 BRUSH UP

For the background, use the Brush tool and a Soft Round preset on 80% opacity with a high Master Diameter.

Press option/alt and click on a dark blue in the girl's top, click Background in the Layers panel and paint a few strokes.

Selecting blue creates color harmony—see pages 12-13 for art concepts for choosing colors.

Meanwhile, because the skin tone is on the orange side, and blue is the color complement—or opposite on the color wheel—of orange, the two colors go together well.

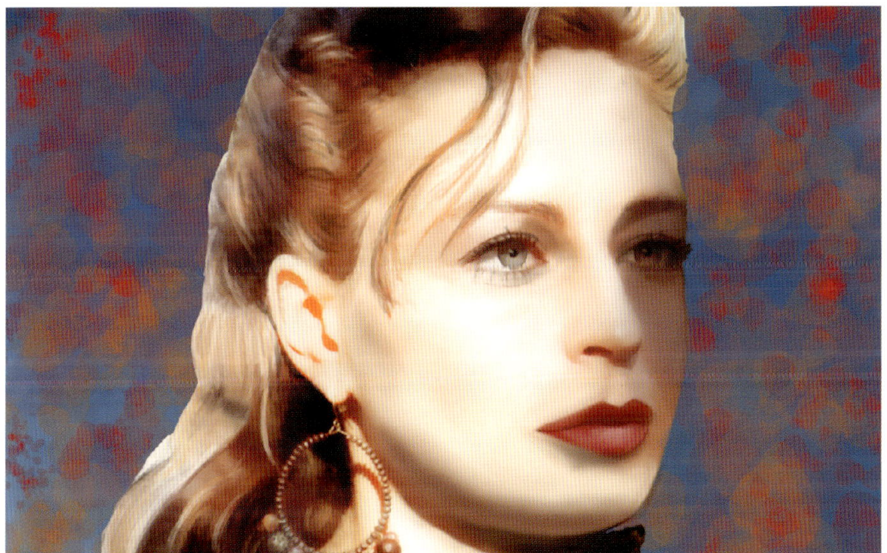

6 A NEW LEAF

Switch to an Airbrush Soft Round preset and paint more blue in the background to keep some of the texture while eliminating the green because it doesn't fit into the color scheme.

Choose the Scattered Leaves preset on 50% opacity, raise the Scattering sliders in the Brushes panel and paint in the background with red and orange at various Master Diameter settings, creating more color harmony.

Save, and then choose File: Save As and create a new version.

Then flatten (Layer menu: Flatten Image). Now you can do the final touchups.

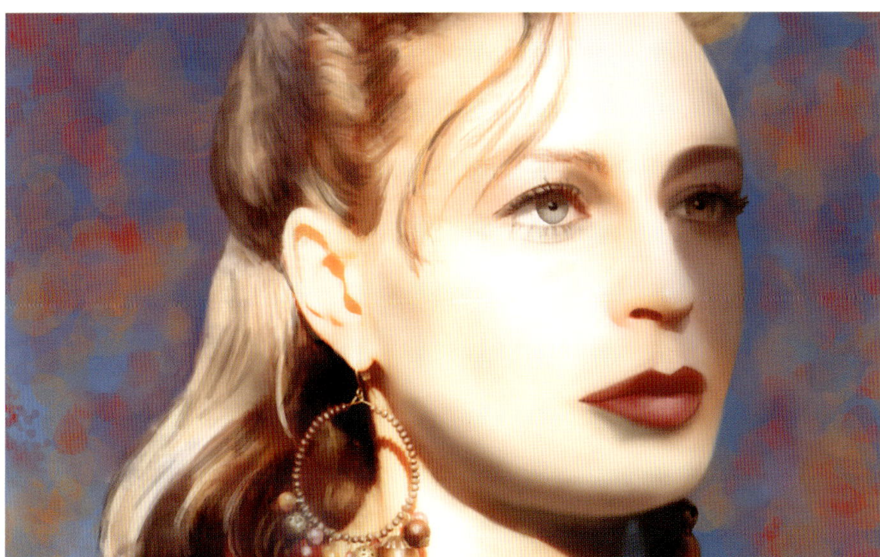

7 WITH A SMEAR

To extend the hair and to blend it with the background, paint some hair strands with the Brush tool and the Rough Round Bristle preset.

Press option/alt and click on a color in the hair and either paint with it or choose a lighter or darker tone of it, depending on what you see in the source image. Pick up background colors and paint into the hair, also to blend the hair with the background better. Use the Smudge tool and the Oil Medium Wet Flow preset to blend some of the background elements and to blend the hair with the background even more.

PHOTOREALISTIC PORTRAITS

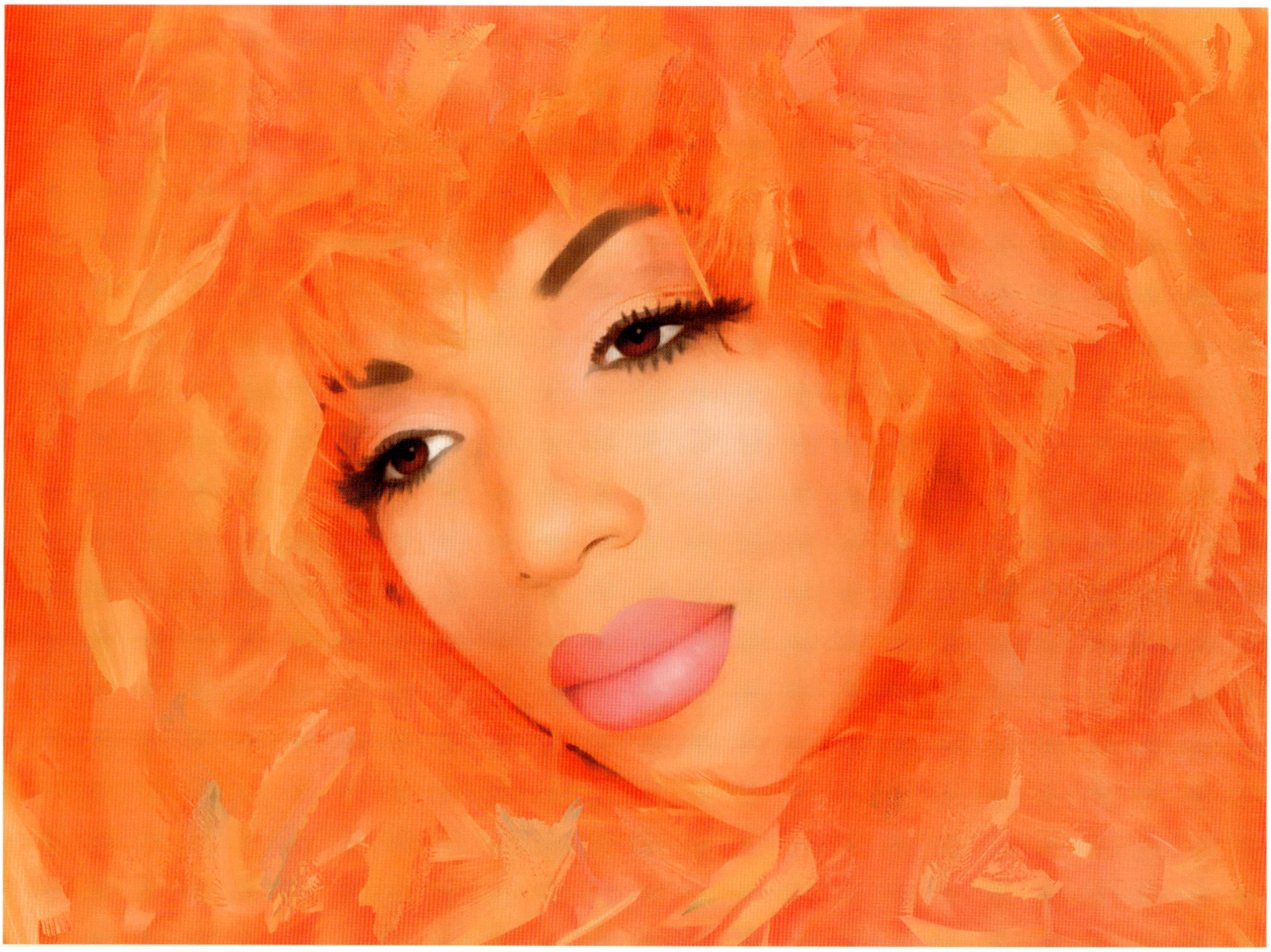

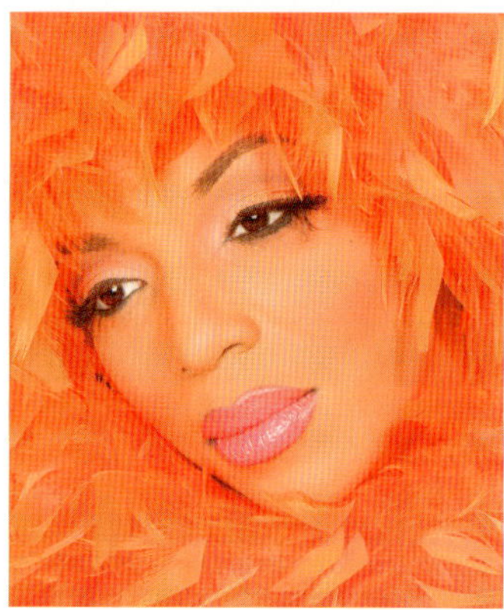

Photorealistic Portrait
PAINTING BY KAREN SPERLING
FROM A PHOTO BY JACKIE HICKS.

The Photorealism art movement first appeared in the late 1960's.

Its members created paintings that were so realistic, they could have been photographs.

I call a digital portrait or landscape from a photo photorealistic if the painting looks like the photo, as opposed to other portraits and landscapes that include only some parts of the photo.

Photorealistic portraits are very popular among photographers offering painted portraits to their clients.

Photographer Jackie Hicks commissioned me to paint the painting on this page from her beautiful photo.

Her instructions were: "Paint it lightly." She wanted it to look just like her photo, but with a painterly touch.

To set up the photo to paint in Painter:

1. Open the photo in Painter (File: Open) and choose File: Clone.
2. Name this clone copy (File: Save As).
3. Resize and reposition the original and the clone so that they are side by side on the monitor.
4. Choose the Underpainting palette in the Window menu and use Smart Blur on the clone.
5. Save the smart blur version, then choose File: Clone and paint.

1 THE EYES HAVE IT

Paint the face with the art concepts on pages 18-19 in mind. Begin painting the eyes using the Chalk's Sharp Chalk. Press option, Mac; alt, Windows, and click on a dark brown in the image and paint an outline around the irises.

Next, press option, Mac; alt, Windows and click on the reddish brown in the right eye.

Paint the irises of both eyes within the dark brown edges.

Choose a darker tone in the Colors palette and paint the pupils.

Choose the Chalk's Square Chalk, lower the Size slider and paint the eyelashes.

Darken the area below the eyelashes by painting with the Chalk's Sharp Chalk. Press option/alt and click on colors already in the image and paint with them.

Blend all the transitions between colors by painting with the Blenders' Just Add Water.

With the Digital Watercolor's New Simple Water chosen, with opacity set to 4%, paint a shadow at the top of each iris.

Choose Layers menu: Dry Digital Watercolor when done.

With the Chalk's Sharp Chalk, paint the catchlights.

Turn the Sharp Chalk into a blender brush and blend the eyelash shadows and the irises.

With the Square Chalk set up as a blender, add texture on the eyelids and under the eyes.

See page 24 for steps for creating and saving blenders.

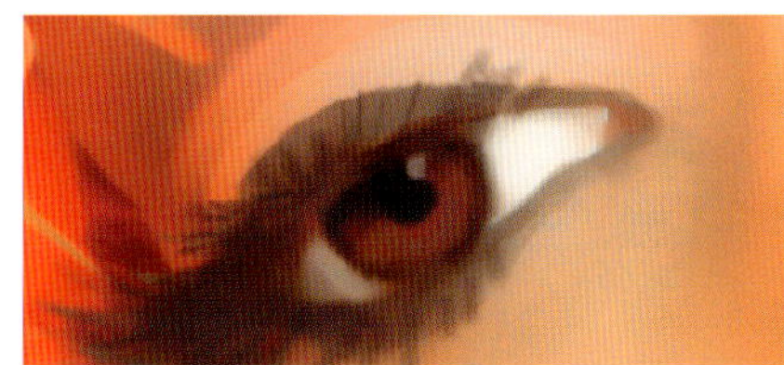

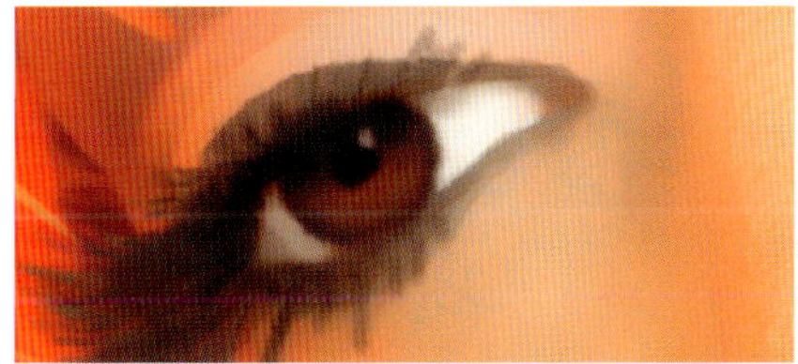

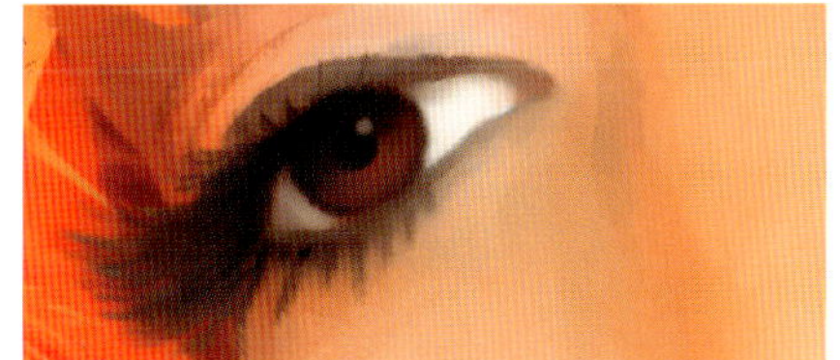

2 LIPS

Use the Chalk's Square Chalk to paint the lips. Press option/alt and click on the pink at the top of the bottom lip and paint over the white, shiny part to even up the tone.

Choose a darker pink in the Colors palette, paint the outlines and add the dark color in the shadows. With the Blenders' Smudge, blend the strokes and smooth out the transitions.

Continue to paint, adding tones and blending them based on the tones in the photograph.

Don't blend too much—letting brush strokes show makes the image look more painterly.

Add a dash of white with the Sharp Chalk on the lower lip and blend with the Smudge.

See page 19 for art theories for painting lips.

That's a good trick for lightening areas in general—paint with the chalk then blend with a blender.

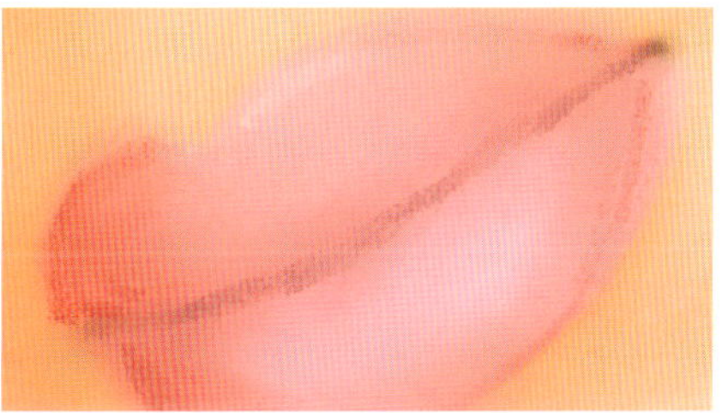

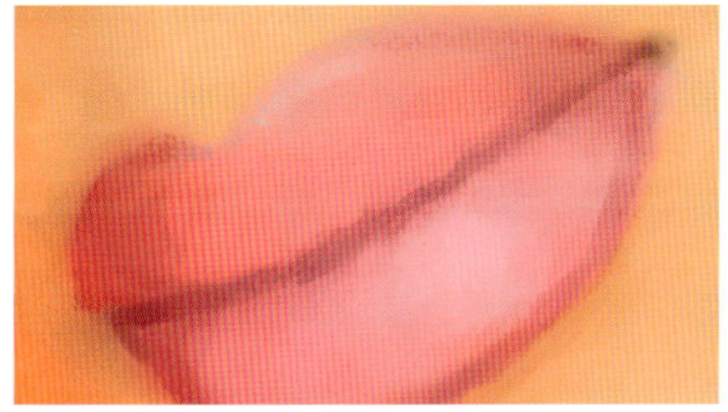

3 FINE FEATHERS

The feathers got a little too smooth in the blur step. To paint some texture back into them, create a custom brush tip (see inset at right) for the Artists' Sargent Brush—with the Sargent Brush selected, press lightly to get the thin strokes and press heavily for the wider strokes.

See page 27 for information about creating a custom brush.

Paint with the custom-tip brush with the rubber stamp selected in the Colors palette to pick up colors from the source image and with it deselected to choose your own colors.

Add strokes to the face with the default Square Chalk and then blend them with the Square Chalk on the blender settings you used earlier.

Press option/alt and click on the cheeks, choose a lighter tone in the Colors palette and paint on the cheeks to lighten them a bit.

Add some brush strokes on a low opacity throughout.

Last, choose the Cloners' Soft Cloner variant and paint lightly on some of the feathers to bring back a little detail, especially around the face.

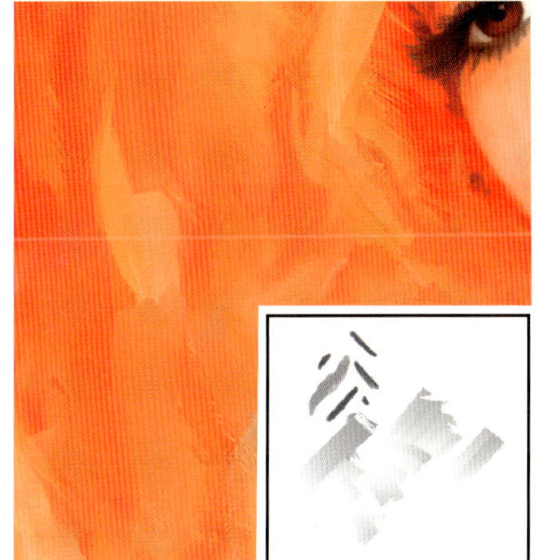

AUTO-PAINTED PORTRAITS

If *Painting for Photographers* were an album, then this painting of mine, which everyone has named "Degas Dancers," would be the title song.

I invited photographers to send their photos for me to paint for tutorials for both this book and for my e-zine, Artistry Tips and Tricks.

Felicia Tausig, a professional photographer who has studied painting with me, submitted her photo with a bunch of others, and I selected this one to paint originally for an issue of Artistry Tips and Tricks.

I chose this photo to paint because it was taken from slightly above the dancers. This angle gave the dancers an interesting layout and it made them look like they were touching, a characteristic of good composition (see pages 16-17 for others). And the dancers' positions formed interesting triangles, which, combined with the other characteristics, made this photo a good one to turn into a painting.

What also made this photo a good painting candidate was that it had a limited number of colors and good contrast. I pushed the contrast even more by choosing Effects: Tonal Control: Equalize (in Painter). I used the default settings and clicked OK.

I also chose Effects: Tonal Control: Brightness/Contrast and raised the top slider a bit and clicked OK.

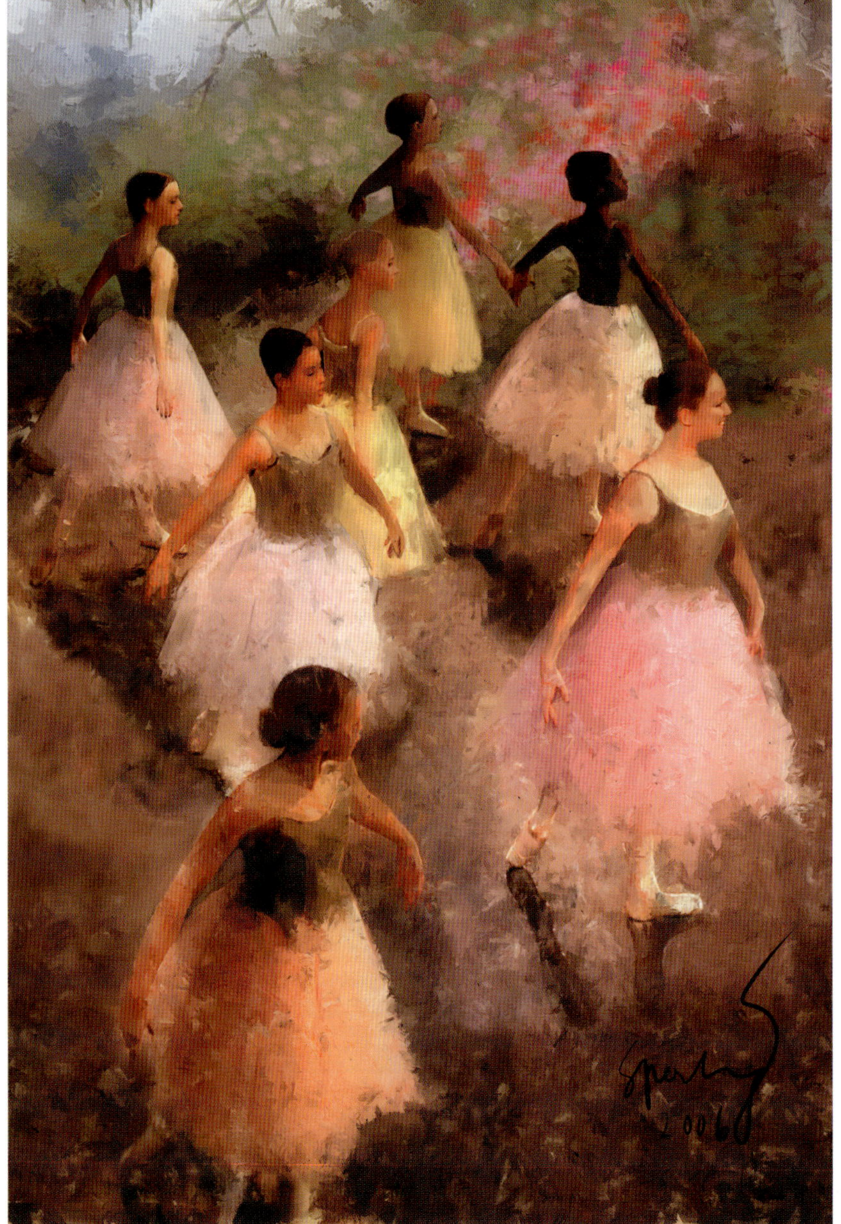

Degas Dancers

PAINTING BY KAREN SPERLING FROM A PHOTO BY FELICIA TAUSIG.

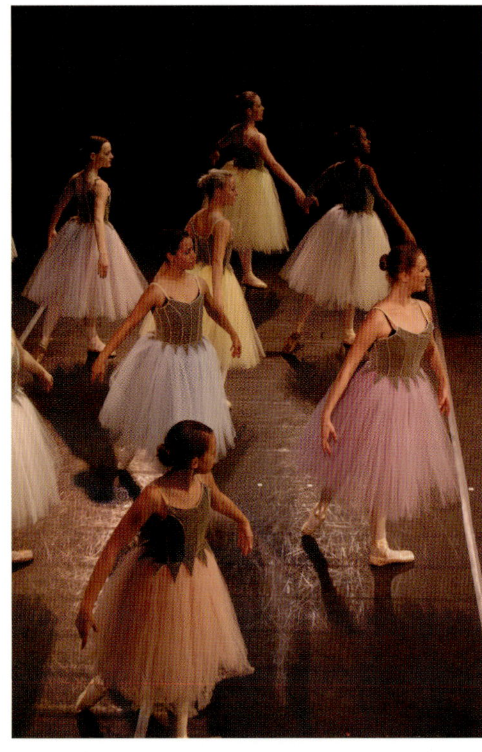

1 EFFECTS: FILL

Like pastel artists using colored paper for their drawings (see page 51), oil painters apply a midtone coat of paint to their canvases to create color harmony and to save painting time.

Clone the photo (File: Clone). Then choose a medium beige in the Colors palette and chose Effects: Fill (command+f, Mac; ctrl+f, Windows). Click next to Current Color in the dialog if it isn't already selected, then click OK. You now have a first coat of beige paint, technically called an underpainting in art terminology. You could turn on Tracing Paper from here, but you don't need it, yet.

2 AUTO-CLONING

Next, you'll apply Auto Clone to speed up painting.

Choose the Artists' Impressionist variant.

Edit the Impressionist variant so that its strokes go in one direction instead of in multiple directions, which is the default setting, by moving Window: Brush Controls: Angle palette: Ang Range and Ang Step sliders to 0°.

Raise the Size slider and lower the Opacity slider in the Property Bar to get large, transparent strokes to build up the effect gradually.

Last, in the Colors palette, click the rubber stamp icon, which will make the brush strokes lift the color from the source image.

Choose Effects: Esoterica: Auto Clone. Brush strokes appear, bringing in the photo as a painting.

To stop Auto Clone, click anywhere in the image.

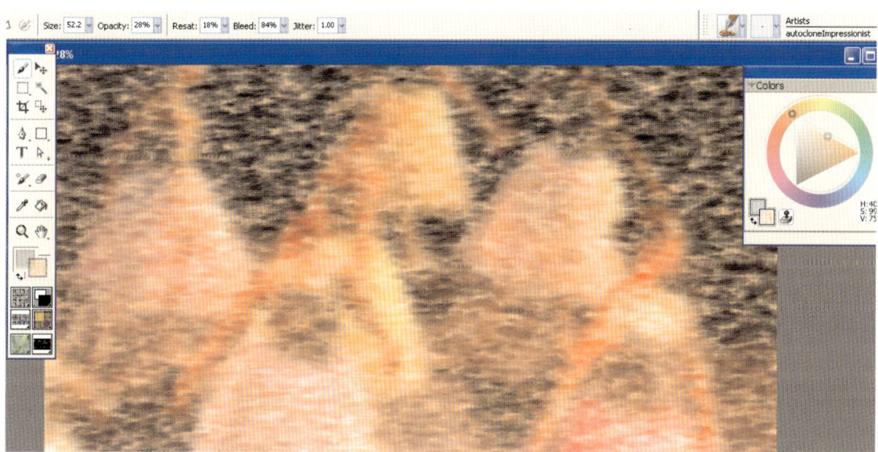

3 AUTO-PAINTING

Auto-Painting comes next. See page 25 for information for working with Auto-Painting.

Paint a custom stroke with the Artists' Sargent Brush—you see the stroke at right—name it bd, then Auto-Paint with it on various slider settings in the Auto-Painting palette, with the check boxes below Randomness deselected.

Run Auto-Painting, change the sliders, run it again, change again.

By adjusting all these sliders, running Auto-Painting, stopping it, adjusting the sliders, and running Auto-Painting some more, the brush strokes build up in a painterly way.

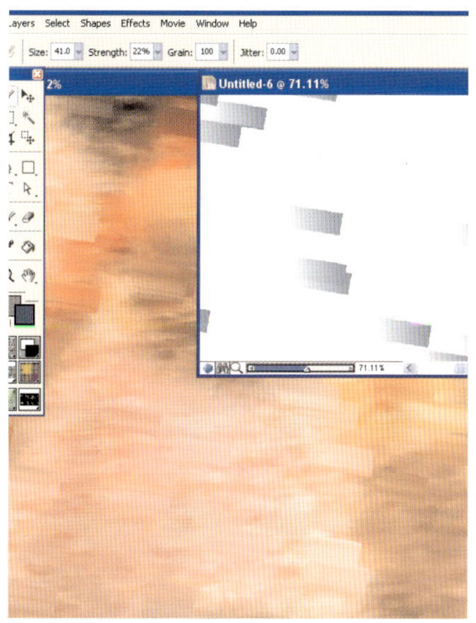

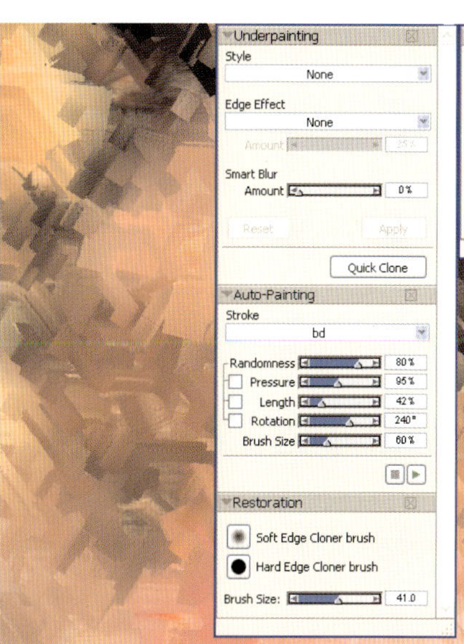

4 SCRIBBLE

Switch to the Scribble stroke in the Auto-Painting palette. Check the Randomness boxes for all the parameters and run Scribble for awhile, stop it, adjust the Brush Size slider in the Auto-Painting palette, then run Scribble again, for just enough brush stroke variety.

5 IMPRESSIONIST BRUSH

Choose the Artists' Impressionist variant. Choose Brush Selector menu: Restore Default Variant to get back the original settings. Click the rubber stamp in the Colors palette and run Scribble with the Randomness boxes checked. Run Scribble for awhile, stop it, adjust the Brush Size slider in the Auto-Painting palette, then run Scribble again, for even more variety. Repeat several times.

6 CLONING

Choose the Soft Edge Cloner brush in the Restoration palette (which is a short cut to the Cloners' Soft Cloner variant, by the way).

Here's where art concepts come into play.

Your first thought might be to simply paint back elements like faces.

Instead, concentrate on restoring edges of contrast between light and dark because the more areas of contrast that a painting has, the more interesting it is.

In the bottom, right image, for instance, paint the edges between light and dark on the dancer's tutu.

Turn on Tracing Paper to follow the photo while painting, turn off Tracing Paper to see the results.

See page 27 for more information about Tracing Paper.

Lower the Size slider in the Property Bar to bring back a smaller amount of the original so that you don't wipe out all the brush strokes.

Don't worry about painting back every detail. A photo is more detailed than a painting, so your image will look more painterly if you leave out detail. Just bring in enough to suggest your subject.

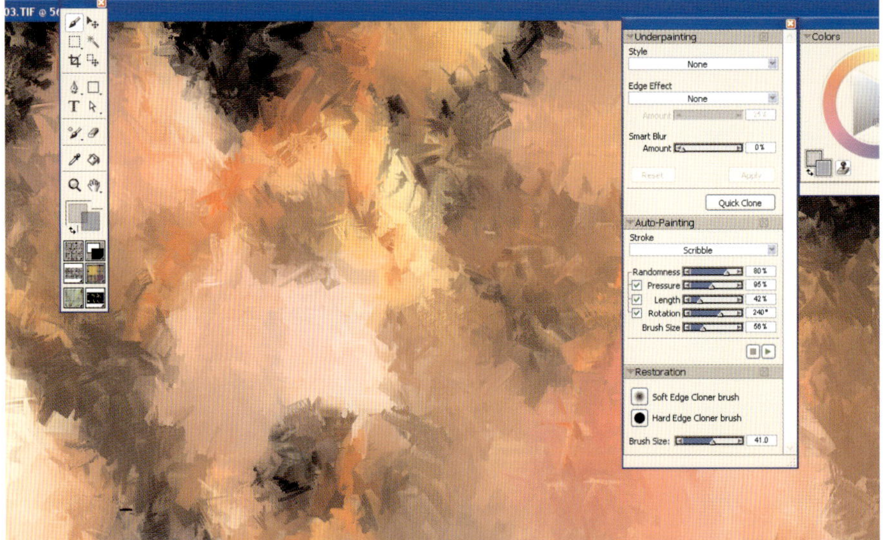

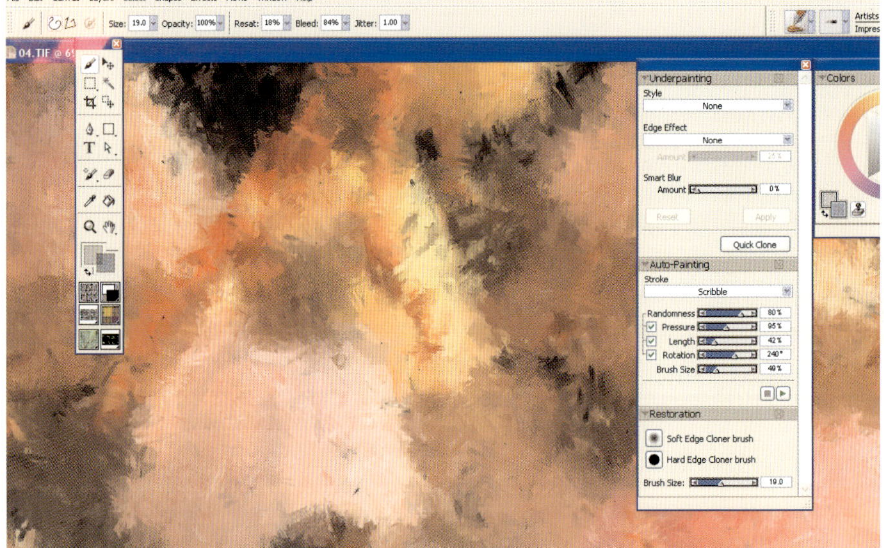

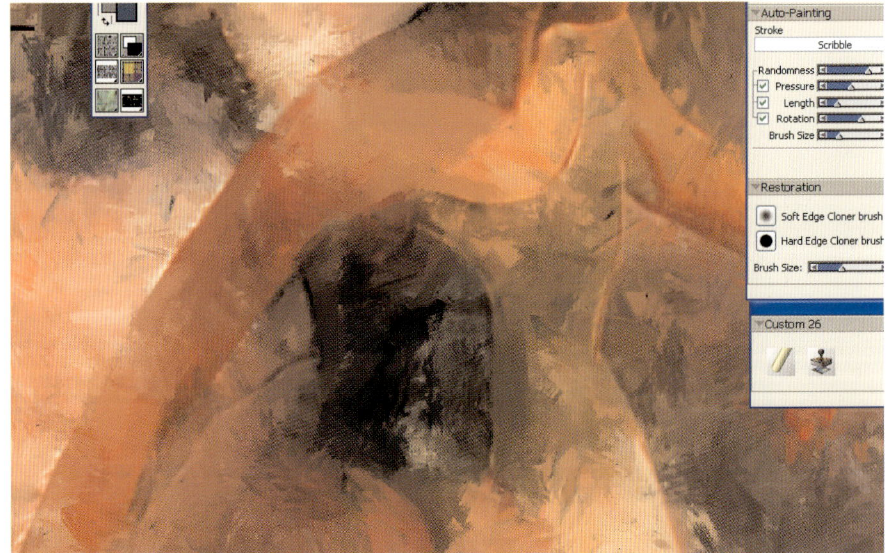

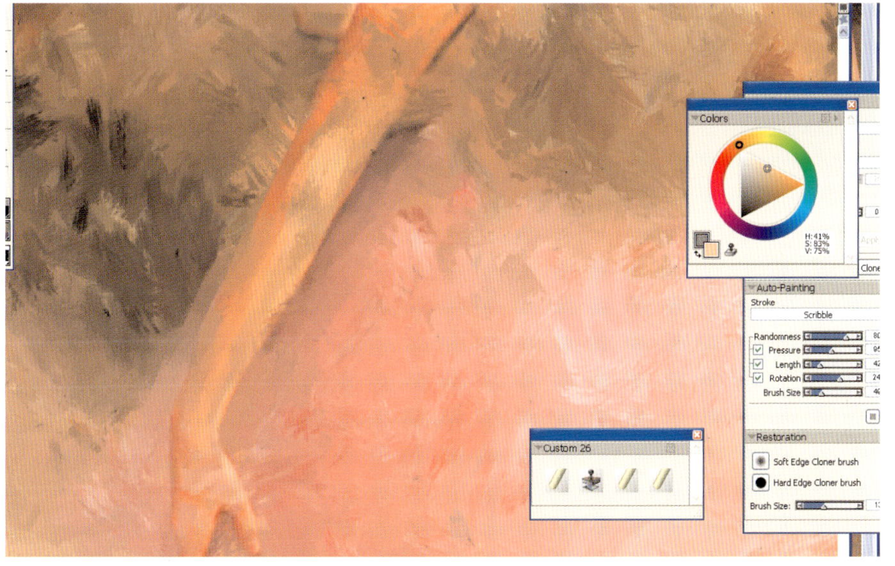

7 ADDING COLOR

In some places, the Auto-Painting strokes bring the wrong color into an area. Add the right color with the Chalk's Square Chalk. Choose Brush Selector menu: Restore Default Variant to bring back the brush's original settings. Then either choose a color and paint, or use a color from the photo by clicking the rubber stamp in the Colors palette. Then blend with the Square Chalk as a blender (see page 24 for steps).

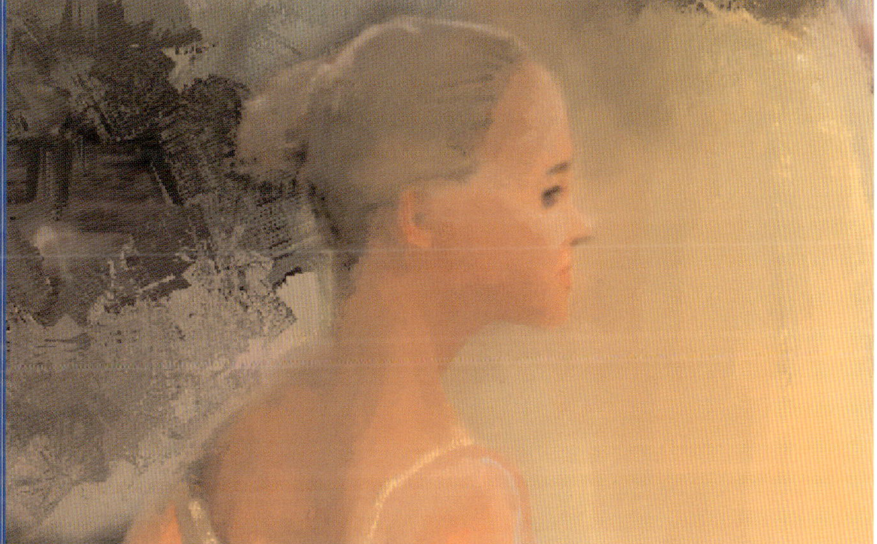

8 LET'S FACE IT

Next paint the faces, hair, hands and shoes. First smooth over the strokes by painting with the Square Chalk as a blender with the Size slider in the Property Bar on a low setting to get a narrow stroke.

With the Soft Cloner also on a very low size setting, paint the eyes, noses and lips from the original. Just paint the photo in slightly—you don't want to lose the painterly look.

Then, using the photo as your guide, add color with the Square Chalk, painting in lights and darks on the face where you see them in the photo.

Last, blend the strokes with the Square Chalk as a blender.

This is a back-and-forth process. You paint the color a little, you blend a little, you paint with the Soft Cloner a little, you blend a little. You keep repeating till you're done.

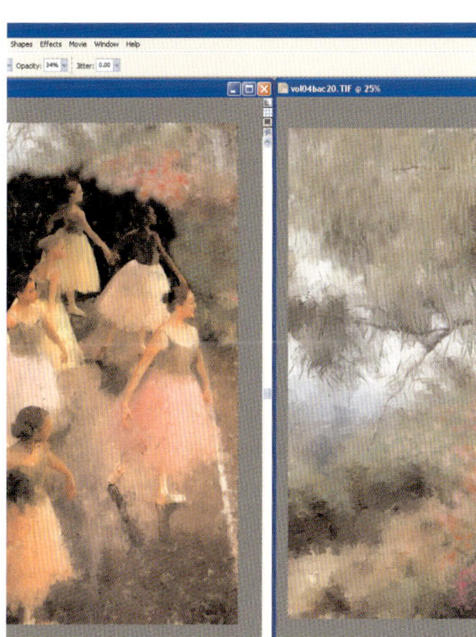

9 LAST STEPS

Add the background by cloning from a backdrop from the Artistry Scenes Backdrops Volume 1 CD (visit http://artistrymag.com/ for details) or from any other landscape.

Resize the backdrop window and put it on the right-hand side of your screen, and resize the dancers window and put it on the left (see image, left).

Then with the Cloners' Soft Cloner selected, press option, Mac; alt, Windows, click on a place to start cloning from in the backdrop image and paint in the dancers image.

After you paint from the backdrop, extend the stage by pressing option, Mac; alt, Windows and clicking on a part of the stage in the image's foreground and painting in the background. You can see where the stage was in the original photo and how I extended it in the image on page 60.

Last, touch up various parts of the image.

Press option/alt and click on a part of the image to paint from and paint where you want to do the touchup.

For instance, I eliminated the dancer all the way to the left who was cut off and also eliminated some of the dark spots of color on some of the costumes.

I also added to the foliage in the back.

IMPRESSIONIST PORTRAITS

Impressionism began officially in Paris in 1874 by artists including Edgar Degas, Claude Monet and Pierre-Auguste Renoir, who painted how they perceived nature and how light affected their subjects.

Take Monet's Haystacks, for instance, which he painted at different times of day, in different seasons and under varying weather conditions (do a google.com search).

The series is a perfect example of the philosophy presented in this book that you're painting areas of light and dark, not objects.

Monet was able to create great art from a subject that might have been considered uninteresting by those who think art is about objects instead of lights and darks.

If you want your paintings from photos to really look like paintings, take a cue from the Impressionists—think in terms of painting your perceptions of a scene, not the scene itself.

The photo is the exact record of the scene.

Impressionist Portrait
Painting and photo by Karen Sperling. Photo taken at Butterfly House, Topanga, CA.

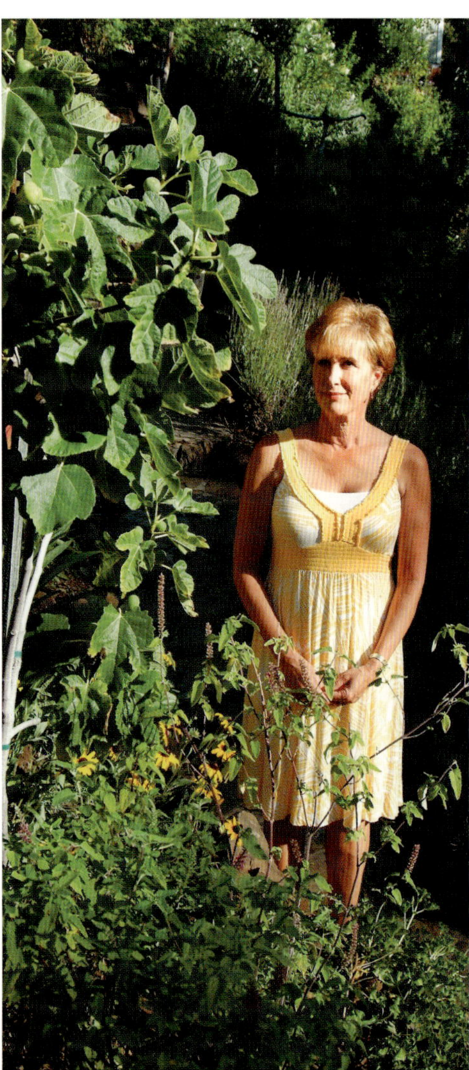

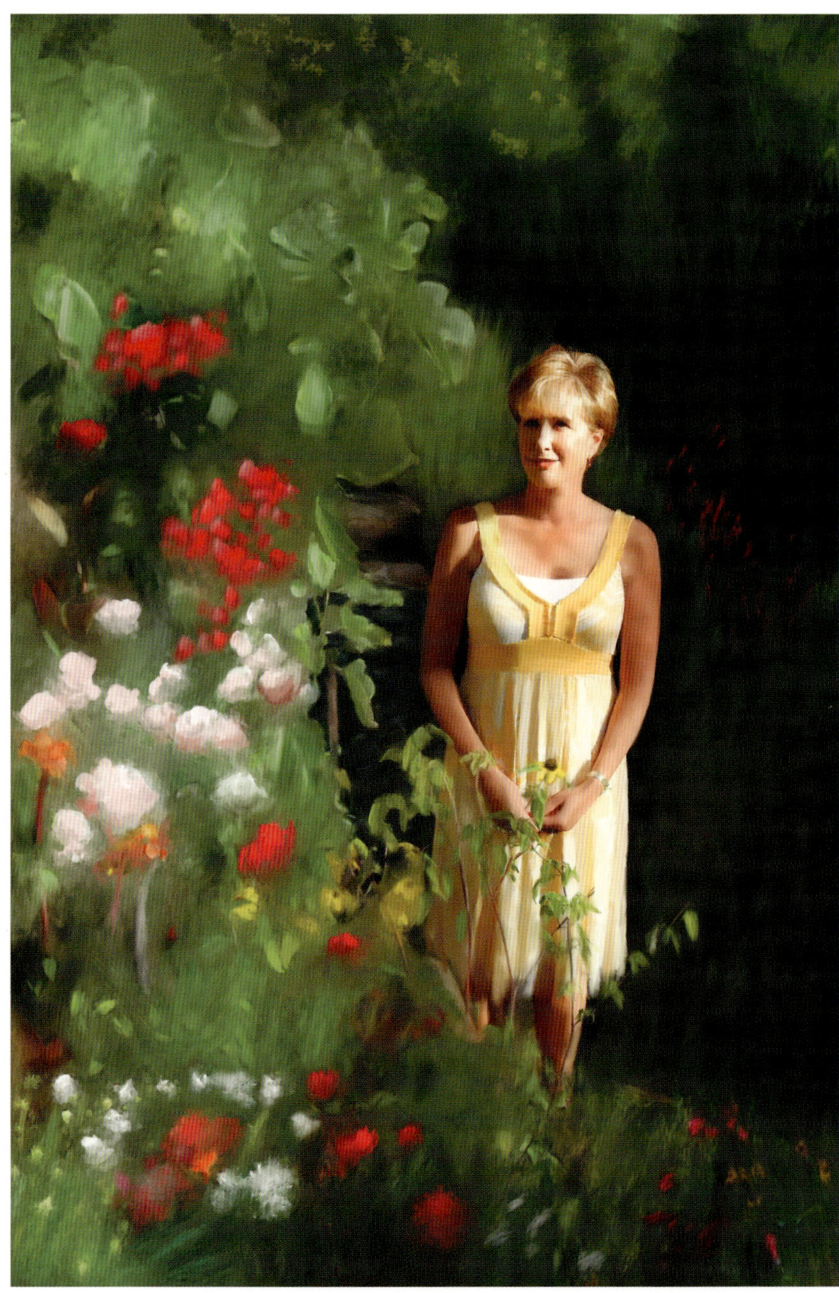

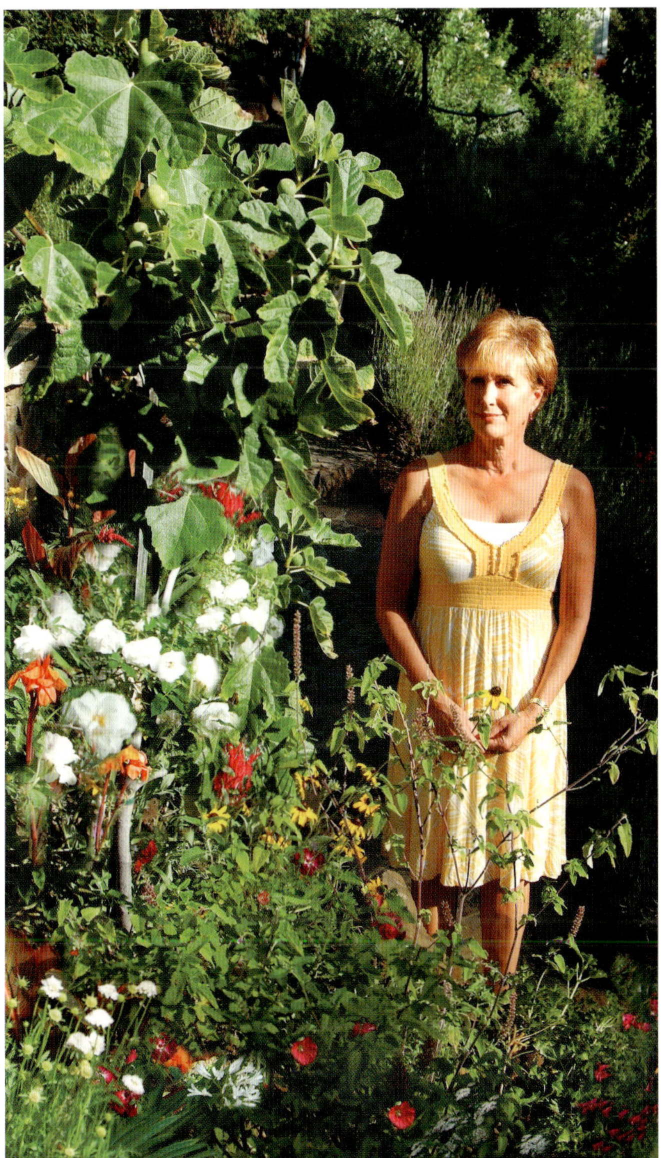

1 BOWERS OF FLOWERS

Open a photo in Painter (File: Open), clone it (File: Clone) and name it (File: Save As).

To add flowers, open other photos and clone flowers into this photo, using either the Cloners' Soft Cloner or xScale 2P variants. See page 26 for steps for using the xScale 2P.

To clone with the Cloners' Soft Cloner:

1. Press option, Mac; alt, Windows.
2. Click on a flower or anything else you want to clone.
3. Paint where you want the flower to appear.

Repeat flowers from one part of the photo in other parts.

Clone one of the yellow flowers onto a stem next to the figure's hand to make it look like she is holding a flower. To place the stem that is next to the hand into the hand, choose the Chalk's Sharp Chalk variant, press option, Mac; alt, Windows and click on the hand to pick up the color, then paint over the stem, making it look like it is inside the hand. Blend the color a little with the Blenders' Smudge.

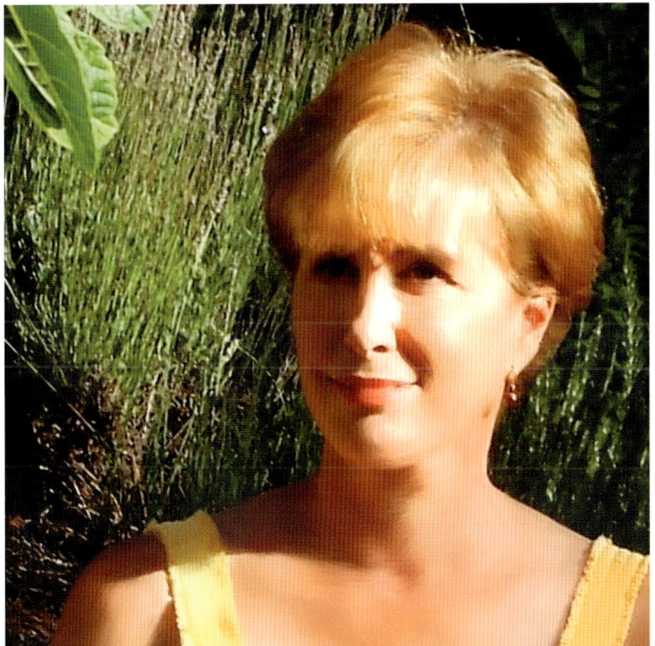

2 BRUSH STROKES

Paint the figure with the Acrylics' Opaque Acrylic variant with these settings in the Property Bar: Opacity: 10%; Resat: 0%; Bleed: 49%.

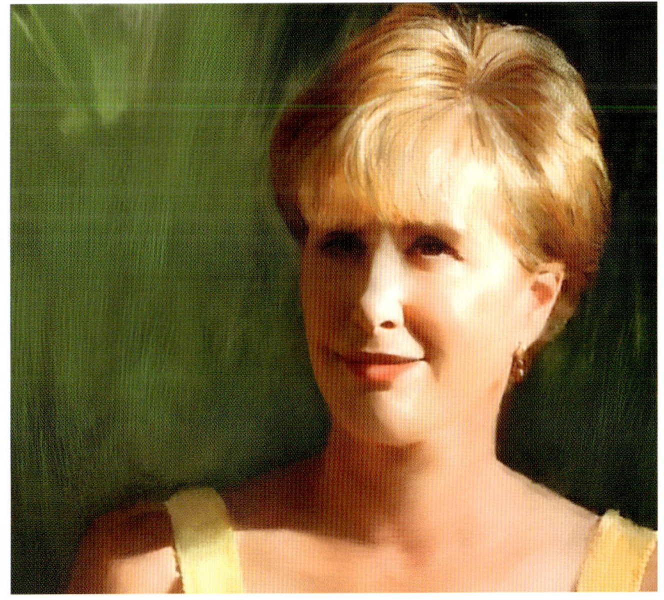

3 TONE CONTROL

Paint with the Chalk's Sharp Chalk variant to add lights and darks to the hair; eliminate the shadow at the top of the nose; and add some color to the lips. Press option, Mac; alt, Windows and click on a color in the image, choose a lighter or darker tone in the Colors palette and paint. Then blend with the Blenders' Smudge variant. See pages 18-19 for the art concepts for painting faces and hair.

4 PAINTING FLOWERS

To paint the flowers and the backgound textures, use many brushes—they're listed below and on the opposite page.

I painted everything on the Canvas. I know some people like to use layers, and I use them sometimes, but in general, I find painting without layers is easier—you don't have to keep track of which layer is which.

Instead of keeping experiments on layers, I save them in separate images. That way, I can use something from a previous step and still avoid layers.

To save an interim step, save (File: Save), then choose File: Clone, name the clone (File: Save As) and close the previous version you saved before you cloned. Then you can borrow elements from the saved image.

For instance, let's say you have saved five interim versions. And let's say you like the way you did a flower in version three of the image.

With the current version as the active window, and with version three also open, choose File: Clone Source: version three.

Once the files are attached in this way, you can use the Cloners' Soft Cloner variant to paint in the current version whatever you like from version three.

See page 26 for more information about clones and clone sources.

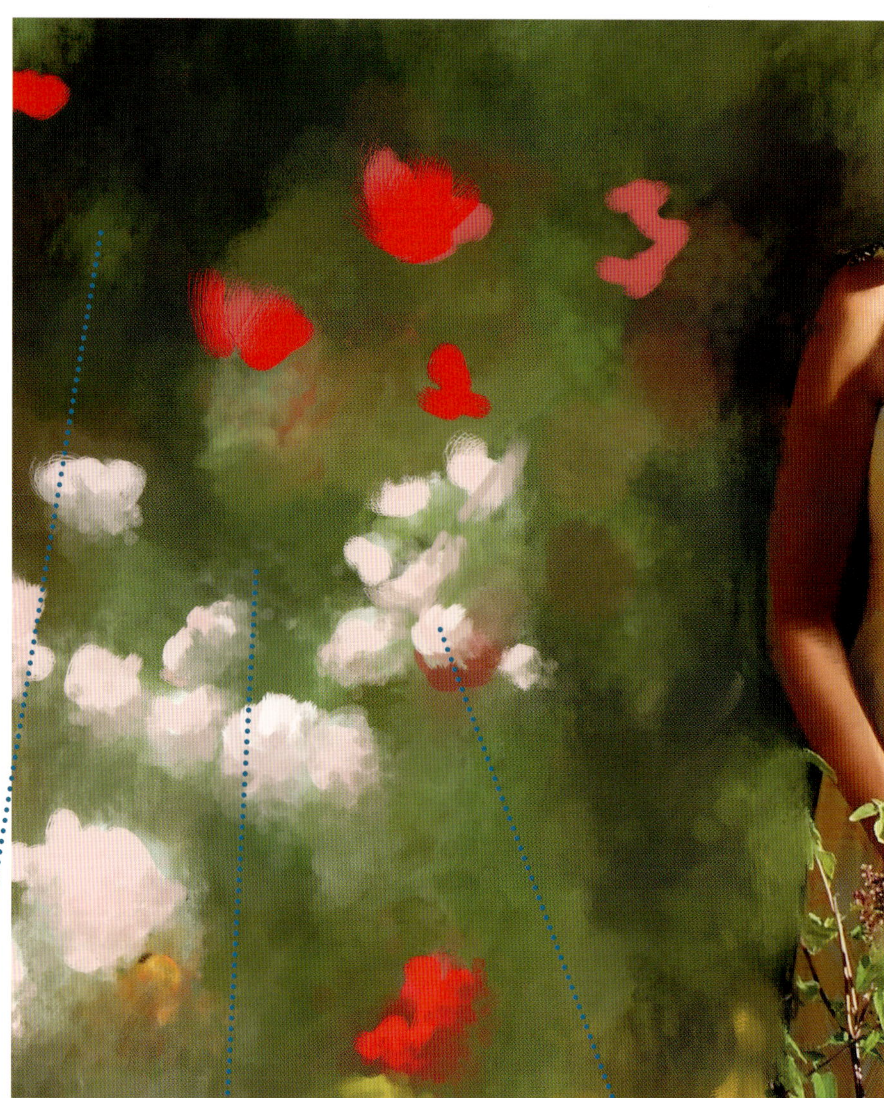

CHALK'S SQUARE CHALK
Opacity: 72%; Resat: 39%; Bleed: 73%; Jitter: 2.49; Colors palette rubber stamp: checked. Paint a bunch of strokes for a texture effect.

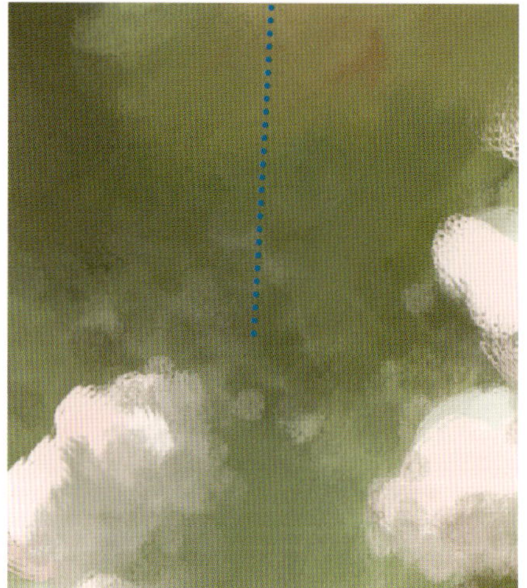

SPONGES' SMEARY WET SPONGE
Opacity: 85%; Pull: 26%; Jitter: 2.15; Colors palette rubber stamp: checked. Paint a bunch of strokes for another texture effect.

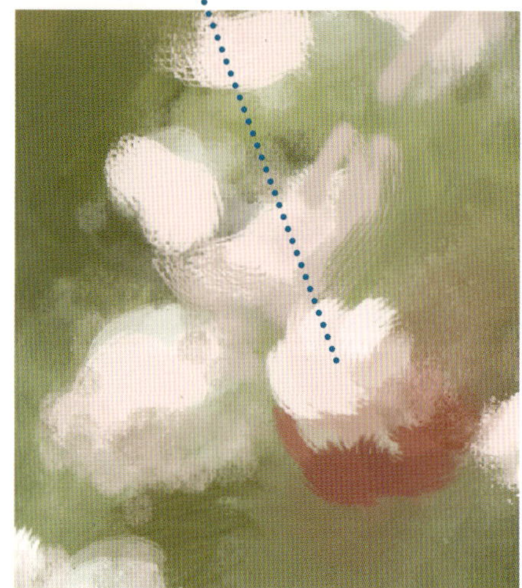

ACRYLICS' OPAQUE ACRYLIC
Opacity: 60%; Resat: 30%; Bleed: 49%; Colors palette rubber stamp: checked. This bristly brush adds a nice painterly touch.

5 Different Strokes

Continue to paint, building up the artwork based on where you see highlights, midtones and shadows in the source photo.

Use the brushes listed on this page and on the opposite page.

One way to make your photos look like paintings is to use different brushes and strokes throughout.

Exploring all the different textures and effects created not only with Painter and Photoshop's brushes, but also with traditional oils, acrylics and other media, is one of the joys of painting.

I discovered all the ideas and suggestions in this book by playing around with tools and media.

I appreciate it when artists, photographers and teachers mention me when they use my techniques.

Reading this book is a great way for you to save time by using my ideas in your own paintings.

Meanwhile, take some time to play around with brushes, variants and presets in Painter and in Photoshop not listed in this book.

In addition, get a small canvas and some of the acrylics and oils listed later in the book and just experiment.

You'll discover media and techniques and will have fun along the way.

Just keep in mind: Write down brushes and procedures that you enjoy as you test drive tools—you may not remember the steps later!

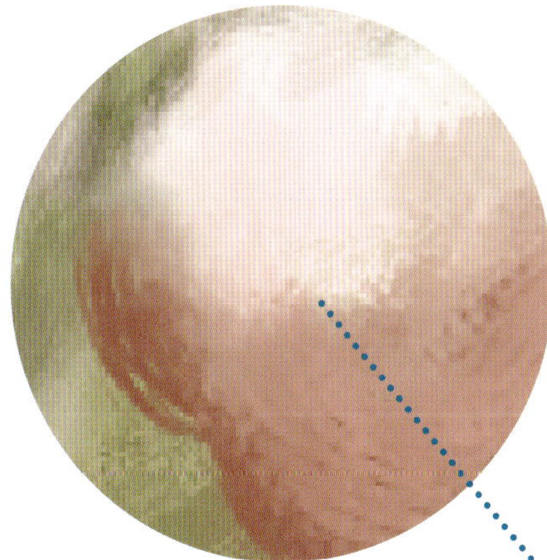

BLENDERS' SMUDGE
Blend a little, leave part of the strokes showing.

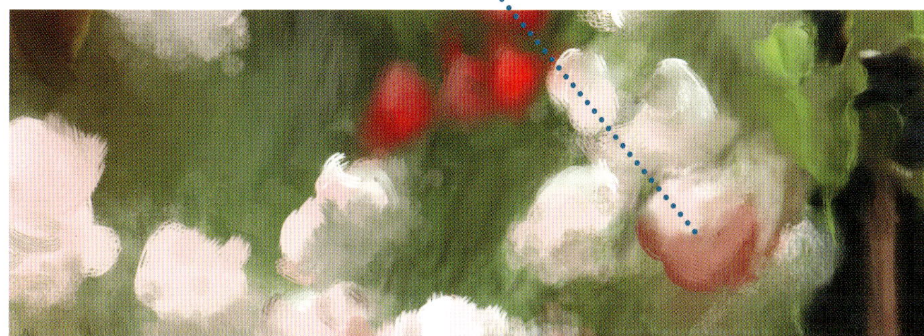

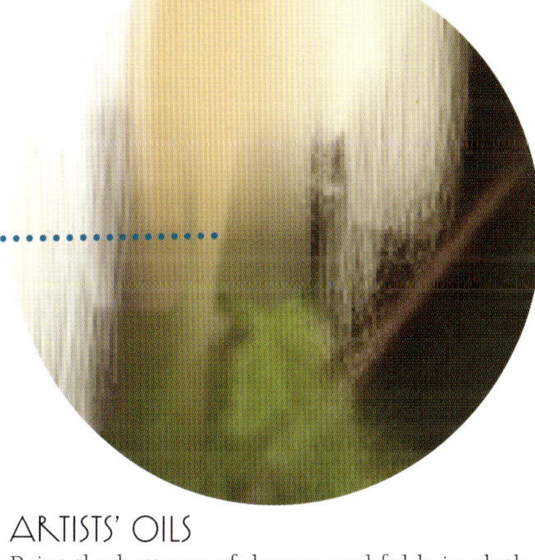

ARTISTS' OILS
Paint the bottoms of dresses and folds in clothing with the Blender Palette Knife.

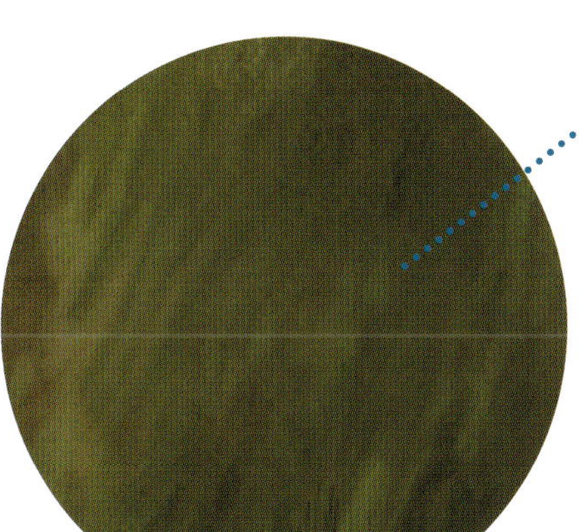

ARTISTS' IMPRESSIONIST
Low size and opacity. Paint texture between things like flowers for the Impressionist look.

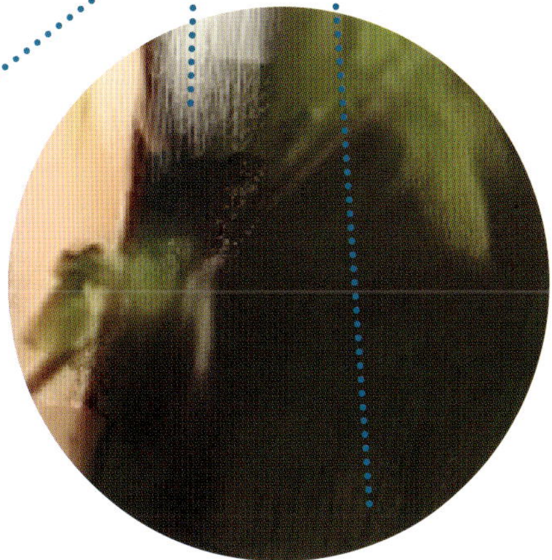

REALBRISTLE BRUSHES
Real Oils Short. Opacity: 65%; Feature: 13.4; Blend: 13%. Paint grass and dress hems.

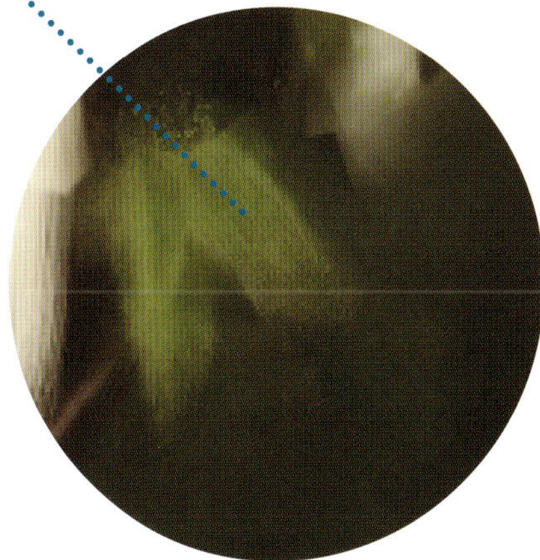

CLONERS' WET OILS CLONER
Feature: 3.7. Bring in some details like leaves and the path.

TONAL PORTRAITS

I've been going to a lot of gallery openings here in Los Angeles recently, and most of the artists today, it seems, paint with light hues and tones.

When I started this painting from Michelle Lamberth's beautiful photo, I had the idea that I wanted to capture the light, airy feeling of the paintings I've seen recently.

That's why I called this chapter "Tonal Portraits."

You're going to use a layer to lighten the photo's tones, making the background lighter than the figure, which, maybe or maybe not coincidentally, is a popular look for painted portraits nowadays.

As you learned in the Tones and Focal Points chapter on pages 14-15, the focal point, or subject, is the area of greatest contrast between light and dark.

Since in a portrait you want the figure to be the subject, then you will make the subject either lighter or darker than the background—in this painting, darker.

In Painter, check your photo's tones with Effects: Tonal Control: Adjust Colors. Move the Saturation slider all the way to the left to shut off the photo's colors, revealing the tones. Choose Edit: Undo to get the colors back again when you're done.

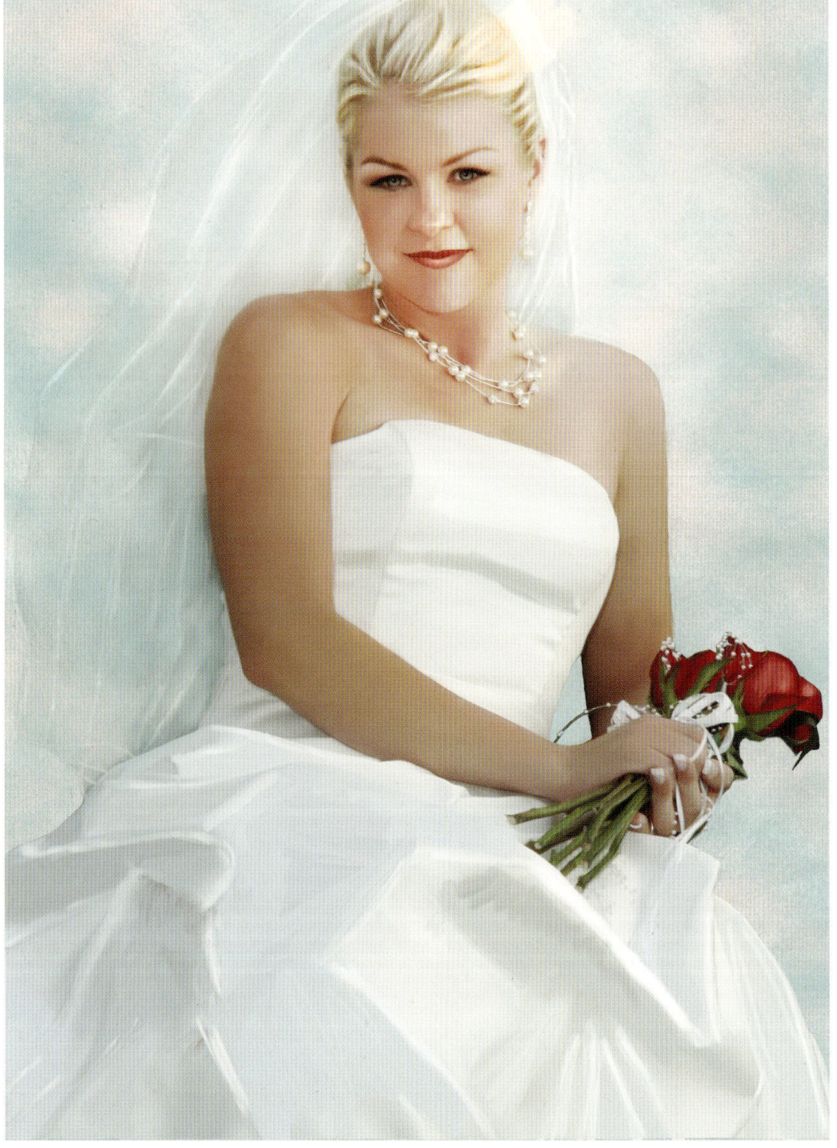

I started this painting by opening the photo in Painter (File: Open) and then choosing File: Clone and naming the clone (File: Save As).

The first step was painting the figure, as you're about to see.

See pages 18-19 for the art concepts for painting facial features and hair.

Tonal Portrait

PAINTING BY KAREN SPERLING FROM A PHOTO BY MICHELLE LAMBERTH.

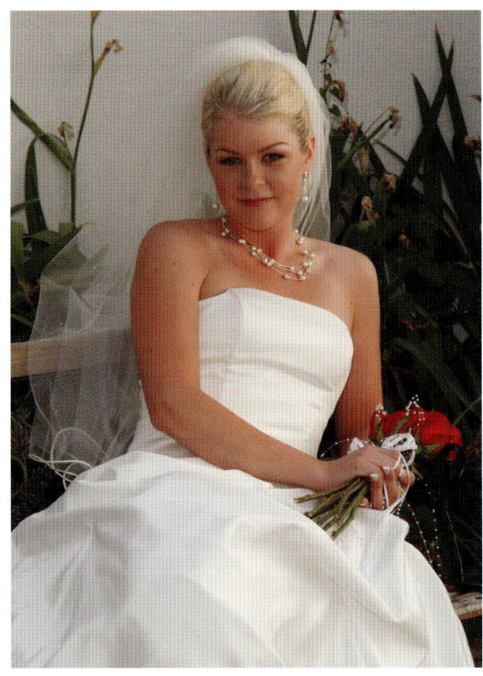

1 THE PERFECT BLEND

Start the portrait by painting with the Blenders' Just Add Water and blending out details. Paint on a lower opacity in the Property Bar on the face and on a higher opacity in other areas.

Blend the irises with Just Add Water on a low size setting in the Property Bar. Then paint out the highlights in the eyes with the Chalk's Sharp Chalk on low size and opacity settings in the Property Bar. Paint the iris outline by pressing option, Mac; alt, Windows and clicking in the iris to pick up color, then choosing a darker shade in the Colors palette and painting.

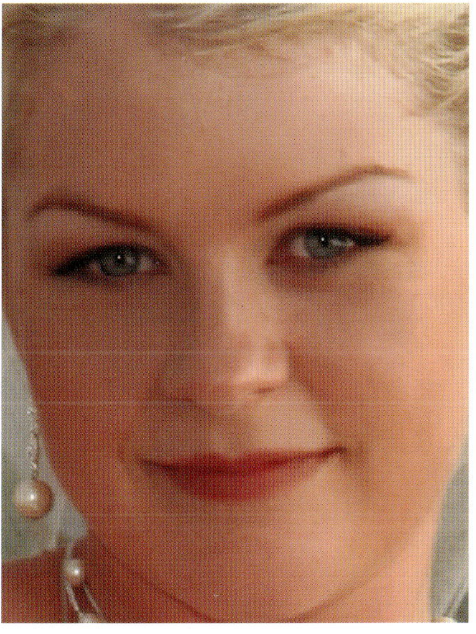

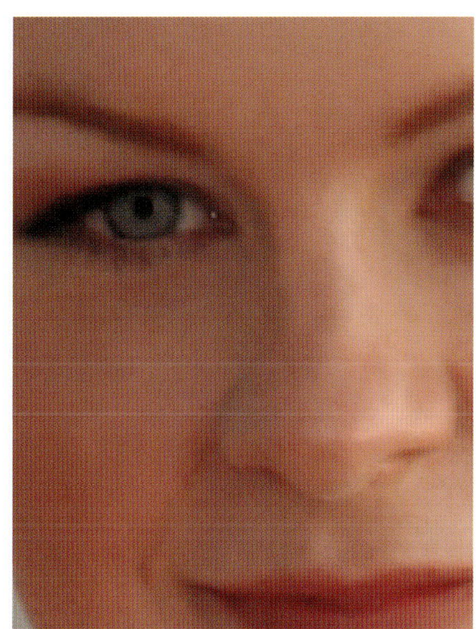

2 IN THE SHADOWS

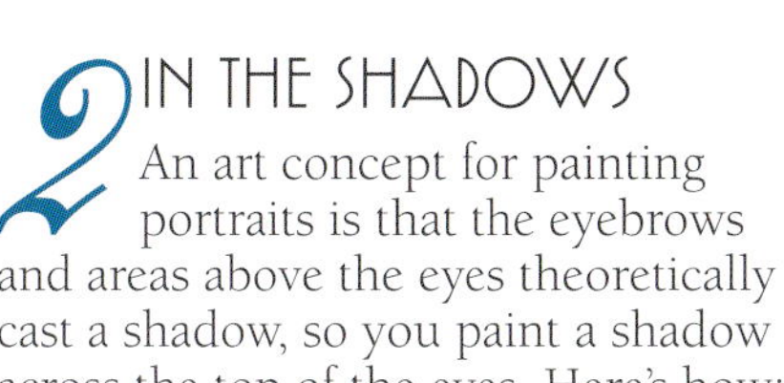

An art concept for painting portraits is that the eyebrows and areas above the eyes theoretically cast a shadow, so you paint a shadow across the top of the eyes. Here's how:

1. Choose the Digital Watercolor's New Simple Water.
2. Choose low size and opacity settings in the Property Bar.
3. Press option/alt and click on the iris to pick up the color.
4. Choose a darker shade in the Colors palette.
5. Paint across the top of the eye.
6. When finished painting with the New Simple Water, choose Layers menu: Dry Digital Watercolor.

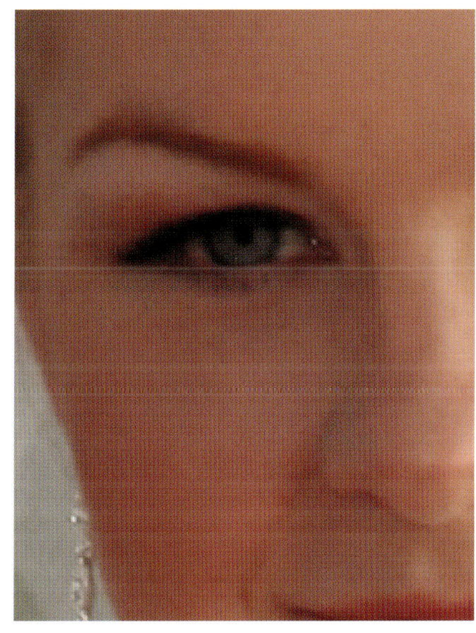

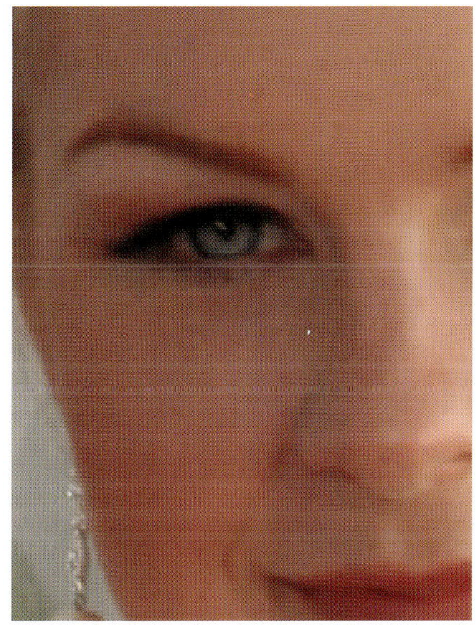

3 THE IRISES HAVE IT

Paint with Just Add Water to blend the line between the darker top and lighter bottom of the eye. Then paint with the Photo's Dodge variant on low opacity to lighten the bottom of the irises.

You can paint back a little color with the New Simple Water if the dodging makes the irises too white, then choose Layers menu: Dry Digital Watercolor.

Paint with Just Add Water to blend the corners of the eyes to eliminate details.

Paint highlights on the face. Here's how:

1. Choose Layers menu: New Layer. Deselect Preserve Transparency in the Layers palette.

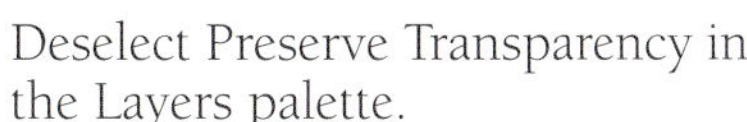

2. Choose the Airbrushes' Digital Airbrush variant; lower opacity in the Property Bar.
3. Press option/alt and click on a highlight to pick up the color.
4. Choose a lighter tone of it in the Colors palette.
5. Paint where you see highlights in the photo to lighten them.

Then blend the paint.

1. Choose the Blenders' Just Add Water. Lower the Opacity slider.
2. Check Pick Up Underlying Color in the Layers palette.
3. Paint to soften edges and blend.
4. Flatten the layer (Layers: Drop).

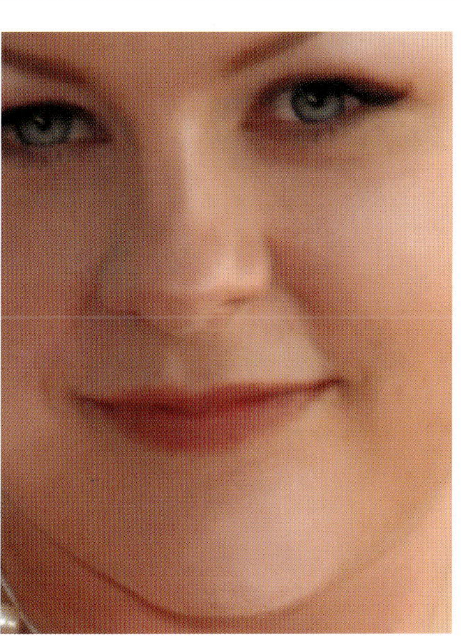

4 LIPS AHOY

With the Digital Airbrush on low size and opacity settings, press option/alt and click on the upper lip, choose a darker tone in the Colors palette and paint on the upper lip.

Then Press option/alt and click on the lower lip, chose a lighter tone and paint.

Lower the size even more and paint a darker tone between the lips and around them as outlines. To fix edges, press option/alt and click on a color outside of the lips, like the chin, for example, and paint next to the lips to adjust the lips. Then paint with Just Add Water to blend.

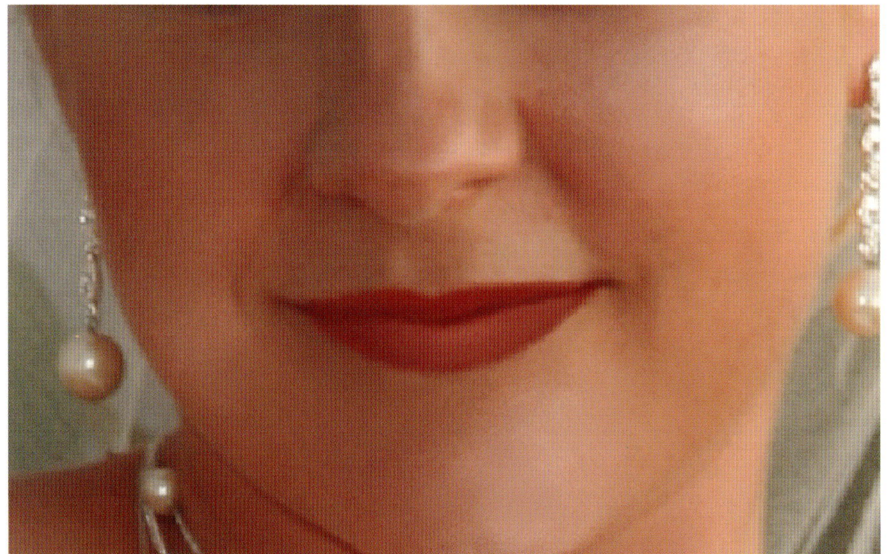

5 HAIR AND THERE

For the hair, paint broad areas of highlights, midtones and shadows and just suggest individual strands.

Start by blending strands with Just Add Water on low opacity, creating tonal areas based on the photo.

Then with the Oils' Smeary Round variant, press option/alt and click on a highlight, choose a lighter tone in the Colors palette and paint. Do the same with shadows and darker tones. Then blend some more with Just Add Water. Repeat the process till you have areas of color with suggestions of hair strands, as you see in the image at right.

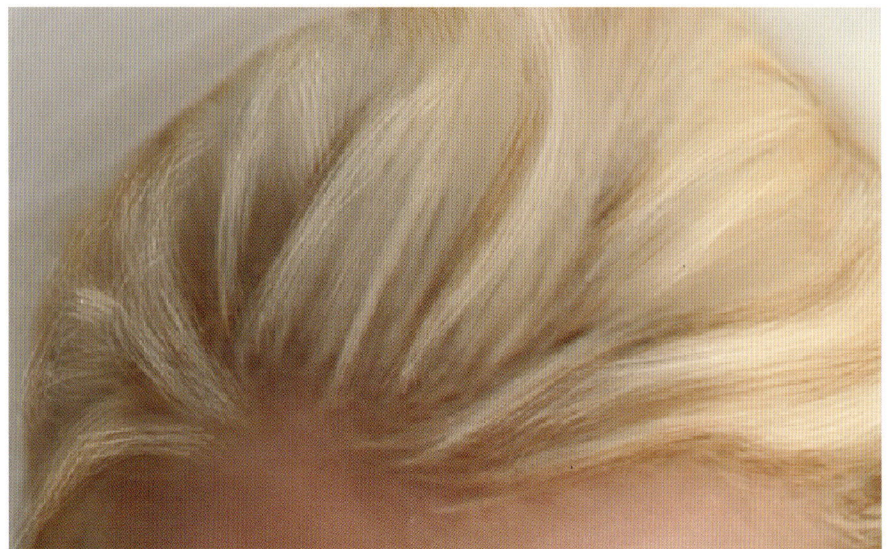

6 LAYER EFFECT

Open the painting in Photoshop, select the figure with the Magnetic Lasso tool, then open the painting in Painter and make the figure into a layer. See pages 30 and 36 for steps. Click the Canvas in the Layers palette and choose Select: All and delete, Mac; backspace, Windows, which clears the background. Then reattach this image to the photo for Tracing Paper—see page 26 for the steps.

As for colors, the main color in the skin is red-orange, therefore, use blue-green—the complement, or color opposite the color in the color wheel—for the background.

7 GRADIENTS

Fill the background with a gradient. See page 29 for steps for creating and editing gradients.

Here's how to get the circle behind the bride's head (see image at right):

1. Click in the Canvas in the Layers palette (the bride is a layer).
2. After you create your gradient, click the sphere icon in the Gradients palette.
3. Click on the paint bucket in the toolbox. Click on the bride's face in the image. The color goes behind the bride forming a halo around her head. If you don't like the gradient's position, choose Edit: Undo and try again.

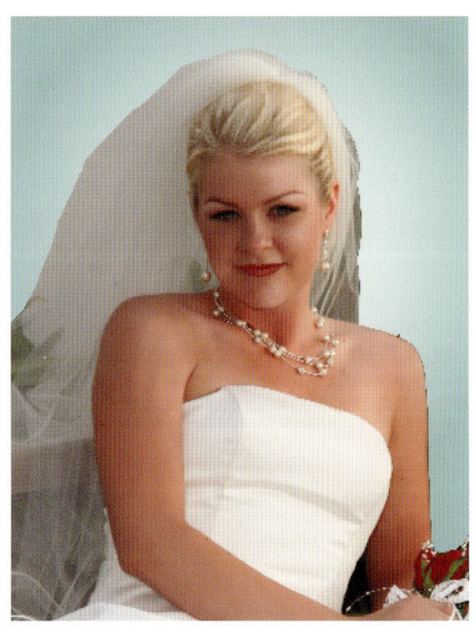

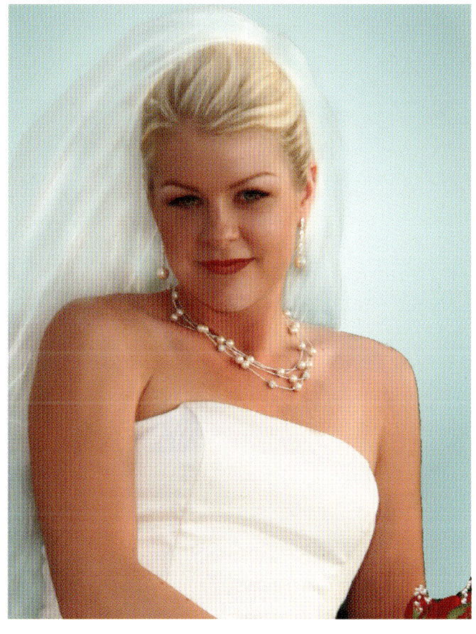

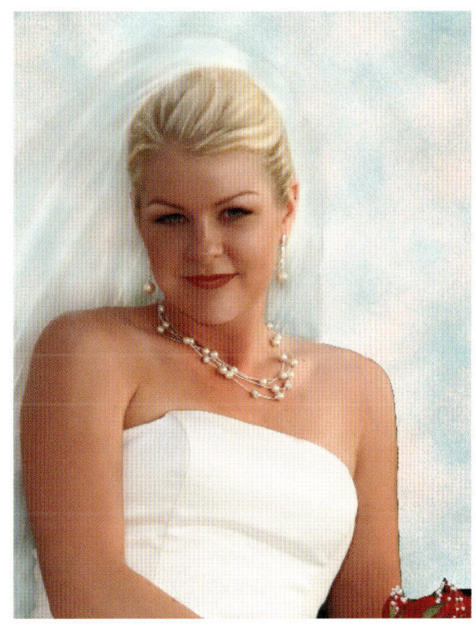

8 LIGHT FANTASTIC

Use layers to make the background lighter than the figure. Here are the steps to do so.

1. Click in the Canvas in the Layers palette.
2. Choose Select: All.
3. Press option, Mac; alt, Windows and choose Select: Float. You get a layer copy of the Canvas.
4. In the Layers palette, choose Overlay to reveal the bride and lower opacity to turn down brightness.

Here's how to get the texture:

1. Shut the eye next to the new layer in the Layers palette.
2. Click Canvas in the Layers palette.
3. Choose white in the Colors palette.
4. Choose the Chalk's Square Chalk.
5. Choose the Auto-Painting palette in the Window menu. Select Medium Dab in the Stroke menu.
6. In the Property Bar, raise the Size slider and lower the Opacity slider.
7. Click the green arrow to run Auto-Painting. Click in the image to stop. See page 25 for more information about Auto-Painting.
8. Click the eye open next to the top layer.

Click the figure in the Layers palette and darken tones in the eyes, lips and hair by painting with the Digital Watercolor's New Simple Water. When done, choose Layers menu: Dry Digital Watercolor.

Paint highlights in the hair with the Photo's Dodge variant.

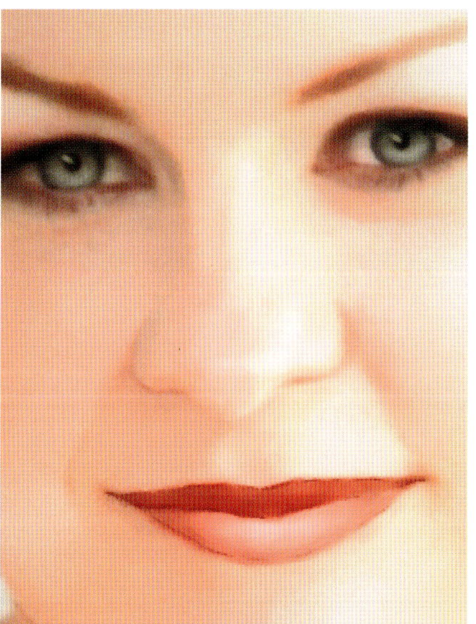

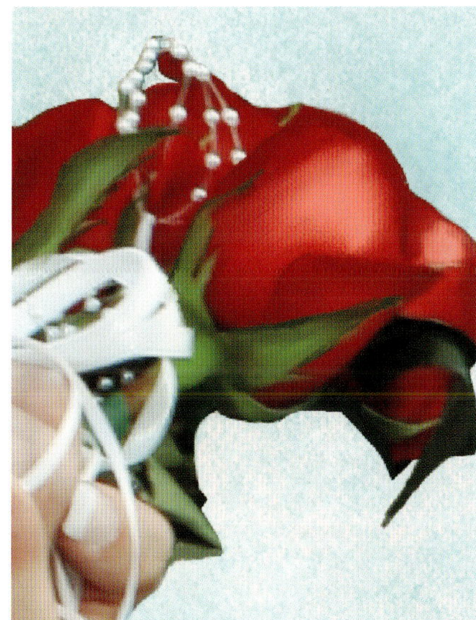

9 OH VEIL

Paint the veil using Tracing Paper as your guide. See page 27 for steps for using Tracing Paper.

With the Airbrushes' Digital Airbrush variant chosen, press option/alt and click on the blue-green in the Canvas and paint on the veil in the figure layer to make the veil look transparent.

Paint the white highlights with the Photo's Dodge and blend them slightly with Just Add Water.

Reveal some of the background in the veil, and clean up the figure's edges, by painting in a layer mask — see the steps for using layer masks on page 31.

Paint the dress using the RealBristle Brushes' Real Oils Short variant. Press option/alt and click on the colors and paint to create sharp edges between areas of light and dark. Then Press option/alt and click on colors; choose lighter and darker versions in the Colors palette; and paint to enhance highlights and shadows.

Paint the flowers with the Chalk's Sharp Chalk. Press option/alt and click on a color in the image, choose a lighter or darker version of it in the Colors palette and paint.

Blend with the Blenders' Grainy Water.

Painting Backgrounds

I like to look at web sites to see what people are doing with painted portraits nowadays.

A lot of the web sites I've visited show portraits with painted backgrounds like you see here.

In this chapter, you'll find out which brushes to use in Painter to create painterly backgrounds for portraits.

Once you know which brushes to use, it's easy to experiment with different looks and techniques.

The portrait on this page is just one example of what you could do with the brushes listed in this chapter.

Experiment with the strokes and textures to devise your own creations.

If you feel a little stumped about how to design your own backgrounds, seeing how other artists handle brush strokes can help.

Visit galleries and museums, or look at books and web sites.

Then play around with your own looks—you'll be surprised how easy it is.

Meanwhile, about this photo of Oprah—I had in the back of my mind that I wanted to include a celebrity portrait in this book, and while surfing the internet looking at art, I came across this photo, which I thought was one of the best I'd seen of her.

The photo had a byline, Evan Agostini.

I did a google.com search and found Evan on Facebook.

I requested permission to use the photo and he agreed.

Thanks, Evan!

For the painting, start by opening the photo in Painter (File: Open). Choose File: Clone and name the clone (File: Save As). Close the original to keep it intact, and paint in the clone.

Painting Backgrounds
PAINTING BY KAREN SPERLING FROM A PHOTO BY EVAN AGOSTINI.

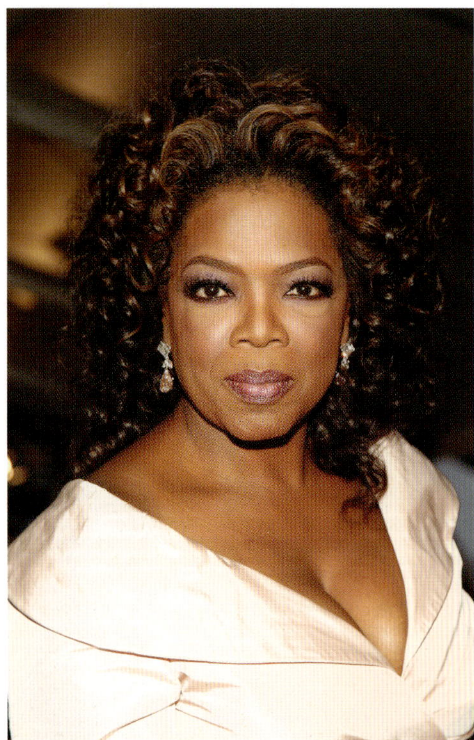

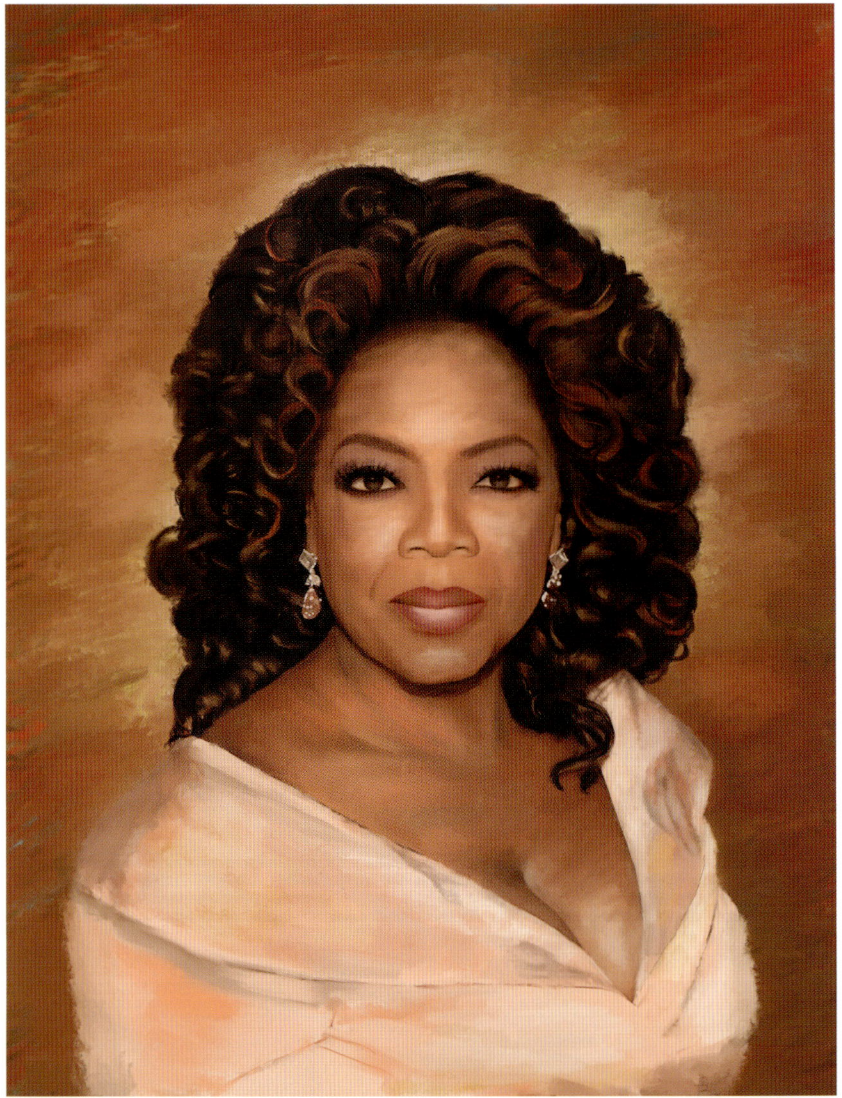

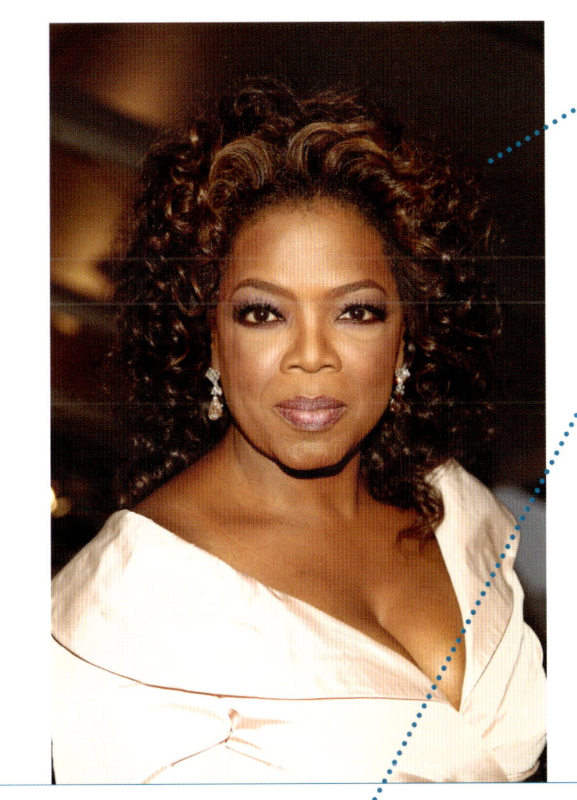

1 ADD PIXELS

First, add pixels by choosing Canvas: Canvas Size and typing 300 pixels on the left, right and top.

2 SELECT THE FIGURE

In Photoshop, select the figure using the Magnetic Lasso. It was a little tricky—I needed to lighten the photo to see the hair to select around it, but I didn't want the lightened figure. The solution was to make a layer (command+j, Mac; ctrl+j, Windows); lighten the layer (Image: Adjustments: Brightness/Contrast); make the selection and save it (see page 36 for instructions); delete the layer; and save the image in the .psd file format.

3 COLOR SCHEME

Give the image a unified color scheme using a layer. Open the file in Painter, choose Select menu: Load Selection. Choose Select: Invert and press delete, Mac; backspace, Windows to clear the background. Choose Layers menu: New Layer. Press option, Mac; alt, Windows and click on the clothing to pick up a color. With Preserve Transparency deselected in the Layers palette (the layer should be highlighted, too), choose Effects: Fill. The layer fills with the color. Move the Opacity slider in the Layers palette to 44% and choose Color in the drop down menu, and you now have a color scheme. Choose Layers: Drop to flatten the layer, load the selection again and choose Select: Float to make the figure a layer.

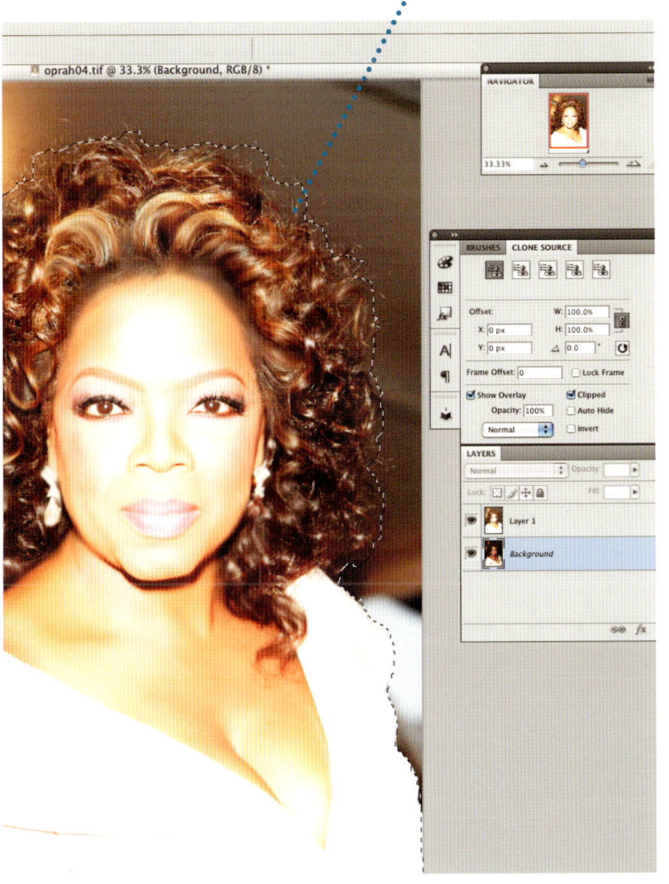

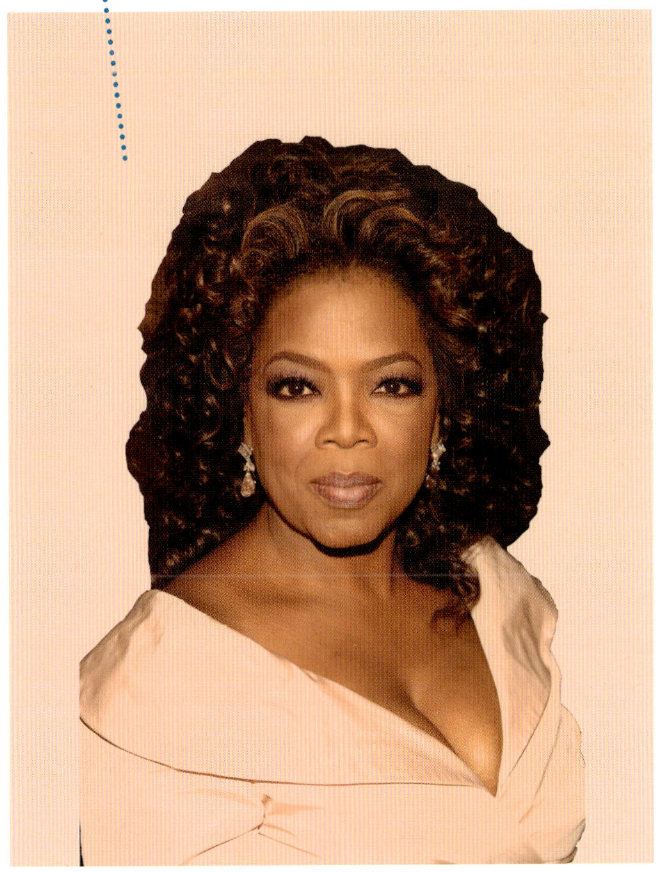

4 Adding Texture

Click the Canvas in the Layers palette and paint the background. On this page are the brushes to use.

The basic process is: Paint color, then blend it.

Create new brushes and edit existing ones to build up the textured effect.

As you paint, keep in mind that the figure is the focal point, or area of greatest contrast between light and dark. That means that the area next to the figure is light. You could also make the adjacent area darker than the figure—as long as it contrasts.

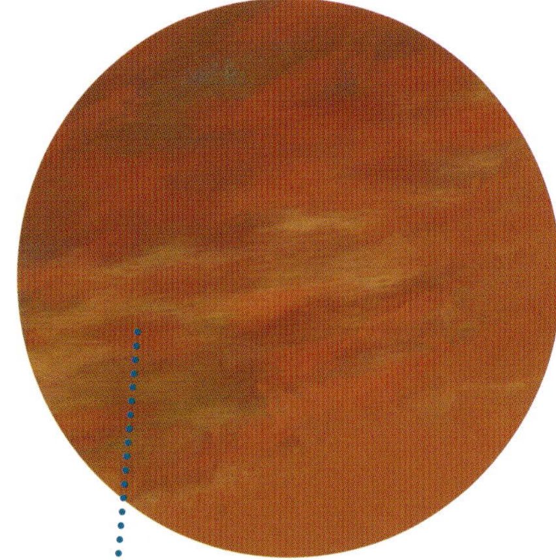

Artists' Impressionist

Good for texture. Soften the effect by painting with the brush as a blender—see page 24 for steps for setting up and saving blenders.

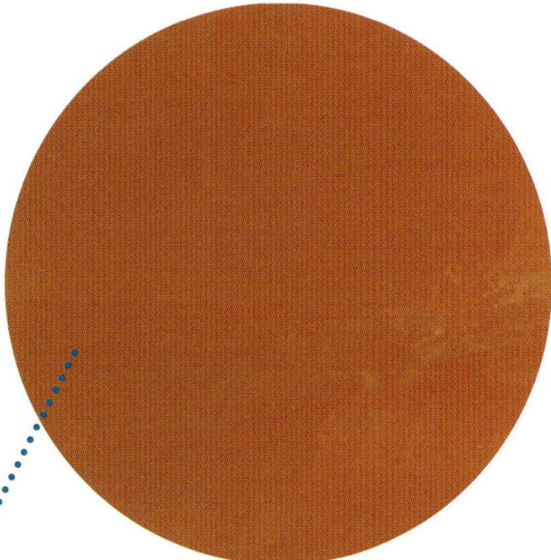

Chalk's Square Chalk

Paints "flat" strokes with a little texture. Use this brush for blending, too—see page 24 for steps for setting up and saving blenders.

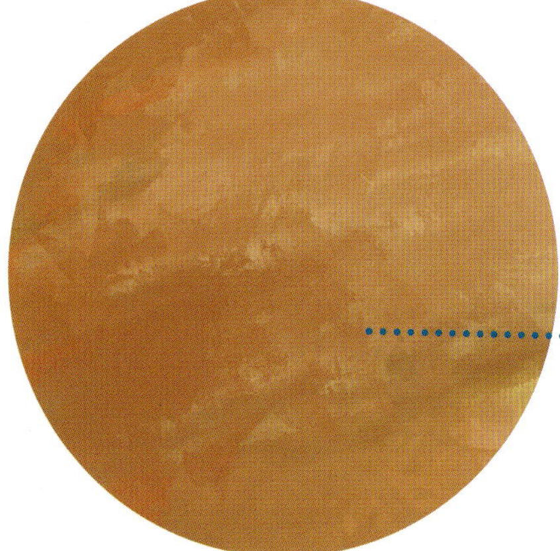

Cloners' Soft Cloner

No need to paint all background strokes from scratch. When an area that you've painted looks good to you, press option, Mac; alt, Windows and click on it with the Soft Cloner chosen, then paint elsewhere. Repeat many times in different areas to build up the background.

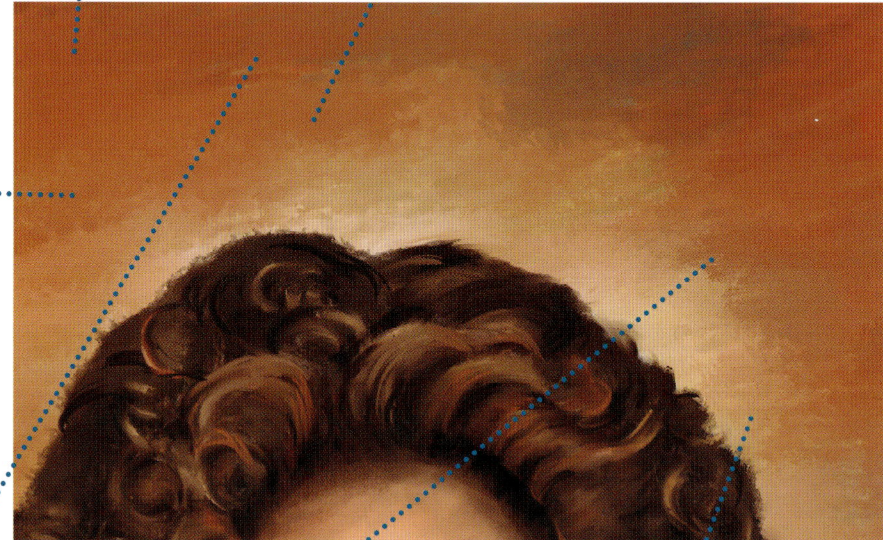

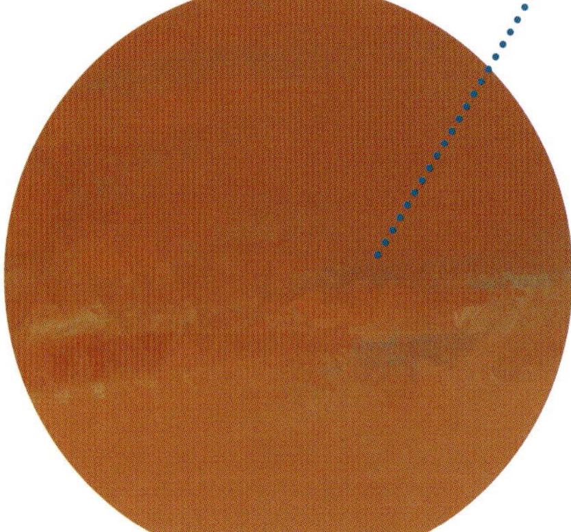

Blenders' Just Add Water

Blend without texture by painting with the Just Add Water. Lower opacity for a more subtle result. Paint with the Blenders' Smudge to blend with texture. To blend with medium texture, paint with the Blenders' Grainy Water variant.

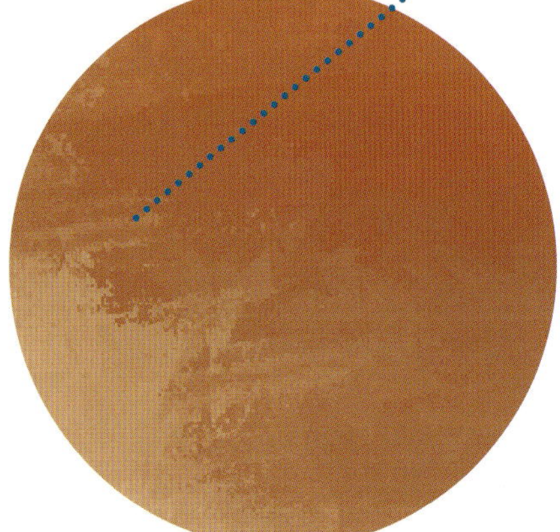

Blenders' Water Rake

Property Bar: Opacity 22%, Grain 13%, Resat 8%, Bleed 49%, Jitter 0.63. Window: Brush Controls: Rake: Contact Ang: 40°, Brush Scale: 273%, Turn Amount 5%, Bristles, 20, Spread Bristles and Soften Bristle Edge: checked.

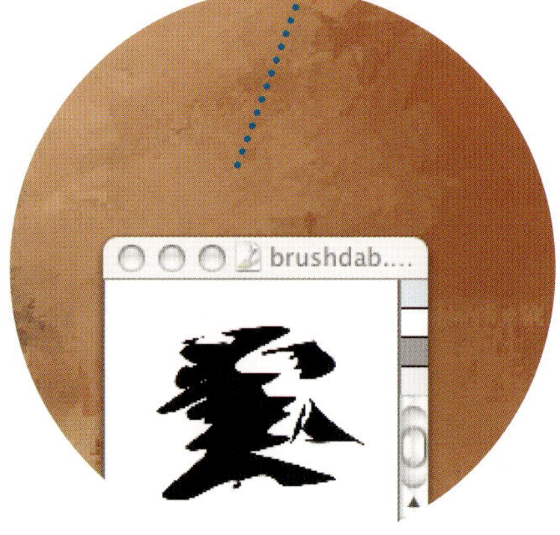

Custom Sponge

Create a texture brush by adding a new tip (pictured above) to the Sponges' Smeary Wet Sponge. Name it Custom Sponge. Create the tip with lasso selections filled with black. See page 27 for instructions.

5 Figuratively Painting

Click the figure layer in the Layers palette and paint the face and hair using the techniques described in the previous chapters.

Use some of the background brushes to paint the clothing and skin.

Use colors from the background in the figure and from the figure in the background for color harmony—press option, Mac; alt, Windows and click on a color to pick it up, then paint with it.

When the figure is done, choose Layers menu: Drop to flatten.

Paint with the background brushes to blend the figure with its surroundings by roughening up the figure's edges and painting to extend some of the hair.

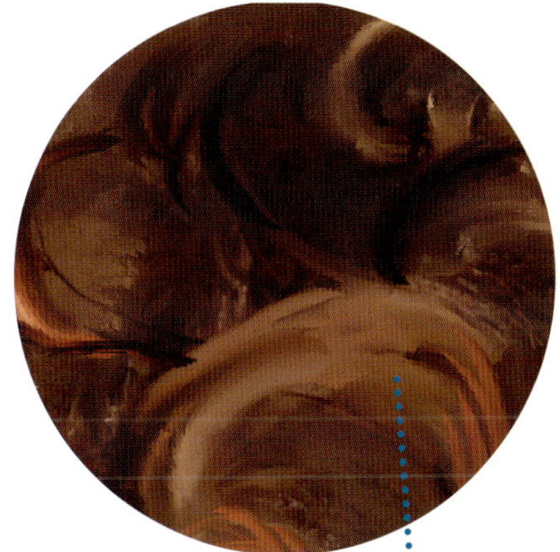

CHALK'S SHARP CHALK
Blend with the Water Rake to create light and dark areas. Then paint a few strands with the Chalk's Sharp Chalk, then blend again.

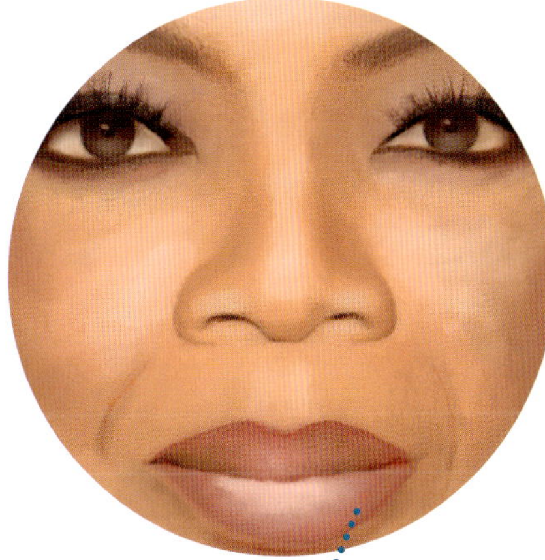

AIRBRUSHES' DIGITAL AIRBRUSH
Paint the eyes and the lips with the Digital Airbrush. Add a little texture to the lips with the Square Chalk. See page 18 for art tips for faces.

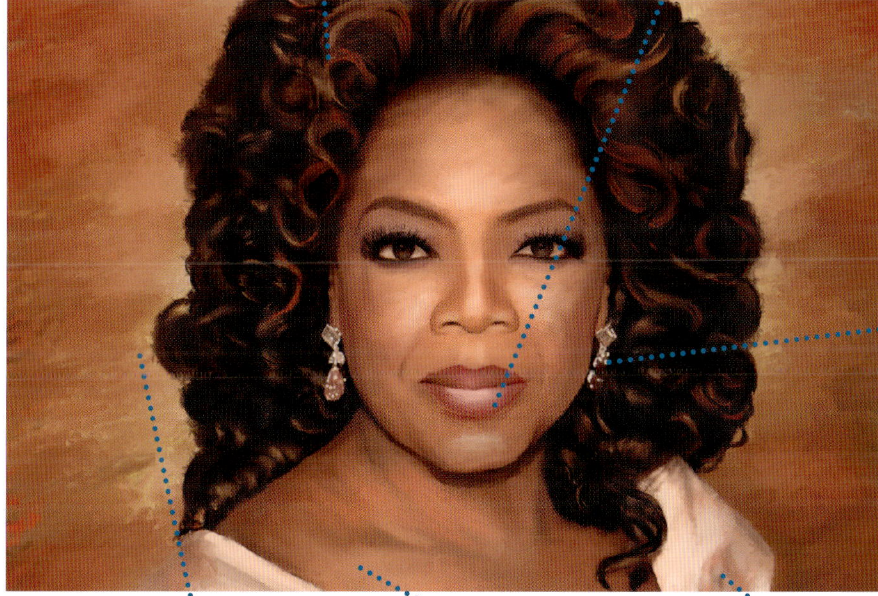

PENS' SCRATCHBOARD TOOL
Paint jewelry highlights and shadows with the Pens' Scratchboard Tool.

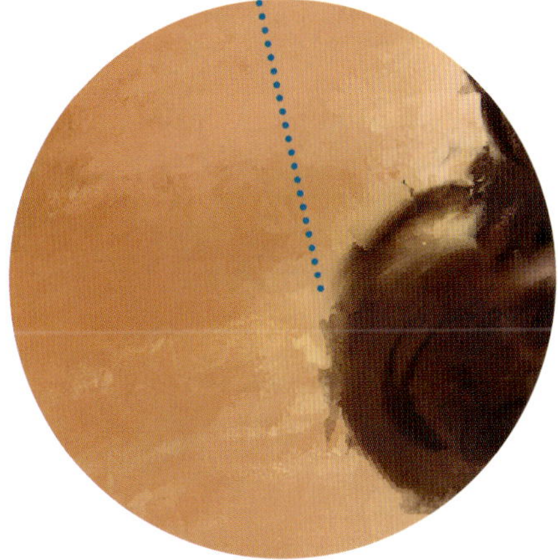

CUSTOM SPONGE
After flattening the figure layer, use the Custom Sponge (see opposite page) to create a soft transition from the hair to the background.

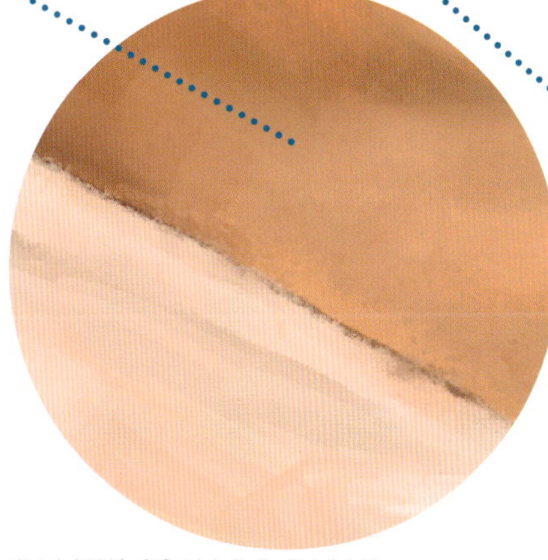

CHALK'S SQUARE CHALK
Paint color on the skin with the Square Chalk, then blend—see page 24 for steps for setting up and saving blenders.

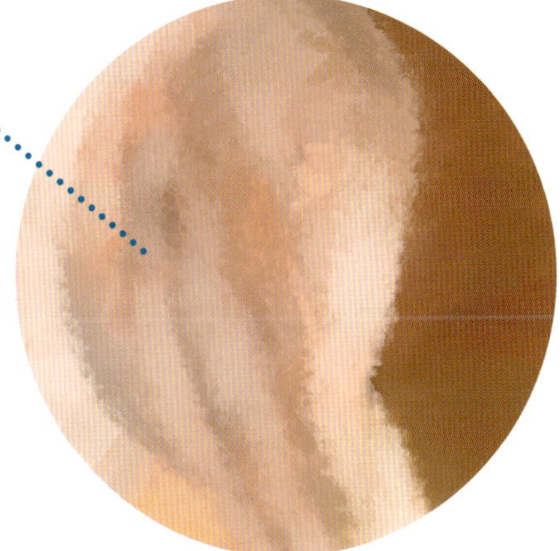

CUSTOM SPONGE
With the Custom Sponge, add highlights and shadows in the dress using the photo as your guide, then blend with the Smudge.

PAINTERLY PORTRAITS

Many photographers prefer painting photorealistic portraits, I guess because they think they're easier to do than portraits painted from scratch.

The thought of painting a blank image intimidates them.

Despite the popularity of photorealistic portraits from photos, there are those who prefer the look of the painted portrait created on a blank canvas.

Using Painter's Tracing Paper to guide you and keeping in mind the art concepts that you've learned in this section and in the one on art theories should make painting portraits without photo elements pretty easy!

In case you're wondering, yes, this is a self-portrait. I chose to paint this photo because I wanted to feel free to experiment—I didn't want to have to worry about how someone else would feel about the results. I like the way it came out, and since I'm the subject, the portrait was a success!

After deciding to paint this photo, I looked at the colors and thought they'd lend themselves to an adjacent color scheme (see pages 12-13 for information about choosing colors).

As for the tones, you now know that you want the background to be either lighter or darker than the figure to make the figure the subject, or focal point, or area of greatest contrast between light and dark.

In the photo, there was contrast between the face and the hair, but the hair blended into the background.

In the painting, the subject is still the face, which is the area of greatest contrast between light and dark.

However, I made the background lighter to contrast with the hair and sweater, which made the painting more interesting—the fewer colors and the more contrast you have, the more dramatic your paintings will be.

See pages 14-15 for information about working with tones.

Painterly Portrait

Painting by Karen Sperling from a photo by Zarek.

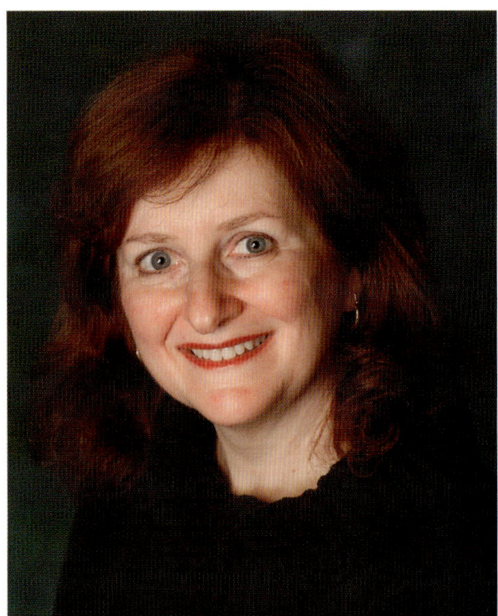

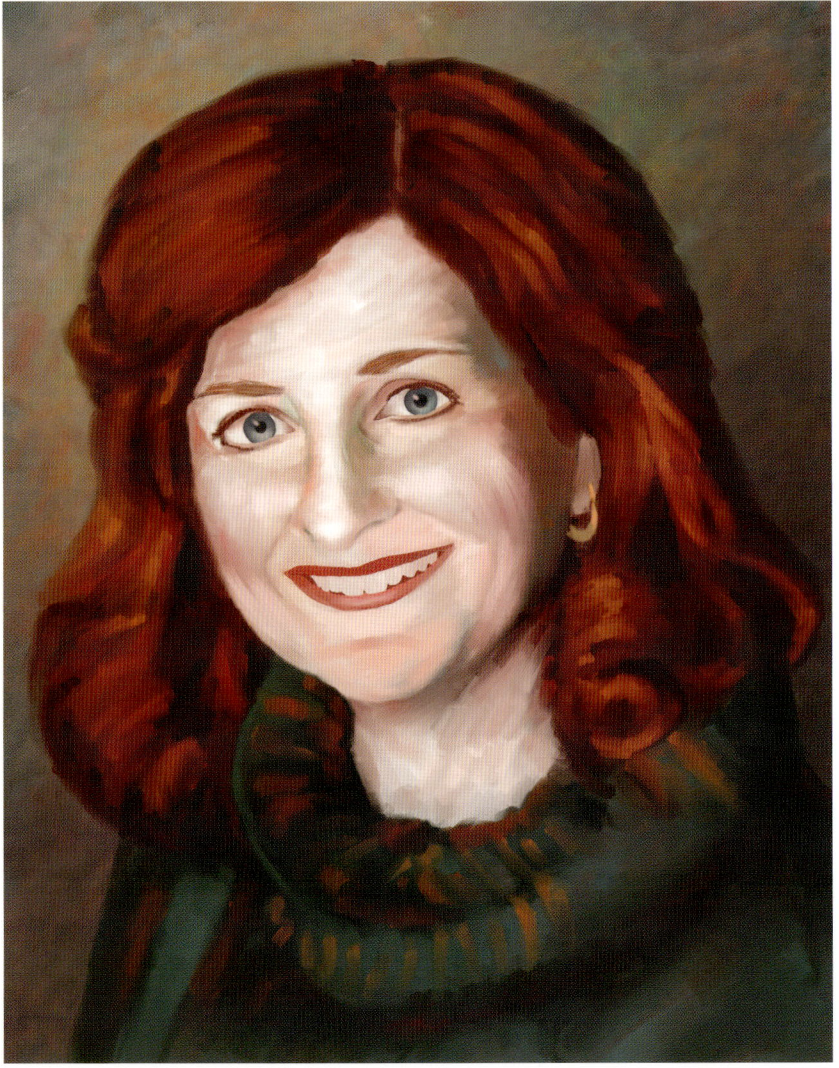

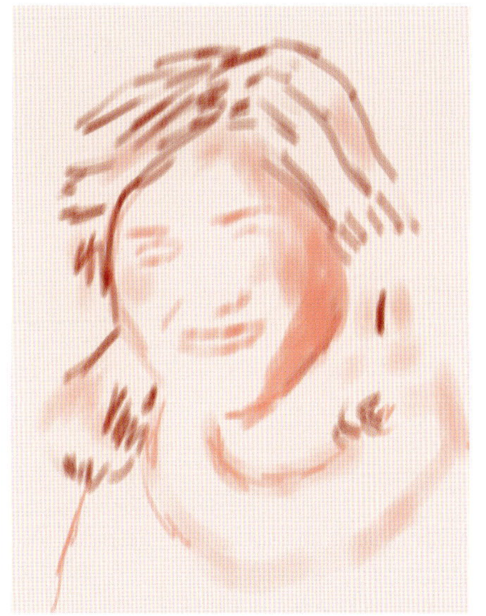

1 FILLING AND ABLE

With the photo open in Painter, choose (File: Clone). A clone of the photo appears. Choose a medium pink in the Colors palette and choose Effects (Edit in Painter 11): Fill (command+f, Mac; ctrl+f, Windows). Click next to Current Color if it isn't already selected, click OK. You now have a first coat of pink paint, technically called an under-painting. Turn on Tracing Paper (see page 27 for instructions). Choose a darker tone of the pink and start by painting dark areas with the Acrylics' Real Wet Brush (in Painter 11-in Painter X use the Acrylics' Dry Brush) on 17% opacity.

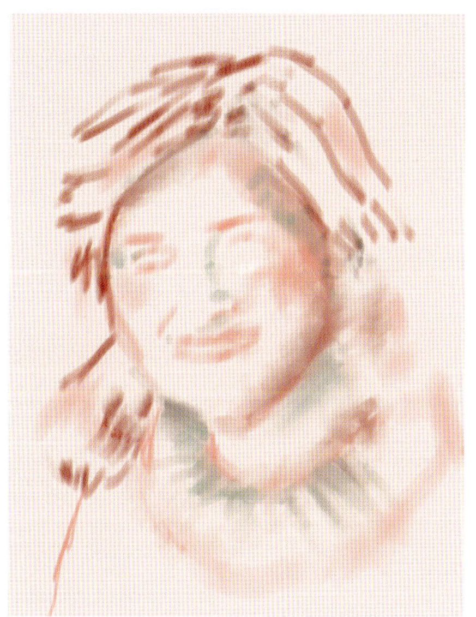

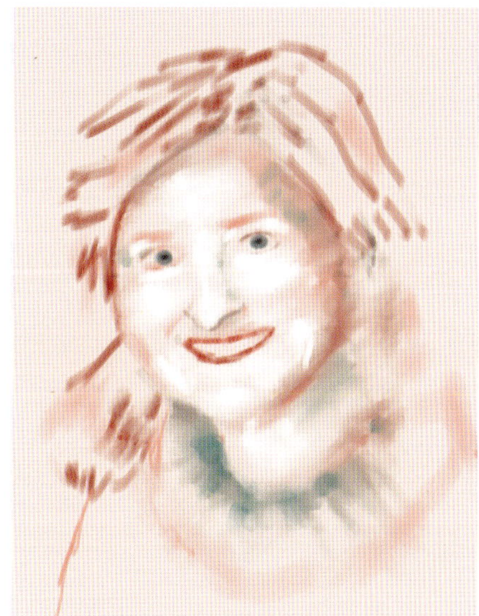

2 MY COMPLEMENTS

Switch to green and the Artists' Oils' Blender Bristle on 43% opacity and continue to paint dark tones. Painting with a complementary color in the shadows is a way to add color harmony, where you repeat colors throughout the painting.

Choose a light tone of pink in the Colors palette and start to paint where you see highlights in the photo.

Paint the eyes and lips with the Chalk's Sharp Chalk and blend with the Blenders' Just Add Water. You're not painting objects, you're painting where you see light and dark tones in the photo.

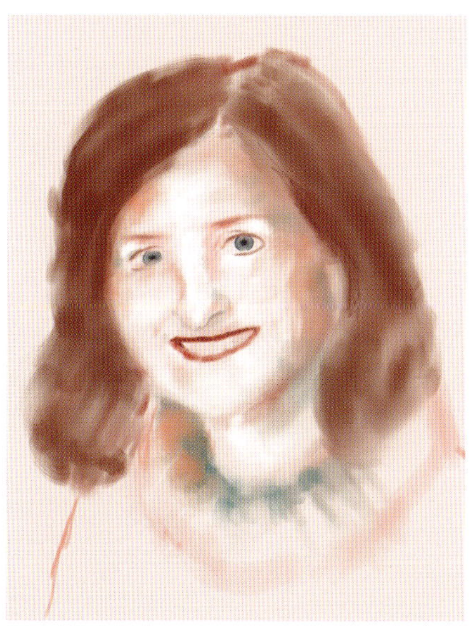

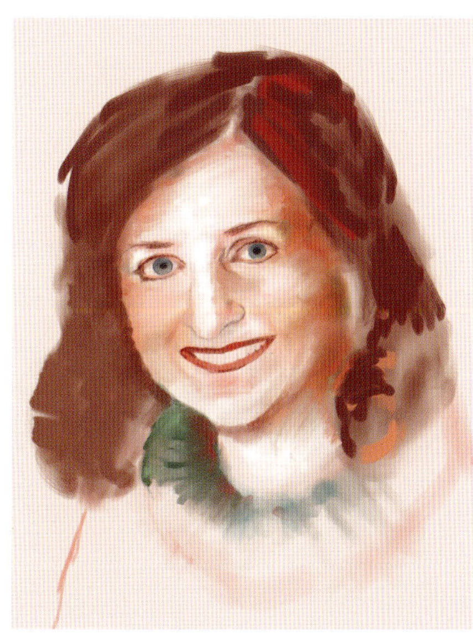

3 HAIR TODAY

Continue to paint tones based on where they appear in the photo, using the brushes mentioned above.

When painting hair, the idea is to paint broad areas of lights and darks.

Then, lower the size setting and paint suggestions of hair strands.

Paint the creases above the eyelids using the Sharp Chalk. Then blend with the Blenders' Just Add Water.

Paint the shadows at the top of the eyes with the Digital Watercolors' New Simple Water on a low opacity and choose Layers: Dry Digital Watercolor when done.

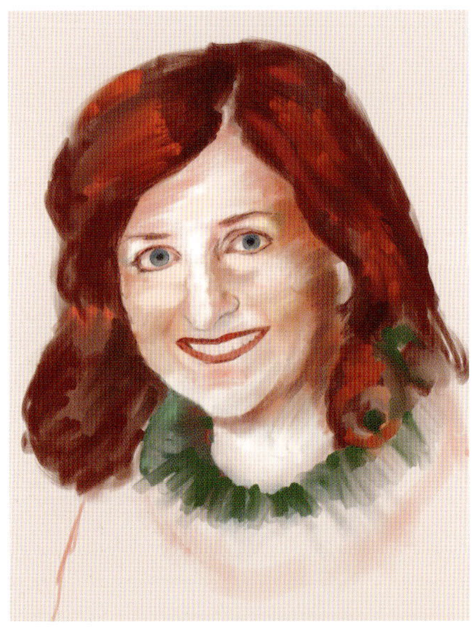
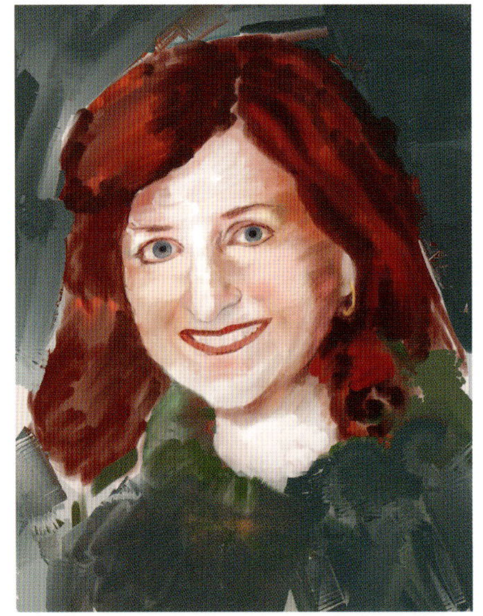

4 MORE COLORS

Alternating between the Artists' Oils' Blender Bristle and the Artists' Sargent Brush, add more colors in the adjacent color scheme to the sweater, face, hair and background, continuing to paint where you see lights, darks and midtones in the photo with Tracing Paper turned on. Turn off Tracing Paper to see the results and turn it on again to paint.

If you can't tell how the tones look, use Effects: Tonal Control: Adjust Colors and lower the Saturation slider, click OK. When done, choose Edit: Undo to get back the colors and keep painting.

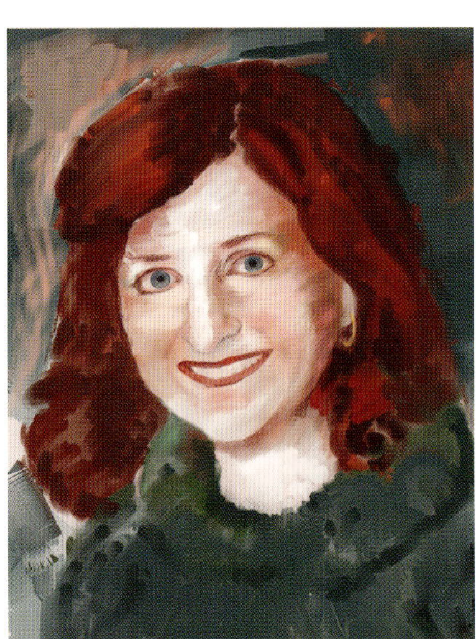
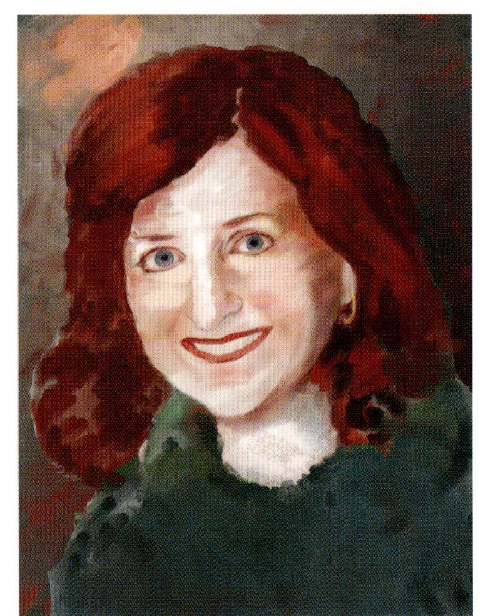

5 FIGURE PAINTING

At this point, make the figure a layer by selecting with the lasso—it doesn't have to be an exact selection because you are going to be painting the edges anyway—and choose Select menu: Float.

Click Canvas in the Layers palette and, using the Blender Bristle, the Sargent Brush and the Artists' Impressionist brush, add colors to the background using adjacent colors in the color wheel (see page 12).

Click the figure layer and continue to add colors, painting lights and darks where you see them in the source photo.

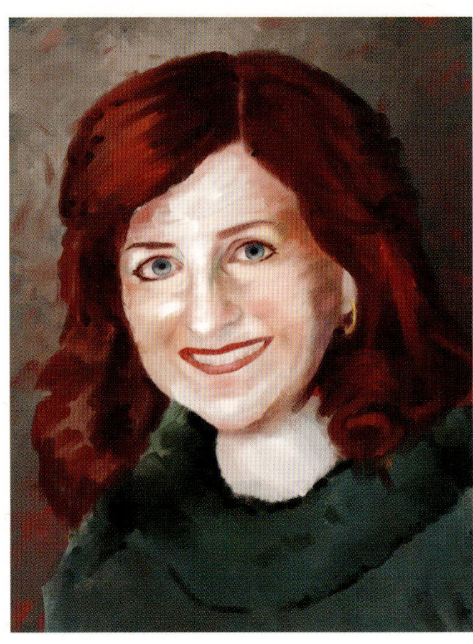
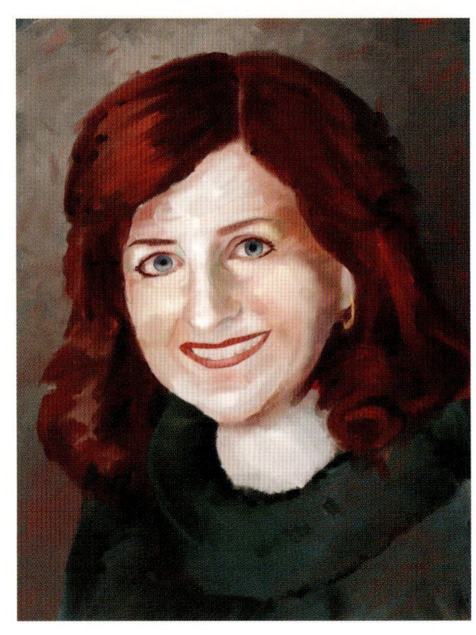

6 BUILDING UP TONES

Using the same brushes, continue to paint with colors and tones in the color scheme on the hair and on the sweater.

Continue to paint, following the areas of light and dark that you see in the photo with Tracing Paper turned on; turn Tracing Paper off to check your progress; then turn it back on again and proceed to paint.

Add some red, the complement of green, in the sweater shadows.

Also add a darker tone of green in the shadows, lower the Size slider and paint some lines around the collar. Still think of them as tones—notice they're in the photo!

7 RANDOM ACTS

Add some more color harmony by painting with the green in the face and adding shades of red in the background.

Paint in the background with the Impressionist brush and the Chalk's Square Chalk.

Raise the Jitter slider in the Property Bar to get the randomized strokes you see in the background at right.

Use the brushes to paint with color and also to blend (see page 24 for information about setting up brushes as blenders).

Paint with the idea of keeping the area around the head lighter than the rest of the background.

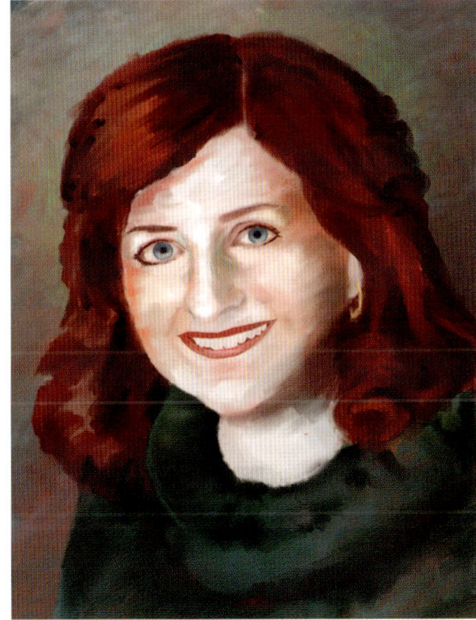

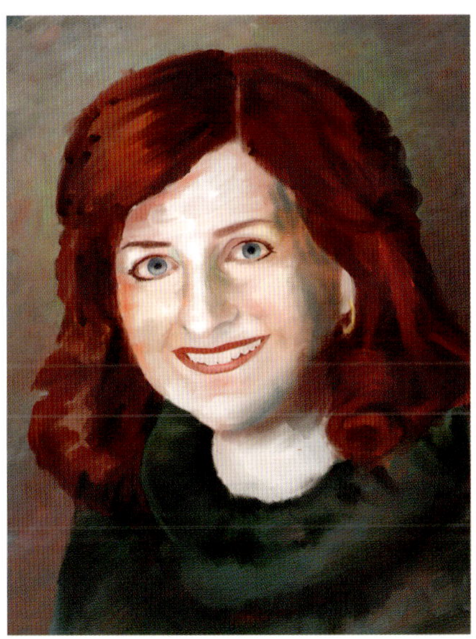

8 HUE BET

Add yellow-orange in the hair, sweater and background to liven things up.

Choose yellow-orange because it is in the adjacent color scheme, or colors next to each other in the color wheel.

Paint with the Blender Bristle on the figure and with the Square Chalk and Impressionist brush on high jitter settings in the background.

Add more tones to the face by painting with the Blender Bristle and Sargent Brush. Blend a little with the Square Chalk as a blender, but mostly blend by scribbling with the Blender Bristle.

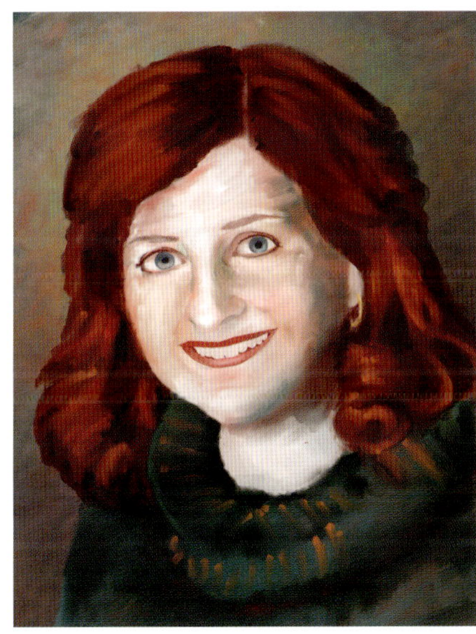

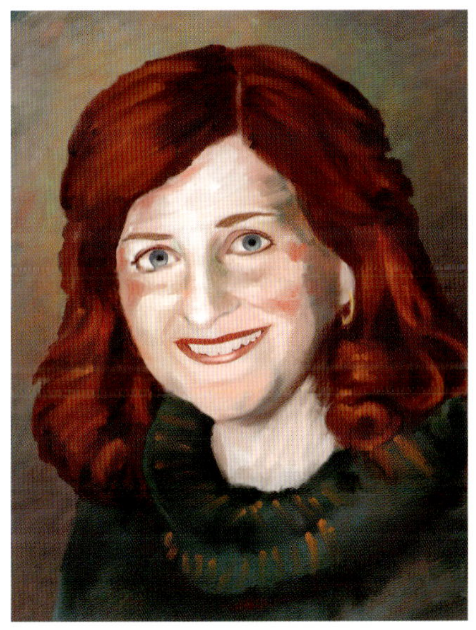

9 LAST STEPS

In the final steps, add some more colors to the sweater and hair. Also, edit the tones in the face based on the tones in the photo by painting with the Chalk's Sharp Chalk and then blending with the Blenders' Just Add Water.

Paint deep tones around the teeth with the Sharp Chalk and blended with Just Add Water.

Then choose Layers menu: Drop, which flattens the figure layer.

Paint on the hair with the Sharp Chalk and Blender Bristle to blend it in with the background.

And that's how I painted a "painterly" portrait in Corel Painter!

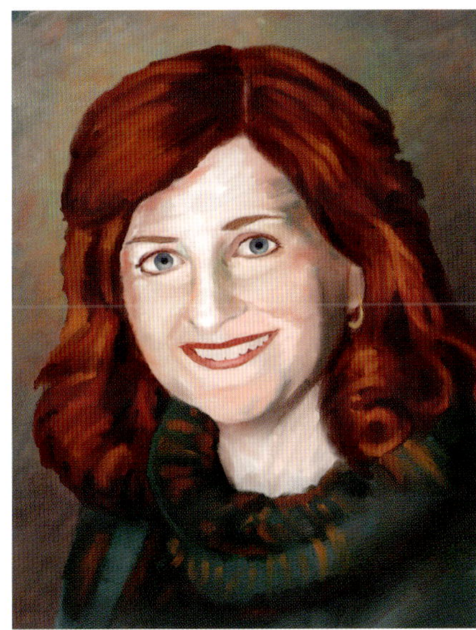

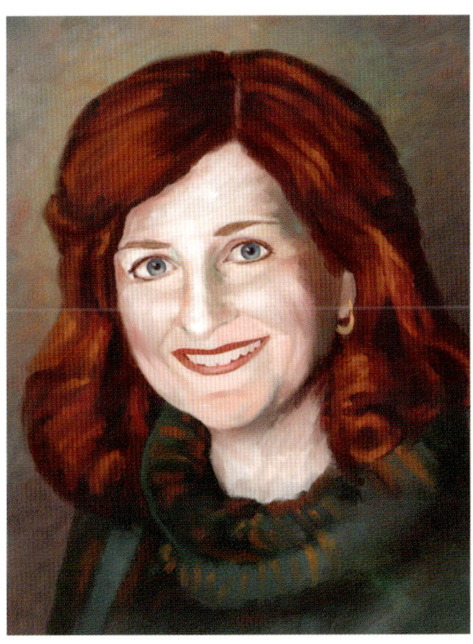

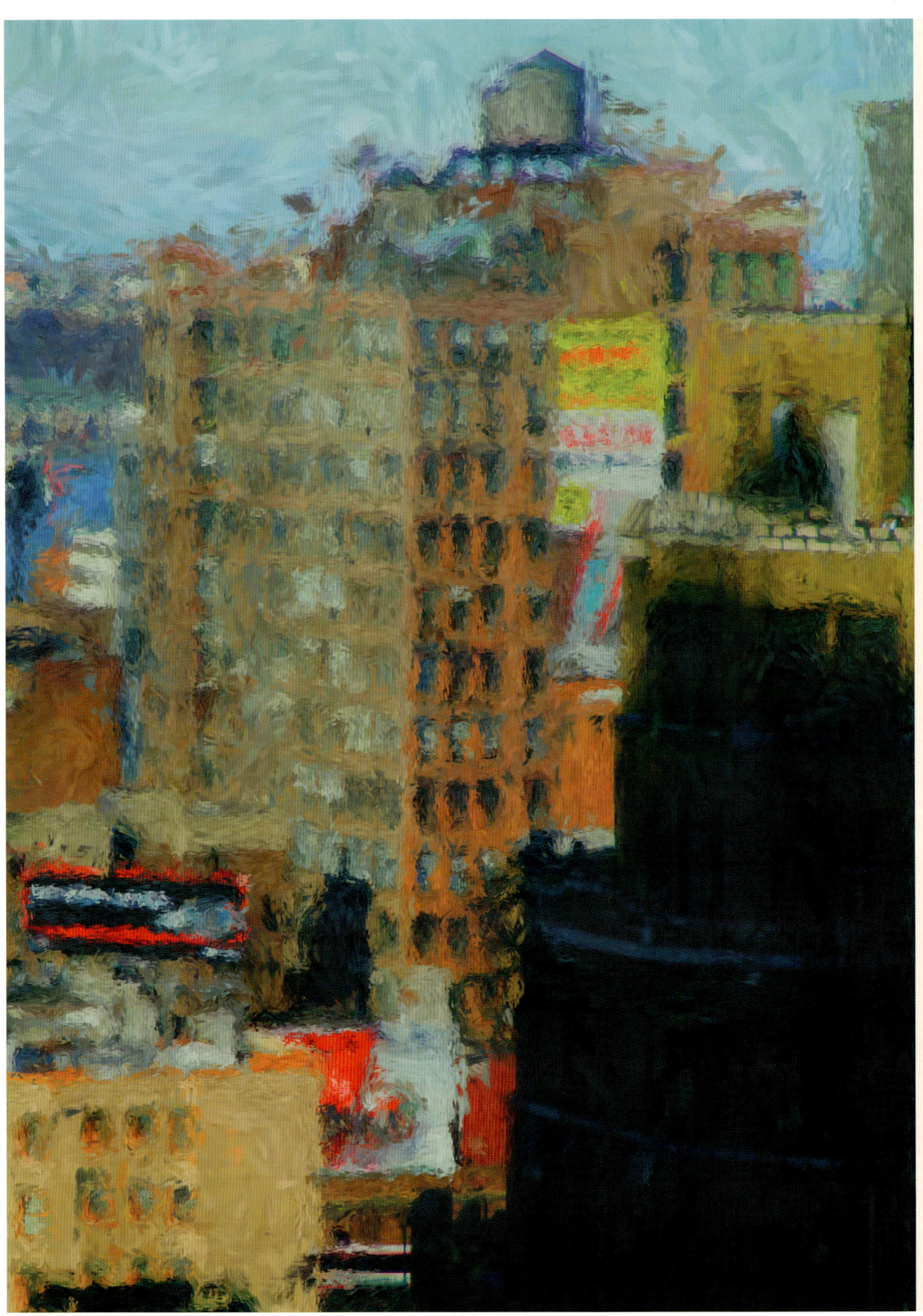

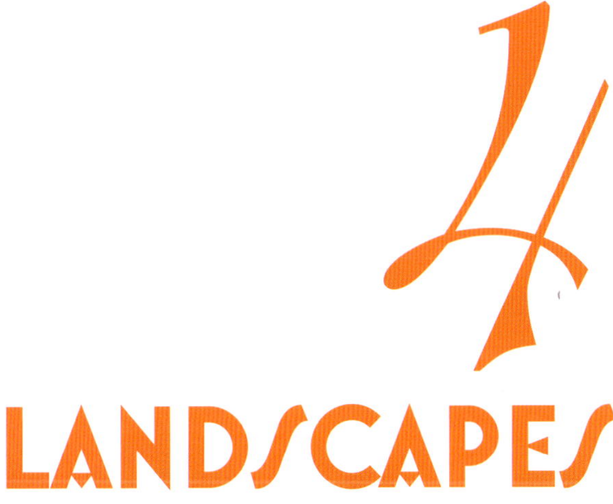

4 LANDSCAPES

Painting landscapes should be easy. You take a photo and you clone it into a painting, right? Nothing to it!

The trouble is, not every photo lends itself to being painted.

Once you know which landscape photos are the best candidates for being painted, and how to fix them if they're not, you'll be painting landscapes quicker than you can say Winslow Homer.

In this chapter, you'll discover what to look for in your photos to turn them into landscapes, how to edit them if they're not ideal and then which Corel Painter and Adobe Photoshop brushes to use for oils, watercolor and pastel effects.

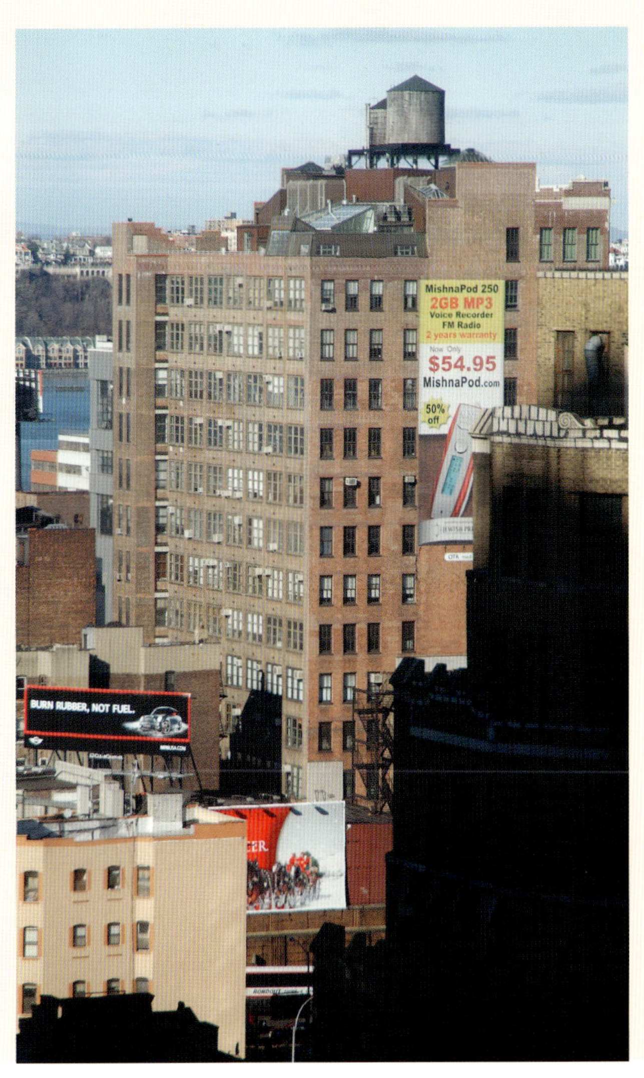

Cityscape

Photo and painting by Karen Sperling, featured in the April 2007 issue of Artistry Tips and Tricks, http://www.artistrymag.com/

OIL-PAINTED LANDSCAPES

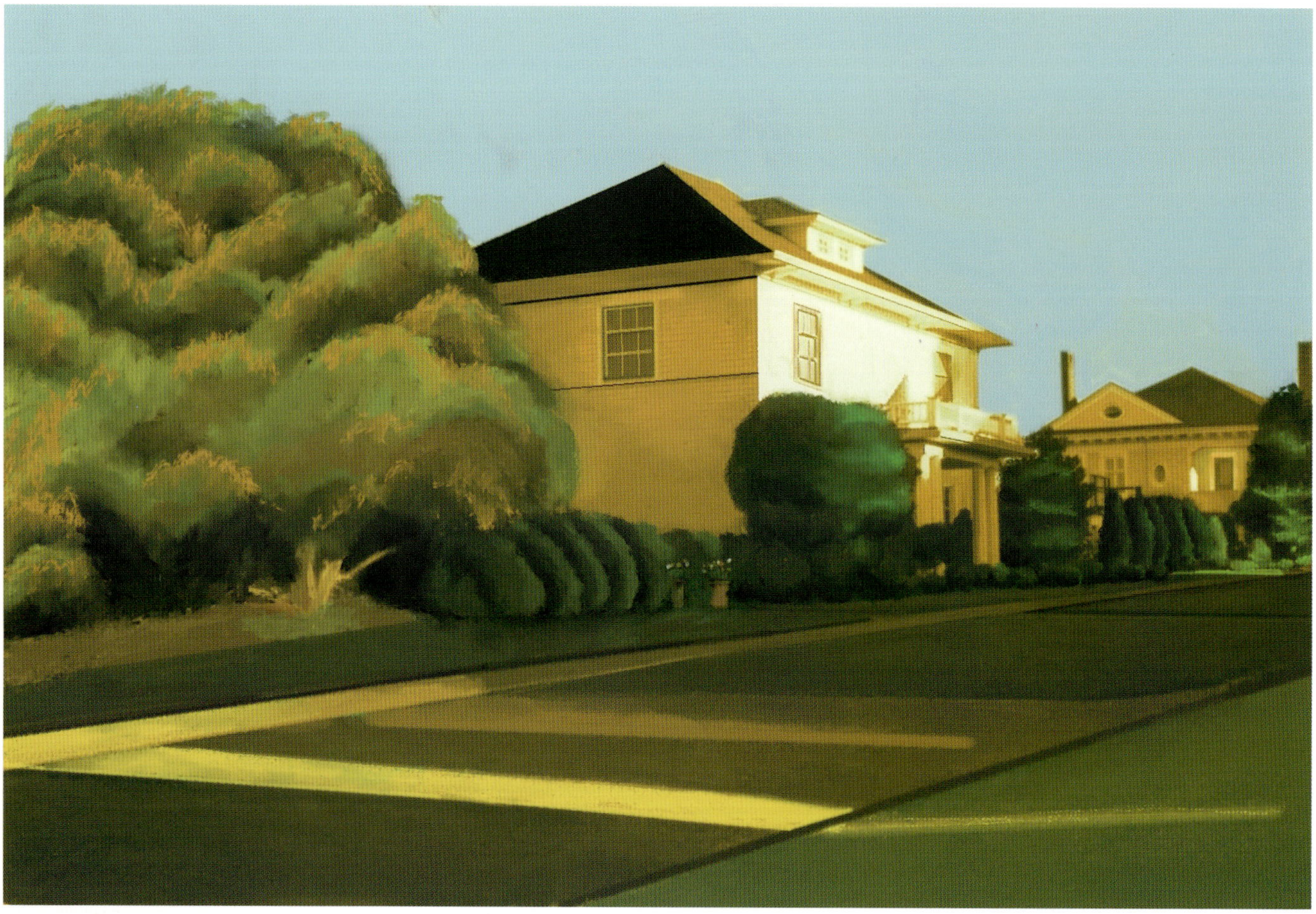

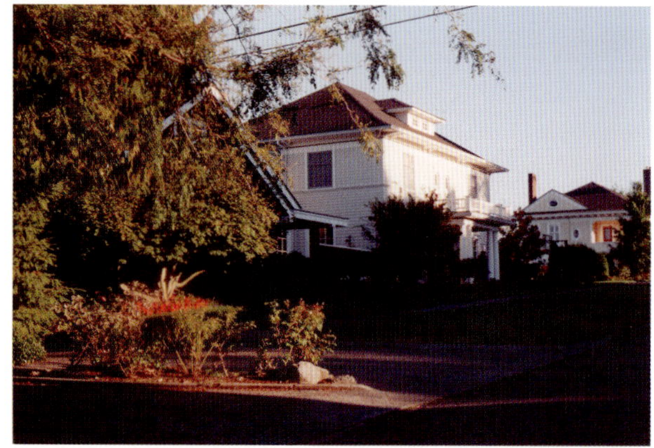

Oil-Painted Landscape
PHOTO AND PAINTING BY
KAREN SPERLING.

The more tones you have and the fewer colors, the more dramatic your paintings will be. This painting from a photo that I took in Tacoma, WA, is a perfect example. I have exhibited this painting in galleries, and collectors have bought it.

I used an adjacent color scheme—compare the painting to the color wheel on page 12 and you'll see that I used the colors next to each other starting with yellow-orange and moving clockwise through yellow, yellow-green, green and blue-green.

I used the tones in the photo, which I took late in the day, creating strong highlights and shadows, which I painted, including the crisp divisions between tones, like the highlights on the grass.

Another art concept that I used to paint this painting was the idea that a painting has less detail than a photo.

Notice that I eliminated the first house, all the way to the left, made the tree shorter, eliminated all the shrubbery in the lower left-hand corner and painted out the branch on top.

I got the idea to make all the foliage geometric shapes by looking at the works of Hopper and Cézanne.

1 MADE IN THE SHADE

Choose File: Clone to save the original photo intact. Close the photo.

Give the clone a new color scheme by using Express in Image, explained on page 29.

At right you see the way the Colors and Gradients palettes were set up to get the result in the image.

Next, save this version and choose File: Clone again, and name this new clone (File: Save As).

The previous version is now the source image and this new clone is the painting.

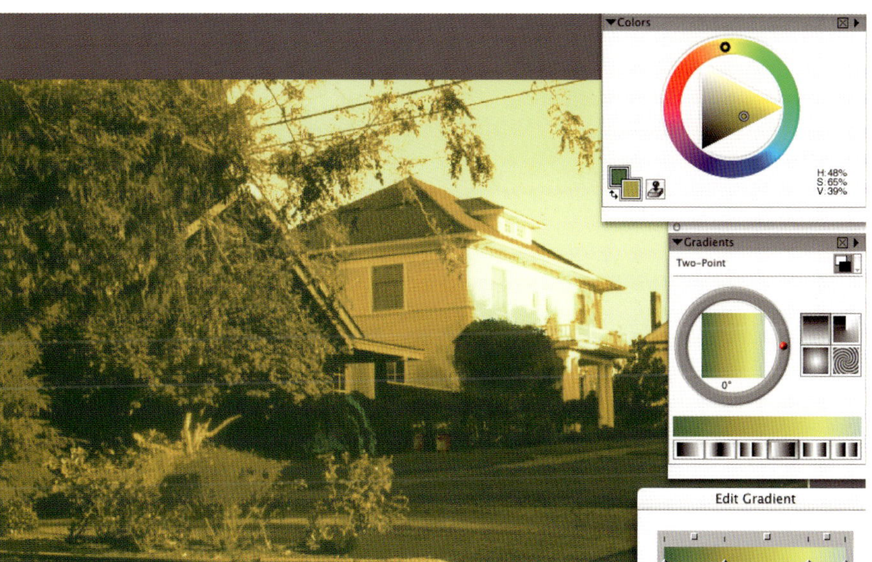

2 BLUE-GREEN SKIES

Express in Image does a pretty good job of filling in colors, but it made the sky yellow.

Paint the sky blue-green using the Airbrushes' Digital Airbrush. I prefer to stay away from selections and layers when I can, so to paint edges, lower the Size slider in the Property Bar and draw outlines as you see in the image at right, then raise the Size slider and paint in between the outlines to fill the areas with color. To paint or draw with a straight line, type v, click one end of the line, then click the other end of the line. To finish the line, type b. You can also press Shift, then paint, which constrains your stroke to a straight line.

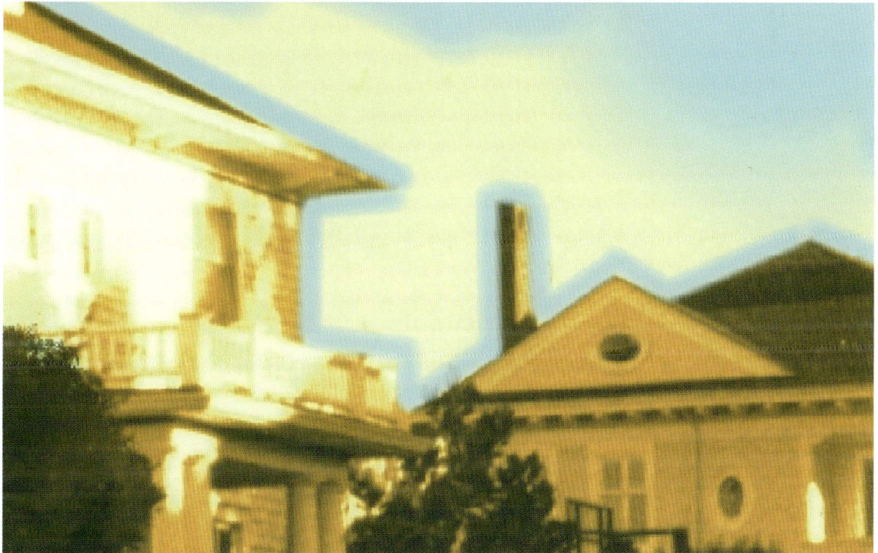

3 PAINTING HIGHLIGHTS

Eliminate the front, left-hand bushes by painting with the Chalk's Square Chalk variant.

Press option, Mac; alt, Windows, click on the color next to the bushes, then paint on top of the bushes, making them disappear.

Blend the Chalk strokes using the Blenders' Smudge variant to create an oil-painted effect. When you don't blend, the strokes look like pastels.

Paint the highlights and shadows on the walks and lawns with the Square Chalk, making distinct edges between light and dark areas.

Use the methods described in step 2 above for keeping the lines straight.

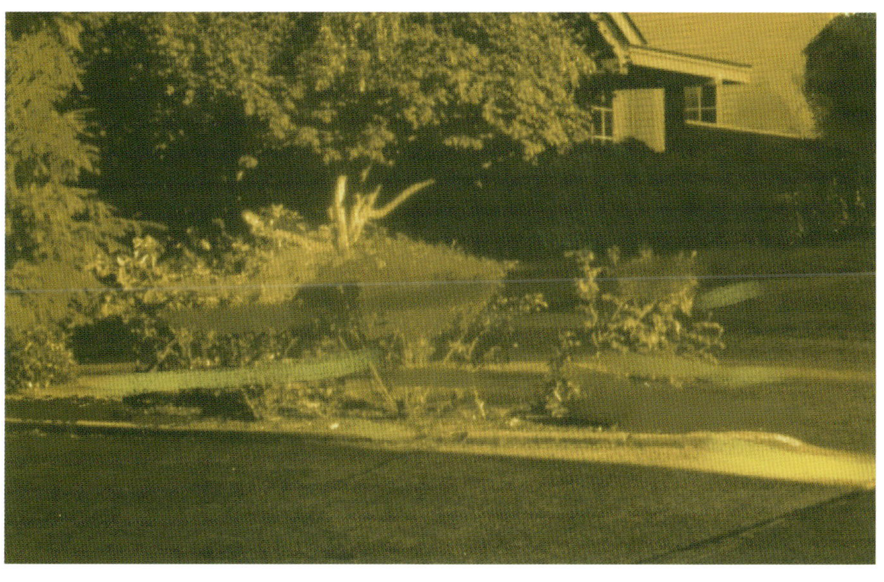

4 NOW YOU SEE IT

Paint out the tree and the house on the left and the branches on the house next to them the same way that you eliminated the front bushes, that is, with the Square Chalk selected. Press option, Mac; alt, Windows, click on the color next to what you want to eliminate, then paint on top of the objects, making them disappear.

Blend the Square Chalk strokes with the Blenders' Smudge variant to create an oil-painted effect.

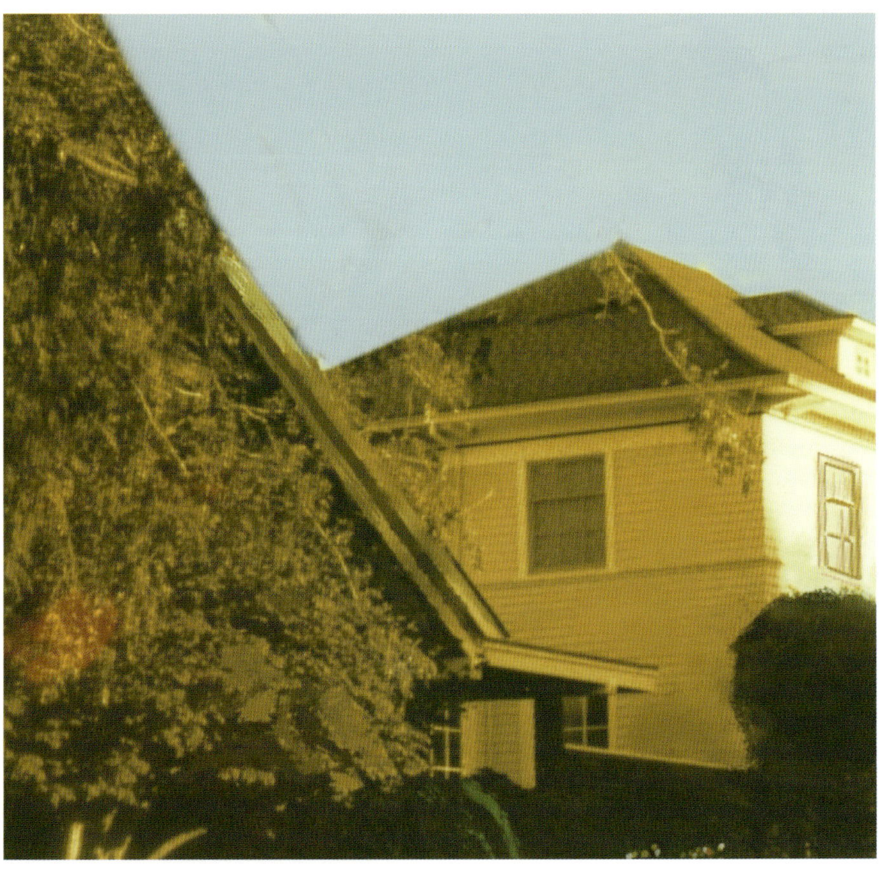

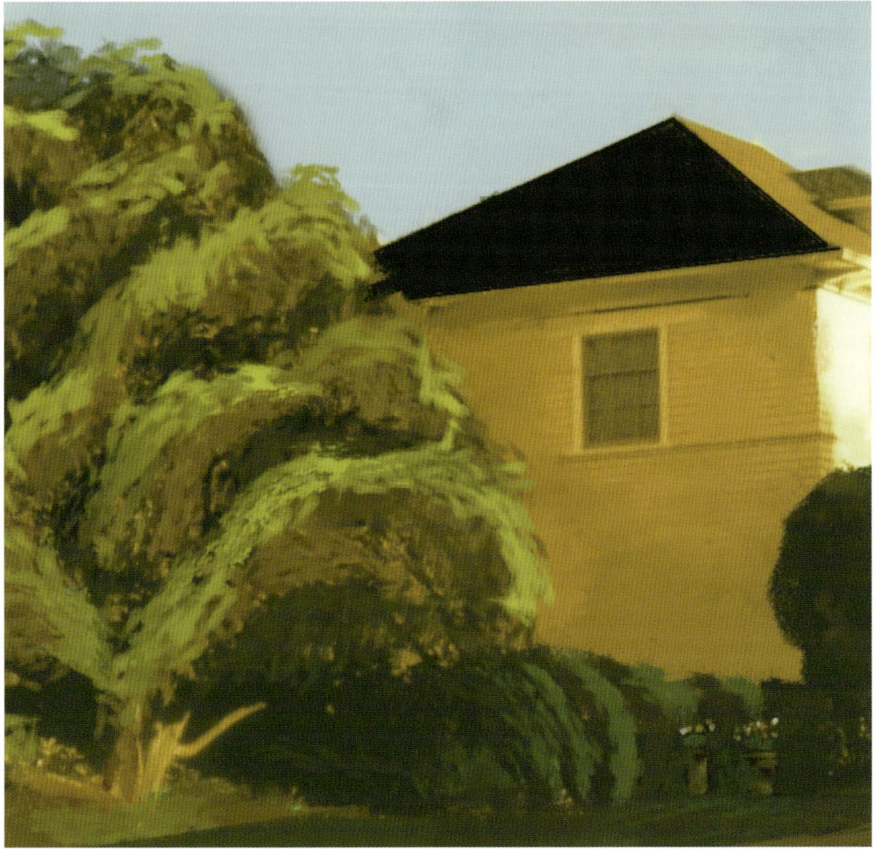

5 NOW YOU DON'T

After you finish painting out the extra branches and the house, paint the tones on the roof to darken them using the Square Chalk.

Paint tones based on the light source. In this case, the light is coming from the right, so the areas facing away from the light, like the roof, are dark.

Then paint the large tree on the left using the Artists' Impressionist brush.

In general, when you paint landscape areas like trees, mountains and boulders, you paint patterns created by the highlights and shadows, using the colors in your color scheme. The wavy pattern that you see in the tree is in the photo. Emphasize it by painting lighter tones where you see highlights and darker shades where you see shadows.

Once you have a few colors that you like, press option, Mac; alt, Windows and click on them to pick them up and paint with them elsewhere.

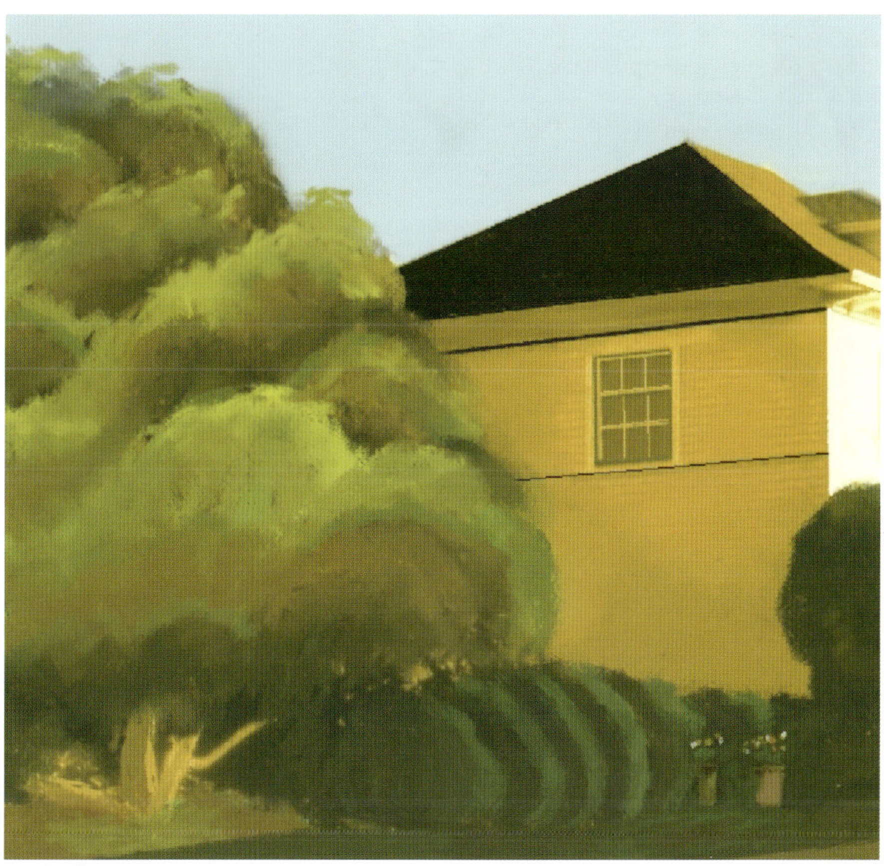

6 TREE'S COMPANY

After you have a few patterns and strokes in the tree, blend using the Artists' Impressionist variant. Continue to paint, switching to the default settings for the Artists' Impressionist variant to add color, then blend again with the blender version.

See page 24 for information about turning brushes into blenders, saving the changes in variants and restoring default variants.

With the Chalk's Sharp Chalk variant chosen, use the straight line painting technique described on page 83 to clean up the house's edges. Paint with whitish yellow on the front of the house to make the bright areas crisper.

7 GRAND FINALE

In the final stage of the painting, adjust tones some more, referring to the lights and darks in the source photo to guide you as you paint.

Use more intense colors in the highlights in the foreground. Having less intense colors in the background creates the illusion of distance.

Paint with a dark green in shadows in the trees and shrubs.

Make the tree and bushes fuller and more defined.

Paint straight lines as described on page 83 in the lawn and walk to make them crisper.

And that's how I turned a photo into an oil-painted landscape in Painter!

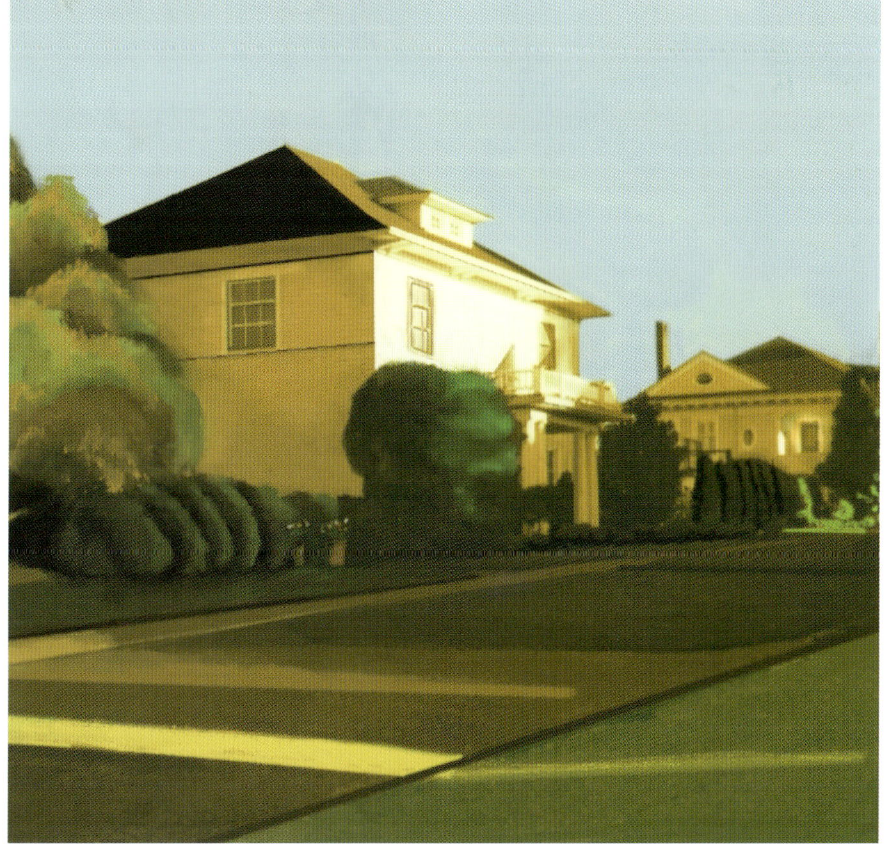

Watercolor Landscapes

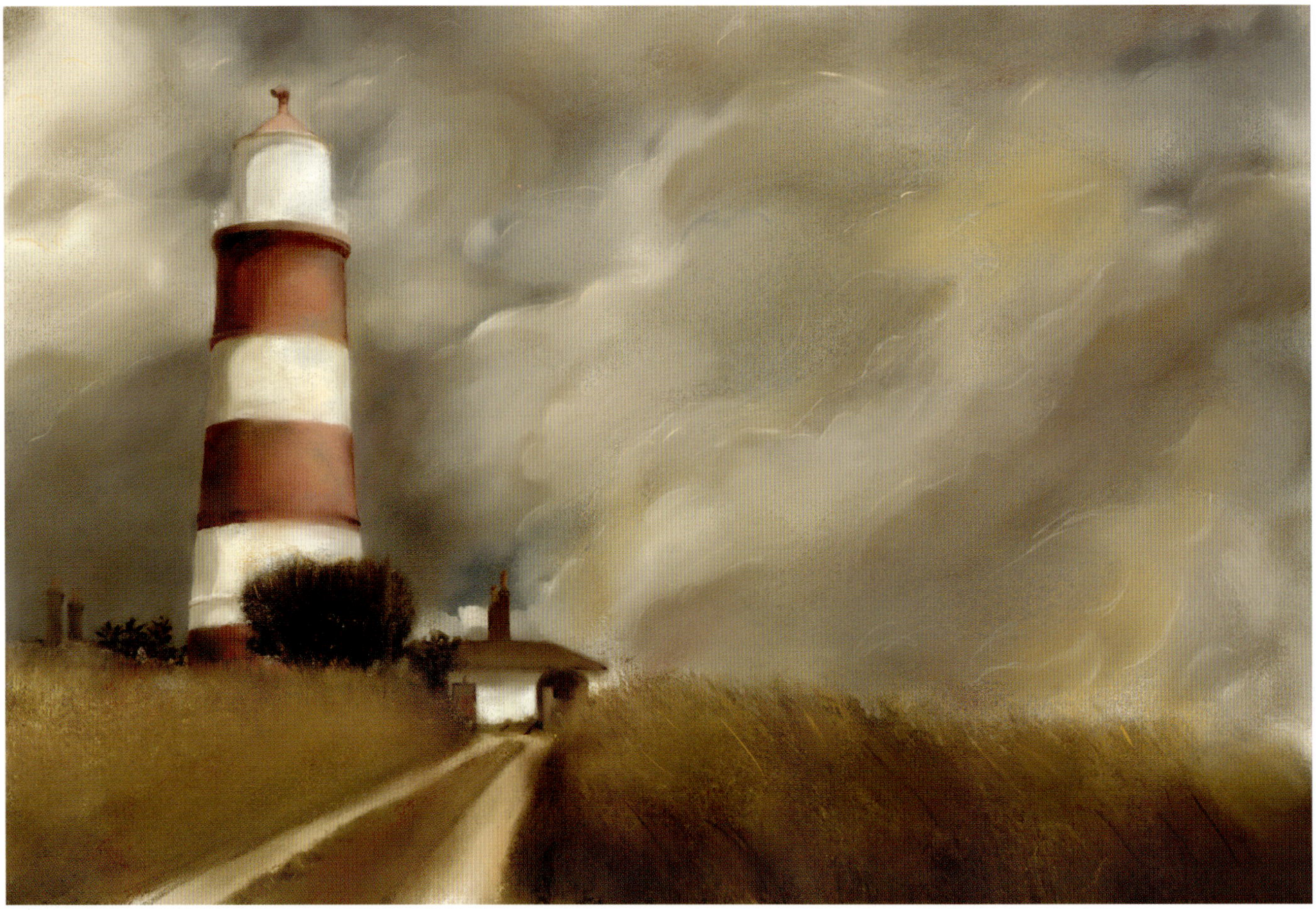

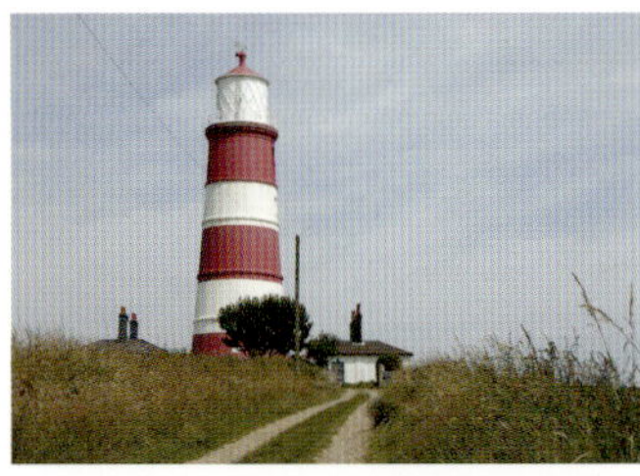

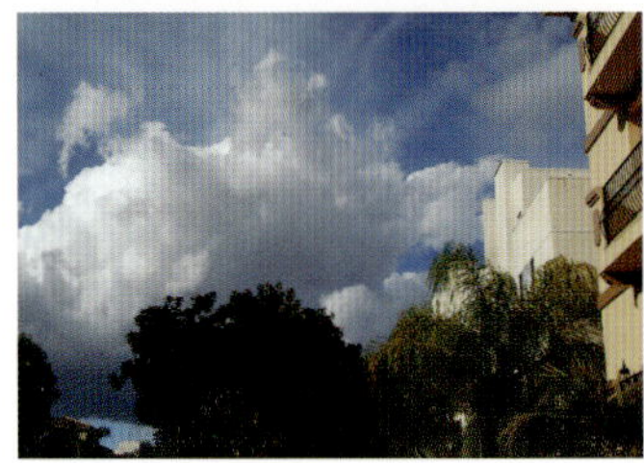

Watercolor Landscape

Painting by Karen Sperling; photos by her (sky) and by Ken Partington (lighthouse).

Ken Partington took this photo of a lighthouse that may be the victim of a vanishing coastline.

"Here in England we have a problem around the coast of Norfolk with sea eroding the coastline," Ken notes. "About a yard per year in some places. Happisburgh (pronounced Hazeborough) is one such place on the east coast of Norfolk. I took this photo because the lighthouse may not be there in a few years' time. I have fancied this adorning my wall for a while now."

Before painting the photo, I adjusted the tones and colors and moved things around a little, as you're about to see.

I also added clouds from photos I had taken where I live in southern California to add interest to the sky, based on traditional English landscape paintings (see page 20).

That's my idea of a good time—driving around, taking photos!

If you haven't already done so, take your own "stock photos" that you can pull from when you need things like clouds, flowers, trees, birds, etc.

Open the lighthouse photo in Painter.

Choose File: Clone, name the clone (File: Save As) and close the original.

The clone is the new source image.

I save in the .psd format if I have layers, or if I'm going to open the file in Photoshop. Otherwise, I save in .tif.

The next step is to clone in clouds, as you're about to see.

1 VARIED-SOURCE CLONE

Resize the cloud photos so that they and this new source image are visible on the screen at the same time.

To resize a window, click and drag in the lower right-hand corner. To move a window, click and drag at the top of the window on the title bar.

Next, bring some cloud formations into the lighthouse photo.

Rather than clone directly, clone a little from here and a little from there.

I based my cloning choices on the art concept that the subject, or focal point, is the area of greatest contrast between light and dark.

The lighthouse was logically the subject, so I wanted to make sure that it contrasted with the background. That meant I'd clone in a dark area around the lighthouse that was darker than both the light and the dark areas on the lighthouse.

The images are different sizes, so use the Cloners' xScale 2P variant, which scales as you clone.

See page 26 in the Corel Painter Tools chapter for information for using the Cloners' xScale 2P variant.

Paint around the lighthouse, bringing the clouds in from the various photos.

To paint next to the lighthouse, first paint an edge on a low size setting, then fill in paint next to this new edge on a high size setting. This eliminates the need for selections and layers.

The dark area that comes in as you paint contrasts well with the light and dark areas of the lighthouse.

2 SAME-SOURCE CLONE

Once your have some clouds that you like, use the Cloners' Soft Cloner to repeat them in other parts of the image. Press option, Mac; alt, Windows and click where you want to paint from and then paint.

You can also use the Airbrushes' Digital Airbrush to paint clouds.

On a low opacity and high size, press option, Mac; alt, Windows and click on a color to pick it up and paint. Notice clouds are lighter on top and darker on the bottom. Paint these tonal differences with the Digital Airbrush—the strokes look like clouds!

3 ON THE MOVE

The image was looking pretty good except for one thing—although the lighthouse wasn't in the middle of the image, the little building and road were, resulting in an undesirable composition (see page 16 for composition art concepts). Therefore, I adjusted their position. To do so, choose Canvas: Canvas Size, type in -400 in the pixels to left box and 400 in the pixels to right box.

This crops the image on the left and adds some space on the right, thereby moving the lighthouse, building and road over to the left, a quicker fix than solving the problem using layers.

Then, using the Cloners' Soft Cloner, press option, Mac; alt, Windows and click in an area to the left of the space and then paint on the space to the right to fill in the blank area created by the added pixels.

4 COLOR SCHEME

To give my painting a color scheme, I opened Croyland Abbey by John Sell Cotman and I used the Color Scheme menu in the Underpainting palette to add the Cotman colors to my newly composited image. See page 29 for information about using the Color Scheme menu to transfer colors between images.

When done, save (File: Save) and then choose File: Clone, name this new file (File: Save As) and close the previous one so that you'll have a copy of this composition intact in case you need to go back to it later.

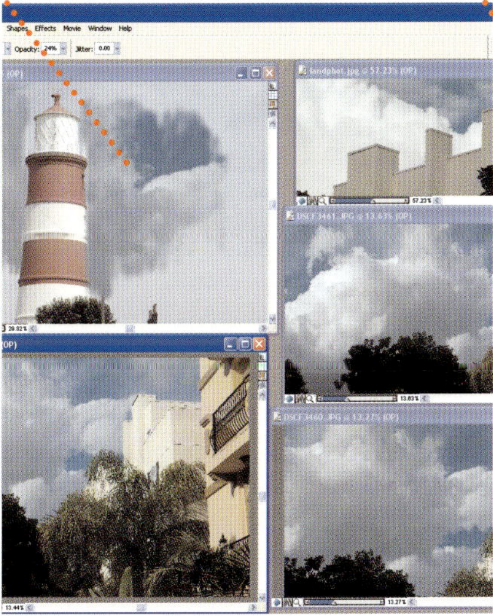

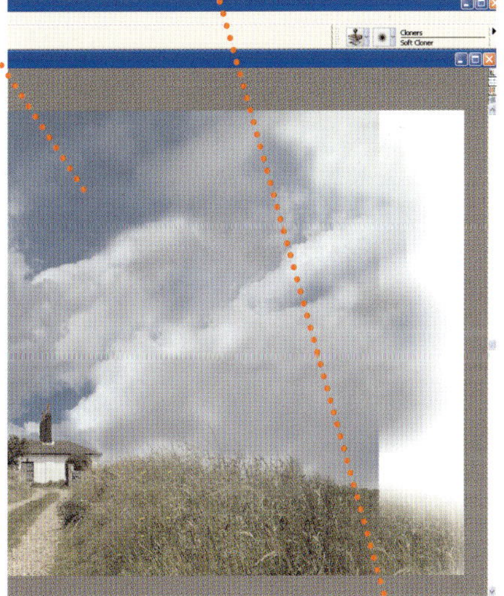

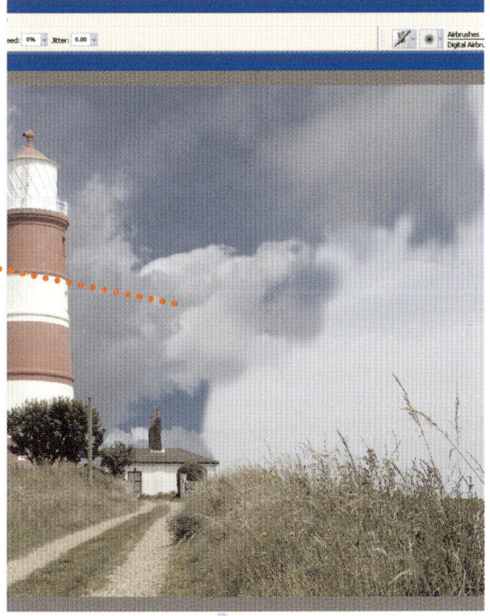

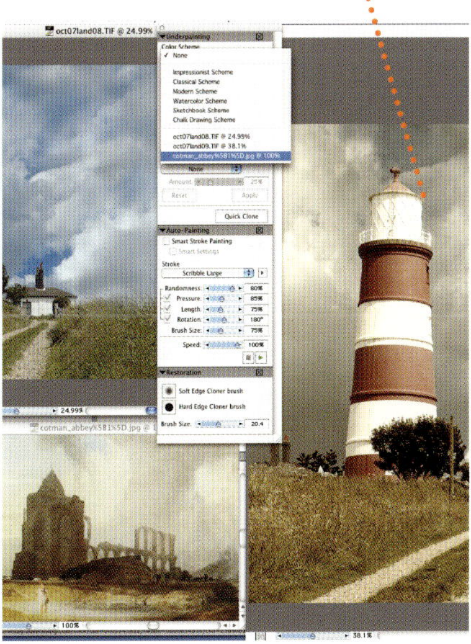

5 ADDING TEXTURE

To eliminate details and create areas of color, set the Smart Blur slider in the Underpainting palette on 100%.

Save this image, then clone the image, clear the contents of the clone and turn on Tracing Paper. See page 27 for the steps for clearing the image and for activating Tracing Paper.

Then add texture by painting with the Airbrushes' Coarse Spray.

Click the rubber stamp in the Colors palette so that the brush will pick up the color from the source image as you paint in the cloned image.

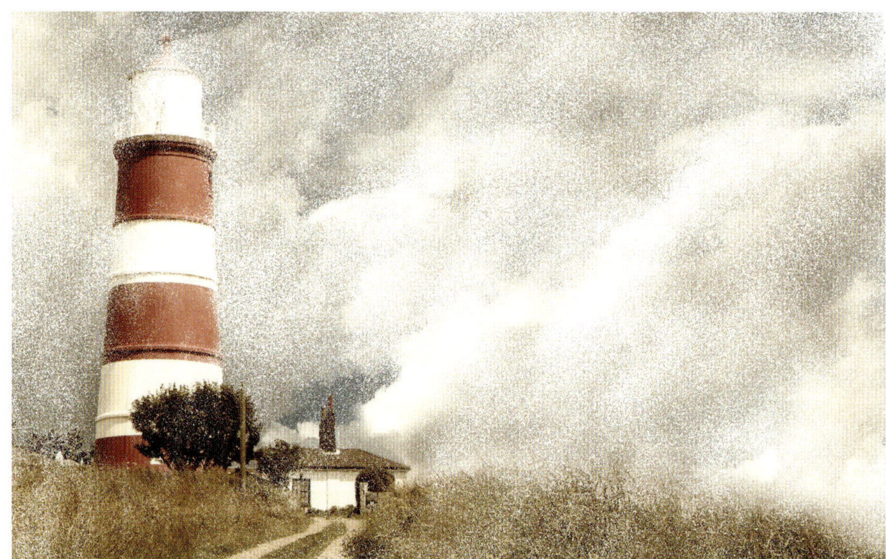

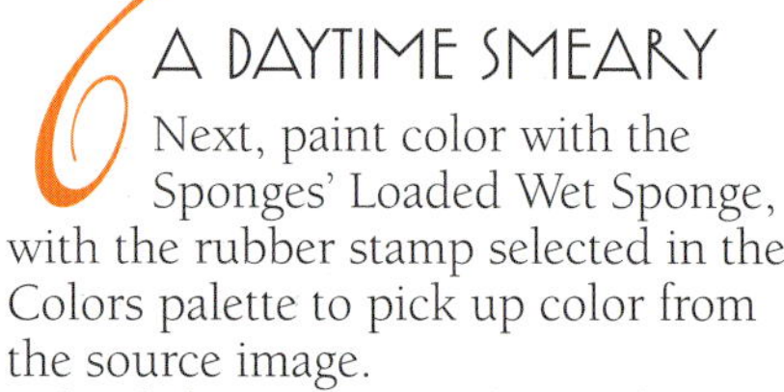

6 A DAYTIME SMEARY

Next, paint color with the Sponges' Loaded Wet Sponge, with the rubber stamp selected in the Colors palette to pick up color from the source image.

Blend the current strokes and add new ones using the Sponges' Smeary Wet Sponge with the rubber stamp selected in the Colors palette.

To get the edge of the lighthouse, first paint on the area next to the lighthouse, then paint on the lighthouse.

The more you paint next to an object and then on the object, the cleaner the edge between the object and the area next to it will be.

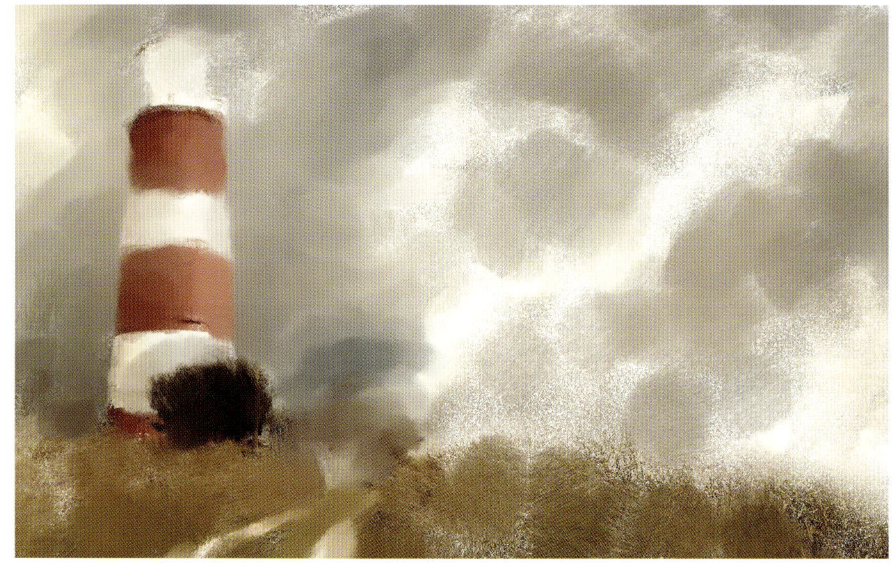

7 WASH OVER ME

Next, use the Watercolor's Soft Runny Wash variant with the rubber stamp in the Colors palette selected.

Paint the house and the tree and some of the lighthouse.

When you paint with the Watercolor variants, they create layers.

Before you move onto your next brush, choose Layers menu: Drop All to flatten the layers. If you don't, and then try to paint with a non-Watercolor variant, you'll get a prompt telling you that you can't paint with other brushes in the watercolor layer.

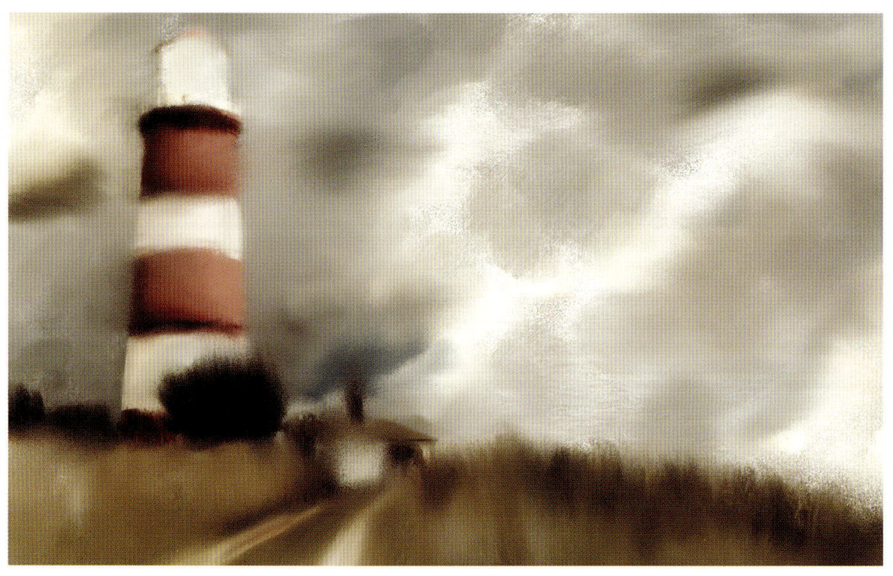

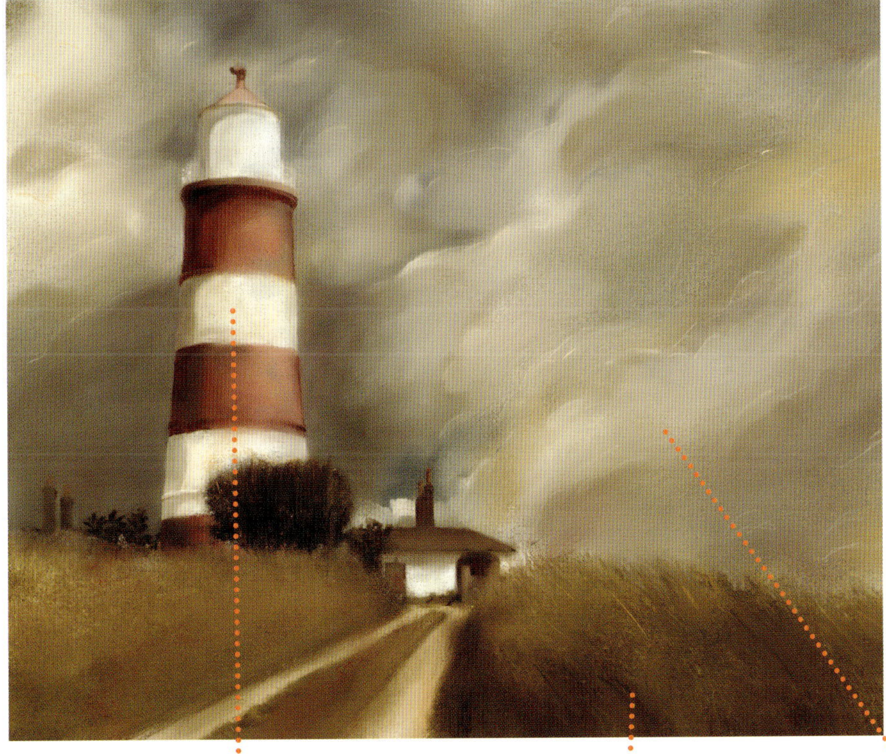

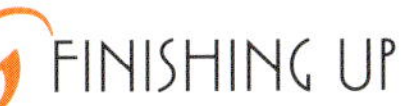

8 FINISHING UP

From here, continue to paint with the same brushes.

Painting is a back-and-forth process. You paint a little with one brush, paint some more with another, go back and paint with the first brush some more, and keep repeating.

As you go along, following the tips below for painting tones, grass and skies, bring in details like edges of the house and the lighthouse from the previous image by painting with the Soft Cloner.

To soften the edges after you paint them with the Soft Cloner, paint with the Blenders' Grainy Blender.

I get a lot of compliments about this image, and it was included in the gallery in the Painter 11 software.

I think that the painting appeals to everyone because it includes the basic art concepts of a limited color palette with color harmony, a clear focal point and a subject that is off-center.

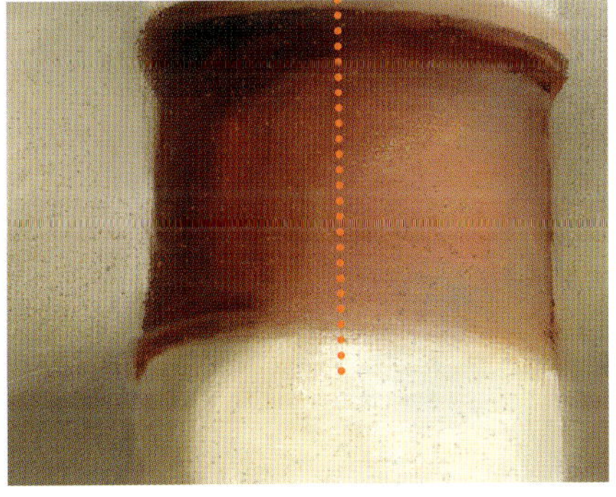

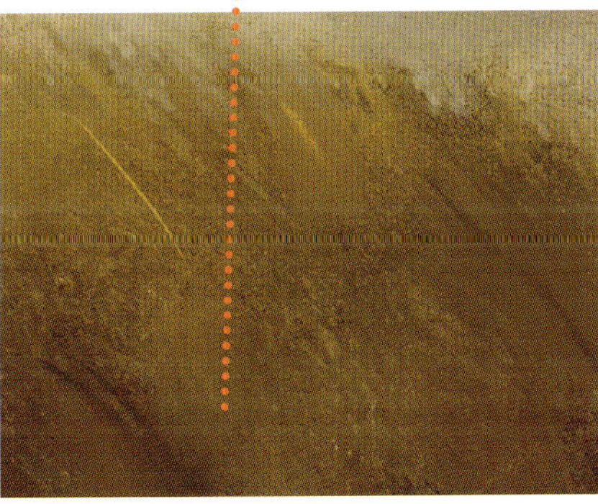

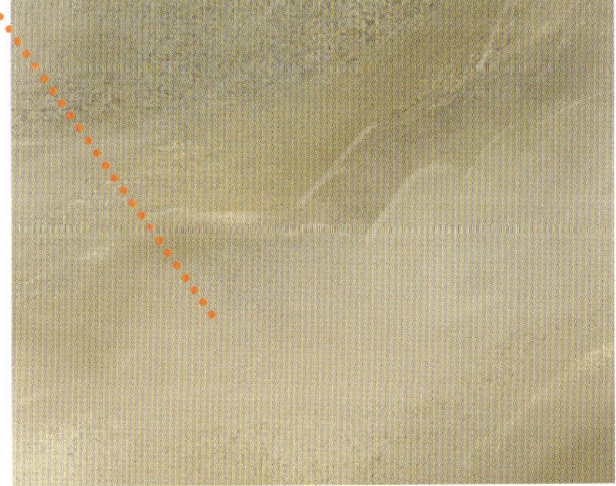

TONES

Paint distinct light and dark tones like on the lighthouse based on where you see them in the photo using the Artists' Impressionist brush with the rubber stamp selected in the Colors palette and the Size and Jitter sliders in the Property Bar turned down.

Then blend the color with the Blenders' Grainy Blender variant.

Painting these light and dark tones with distinctive edges between them gives the image its painterly look.

Add highlights in the sky using the Pens' Scratchboard Tool.

Press option, Mac; alt, Windows and click on a light color in the painting, choose a lighter tone of it in the Colors palette and paint the highlights with Tracing Paper turned on. Turn off Tracing Paper to see the results (see page 27 for information about Tracing Paper).

Then blend the lines a little with the Grainy Blender so that they look like they're part of the painting, but don't overdo the blending.

GRASS

I used many different brushes to create the grass.

First paint with the Sponges' Loaded Wet Sponge with the rubber stamp selected in the Colors palette.

Blend these strokes by painting with the Blenders' Grainy Blender variant.

Add a dash of Artists' Impressionist brush strokes with the rubber stamp selected in the Colors palette and the Jitter slider in the Property Bar turned all the way up.

Then blend again with the Grainy Blender.

Add more texture by painting with the Airbrushes' Coarse Spray on low opacity. Press option, Mac; alt, Windows and click on colors then paint with them.

Painting with colors already in the image creates color harmony, where colors repeat throughout the artwork.

Blend using the Grainy Blender with opacity turned down and size turned up.

Repeat these steps to build up the effect.

SKY'S THE LIMIT

Paint the sky in several steps, using the tones in the source image to guide you, adding texture along the way.

Paint with the Loaded Wet Sponge with the rubber stamp selected in the Colors palette, then blend with the Grainy Blender and the Smeary Wet Sponge.

When blending, turn on Tracing Paper so that you can see the edges separating light and dark areas and blend to make these edges distinct.

Next, paint with the Airbrushes' Coarse Spray on low opacity to add more texture.

Choose colors to paint with by pressing option, Mac; alt, Windows and clicking on them in the image. Paint with the same tones or paint with lighter or darker versions chosen in the Colors palette to pump up contrast.

I find it helps to see how artists in the past handled things, and I did google.com searches on English landscape artists to see how they painted skies to guide me in painting mine.

PASTEL LANDSCAPES

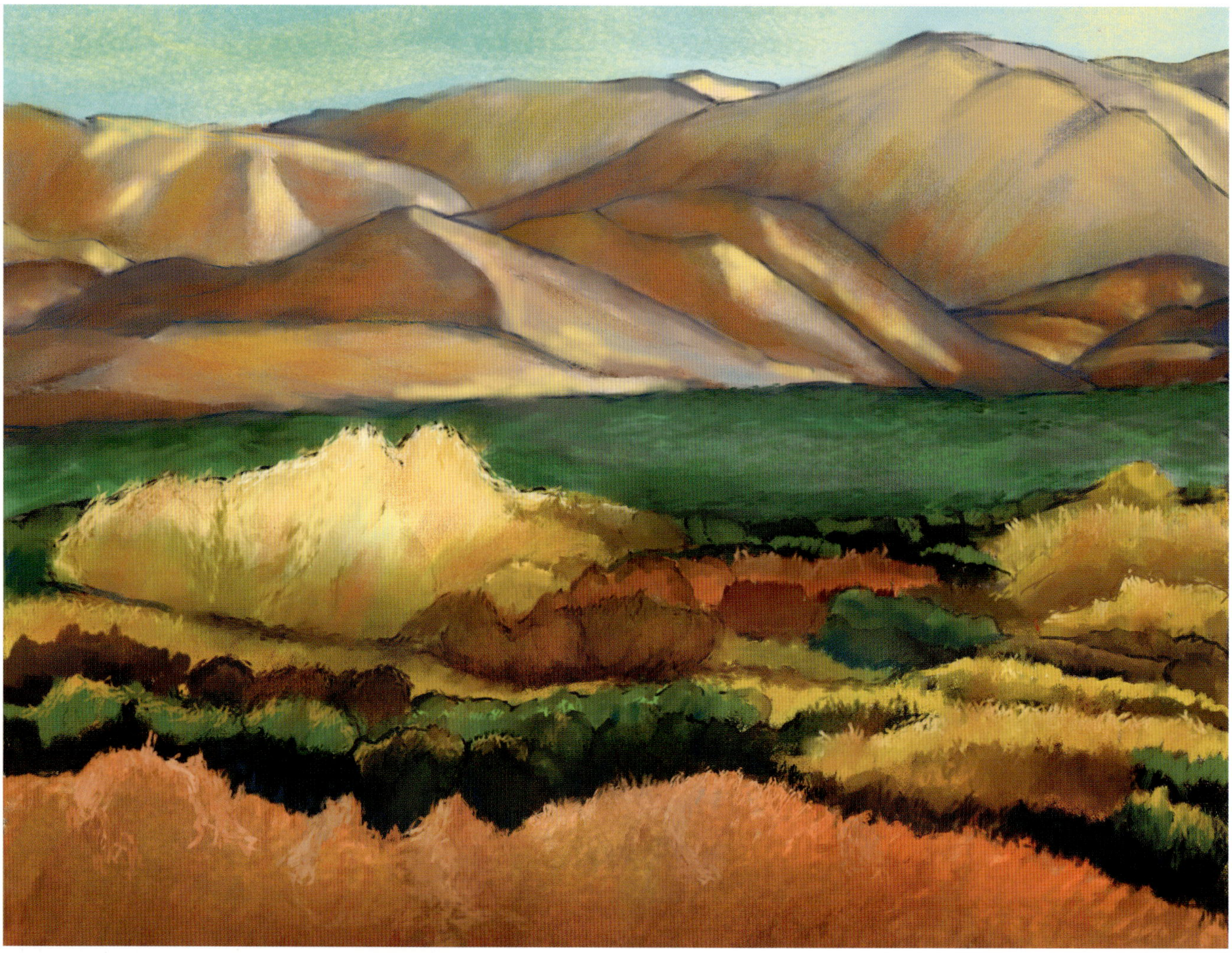

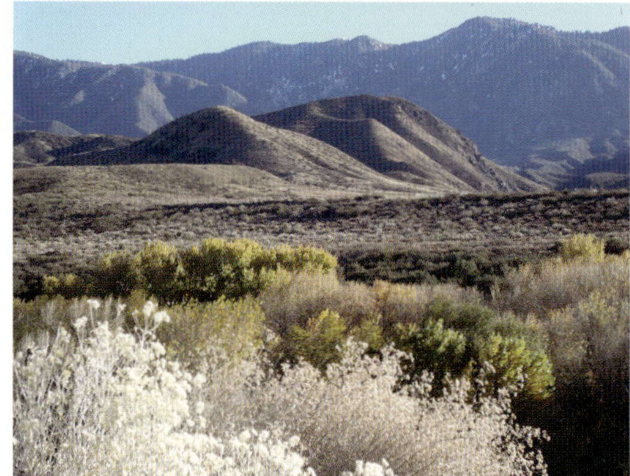

Pastel Landscape
Photo and painting by Karen Sperling.

I created this pastel drawing in Corel Painter from this photo that I took in Soledad Canyon, which is north of Los Angeles.

The white plant in the lower left would make a good focal point if it were closer to the imaginary intersection of the canvas folded in thirds, but it was too far down to fit the bill.

I knew this while I was taking the photo. I tried framing the photo differently when I shot it, but below the white plants was the road I was standing on, so composing the photo differently wasn't an option. I'd have to fix it later.

Also, the photo's colors didn't add up to a color scheme.

I consulted the color wheel on page 12 and decided that the yellow, green and shades of orange (beige tones) could stay. I just had to add shades of red-orange, yellow-orange, yellow-green, green and blue-green, and I'd have an adjacent color scheme.

See page 13 for information about adjacent color schemes.

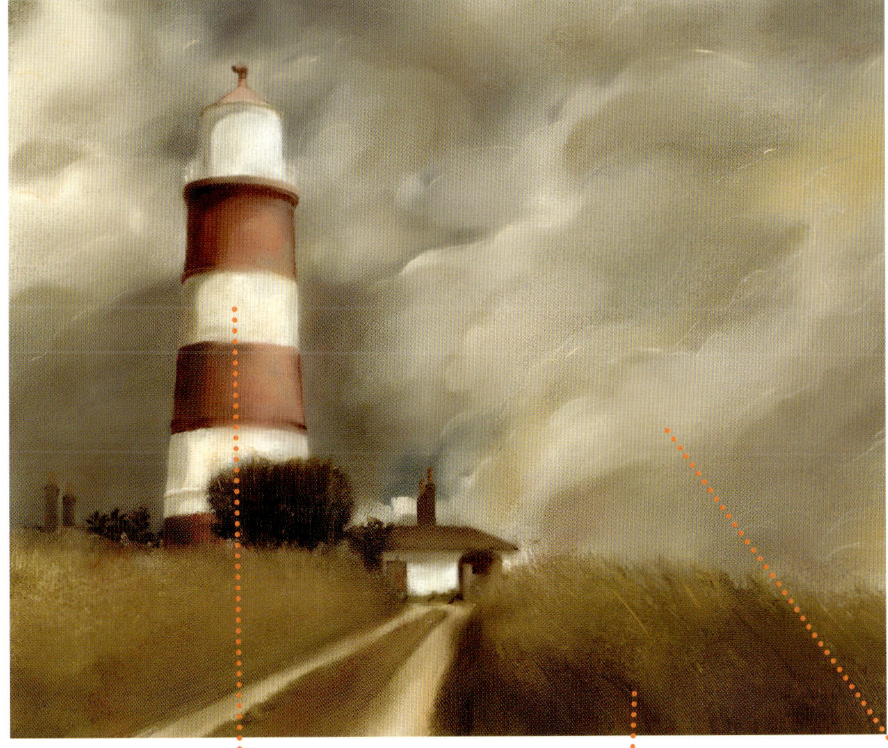

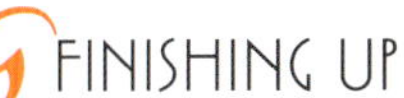

8 FINISHING UP

From here, continue to paint with the same brushes.

Painting is a back-and-forth process. You paint a little with one brush, paint some more with another, go back and paint with the first brush some more, and keep repeating.

As you go along, following the tips below for painting tones, grass and skies, bring in details like edges of the house and the lighthouse from the previous image by painting with the Soft Cloner.

To soften the edges after you paint them with the Soft Cloner, paint with the Blenders' Grainy Blender.

I get a lot of compliments about this image, and it was included in the gallery in the Painter 11 software.

I think that the painting appeals to everyone because it includes the basic art concepts of a limited color palette with color harmony, a clear focal point and a subject that is off-center.

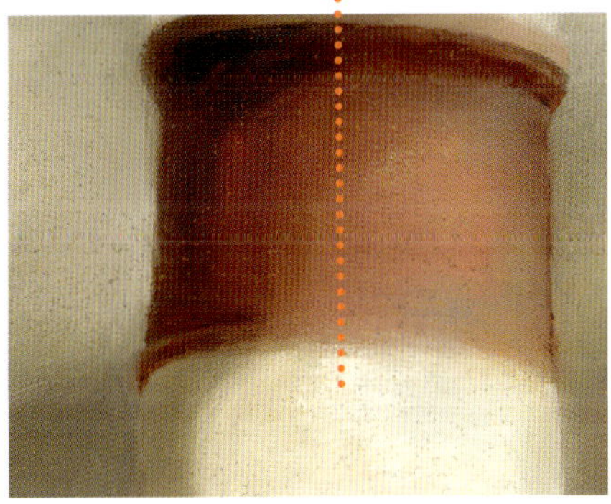

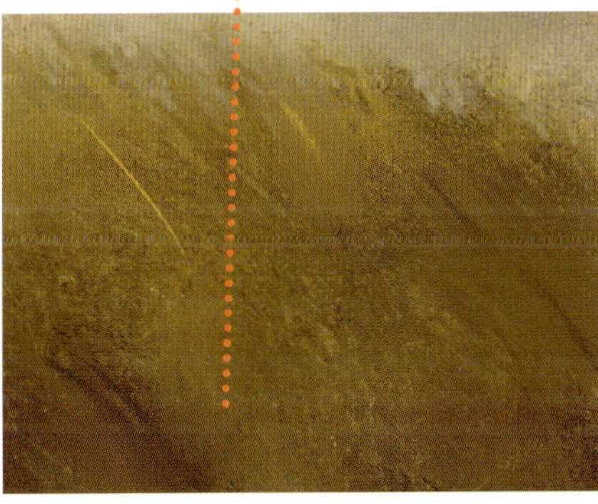

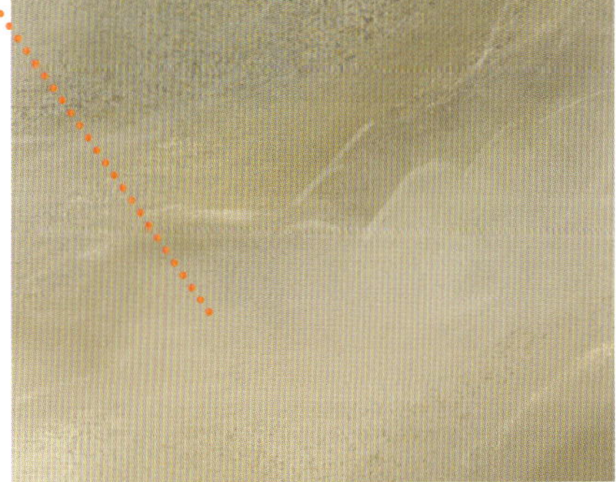

TONES

Paint distinct light and dark tones like on the lighthouse based on where you see them in the photo using the Artists' Impressionist brush with the rubber stamp selected in the Colors palette and the Size and Jitter sliders in the Property Bar turned down.

Then blend the color with the Blenders' Grainy Blender variant.

Painting these light and dark tones with distinctive edges between them gives the image its painterly look.

Add highlights in the sky using the Pens' Scratchboard Tool.

Press option, Mac; alt, Windows and click on a light color in the painting, choose a lighter tone of it in the Colors palette and paint the highlights with Tracing Paper turned on. Turn off Tracing Paper to see the results (see page 27 for information about Tracing Paper).

Then blend the lines a little with the Grainy Blender so that they look like they're part of the painting, but don't overdo the blending.

GRASS

I used many different brushes to create the grass.

First paint with the Sponges' Loaded Wet Sponge with the rubber stamp selected in the Colors palette.

Blend these strokes by painting with the Blenders' Grainy Blender variant.

Add a dash of Artists' Impressionist brush strokes with the rubber stamp selected in the Colors palette and the Jitter slider in the Property Bar turned all the way up.

Then blend again with the Grainy Blender.

Add more texture by painting with the Airbrushes' Coarse Spray on low opacity. Press option, Mac; alt, Windows and click on colors then paint with them.

Painting with colors already in the image creates color harmony, where colors repeat throughout the artwork.

Blend using the Grainy Blender with opacity turned down and size turned up.

Repeat these steps to build up the effect.

SKY'S THE LIMIT

Paint the sky in several steps, using the tones in the source image to guide you, adding texture along the way.

Paint with the Loaded Wet Sponge with the rubber stamp selected in the Colors palette, then blend with the Grainy Blender and the Smeary Wet Sponge.

When blending, turn on Tracing Paper so that you can see the edges separating light and dark areas and blend to make these edges distinct.

Next, paint with the Airbrushes' Coarse Spray on low opacity to add more texture.

Choose colors to paint with by pressing option, Mac; alt, Windows and clicking on them in the image. Paint with the same tones or paint with lighter or darker versions chosen in the Colors palette to pump up contrast.

I find it helps to see how artists in the past handled things, and I did google.com searches on English landscape artists to see how they painted skies to guide me in painting mine.

PASTEL LANDSCAPES

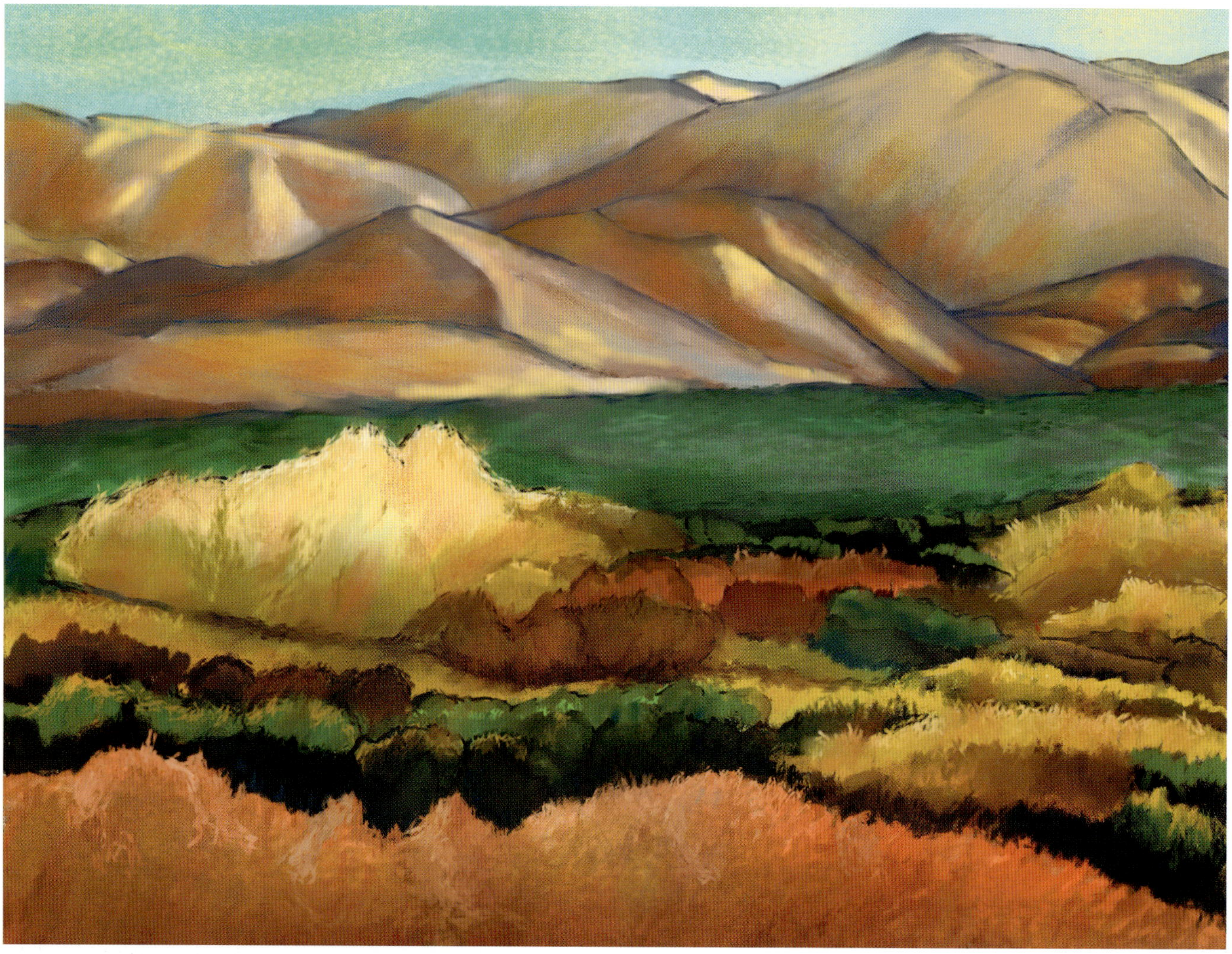

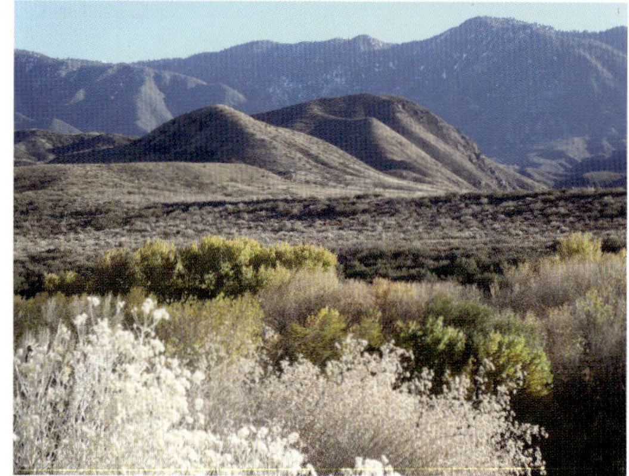

Pastel Landscape
Photo and painting by Karen Sperling.

I created this pastel drawing in Corel Painter from this photo that I took in Soledad Canyon, which is north of Los Angeles.

The white plant in the lower left would make a good focal point if it were closer to the imaginary intersection of the canvas folded in thirds, but it was too far down to fit the bill.

I knew this while I was taking the photo. I tried framing the photo differently when I shot it, but below the white plants was the road I was standing on, so composing the photo differently wasn't an option. I'd have to fix it later.

Also, the photo's colors didn't add up to a color scheme.

I consulted the color wheel on page 12 and decided that the yellow, green and shades of orange (beige tones) could stay. I just had to add shades of red-orange, yellow-orange, yellow-green, green and blue-green, and I'd have an adjacent color scheme.

See page 13 for information about adjacent color schemes.

1 SLIGHTLY REARRANGED

With the photo open in Painter, choose File: Clone and File: Save As to keep the original photo intact. Close the original photo.

In this clone, rearrange elements using layers so that the white plant is near an imaginary intersection of the canvas if it were folded in thirds. Spread out the beige plants to run along the bottom of the image.

I wasn't trying to make the source image perfect. If you look closely at the image at right, you see the layers. Since I was going to paint it anyway, I was only interested in giving myself a rough basis for the painting—sort of a first draft of the finished image.

See page 30 for information about working with layers in Painter.

This is now the source image. Save, then choose File: Clone and File: Save As. The clone is the painting.

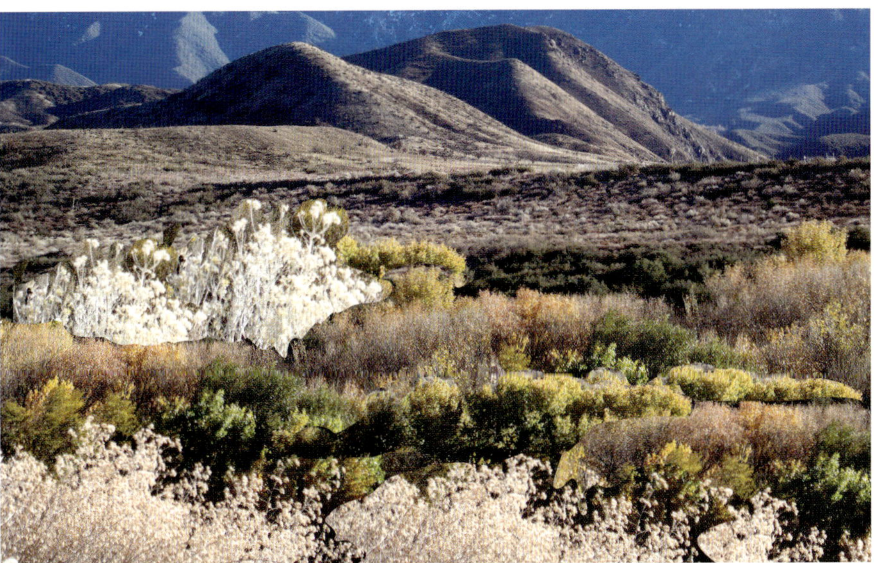

2 CHALK ONE UP

Start adding colors using the Chalk's Square Chalk. Add brush strokes to the image based on the colors that are in the photo and based on the color scheme.

Paint where you see lights and darks in the photo, adding even lighter strokes where you see highlights and deepening the darker tones where you see shadows.

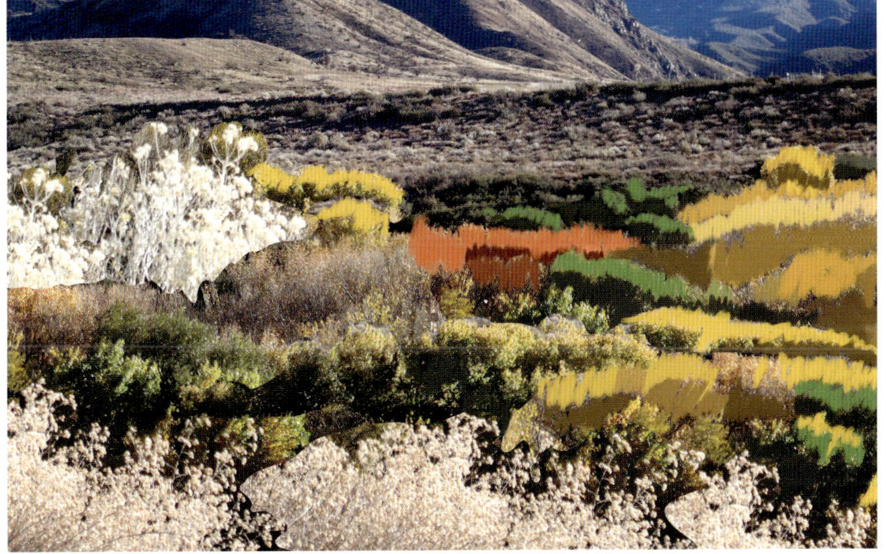

3 PAINTERLY TONES

Continue to paint, choosing saturated tones from the Colors palette to make the image more painterly.

After you have painted some colors, you can pick up colors in one part of the image by pressing option, Mac; alt, Windows and clicking and then painting them in other areas rather than choosing them in the Colors palette.

Using existing colors creates color harmony, where, as you've seen, colors are repeated throughout the art.

Make up the colors using your color scheme. Try to follow the tones that you see in the photo, as you can see in the image at right.

Getting better at painting means getting better at recognizing which tones to paint.

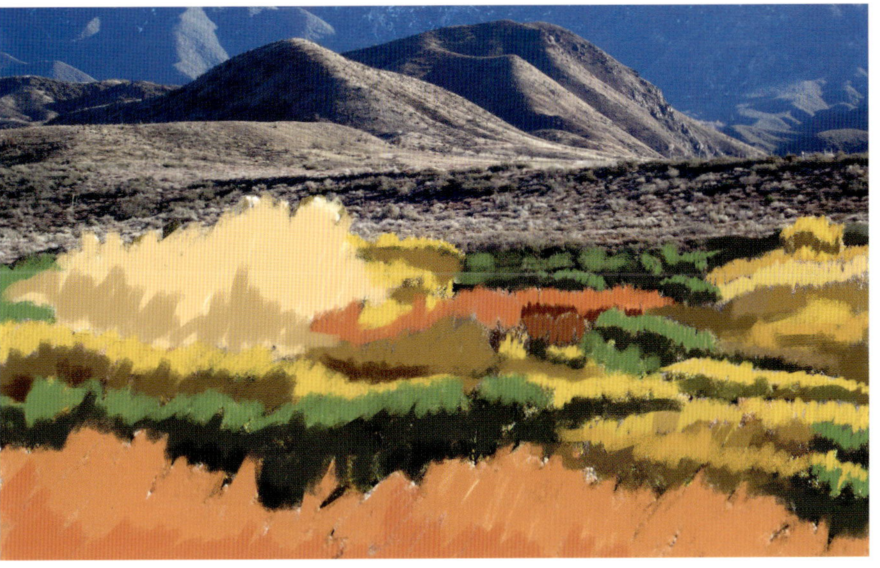

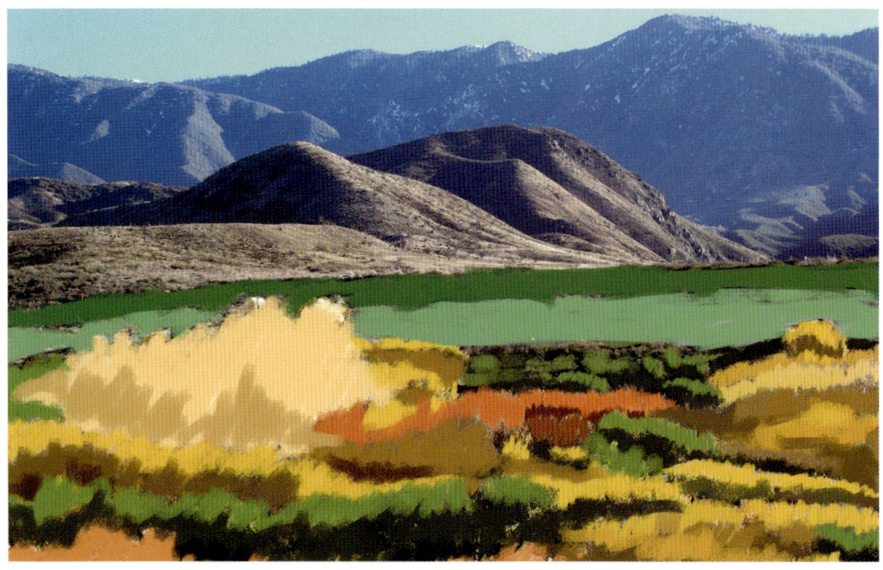

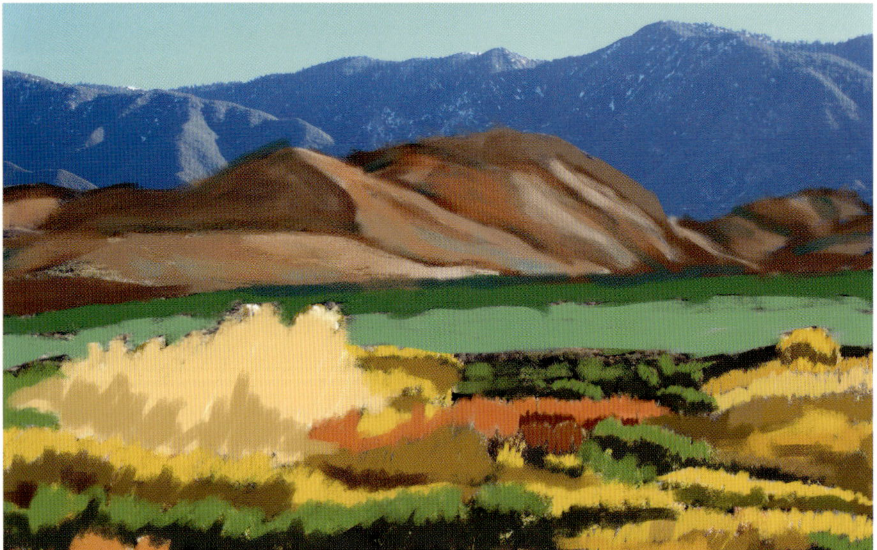

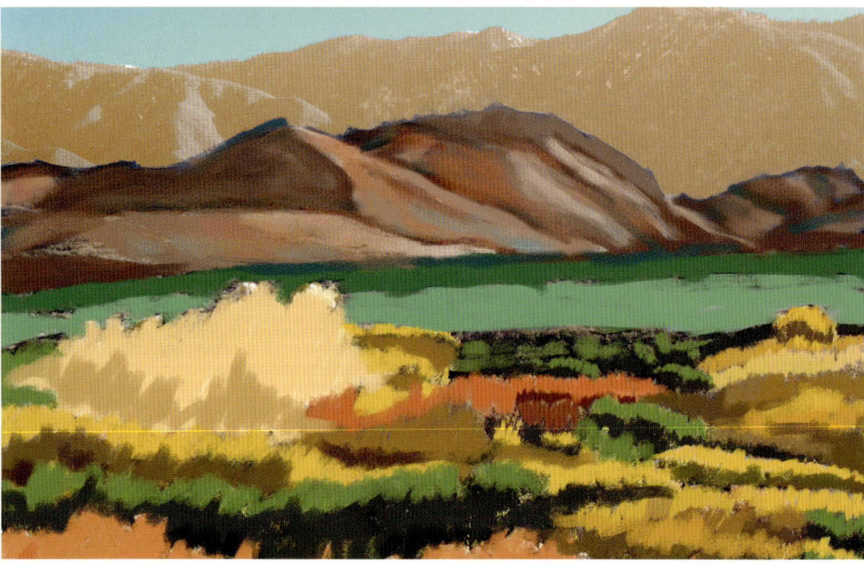

4 DEEP BACKGROUND

Paint the middle ground next, still using the Square Chalk variant.

A traditional painting technique is to show more details in the foreground and fewer details in the middle ground and in the background to create the illusion of distance.

Therefore, to make your paintings from your photos look more painterly, make backgrounds less detailed.

5 WITH A TRACE

Have the painting and the photo open side by side while you draw so that you can see the areas of light and dark in the photo and paint them in the painting.

Also use Tracing Paper to help you see these contrasts to paint them.

See page 27 for information about working with Tracing Paper.

After you have some colors in the mountains, paint with the Chalk's Square Chalk on a low opacity setting in the Property Bar to tint colors. Include some blue-green in the mountain to create the illusion of distance.

6 SELECTION PROCESS

Next is the mountain in the back. You'll make it lighter and less saturated than the elements in the foreground to create the illusion of distance.

Since it has a unique color, it is easy enough to select the mountain with the magic wand in the toolbox.

Deselect Contiguous in the Property Bar to select all the color-related pixels in the image area.

To select more pixels in the range, press shift and sort of scribble on all the areas to add to the selection.

Then edit the color. To do so:

1. Select Effects: Tonal Control: Adjust Colors. The Adjust Color dialog box appears.
2. Move the Hue Shift slider to change the color.
3. Move the Saturation slider to the left to make the color less "juicy."
4. Move the Value slider to the right to lighten the color.
5. Click OK.

The mountain is now lighter and a different color.

7 NICE SHADES

Add some shading to the mountains in the back by drawing with the Chalk's Square Chalk and add outlines with the Chalk's Sharp Chalk.

Use a low opacity setting for both in the Property Bar.

Use for the shading and outlines blue-green, which is the complement—or opposite on the color wheel—of the tone of red-orange used as the mountain's new base color.

Add beige highlights and dark brown shadows—both beige and dark brown are tones of red-orange.

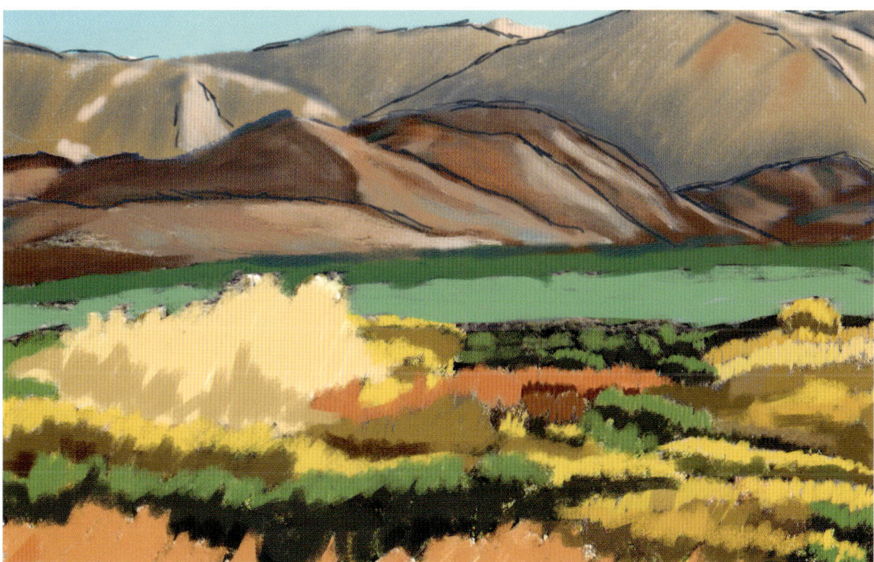

8 BLENDING IN

Add definition using the Artists' Impressionist brush.

Lower opacity and size, press option/alt and click in the image to pick up colors and paint, following areas of light and dark that you see in the photo.

Create a custom palette to access the brushes more quickly than using the Brush Selector.

See page 25 for information about creating custom palettes.

Raise the Size slider and paint on the part just below the mountains with the Artists' Impressionist brush.

Doing so adds texture, suggesting all the plants without actually painting each plant.

Turn the Square Chalk, Sharp Chalk and Impressionist variants into blenders, blend and save the settings as variants—see page 24 for steps.

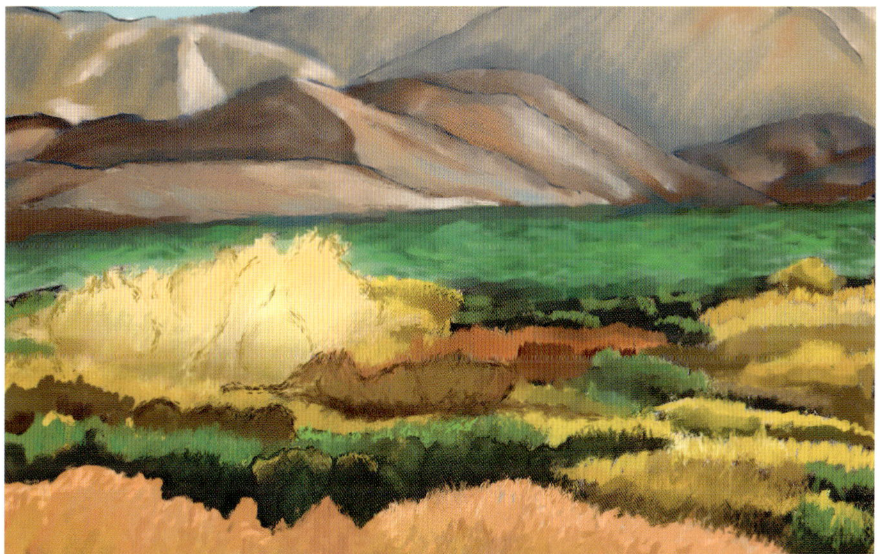

9 TONAL ADJUSTMENT

Last, adjust tones. Paint with the Square Chalk on a very low opacity to tint strokes.

Add yellow and orange to the mountains for color harmony.

Darken tones using the Digital Watercolor's New Simple Water on low opacity. Choose Layers: Dry Digital Watercolor when done.

Paint with the Photo's Dodge tool on the rear mountain to make it look further away and paint with the Burn tool on the foreground to make it look closer.

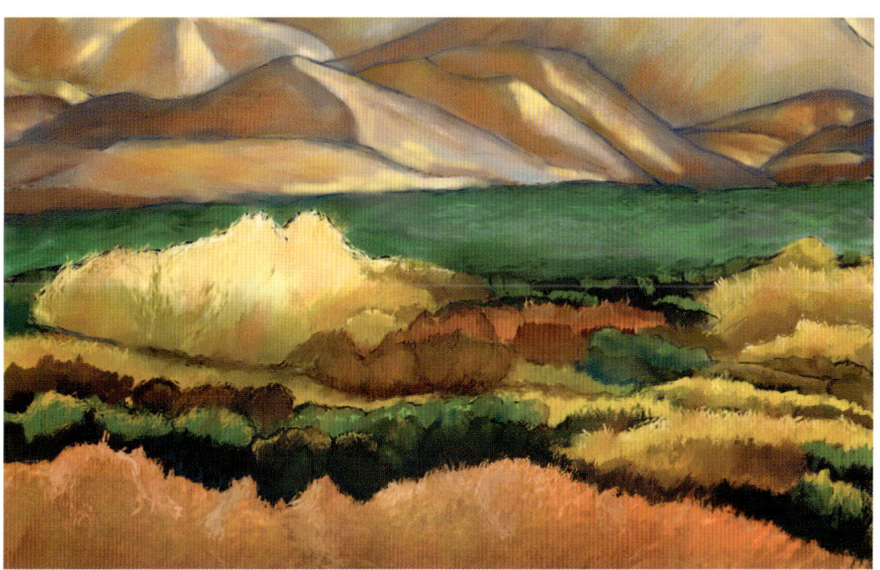

PHOTOREALISTIC PAINTING

Not surprisingly, many photographers want their paintings to look like their photos.

They like their photos, why can't the paintings look like them?

The reason is that usually the photograph doesn't have the qualities that go into a painting, namely a clear focal point and a chosen color scheme.

See pages 12-13 for information about color schemes and pages 14-15 for the lowdown on focal points.

Yet, it is possible to shoot a photo that lends itself to a painterly treatment.

Once in awhile, if you think about your imaginary folds and your tones, and if the colors happen to fall into a color scheme, you can take a photo that will lend itself to being turned into a painting with very little preparation.

The photo on this page is an example.

I took this photo in Palos Verdes, CA. The white roof, the paths and the horizon were the focal points, or areas of greatest contrast between light and dark.

I increased saturation and contrast slightly, and I was able to use the colors in the photo for my painting.

That's why I call this a photorealistic painting, because the painting is pretty much like the original photo, except with brush strokes.

The following pages show how I painted the painting.

With the photo open in Painter, choose File: Clone and File: Save As. Close the original—the clone is now the new source image.

Photorealistic Landscape
PAINTING AND PHOTO BY KAREN SPERLING.

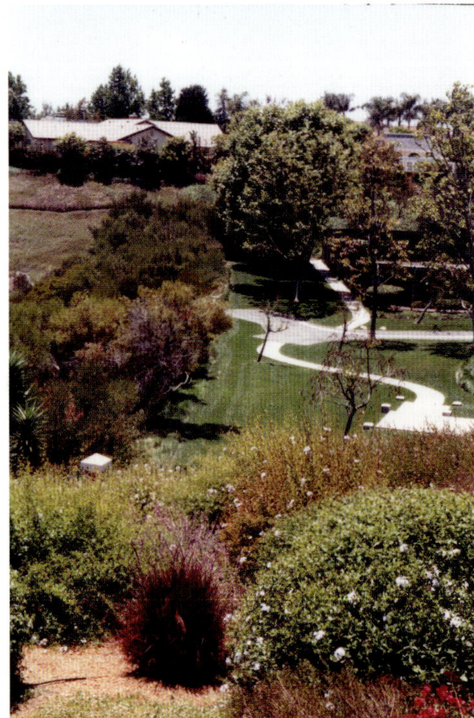

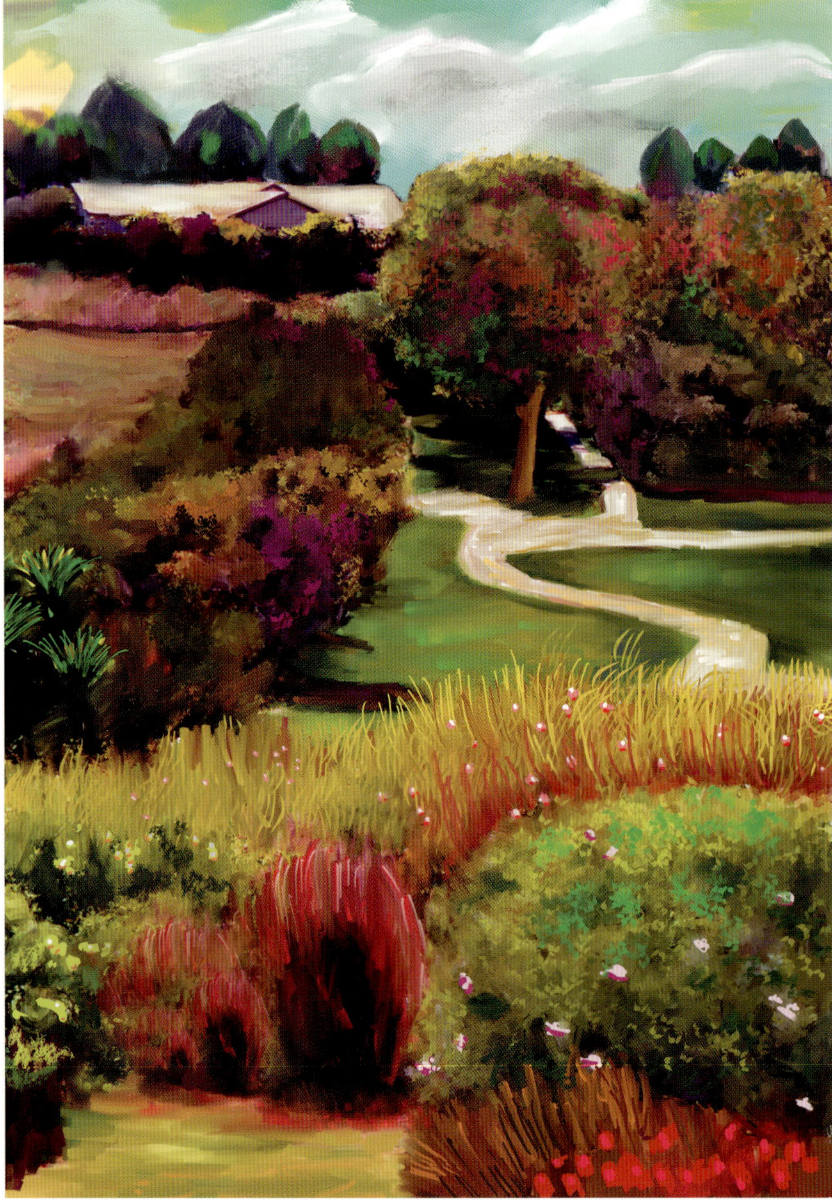

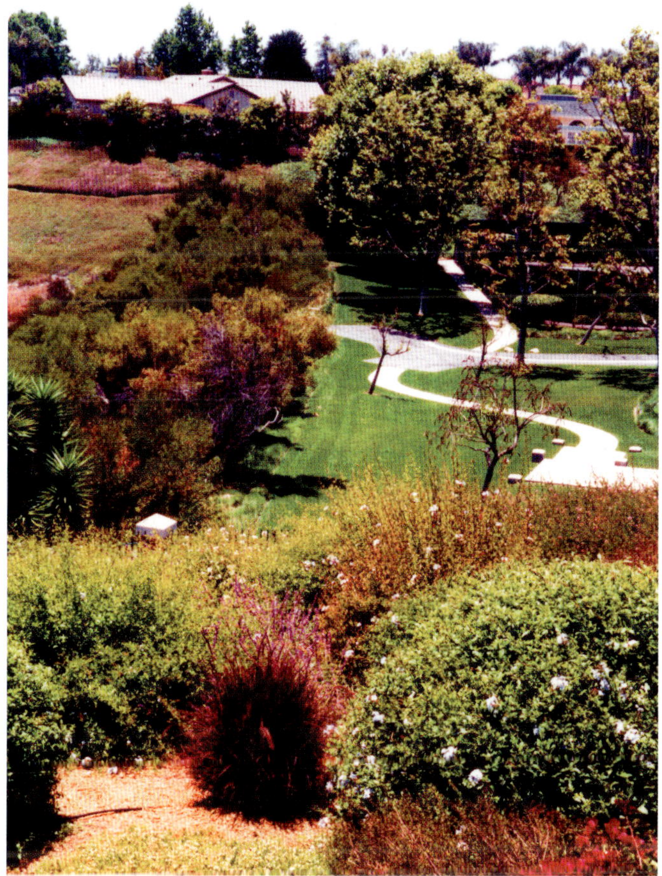

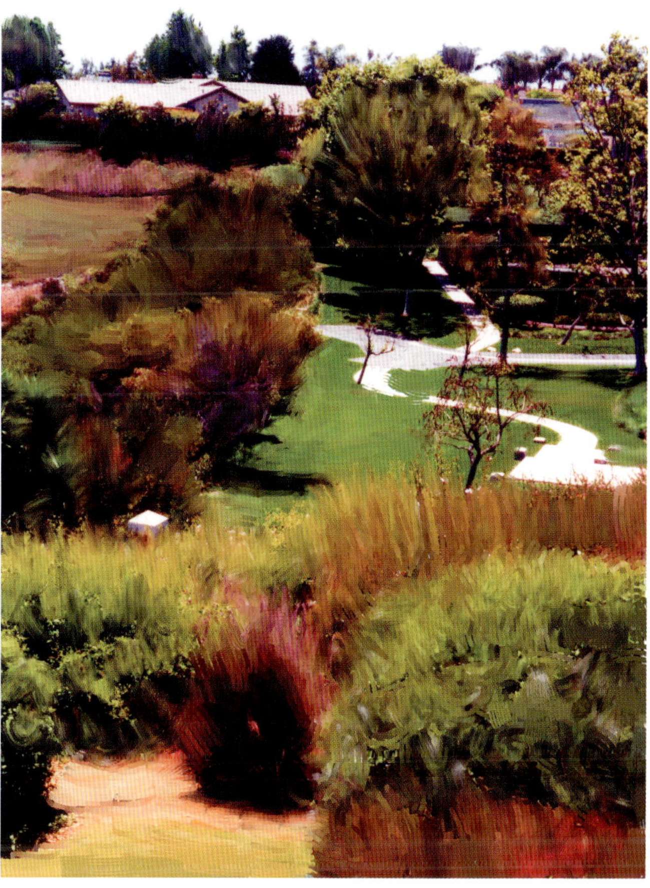

1 SATURATE

In Painter's Underpainting palette (found in the Window menu), choose Saturate in the Photo Enhance menu, click Apply, then choose Increase Contrast in the same menu and click Apply again.

The result is not only colorful, but also falls into an adjacent color scheme, starting with blue-violet and going clockwise to green. See pages 12-13 for information about choosing colors and about adjacent color schemes.

Save this version, then choose File: Clone and File: Save As.

The previous version is now the source image and this new clone is now the painting.

2 PAINT OUT DETAILS

One of the differences between a photo and a painting is that a painting has less detail.

Paint out details using the Blenders' Water Rake.

Choose the following settings in the Property Bar:

Opacity 26%
Grain 23%
Resat 24%
Bleed 49%

Click the rubber stamp in the Colors palette.

Using these settings means the strokes will have a little bit of color brought in from the source image and a little bit of texture.

Lower the Bristles slider to 7 in the Window menu: Brush Controls: Rake palette.

This creates a little space between the bristles so that bristles show up in the brush strokes.

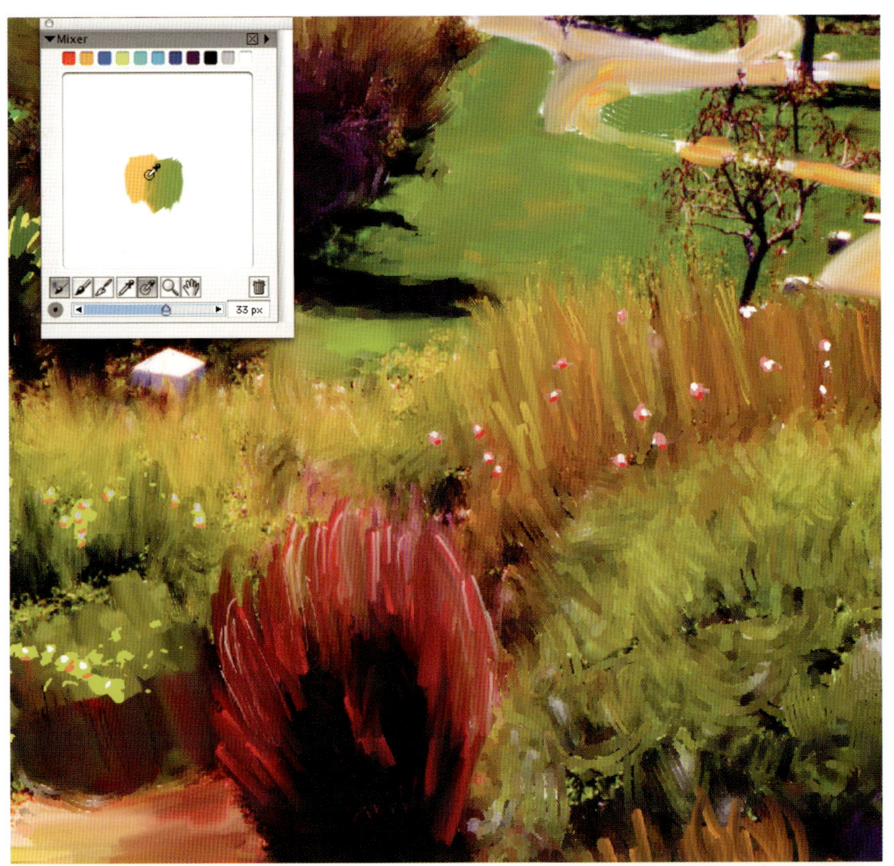

3 Bring Back Details

After painting out details, bring some back in a painterly way. Paint the yellow plant lines with the Pens' Scratchboard Tool on a low size setting. Press option, Mac; alt, Windows and click in the image to pick up colors and paint.

Also paint the little flowers with the Scratchboard Tool. Turn on Tracing Paper (see page 27) to see where the flowers are in the photo, then paint a midtone, like pink, then a lighter color like white, and then a darker tone of the middle color to add a little depth.

Paint the grass areas, paths and plants with the Artists' Oils' Dry Bristle and Blender Bristle. Get a few colors at once using the Mixer, found in Window: Color Palettes. Press option/alt and click in the image to pick up a color and with the brush icon selected in the Mixer, paint the color in the white space. Pick up another color and paint. With the tool with the circle, click at the intersection of the colors and paint in the image.

4 Custom Forms

Use custom brushes to add foliage and shrubbery and to add to the yellow stalks. See page 27 for information for customizing brushes in Painter.

Press option/alt and click to pick up colors from all over the image and paint them everywhere else. Repeating colors throughout an image creates color harmony.

Also, paint in the upper right-hand side of the image with the custom brushes. Compare the photo and painting on page 94, and you'll see what I mean.

The upper-right hand part of the photo wasn't recognizable. Since I decide to keep details based on whether they add to our knowledge of what we're looking at, I decided that what was in the photo could be eliminated. Foliage worked just as well, and was easy to paint with a custom brush.

Paint out the tree in the middle of the image by painting over it with the Artists' Oils because it is standing by itself, unrelated to anything else.

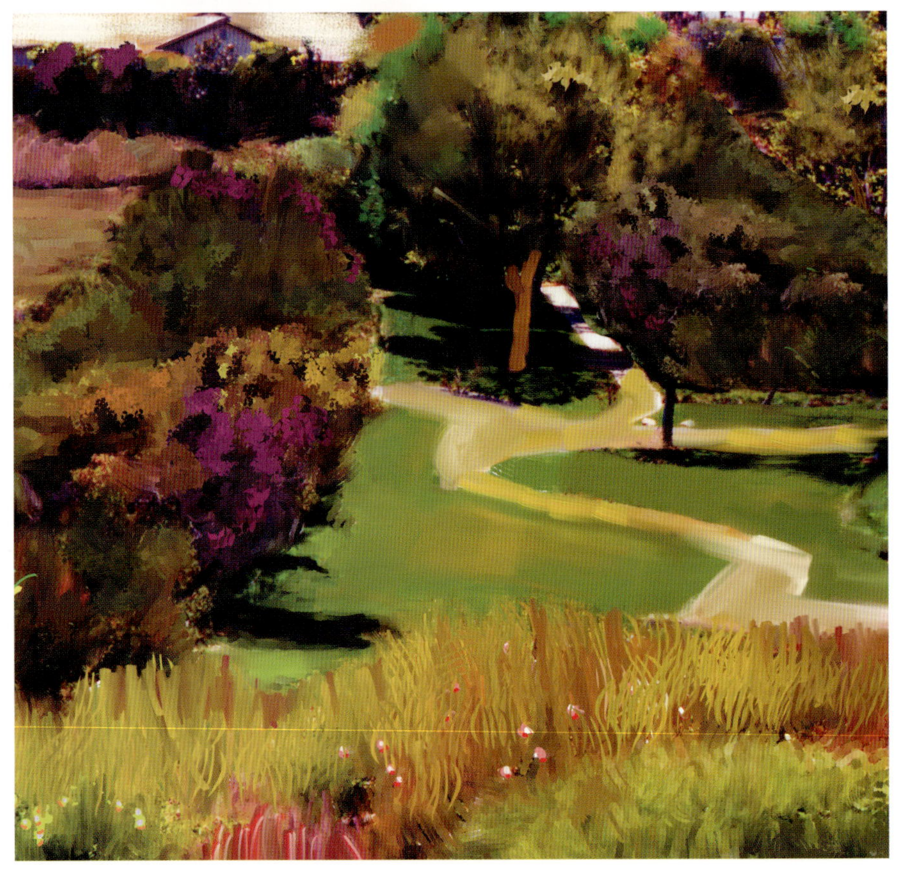

5 Painting in the Grass

Paint the paths and the grass areas some more with the Artists' Oils' Dry Bristle and Blender Bristle variants to build up colors, using the tones from the photo to guide you and colors from the color scheme.

Your images will look even more painterly if you have many tones and colors within areas like grass.

Use the Cloners' xScale 2P variant to paint a few extra red plants in front because having just the one plant looks out of place. It's such an interesting plant that, rather than delete it, repeat it.

See page 26 for instructions for using the Cloners' xScale 2P variant.

Add the green flowers on the left by painting with the Scratchboard Tool.

Press option/alt and click on a light green in the grass, turn on Tracing Paper and paint where you see the flowers in the photo. See page 27 for instructions for working with Tracing Paper.

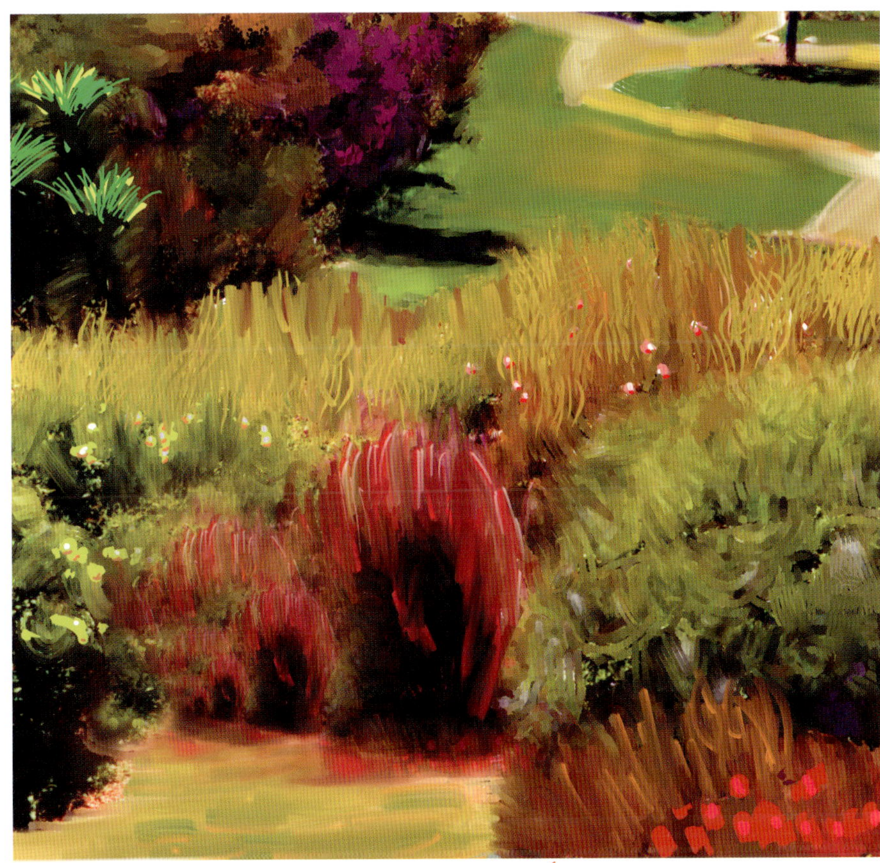

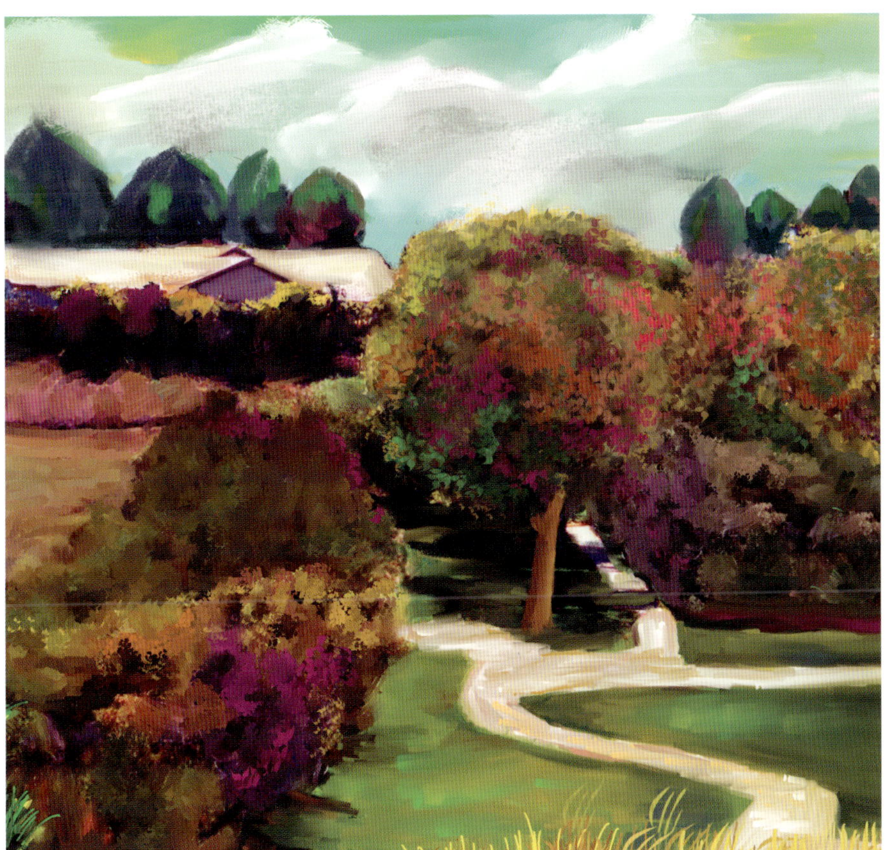

6 Trees a Crowd

Paint the sky by first adding color with the Artists' Oils' Dry Bristle and Blender Bristle variants.

Use green and yellow because they are part of the adjacent color scheme and adding them improves color harmony.

Add white for the clouds using the custom brush on a low size setting.

Add white in the paths and on the roof of the house using the Artists' Oils' Dry Bristle and Blender Bristle variants for color harmony and to make the house and paths the focal points.

Also add the trees in the back, which, contrasted with the light sky, create another focal point.

Last, choose the Acrylics' Captured Bristle variant, reduce opacity to 9%, click the rubber stamp in the Colors palette and paint on the trees and shrubs to blend the leaves a little.

AUTO-PAINTED LANDSCAPES

Auto-Painted Landscape
Photo and painting by Karen Sperling. Photo taken at Butterfly House, Topanga, CA.

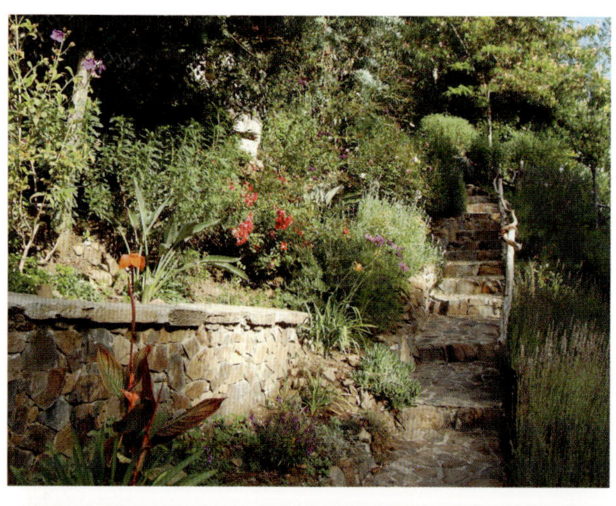

As you saw in the portraits section, Painter's Auto-Painting takes a little manual tweaking to create great effects.

I painted this painting with Auto-Painting using a photo I took in Topanga, CA, at Butterfly House, with some additional painting for details and tones.

I took this photo late in the day, so the sun created great areas of light and dark to paint in the painting.

Unfortunately, as you can see in the original photo, the sun didn't hit the steps in the best way to make them the focal point.

It was easy enough, though, to edit the tones in the final painting.

When painting from photos, using the art concepts to guide you helps!

To start, open a photo in Painter (File: Open) and clone it (File: Clone). Then save the clone (File: Save As).

The photo is the source image and the clone is the painting/destination image.

Use Tracing Paper while painting.

See pages 26-27 for information about source and destination images and using Painter's Tracing Paper.

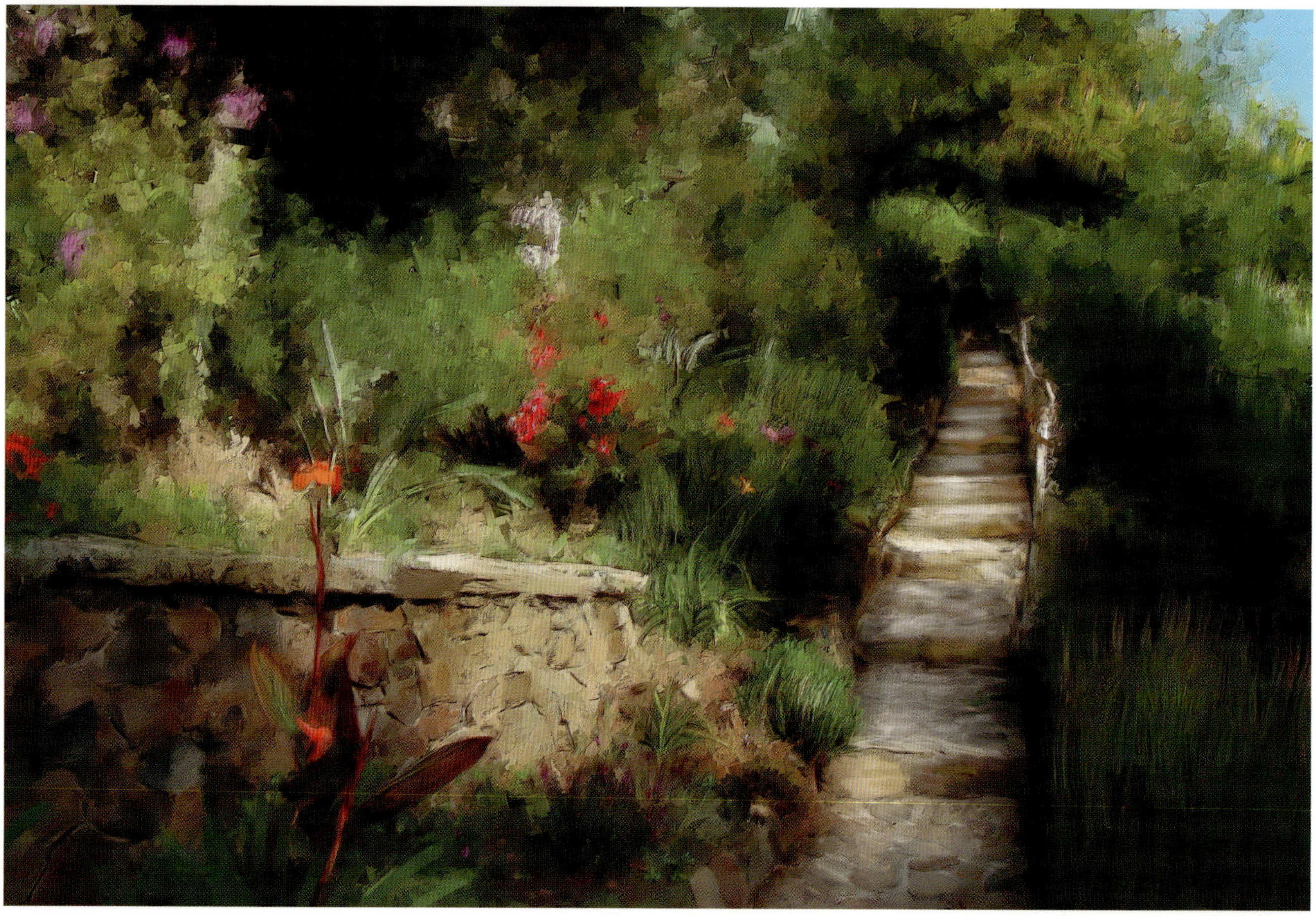

1 STROKE OF LUCK

First, create a custom brush stroke that you will use with the Auto-Painting tools.

1. Open the Auto-Painting palette (Window: Show Auto-Painting).
2. Choose the Artists' Sargent Brush.
3. Click the rubber stamp in the Colors palette, which tells Painter to use colors from the original photo.
4. To create a custom stroke, choose the triangle in the Brush Selector. In the drop down menu, choose Record Stroke.
5. Paint a short stroke like the one in the image at right.
6. Choose Save Stroke in the same menu and type in a name for the stroke in the dialog box that appears. Click OK.

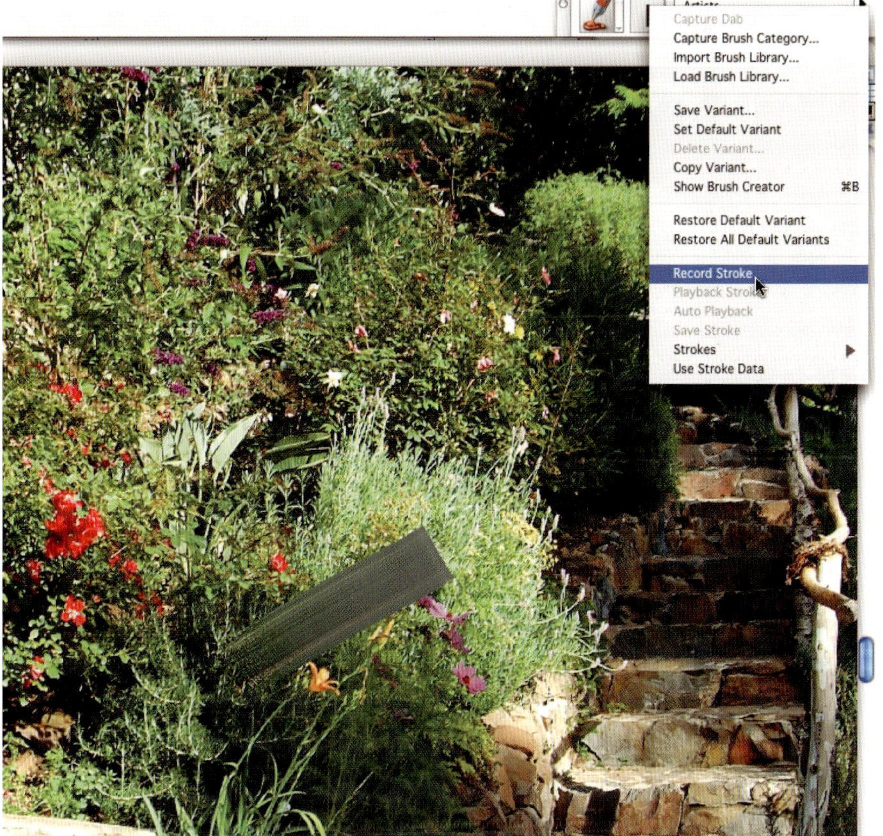

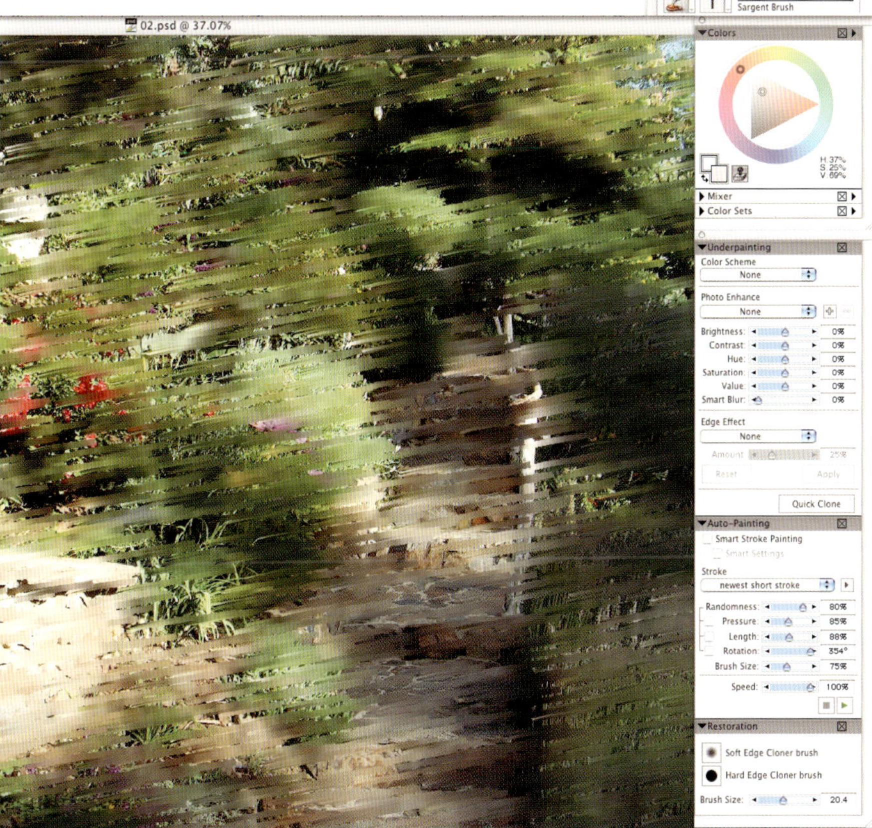

2 AUTOMATIC DEVICE

Next, you'll use this stroke with the Auto-Painting tools.

1. Choose this new stroke in the Stroke drop-down menu in the Auto-Painting palette.
2. In the Auto-Painting palette, deselect the check boxes underneath Randomness, and set the sliders as follows:
   Randomness: 80%
   Pressure: 85%
   Length: 88%
   Rotation: 354°
   Brush Size: 75%
3. Lower the speed slider a little and the strokes will come in more slowly.
4. Click the arrow in the Auto-Painting palette to run the strokes. Run until you have large areas of brush strokes like the ones in the image at left.
5. Click the red button in the Auto-Painting palette or anywhere in the image to stop the strokes.

3 A NEW DIRECTION

Now you'll apply some more strokes with Auto-Painting for a more painterly look.

Adjust the Rotation, Length and Brush Size sliders in the Auto-Painting palette. The settings don't matter, try all different ones to get your own results. Run Auto-Painting again, stop it, adjust the sliders, and run Auto-Painting some more. In this way you build up the brush strokes in a painterly way (see image at right).

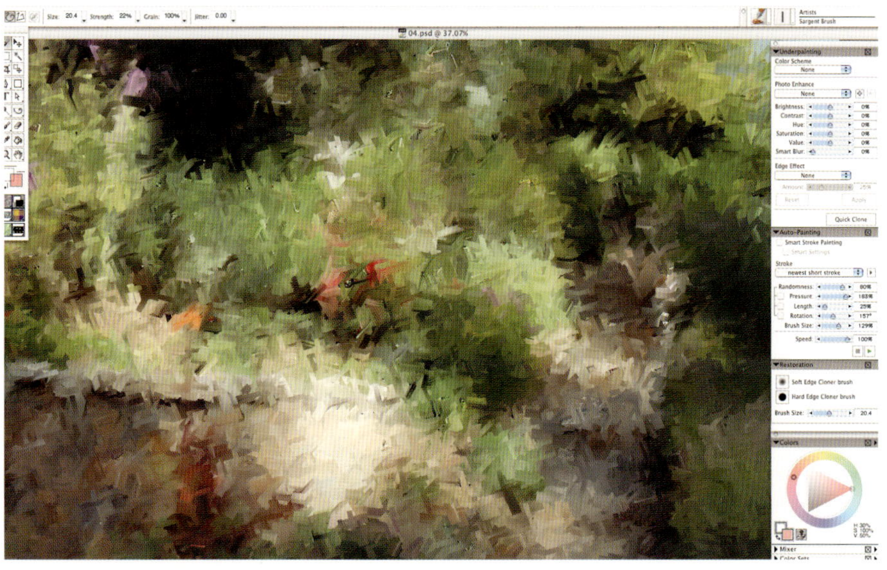

4 RANDOM ACCESS

Next, you'll make the strokes a little more random and less mechanical for a hand-painted look.

1. Choose the Scribble stroke in the Auto-Painting palette.
2. Check the Randomness boxes for all the parameters and run Scribble for awhile.
3. Stop the strokes, adjust the Brush Size slider in the Auto-Painting palette, then run Scribble again for just enough randomness.
4. Switch to the Artists' Impressionist variant, click the rubber stamp in the Colors palette and run Scribble some more, stop it, adjust the Brush Size slider in the Auto-Painting palette, then run it again. Do this several times.

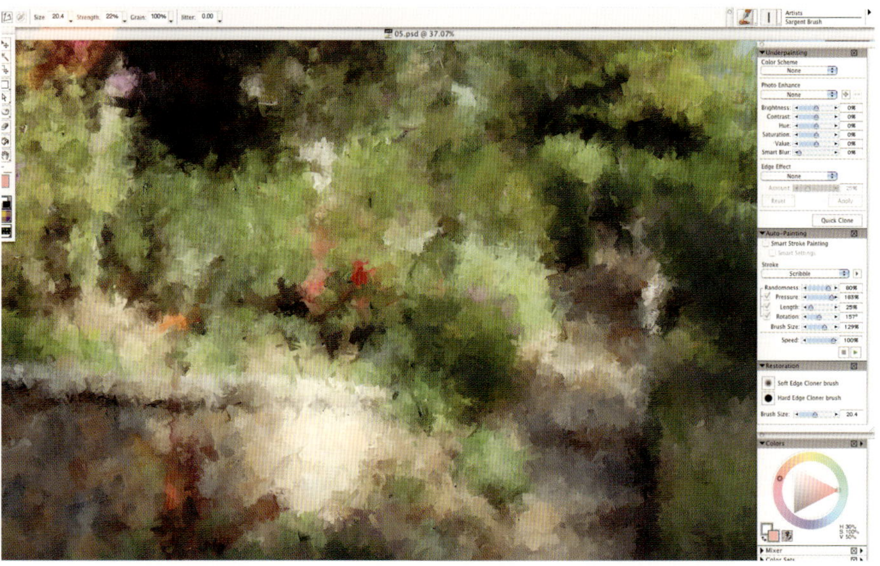

5 BRUSH UP

Next, turn on Tracing Paper and paint details with the Cloners' Smeary Bristle Cloner and the Chalk's Square Chalk with the rubber stamp clicked in the Colors palette.

Turn Tracing Paper off to see your progress, then turn it back on again to proceed.

Paint the edges to emphasize where dark tones meet light tones.

Blend some of the strokes with the Blenders' Smudge.

This is a back-and-forth process. You paint the color a little, blend a little, paint a little, blend a little, etc.

The art will look more painterly if you use a variety of brush strokes, like you see in traditional paintings.

View paintings in local museums and galleries, in books and online, for ideas for your own brush strokes.

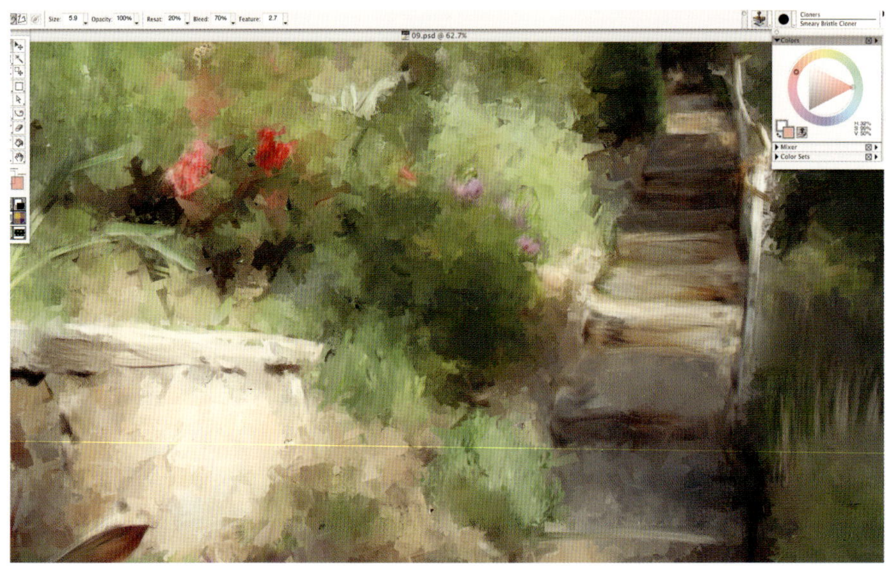

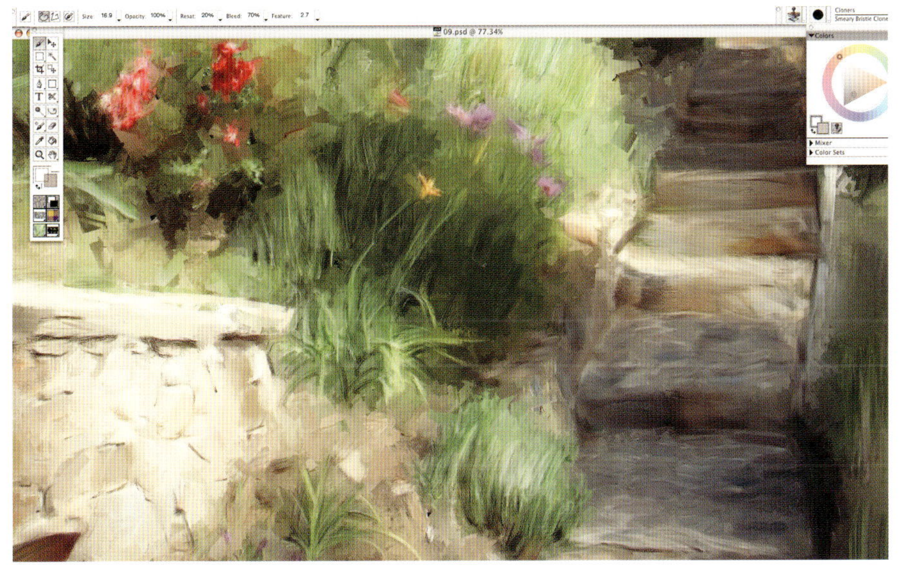

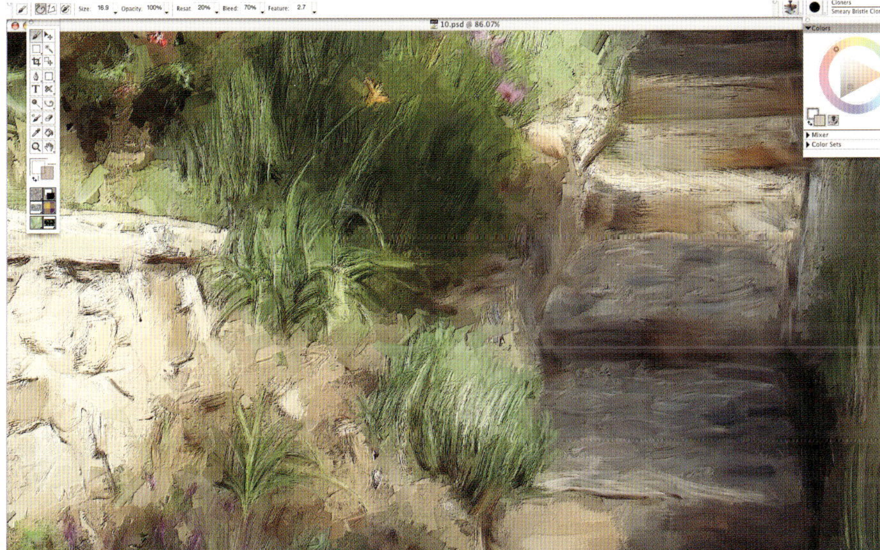

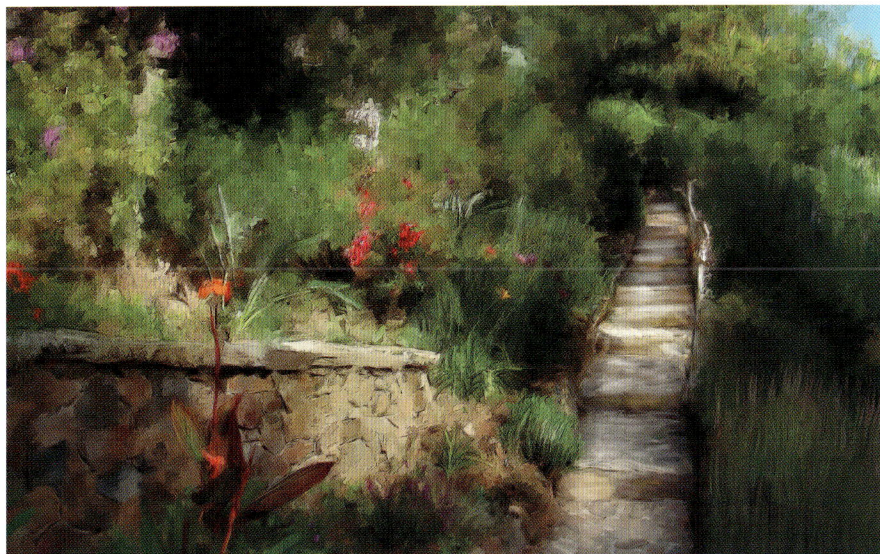

6 Attention to Detail

Paint some details in the foreground while leaving the background less detailed.

Though you might see details in the background in the photo, a traditional art concept is that you leave the background more vague to suggest distance.

Add details in the foreground like the dark lines around the stones by pressing option/alt and clicking on a dark color to pick it up and then painting with the Chalk's Sharp Chalk.

Blend a little with the Smudge. Lower opacity for more subtle blending strokes.

7 On the Surface

Add some texture using Effects: Surface Control: Apply Surface Texture. Choose Image Luminance in the Using menu.

Turn down the Amount and Shine sliders for a more subtle result, then click OK.

8 See the Light

In the final stage, paint with the Photo's Dodge on the steps and with the Photo's Burn on the grass next to the steps to make the steps the clear focal point, or subject, or area of greatest contrast between light and dark.

Also paint with the Digital Watercolors' New Simple Water variant on a low opacity setting on the grass and on the wall in the foreground to darken them a little.

After painting with Digital Watercolor variants, choose Layers menu: Dry Digital Watercolor so that you can paint on top of and blend the Digital Watercolor strokes using other brushes.

Add highlights on the steps by choosing white in the Colors palette and painting with the Oils' Fine Feathering Oils variant where you see highlights in the photo.

Paint with light pressure on the stylus for a more subtle result.

IMPRESSIONIST LANDSCAPES

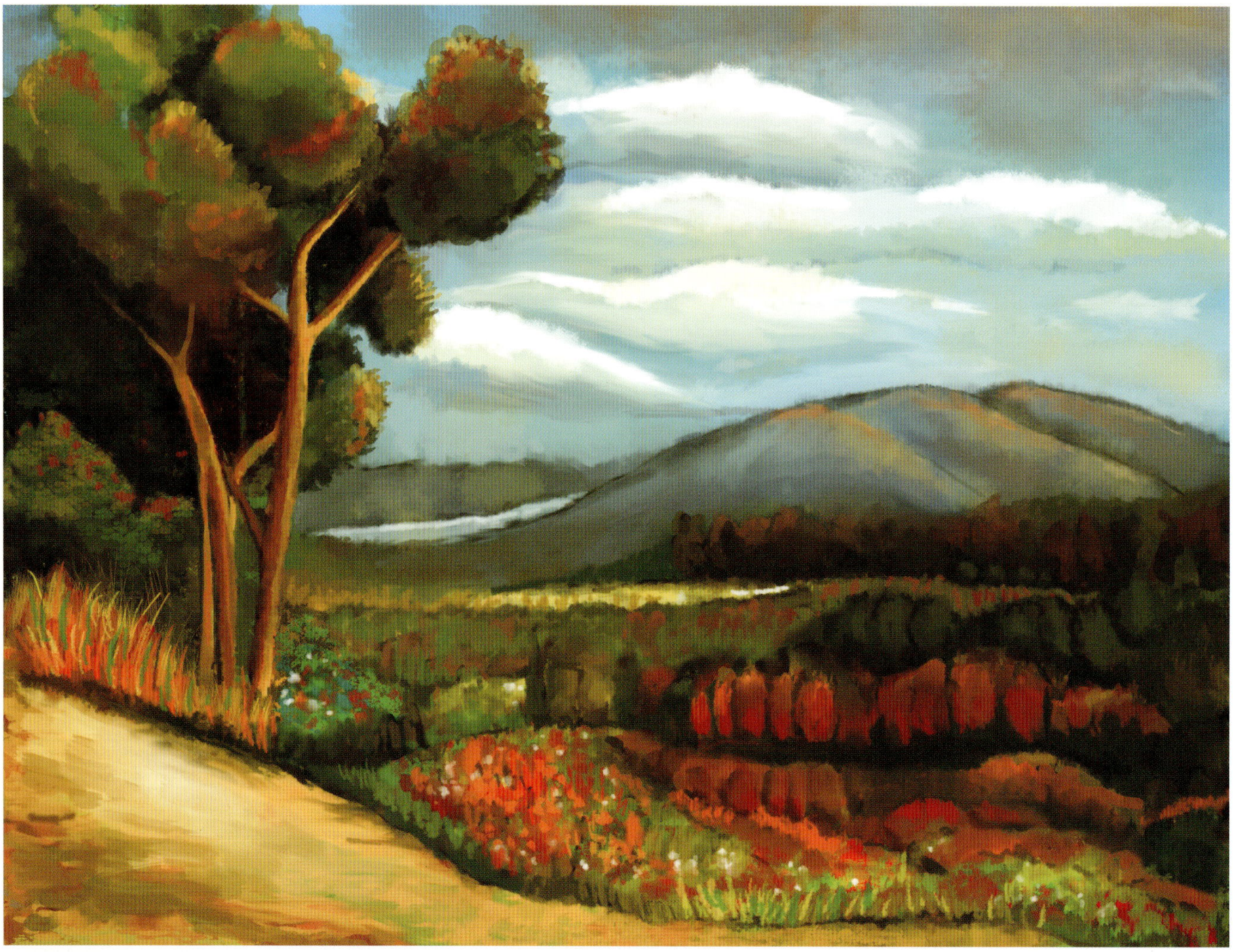

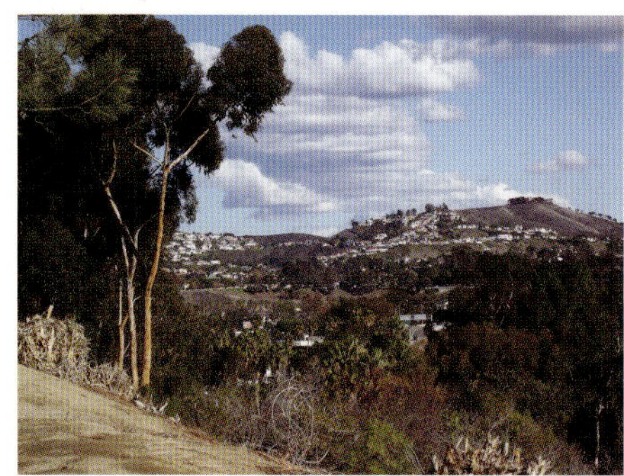

Impressionist Landscape
Photo and painting by Karen Sperling.

I took this photo in Dana Point, CA.

I thought it was a good candidate to be turned into a painting because when I turned the colors off in Painter using Effects: Tonal Control: Adjust Colors and moving the slider all the way to the left, the trees and the mountain were the focal points, or areas of greatest contrast between light and dark. And they fell approximately at the imaginary intersections of paper folded in thirds. See the art lessons starting on page 10 for more information about deciding if a photo is a good candidate to be turned into a painting.

Next, I gave the photo a color scheme in Painter by borrowing colors from Monet. See the steps on page 29.

I opened the color scheme image in Photoshop and chose Image: Duplicate and named the duplicate (File: Save As).

I resized the windows so that the two images were side by side, then I painted on one, using the other as reference.

I made several adjustments in Photoshop to make the painting go more smoothly, as you're about to see.

1 INTERFACE SETUP

When you choose a panel in the Window menu, it brings up a bunch of panels. I find it's easier to close the ones I'm not using.

1. Click and drag out the panel that you wish to close from the group.
2. Click the close button.

This leaves the panels you're using. Click on the panel's name, and it flies out for you to adjust. When done, click the double arrows and the panel gets tucked away again.

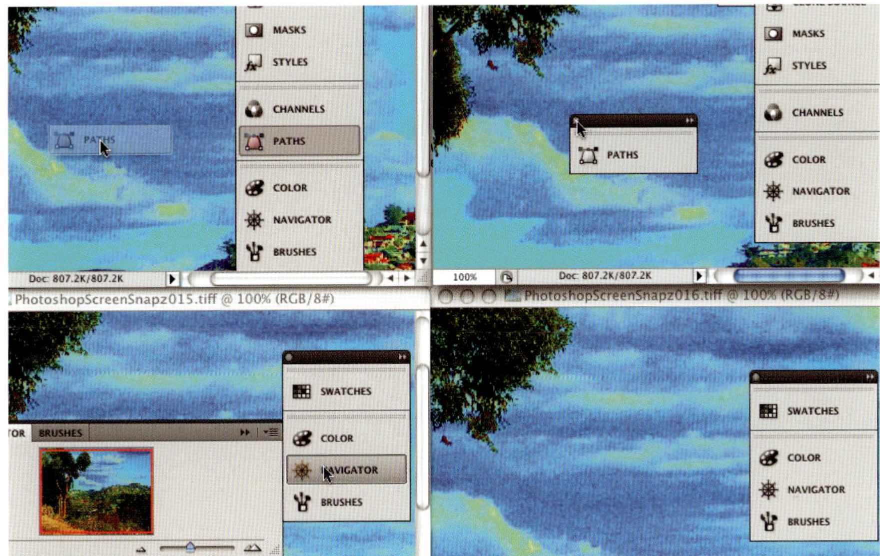

2 BRUSH PRESETS

Click the Brushes panel (A.) and you see the controls for editing presets. Click the little triangle (B.) and choose Text Only in the drop-down menu to see names of presets. Click the choices under Brush Presets to reveal settings on the right-hand side.

I edited Shape Dynamics and Scattering to create my landscape.

Each brush stroke is made up of a bunch of individual dabs, therefore Size, Angle and Roundness in Shape Dynamics refer to the shape of individual dabs. Jitter means randomness, so the more you move the sliders to the right, the more random the dabs are when you paint. Choose Pen Pressure in the Control pop-ups for stylus pressure to affect the results. Minimum Diameter controls stroke width. Move the slider to the left, and pressing lightly on the stylus gives you a narrow stroke and pressing heavily gives you a wide one. The more you move the slider to the right, the wider the stroke is when you press lightly.

Scatter in Scattering controls the space between brush dabs, count determines the number of dabs.

Click the locks to keep the changes after you change presets.

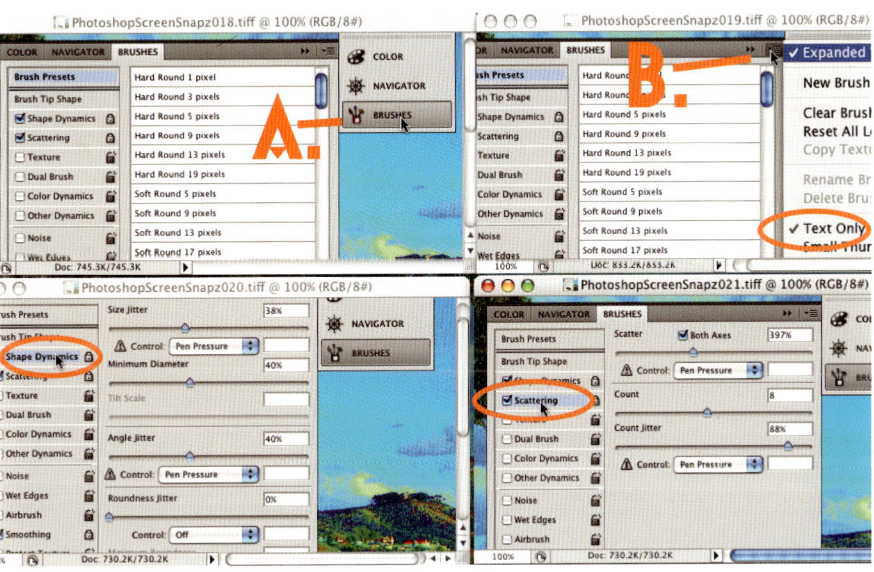

3 BRUSH SIZE SHORTCUT

I find that using the shortcut keys to resize the brush is the quickest way to get a lot of different-sized brush strokes. Press control+option, Mac; right click+alt, Windows, click and drag. You see a circle that represents the stroke width. Adjust by dragging, then let go and paint.

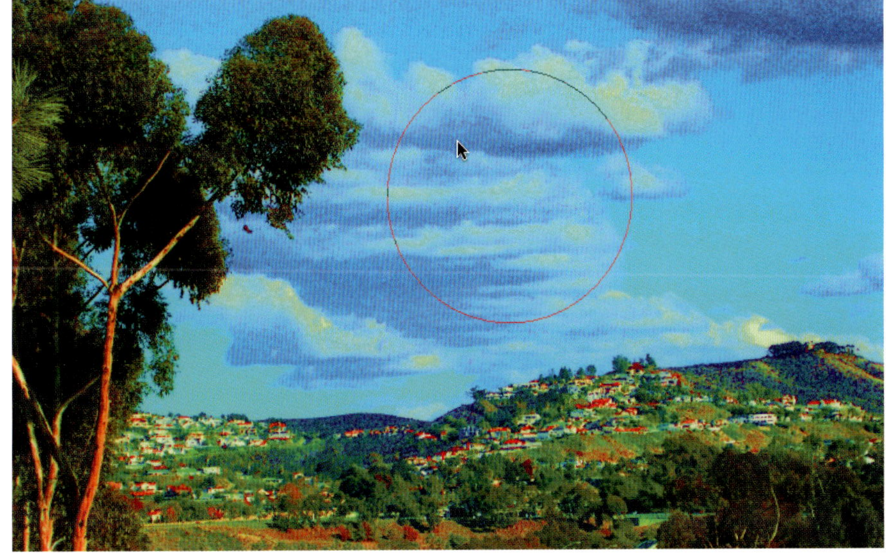

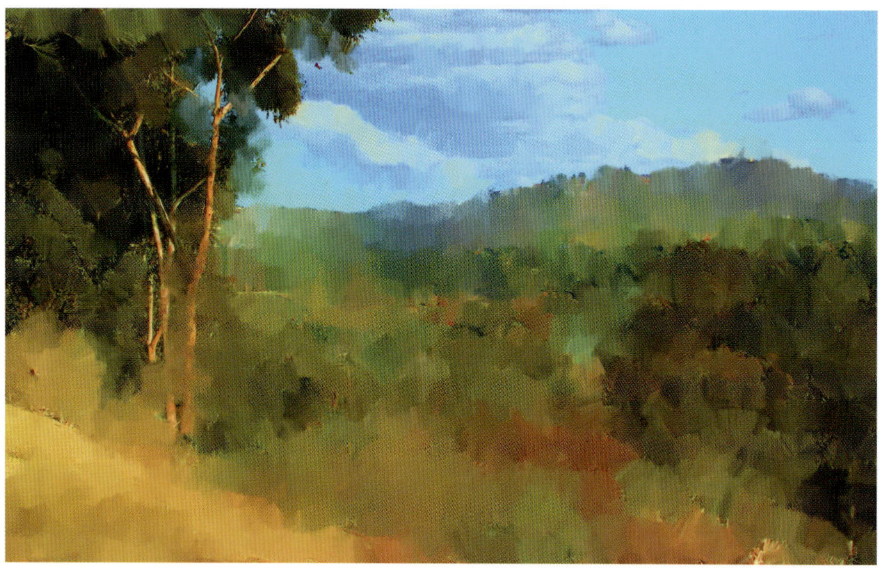

4 ON A BLENDER

After I set up my panels for easy access, it was time to paint. I wanted the painting to look like the photo, but in a colorful, impressionistic way.

I created the painting by adding colors from my color scheme based on where I saw lights and darks in the photo.

Start by blending out details to create patterns of light and dark based on where you see them in the photo using the Smudge tool with the Charcoal Large Smear preset chosen. Move up all the sliders in Shape Dynamics and Scattering with Pen Pressure chosen in the Control pop-up menus and with Smoothing checked.

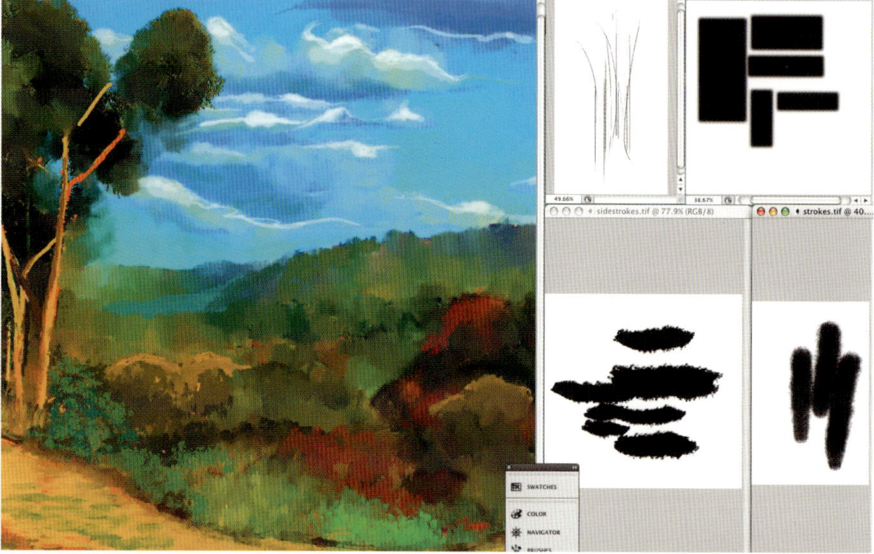

5 CUSTOM-BUILT

I created several custom presets from the silhouettes you see at left—page 35 has the steps. I used them with both the Brush tool and the Smudge tool with the Shape Dynamics and Scattering sliders in various positions. I set up a shortcut key for the Smudge. Here's how:

1. Choose Edit: Keyboard Shortcuts. The Keyboard Shortcuts and Menus dialog box appears.
2. Choose Tools in the Shortcuts For pop-up menu. Scroll down and click Smudge Tool. Type Y.
3. Click OK. Now you can type B to access the Brush tool and Y to access the Smudge tool.

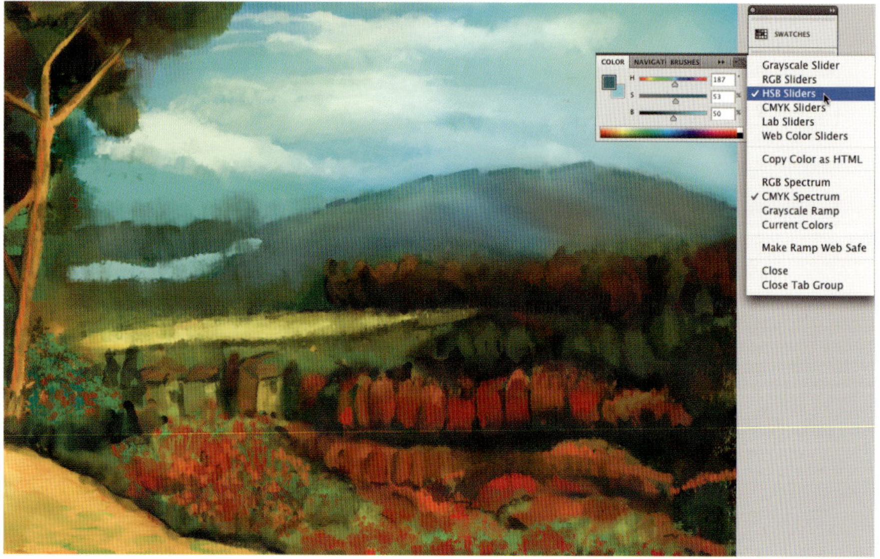

6 EYE ON HUE

I found another way to speed things up was to choose HSB (Hue, Saturation and Brightness) Sliders in the Color panel.

Press option, Mac; alt, Windows and click on a color in the image, then choose a lighter or darker version using the HSB sliders.

Keep painting with the Brush tool, choosing various custom presets, adjusting the sliders in Shape Dynamics and Scattering. Paint where you see lights and darks in the source image open in another window next to the painting.

The three images on this page show my progress as I painted more tones.

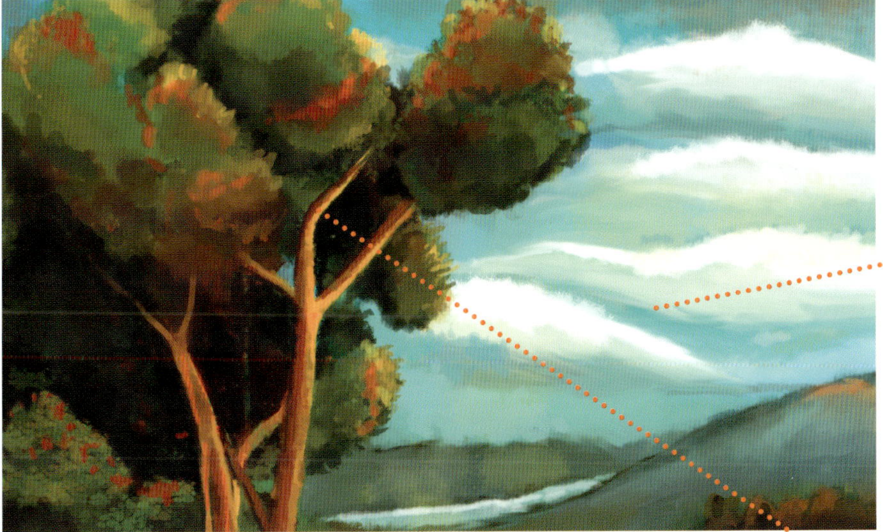

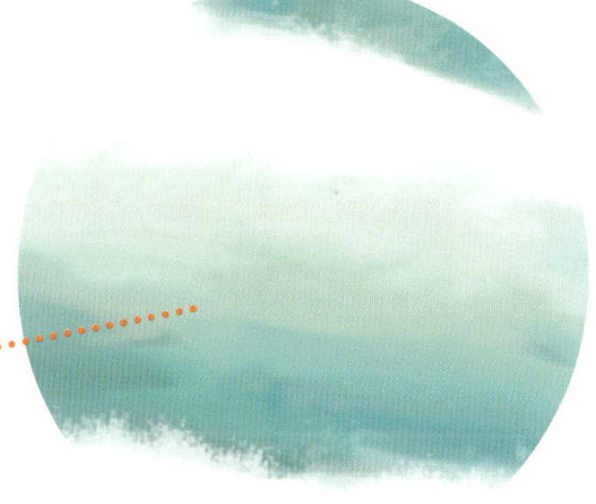

BRISTLE WHILE YOU WORK
For bristly strokes, use a custom side strokes preset (opposite page) with the Smudge tool.

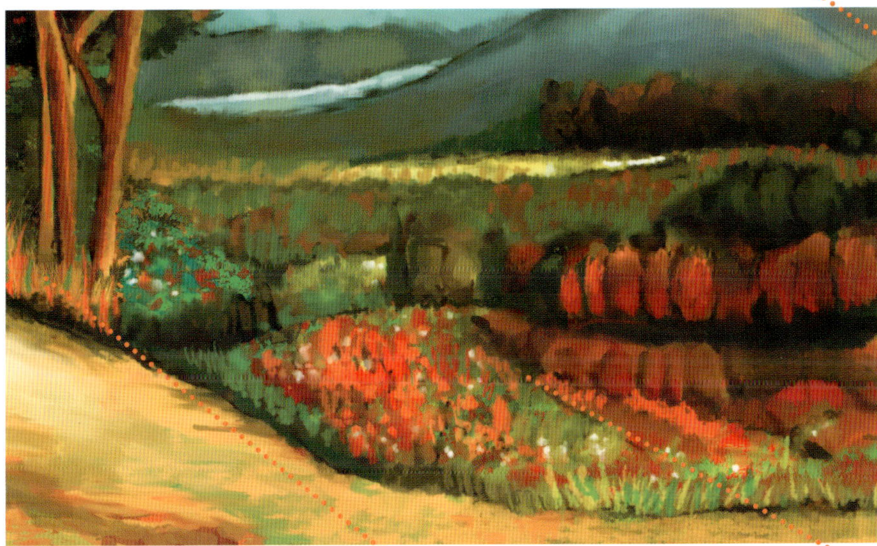

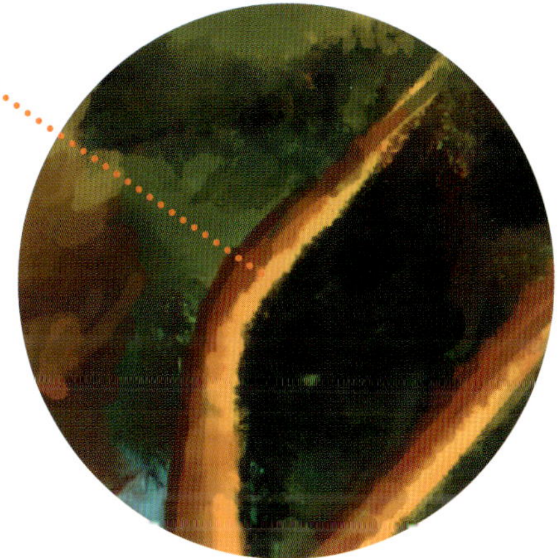

HARD-EDGED
Add edges with the Brush tool and a Hard Round on 50% opacity; build color gradually.

7 FINAL STEPS

Paint the clouds with the Brush tool and a Spatter preset with high Shape Dynamics and Scattering sliders settings and opacity on 70%. You paint a dark stroke at the bottom, then paint a lighter stroke overlapping that and then a white stroke at the top. That's how to paint the different tones for the mountains, too. Add tones based on where they are in the photo. Add yellow and red on 10% opacity in the sky to create color harmony, where colors repeat throughout the painting. Also add a darker tone of the sky's blue-green in the mountains and in the shrubbery. Use the Dodge to lighten up the sky to increase contrast with the mountains and the trees.

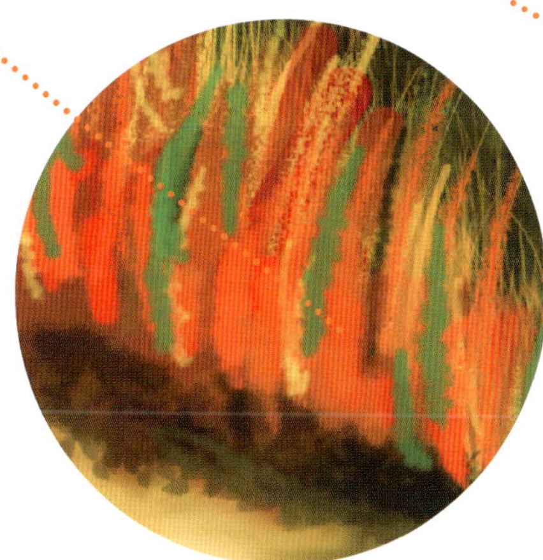

PAINTIN' IN THE GRASS
Paint the grass with the Brush tool, using both a custom preset—I used the top, left silhouette on the opposite page—and a Hard Round preset. Paint the bottom of the grass strokes with the Smudge tool to connect them.

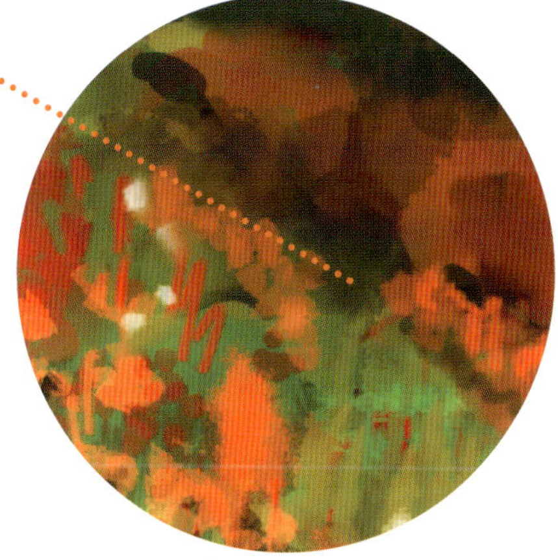

DARK SHADOWS
Paint deep green everywhere you see dark tones in the photo using the Brush tool and a Spatter preset on high Shape Dynamics and Scattering settings. With the Scatter slider all the way to the right, paint with white to suggest flowers for color harmony with the white in the sky.

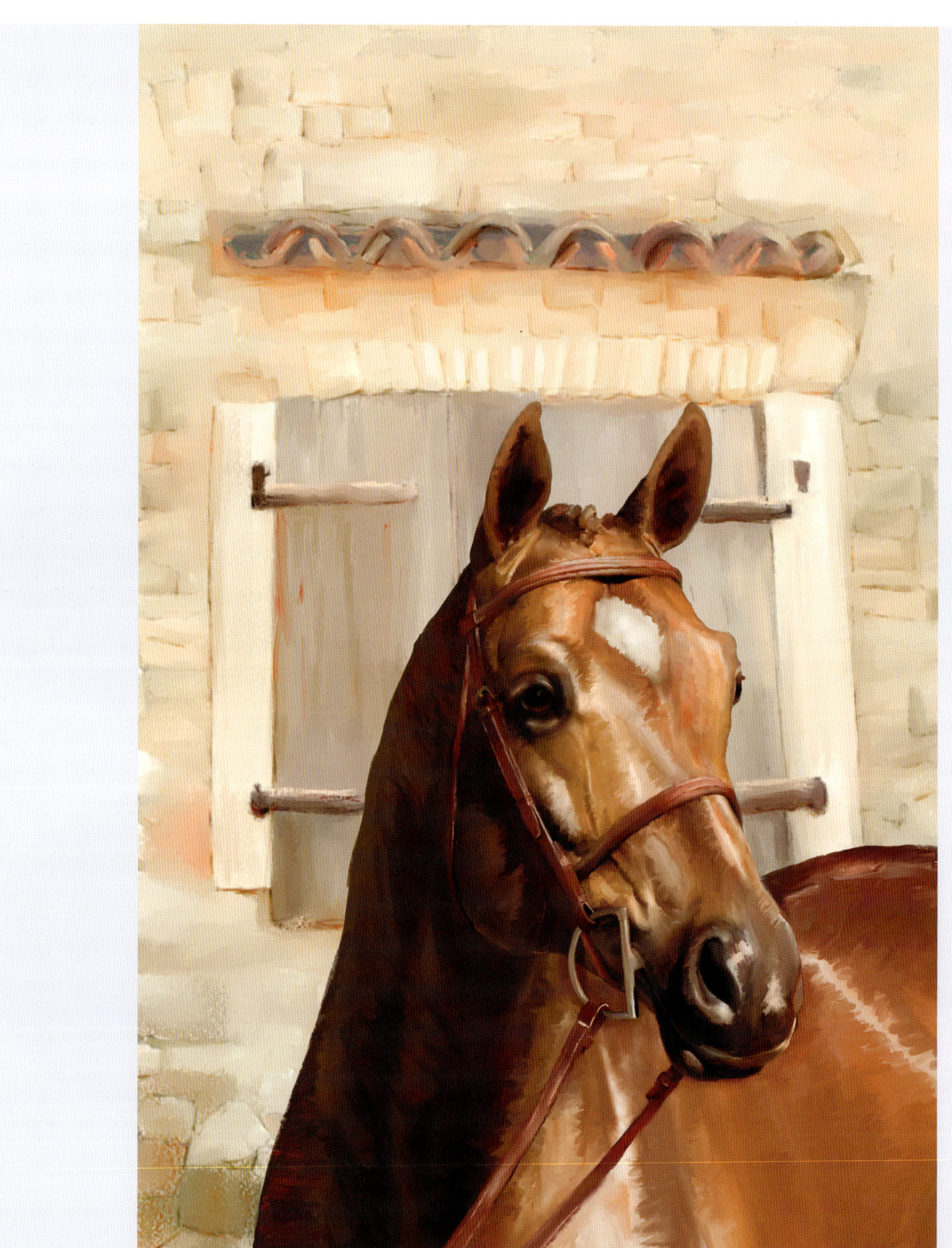

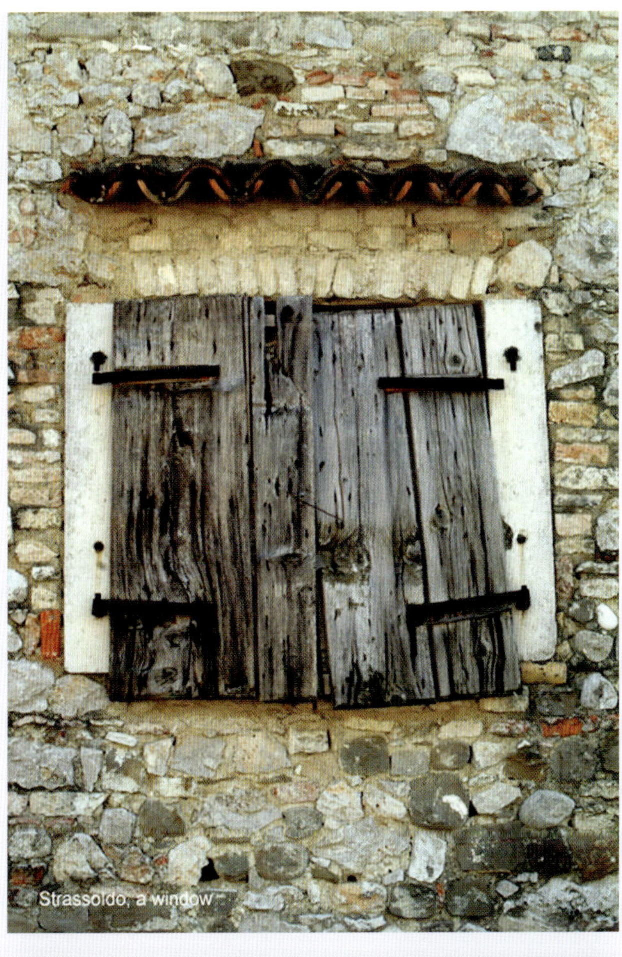

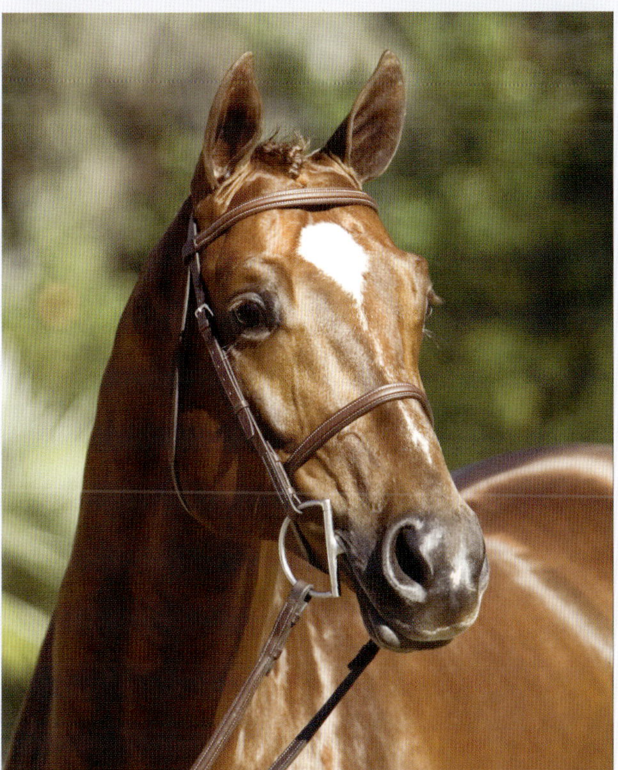

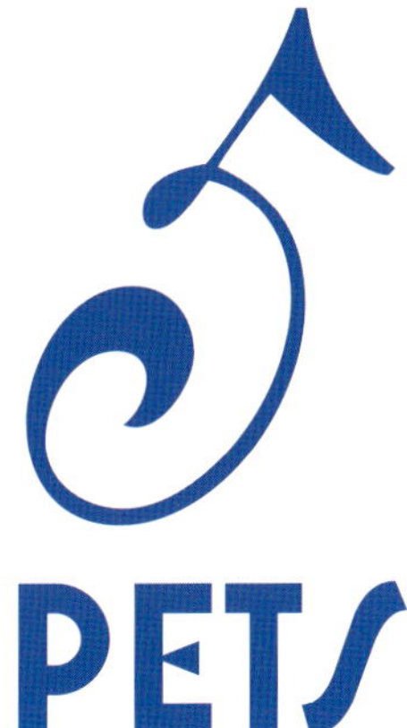

PETS

Perhaps I should have included the following paintings in the portraits chapter. After all, pets are people to those who love them.

If you've read through the book so far, it will come as no surprise that you'll use the same art concepts and Corel Painter and Adobe Photoshop tools to paint pets as you used to paint people and landscapes.

That's because, as you now know, when you paint, you're painting highlights, midtones and shadows, not objects.

In this section you'll find steps for painting dogs, cats and horses.

Horse portrait

Painting (opposite page) by Karen Sperling from photos by Renata Spiazzi (this page, top) and Susan Sexton (this page, bottom), featured in the November 2006 issue of Artistry Tips and Tricks http://www.artistrymag.com/.

PAINTING DOGS

Ellen Roije-Pauwels sent me this photo of her dog, Celine, who passed away last summer. "I hope you can do a tutorial for painting pets with long hair in oils," she said. And here's my painting of Celine.

I started the portrait by checking the tones in the source photo in Painter.

To do so, choose Effects: Tonal Control: Adjust Colors and move the Saturation slider all the way to the left.

With the colors turned off, the dog was lighter than the background, making the dog the clear subject or focal point, or area of greatest contrast between light and dark. I decided to keep the dog lighter than the background to emphasize that contrast in the painting.

Choose Edit: Undo (command+z, Mac; ctrl+z, Windows) to get the colors back again.

Next, I thought about colors.

I looked at the color wheel on page 12 and looked at the colors in the photo to see if they fit into a color scheme.

It turned out the dog had a red-orange tone and the background had a blue-green cast. These colors are complements, or opposites on the color wheel, and therefore good choices for a color scheme, and I decided I would emphasize them in the painting.

Once you decide on how you will paint the tones and colors, you're ready to paint.

With the photo open in Painter, choose File: Clone and name the clone (File: Save As).

I started by creating the background, then I painted the dog into the background.

This portrait is a good example of painting areas of light and dark and just suggesting details, as you'll see.

Dog Portrait

Painting by Karen Sperling from a photo by Ellen Roije-Pauwels.

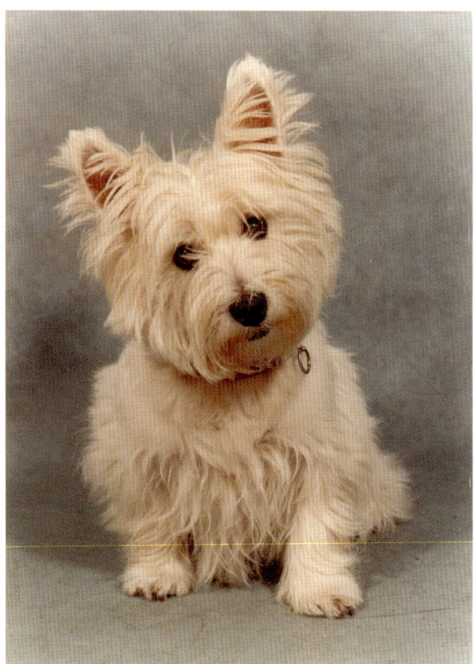

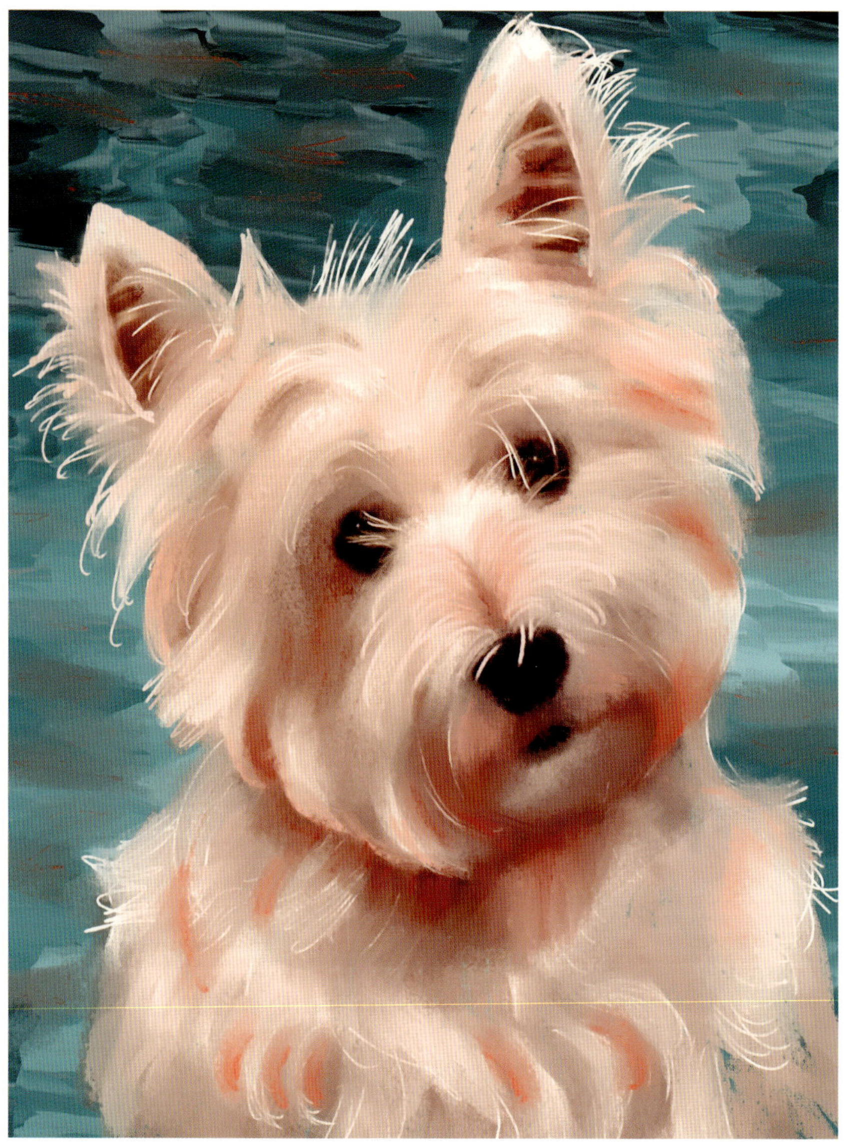

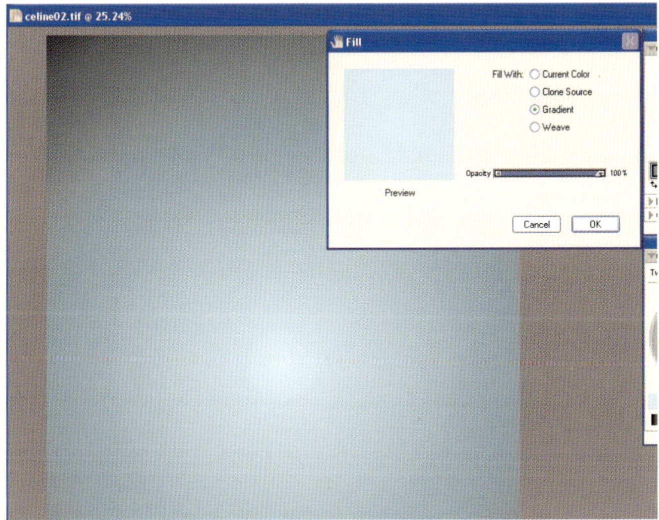

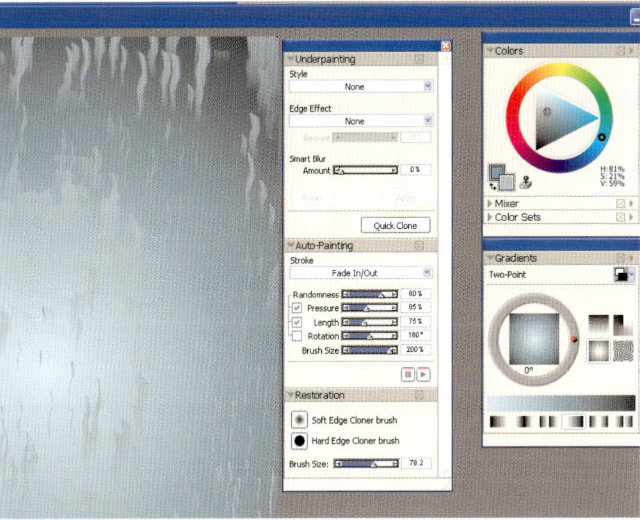

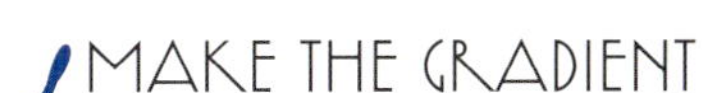

1 MAKE THE GRADIENT

For the background, start by creating a gradient. See page 29 for instructions for creating gradients in Painter.

You can see in the image (above, right) how I set up the colors to get the resulting gradient.

Click the round icon in the Gradients palette to make the fill circular.

To fill the image with the gradient, choose Effects: Fill, click next to Gradient and click OK (above image).

2 BRUSH HOUR

Add some painterly strokes using the Artists' Sargent Brush and the Auto-Painting palette. See page 25 for instructions for using Auto-Painting.

Choose Fade In/Out in the Stroke pop-up menu.

Deselect Rotation under Randomness so that the brush strokes go in one direction. Choose a light blue-green and run this stroke for a little while, till you have some strokes. You see the results in the above image.

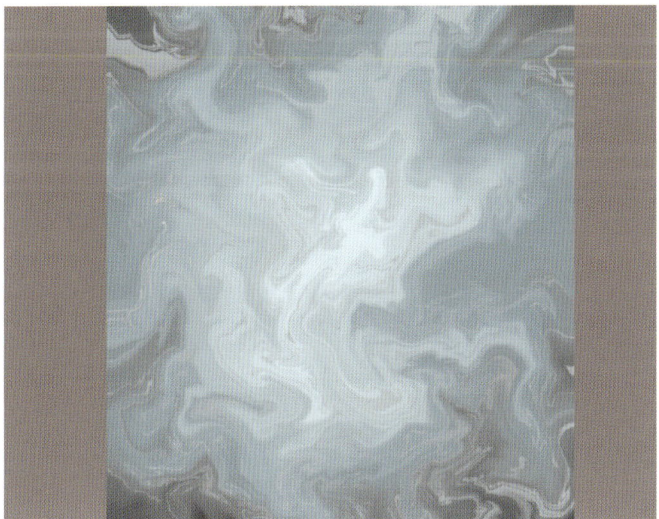

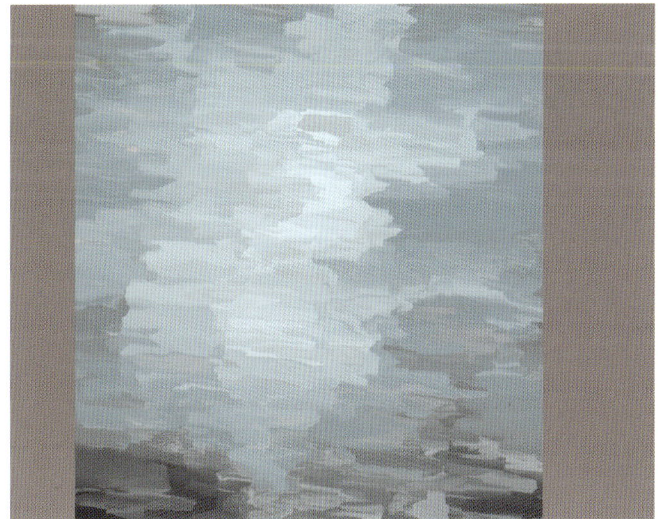

3 STORMY BRUSH STROKES

Make the image more painterly using some Distortion variants with Auto-Painting.

First run Auto-Painting with the Hurricane variant selected and then use Auto-Painting with the Turbulence variant. Alternate between the two brushes, running the strokes, stopping them, changing brushes, running them again. Raise the Size slider in the Property Bar very high for both brushes.

4 FEELING SQUEEGEE-ISH

Make the strokes a little flatter and a little more like traditional brush strokes by running Auto-Painting with the F-X's Squeegee variant chosen.

Choose File: Save to save this version of the background. Then choose File: Save As and create a copy of the background. This way, you have the first version of the background if you need it later. This copy is now the painting and you should still have the source photo open.

5 BRING IN THE DOG

Turn on Tracing Paper—see page 27 for information about using Tracing Paper.

Choose the Chalk's Square Chalk variant. Click the rubber stamp in the Colors palette to pick up colors from the photo. Choose a medium setting in the Property Bar's Size slider and paint to bring in the dog.

The image at right shows my setup as I painted. I had the photo next to the painting (far right) and I had Tracing Paper turned on as I painted (near right).

The secret to painting hair is to paint broad areas of light and dark and to just suggest the strands. Paint strokes in the direction that the dog hair flows, but instead of thinking of it as bringing in strands of hair, paint to bring in areas of light and dark.

At this point you're creating the dog's general shape by painting tones.

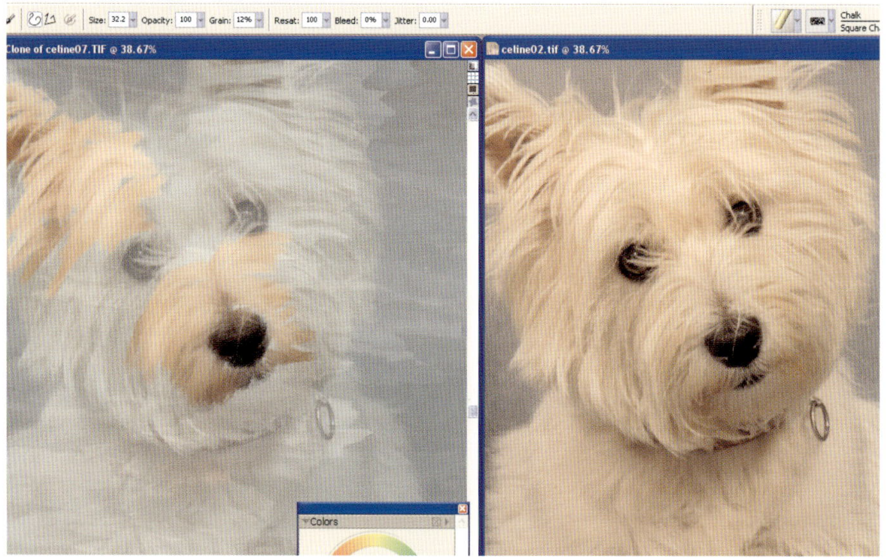

6 DEFINE THE DOG

After you bring in the dog, create definition between light and dark areas by painting with the Blenders' Smudge variant. Leave some of the background color showing in the dog to create color harmony, where colors repeat in the foreground and in the background.

Turn Tracing Paper on and off to see your progress.

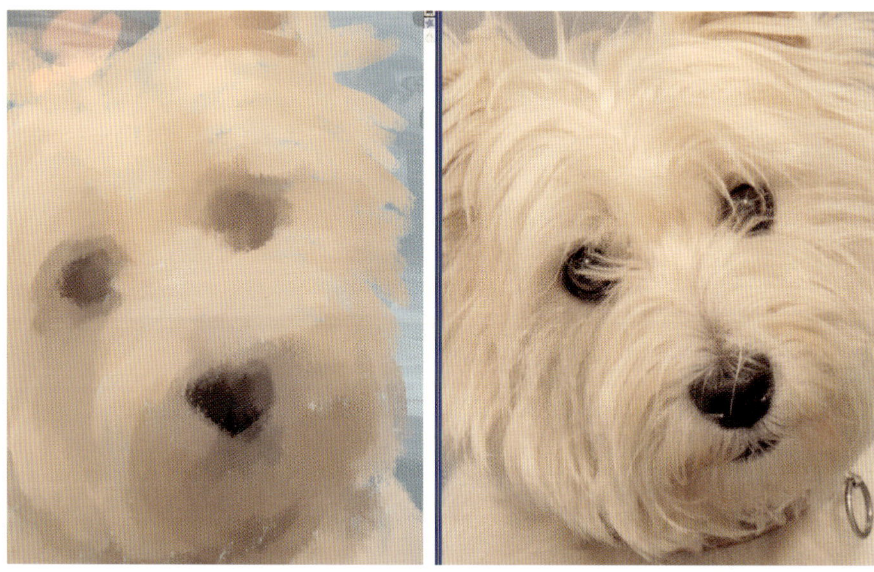

7 MORE DEFINITION

Once you have the basic areas of light and dark, once again choose the Chalk's Square Chalk variant, deselect the rubber stamp in the Colors palette, and paint, emphasizing the areas of light and dark based on where you see them in the photo. Press option, Mac; alt, Windows, click on a color in the image, then choose a lighter or darker version of it in the Colors palette and paint in the image.

You see my progress at right.

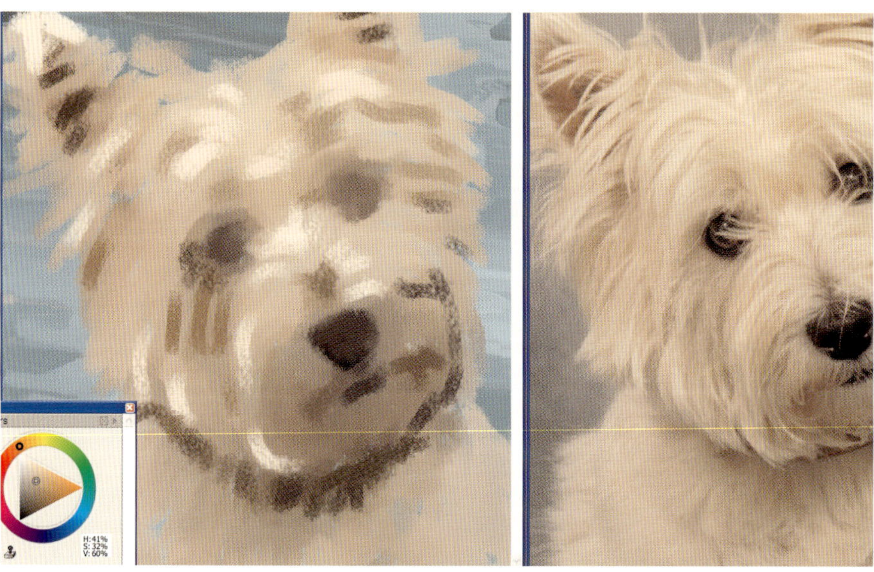

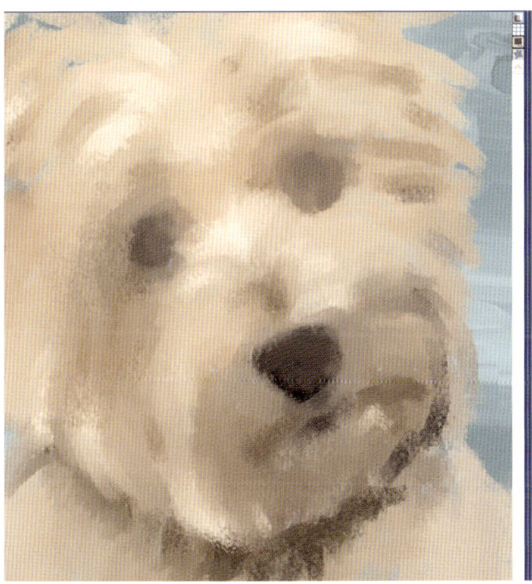
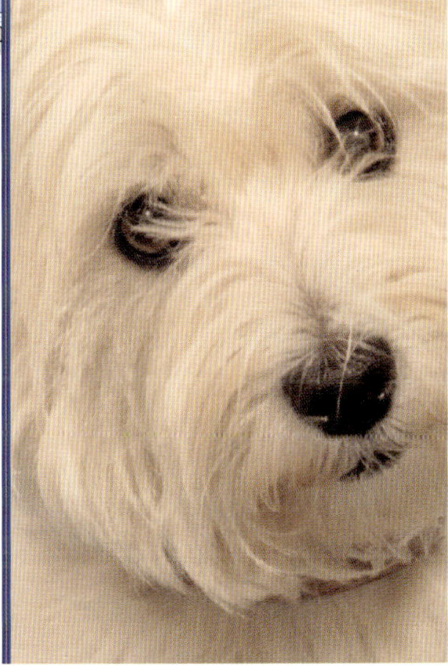

8 Still More Definition

Next, turn the Square Chalk into a blender and blend the areas that you just painted. See the instructions on page 24 for turning brushes into blenders and for saving them as variants.

Using the photo as your guide, blend next to where light areas and dark areas touch, and keep edges between these tones distinct.

Switch back to the original Square Chalk and paint in additional color, then choose the blender version of the Square Chalk that you just created and blend.

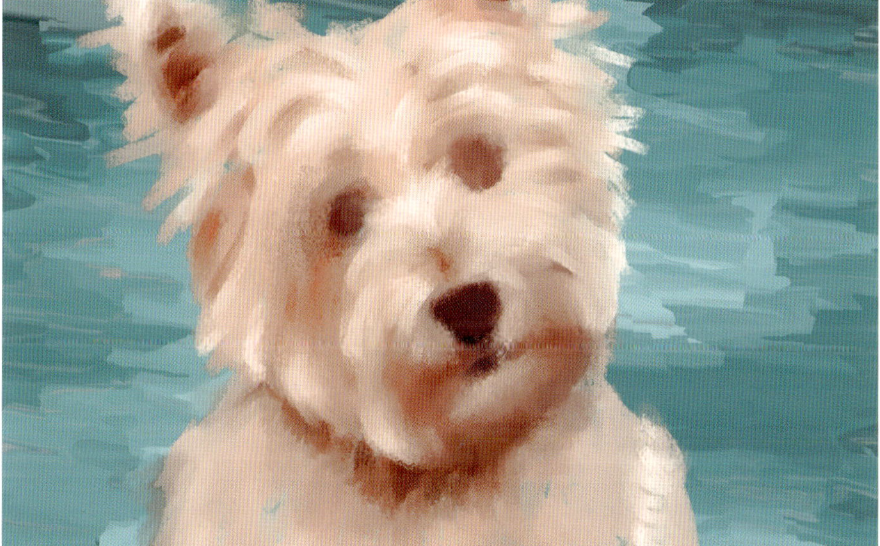

9 Change Colors

Make the dog more red-orange and the background more blue-green because these complementary colors create a more painterly result than using the photo's colors straight out of the box. I also decided to darken the background a little. To change the color and tone:

1. Choose Effects: Tonal Control: Adjust Selected Colors. The Adjust Selected Colors dialog appears.
2. Click on an area in the image.
3. Click and drag in the Preview till you see the same area.
4. Move the Hue Shift slider to adjust colors; move the Value slider to alter tones. Click OK.

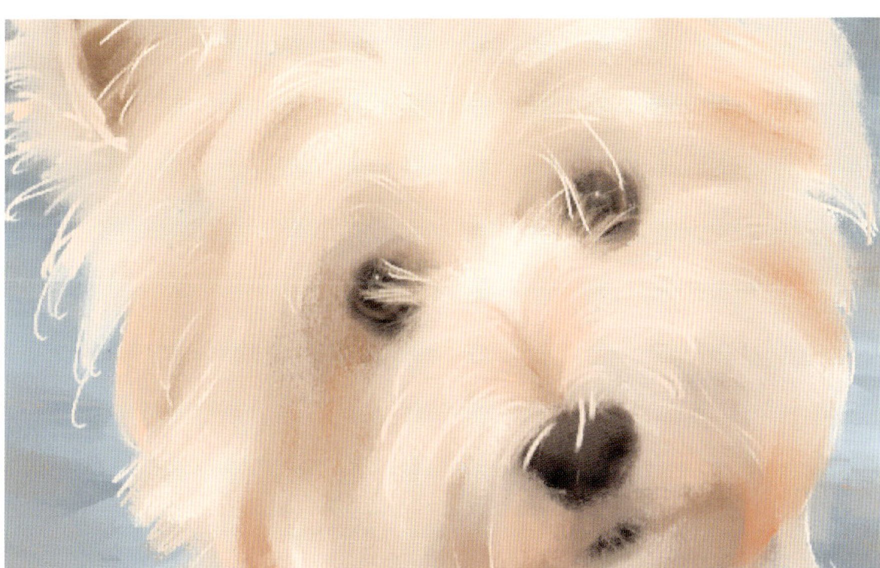

10 Final Steps

Continue to build up tones with the Square Chalk and blend with the Smudge.

Use the Cloners' Soft Cloner to paint in the eyes, nose and mouth.

Switch to the Chalk's Sharp Chalk and draw some lines to suggest hair strands where you see them in the photo. Blend a tad with the Square Chalk blender that you just created.

Add red-orange to the background with the Square Chalk for color harmony. Last, crop with Painter's crop tool. After you select the area you want to keep, click inside the selection to crop. Check page 108 to see how I cropped the final image.

PAINTING CATS

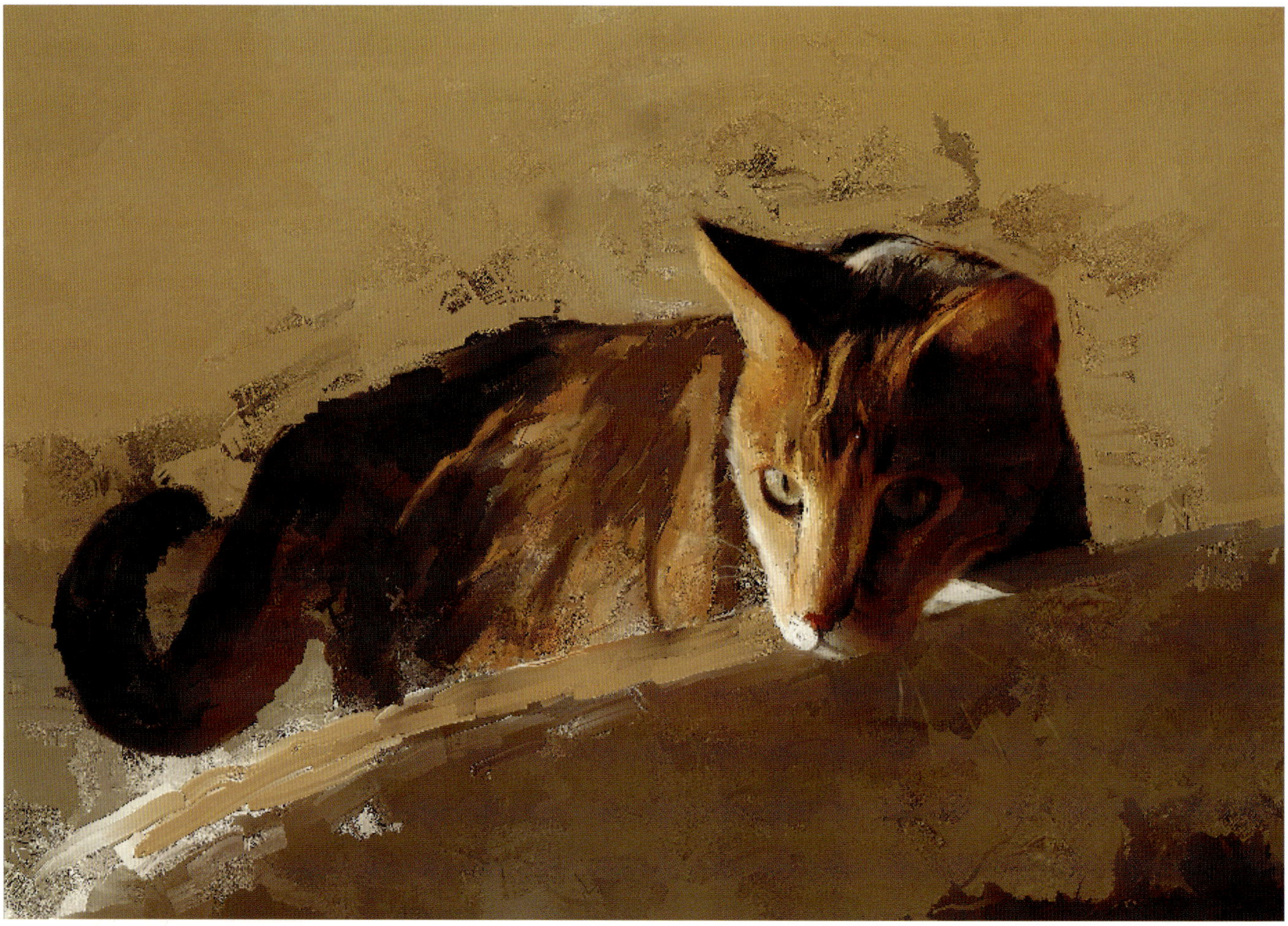

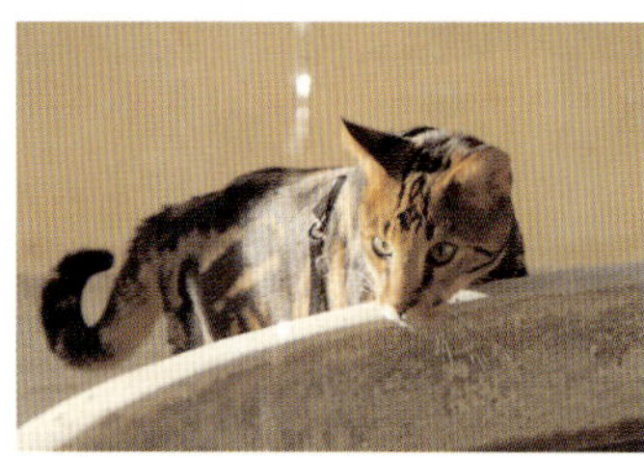

Cat Portrait
Photo and painting by Karen Sperling.

I took this photo on a hot day here in southern California. It was late afternoon, a great time for stark contrasts with tons of highlights and shadows created by the setting sun.

The star of the photo shoot, Norton, the cat, was hiding in the plants in the shade.

We tried to coax him into the sunlight with his toys, but he was no fool.

Finally, as luck would have it, Norton noticed the fountain, which was in the sun, and pouring water. He ventured out of the shade to take a look. I got my photo! It had good composition, and the tones were right for a painting. Part of the face was in light, part was in shadow, and the body, background and fountain all had interesting lights and darks. All this contrast would lend itself to a painting. Of course, it helped that the expression was very cute—cat stalking its prey—a metaphor for me as the photographer stalking mine! It didn't matter that the photo was slightly out of focus because when I painted, the brush strokes would be in focus.

Another good thing about this photo were the colors—they were all in the yellow-orange family, making them useful for the painting.

To start, open the photo in Painter (File: Open). Choose File: Clone and name the clone (File: Save As).

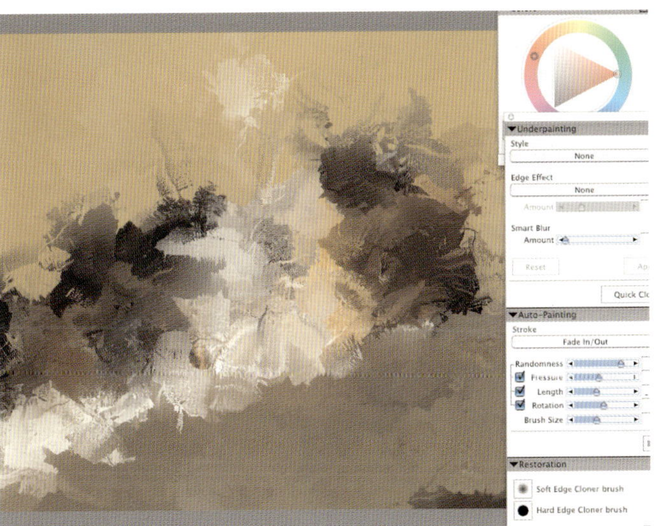

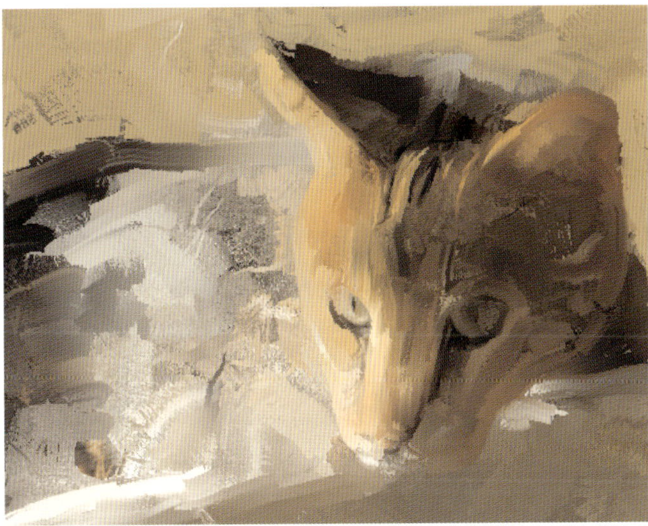

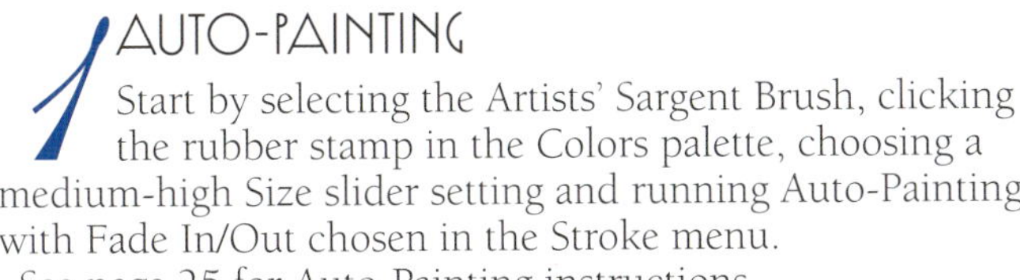

1 AUTO-PAINTING

Start by selecting the Artists' Sargent Brush, clicking the rubber stamp in the Colors palette, choosing a medium-high Size slider setting and running Auto-Painting with Fade In/Out chosen in the Stroke menu.

See page 25 for Auto-Painting instructions.

2 DETAIL

Turn on Tracing Paper and with the Sargent Brush still selected, lower the Size slider and paint details.

Click the rubber stamp in the Colors palette to paint colors from the photo and deselect to choose colors.

Turn Tracing Paper off and then on again frequently to check your progress. See page 27 for Tracing Paper steps.

Paint with the Cloners' Soft Cloner a little to add some detail in the face.

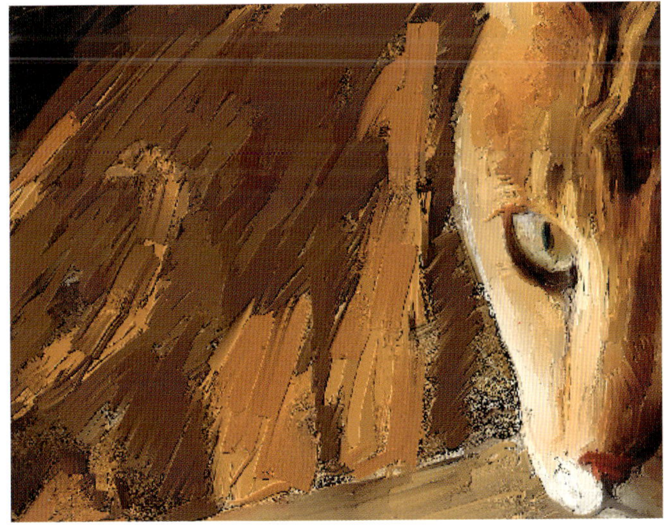

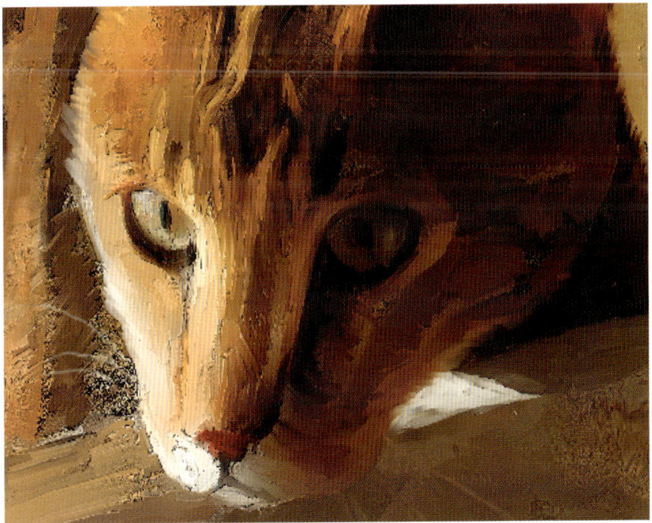

3 TEXTURE

To add some texture to the brush strokes, choose Effects: Surface Control: Apply Surface Texture with Image Luminance chosen in the Using menu.

Paint yellow-orange with the Digital Watercolors' New Simple Water on a low opacity on the gray part on the body to warm it up a bit.

After painting with Digital Watercolors, choose Layers: Dry Digital Watercolor.

4 FUR

To create fur around the head, lower the Size slider in the Property Bar and paint little strokes with the Sargent Brush with the rubber stamp selected in the Colors palette.

Paint a hint of whiskers using the Soft Cloner on a low Size slider setting.

PAINTING HORSES

I went to the Traditional Equitation School in Burbank, CA, to take a photo to paint for this book.

I had in mind a photo of a horse running free, but since it was a school, the horses that were out and about had riders.

I went to the stalls and looked around. All the horses were in shadow, till I rounded a corner, and there was this horse, with the sun shining brightly on his face.

I waited till he turned his head, and now the light face was contrasted with the dark wood—I had my photo!

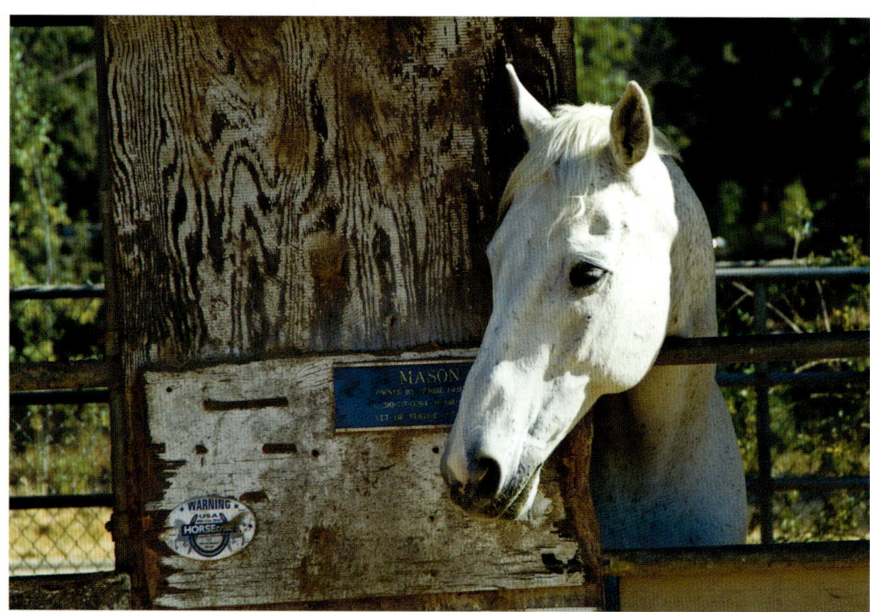

Start by opening the photo in Photoshop. Choose Image: Duplicate and name this copy (File: Save As) to keep the original. Crop the copy to include just the horse and the wood panel. Save—this is your new source image—then duplicate—this is your painting. With the Magnetic Lasso tool, select the horse and make it into a layer (see page 36 for instructions).

In Image menu: Adjustments, use Hue/Saturation, Color Balance and Selective Color to edit the head, then the background, creating a red/red-orange/green/blue-green color scheme. File: Save As in the .psd format.

See pages 12-13 for information about choosing a color scheme.

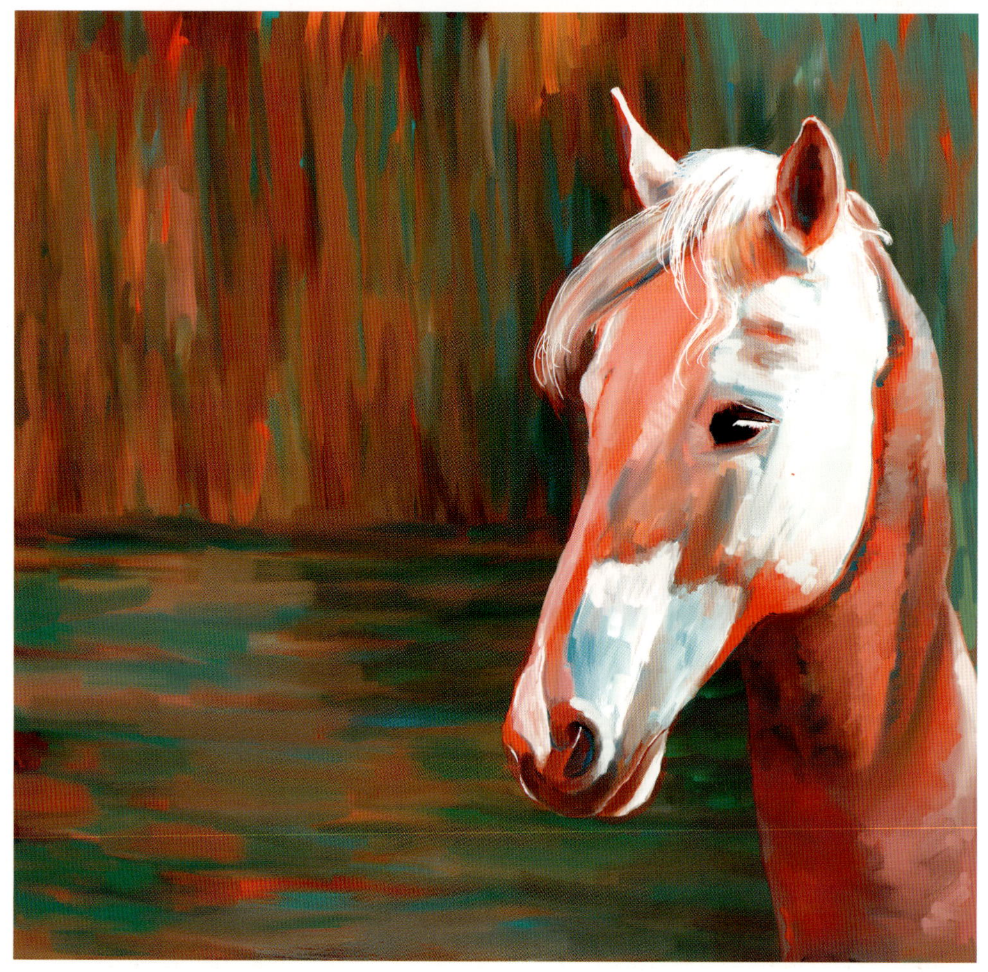

Horse Portrait

Painting by Karen Sperling from her photo taken at the Traditional Equitation School, Burbank, CA.

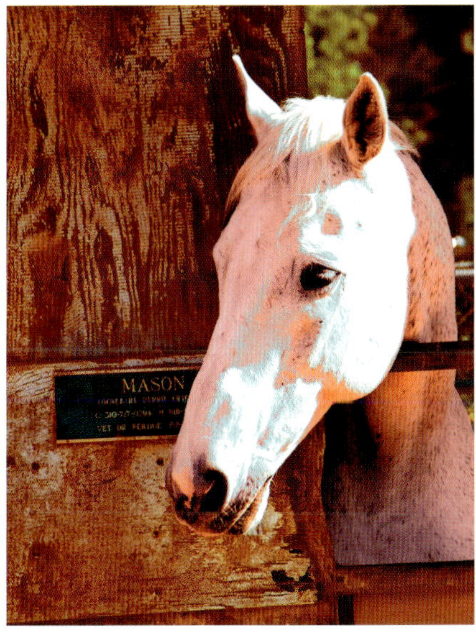

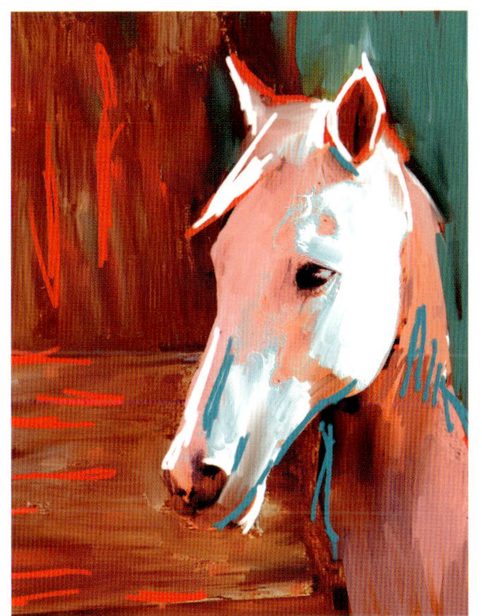

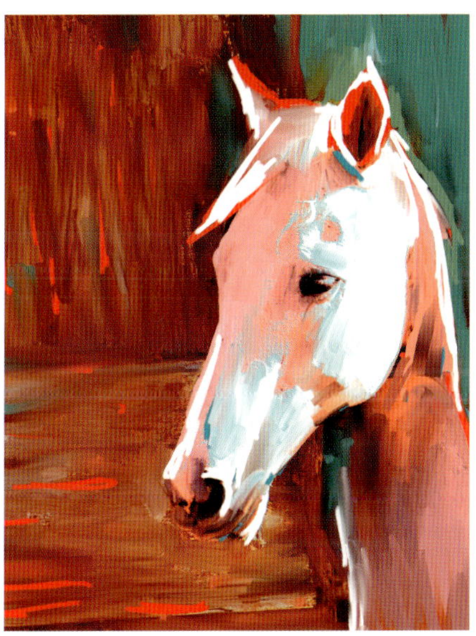

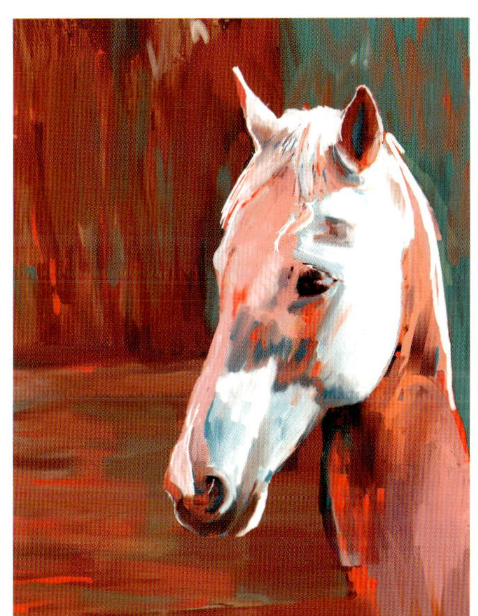

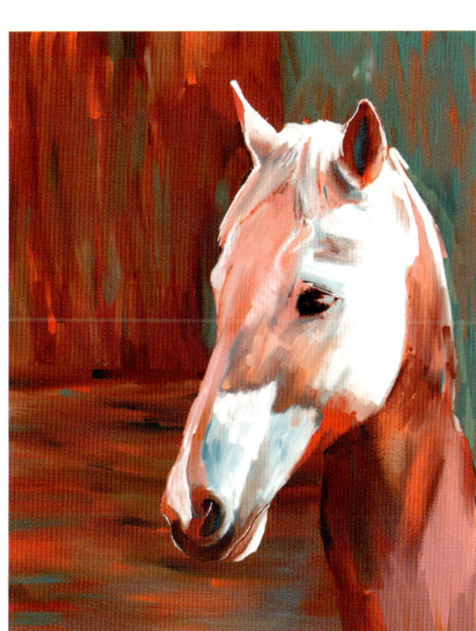

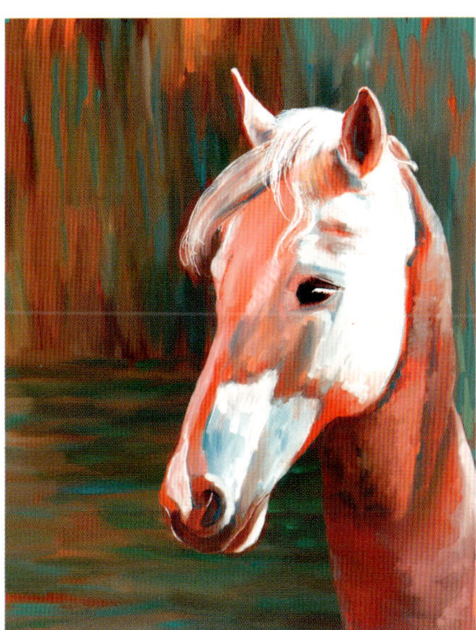

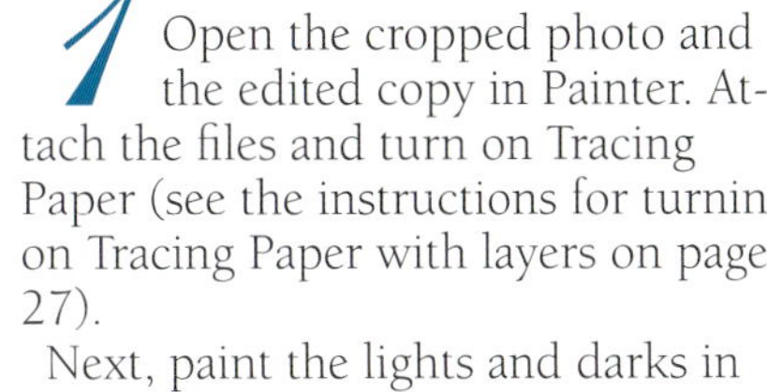

1 COME TO LIGHT

Open the cropped photo and the edited copy in Painter. Attach the files and turn on Tracing Paper (see the instructions for turning on Tracing Paper with layers on page 27).

Next, paint the lights and darks in the image using these brushes:

Pens' Scratchboard Tool for outlines.

Acrylics' Captured Bristle for wide areas of solid color.

Artists' Oils' Blender Bristle for blending strokes.

RealBristle Brushes' Real Oils Short for bristly brush strokes—lower the Feature slider in the Property Bar for solid strokes, raise it for more bristles.

2 LIFT OFF

Paint color with either the Scratchboard Tool (the white outlines) or the Captured Bristle (the red strokes in the wood) and then blend them with the Blender Bristle and Real Oils Short variants.

The Blender Bristle and Real Oils Short variants work in a similar way: You paint and lift, paint and lift, to get pure color, and you scribble to blend the colors. The red strokes on the neck are examples of painting and lifting with the Blender Bristle.

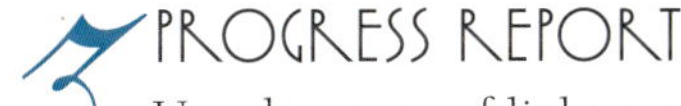

3 PROGRESS REPORT

Use the areas of light and dark in the edited photo to guide you in the painting.

The illustrations on this page show the progression as I built up the colors and tones based on the lights and darks in the edited photo.

Notice how much more interesting the face and neck looked as the darks and lights became more emphasized.

Use the Scratchboard Tool on a low size setting and the Real Oils Short on a high feature setting to paint the mane.

At the end, use Levels in Photoshop to add contrast.

Add green/blue-green next to the horse by editing the brush strokes using Hue/Saturation, Color Balance and Selective Color in Photoshop.

That's how I created a horse of a different color in Painter and Photoshop!

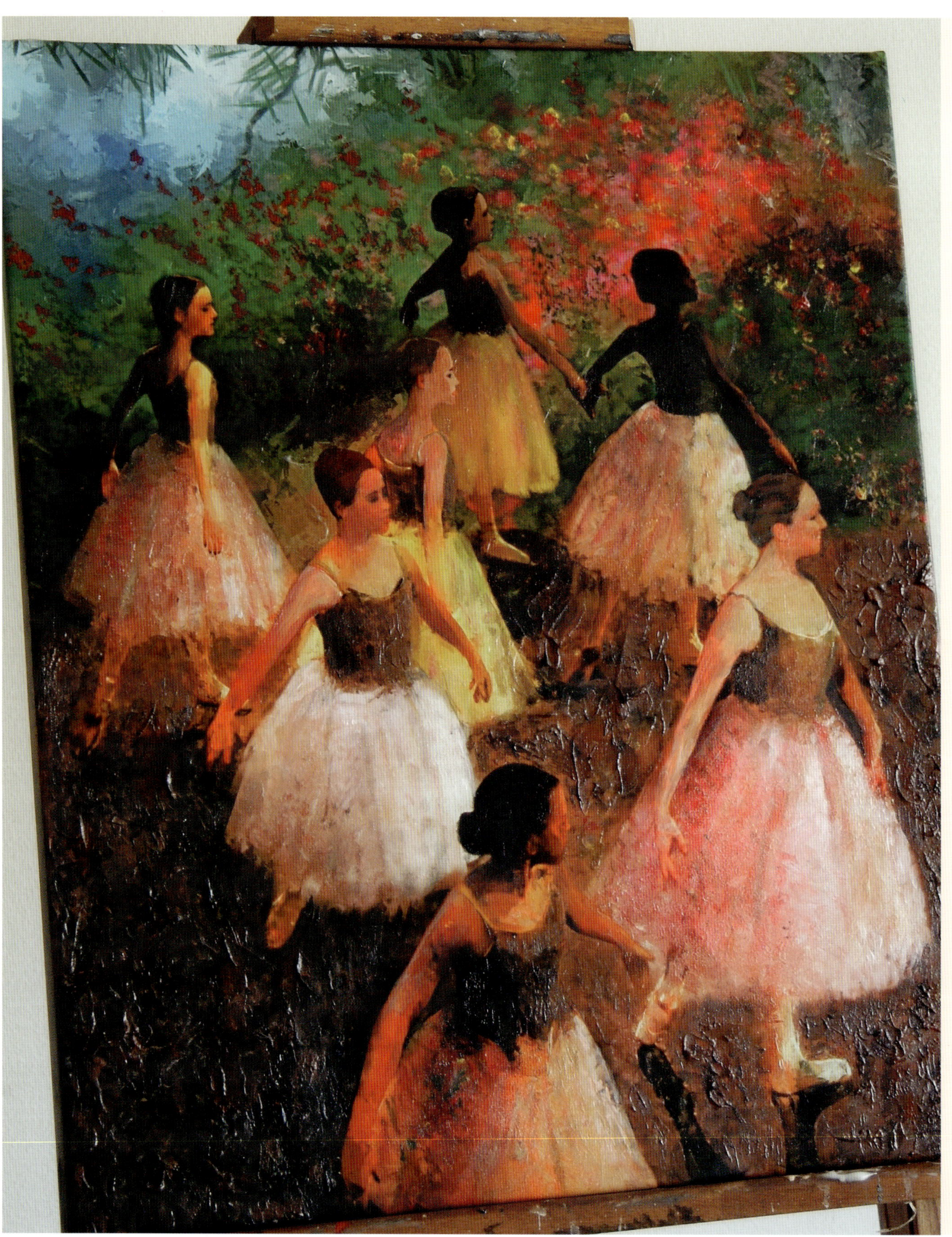

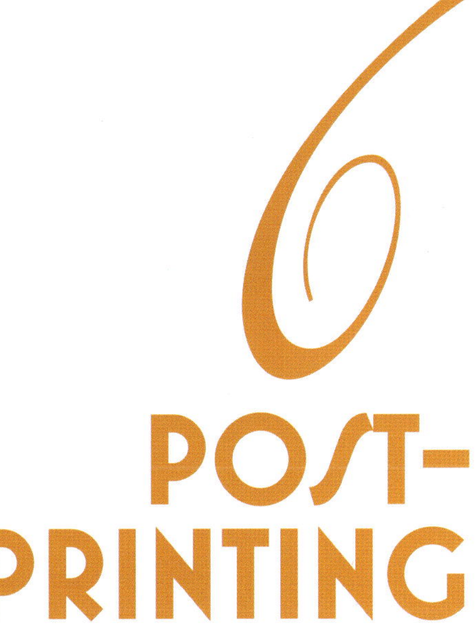

POST-PRINTING

The subject of printing—and all of the considerations about printers, inks and papers—is a vast one, and beyond the scope of this book. Besides, there are already plenty of sources for these topics, both in print and online.

Not as widely covered is the subject of painting on top of the printed canvas, a technique that is gaining in popularity.

This section covers how to apply paint to the canvas after it's printed.

Of course, you can print to watercolor-type paper instead, and you don't have to add paint to canvas prints.

But if you want to paint on canvas after it's printed, this section is for you.

The following chapters will help you get started with painting with traditional media.

Meanwhile, get some canvas boards in an art store and play around with acrylics and oils to get comfortable with them before trying to paint on printed canvas.

I find painting both on the computer and with traditional paint is more about confidence than anything. Getting used to the materials will help you feel more confident.

Remember: If you think you can paint with traditional media, you probably can!

Print

This is a print of the Degas Dancers painting. It's 20" × 24" × 1.50", one of the most popular sizes for canvas prints. The printer was Jacksonville, IL-based J Vee Graphics www.jveegraphics.com. Painting by Karen Sperling from a photo by Felicia Tausig. Photo of canvas print by Karen Sperling.

Applying a First Coat

You have painted your photo in Corel Painter or Adobe Photoshop.

The next step is to print to canvas.

Canvas is the most popular choice for printing out paintings from photos because then you can apply acrylic or oil paints on top of the print.

Photographers have two choices for printed canvases: Either send the files to an outside printing source, or buy a printer and do the printing themselves.

Printing yourself might be more cost-effective monetarily, but you pay the price in terms of quality and time. If you want to print yourself, be ready to not only learn how to do the printing, but also how to do the post-printing.

After the print comes out of the printer, you have to apply a protective coating, whether you're going to hang the print as is or paint on it with acrylics or oils.

I asked three professional printers with whom I've worked what the do-it-yourselfer should do to the canvas after it's printed.

The first thing to do once the print is out of the printer is to let it "cure" or dry for at least 24 hours, says J Vee of Jacksonville, IL-based J Vee Graphics.

"By 'curing' I simply mean drying at room temperature next to a fan set to low. This lets the colors and tones truly stabilize" as well as allowing the surface to accept whatever you apply next, says J Vee.

The next step is to apply a protective coating.

"The easiest method of finishing a canvas is to spray it with a preservative, usually acrylic based," says Alan Zarter of Lawrenceville, GA. "The purpose of the spray is to add durability and display life to the print. I use PremierArt Print Shield, which doesn't alter the look of the print," notes Zarter.

"You can also use Krylon matte, satin, or glossy finishes. Whichever you choose, make sure it is compatible with your canvas and ink and that it also has what are known as UV inhibitors to lessen the long-term effects of exposure to light because your canvas will not be displayed behind glass."

Santa Monica, CA-based Jack Duganne, who invented the term giclée, counsels the do-it-yourselfer to either "use a spray coating like Krylon Workable Fixatif from your local art store or get water based PremierArt ECO Print Shield and roll it on with a foam roller."

Spraying first makes the rolling easier, but it isn't necessary, adds Duganne.

Sprays

Here's a look at the protective coating sprays. Photo by Karen Sperling.

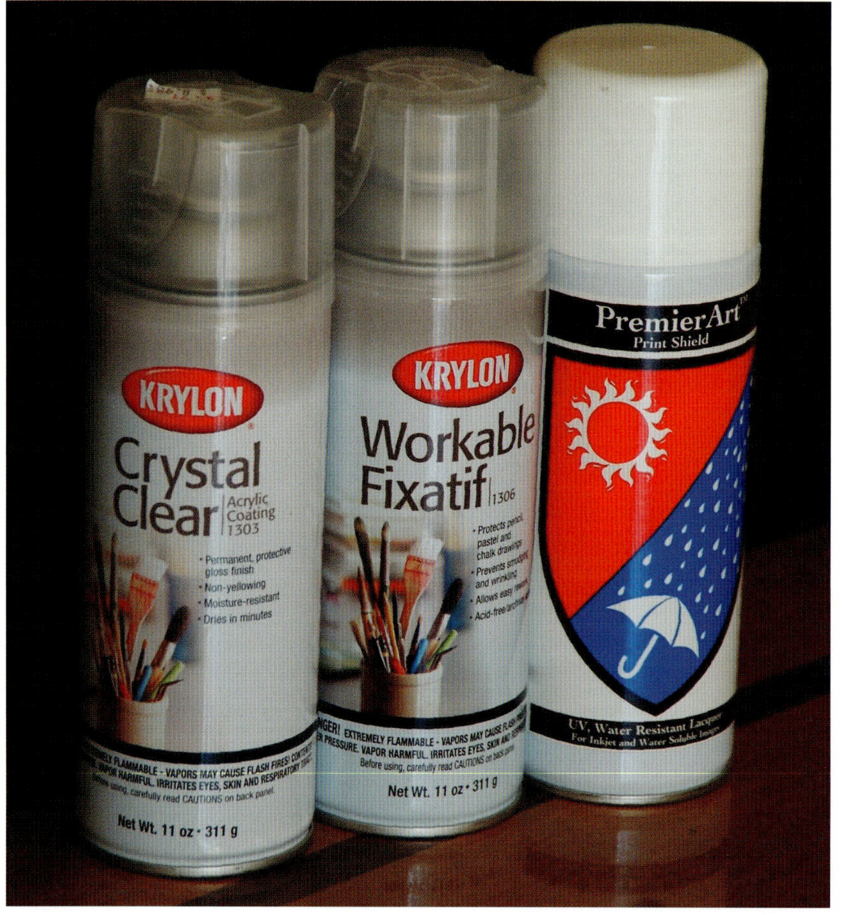

"I've done it both ways and just recently discovered that spraying first was easier, but both ways—spraying first, or just using the roller—work exceptionally well."

Meanwhile, I've used both Krylon Crystal Clear, which is a glossy acrylic coating spray and the PremierArt Print Shield spray.

Using these sprays isn't as simple as you may think.

As Zarter notes, they're smelly and get in your lungs.

I sprayed small portions of a canvas one at a time, letting each one dry, to minimize the amount of spray flying around the room. This can get pretty tedious, though, for a 30" by 40" canvas, which is a common size nowadays.

I have then painted on the sprayed areas after they were dry with good results, so really, this is all you need to know to print your own canvases.

But the canvases I've gotten back from the professionals have an extra depth or feel to them because of additional steps after this first protective coat, or instead of it, not including the actual enhancing of the canvas with acrylic or oil paints.

J Vee, for instance, uses a spray gun found in body shops to apply three coats of varnish after the spraying.

Zarter, meanwhile, will either spray or apply his "favorite finishing technique, which involves coating the canvas with a liquid acrylic either by hand with a roller or sprayed with a compressed-air sprayer."

One of the ways that Duganne treats canvases "is to silk-screen a photo-polymer UV coating onto the canvas pieces and run them through a UV reactor to polymerize and harden them. They are incredibly durable this way and the level of gloss to matte can be controlled extremely well."

The bottom line is, the post-printing process can be as easy as letting the print dry and spraying it, or as complex as having it printed professionally and coated by hand, varnished or silk-screened.

I think you can "get away" with doing it yourself the simple way, but either getting the canvas printed professionally, or learning to do a professional job yourself, will show in the quality of the result.

The experts quoted in this chapter and the next one include:

J Vee-J Vee Graphics
Jacksonville, IL
www.jveegraphics.com
Jack Duganne - Duganne Ateliers
Santa Monica, CA
http://www.duganne.com
Alan Zarter-Alan Zarter Fine Art
Lawrenceville, GA
www.azfineart.com

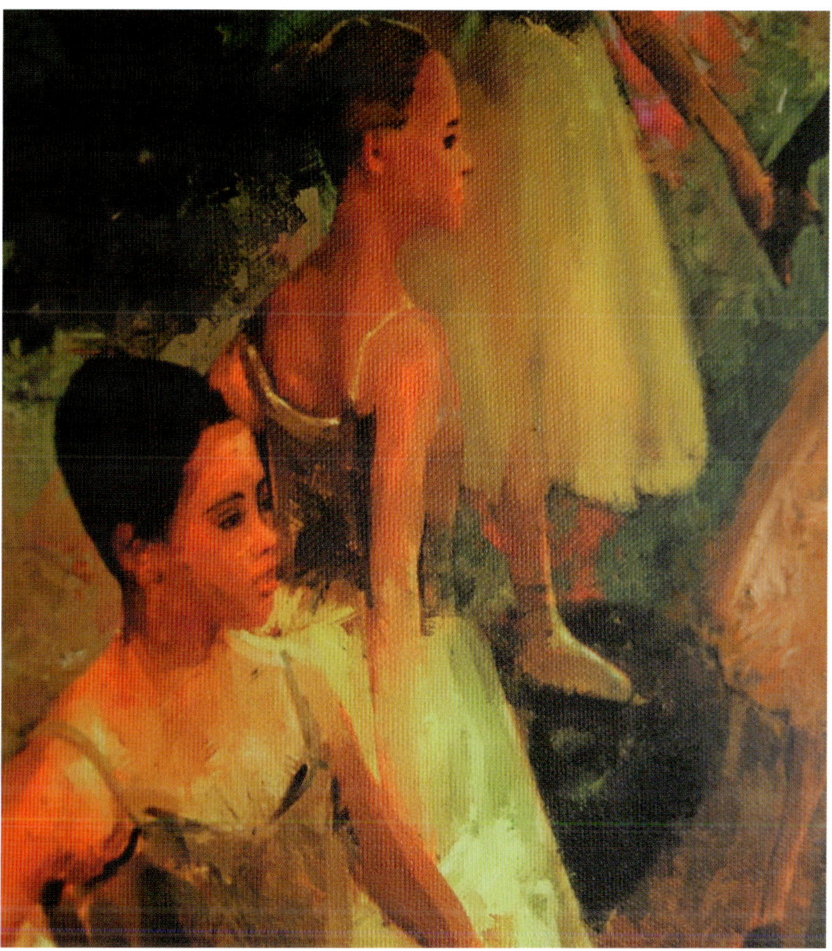

First Look

Here's what the canvas looked like when it arrived from the printer, J Vee Graphics. Painting by Karen Sperling from a photo by Felicia Tausig. Photo of the printed canvas by Karen Sperling.

PAINTING WITH ACRYLICS

I love painting with acrylics.

They're versatile and forgiving.

Make a mistake and wipe it off the canvas with a wet paper towel or rag.

Just do it before the paint dries.

Painting with acrylics, you can paint with any object, paint with any thickness. Brush strokes can be flat or raised.

Throw in tinsel, confetti, sparkles, anything, the acrylic is like glue and everything sticks.

You can paint with brushes or anything that will make a mark.

Brushes range in price depending on whether the hairs are synthetic, natural or a combination of the two.

When you're starting out, you can get by with the less expensive variety.

I have some synthetic brushes, some natural ones and some combinations of the two.

Besides brushes, I use anything else that will create an effect. In fact, for me, like Jean Dubuffet, the abstract expressionist who was one of the early users of acrylics and loved to experiment with them, half the fun is coming up with a new look with a new device.

In addition to brushes and rollers, I've used palette knives; the ridges of cardboard ripped in half; combs; natural sponges; toothbrushes; plastic trowels; paint scrapers; spatulas; credit cards; car windshield scrapers; squeegees; icing applicators; and squeeze bottles.

I have also used clear plastic wrap to rub on acrylics to get a wavy effect like water.

Acrylics are not just added to canvas, but also subtracted.

While paint is still wet, moisten a natural sponge, or a paper towel, and then dab the canvas—some of the paint comes off and some is left behind, creating an interesting textured effect.

Let the paint dry a little and then wipe it up with a wet cloth or paper towel—some remains and some is lifted, leaving

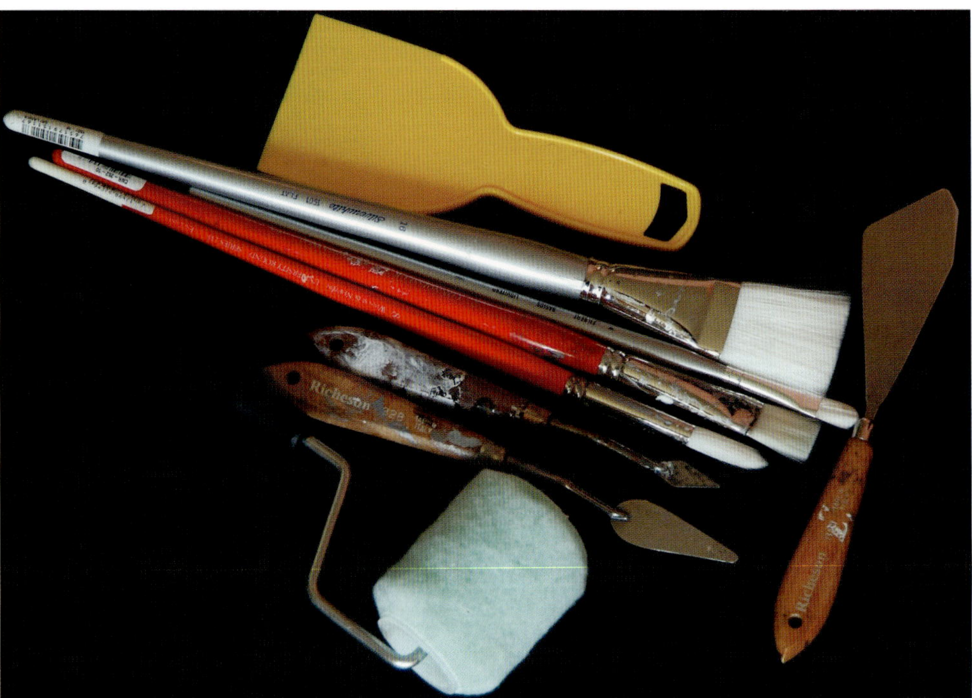

Painting Tools

Use ice scrapers, brushes, rollers, palette knives—anything—to paint with acrylics. Photo by Karen Sperling.

a cool, unique texture.

Use sgraffito, a painting technique where you scratch designs into the wet paint to reveal what's beneath it with something sharp like the other end of a paint brush.

Other things you'll need for painting are rags, paper towels, water, a drop cloth and masking tape to mask off areas to protect them.

Cover an area with masking tape, paint the area next to it, remove the tape, repeat—the result is an unusual work of art. To paint straight lines, apply tape, paint overlapping it, remove the tape.

Make sure you wash painting tools right after you use them.

Acrylics dry quickly, so you can't leave things with acrylics on them, especially brushes—the paint will dry and the brushes will be ruined.

I use plain soap and water and a little dab of a brush cleaner from an art supply store, any one will do, really. When you clean a brush, hold out one hand and push the brush into your palm several times. This releases built up paint next to the ferrule (the metal thing) and makes the brush last longer. Wash with warm water, not hot; rinse with cold.

Next is the paint.

I use the acrylics that come in tubes. Golden and Liquitex are the best-known brands.

Then there's medium. Medium is the generic word for something you mix with the paint.

First, water is a medium for acrylics. You can thin out acrylics simply by mixing them with a little water.

Other, store-bought mediums come in various thicknesses.

Medium is also a product and it is the thinnest (following water, that is).

Gels are the thickest.

Medium comes in all sorts of varieties and thicknesses in between.

Art supply stores have sample cards with examples of all of the thicknesses.

Mediums also come in matte (no shine) and gloss (shine).

I mix matte and gloss mediums because I like a semi-gloss effect.

You'll need something to pour medium into and to mix with paint. You can get a palette in the art store, or you can use old dishes. Sometimes I use plastic plates bought at the grocery store. You'll also need an easel. I got an inexpensive one, but they have big furniture-like expensive ones, too. They also have tabletop easels.

OK, you have all the materials, you're ready to paint.

If you just want to add a coat of shiny paint, do what Jack Duganne and Alan Zarter recommend.

"My favorite finishing technique involves coating the canvas with a liquid acrylic," says Zarter.

"I use Glamour II Giclée Veneer from Breathing Color. I apply the liquid with a roller, but it can also be applied with a brush or compressed-air sprayer depending on the volume you are coating and the finish you prefer. You can choose finishes from matte to glossy or mix them as I do to achieve just the finish you like."

Jack Duganne uses a similar technique to coat the canvas.

Mediums

Mediums come in different thicknesses and in either gloss or matte. Use them by themselves or add to acrylic paint. Mixing the various mediums creates unique effects. Photo by Karen Sperling.

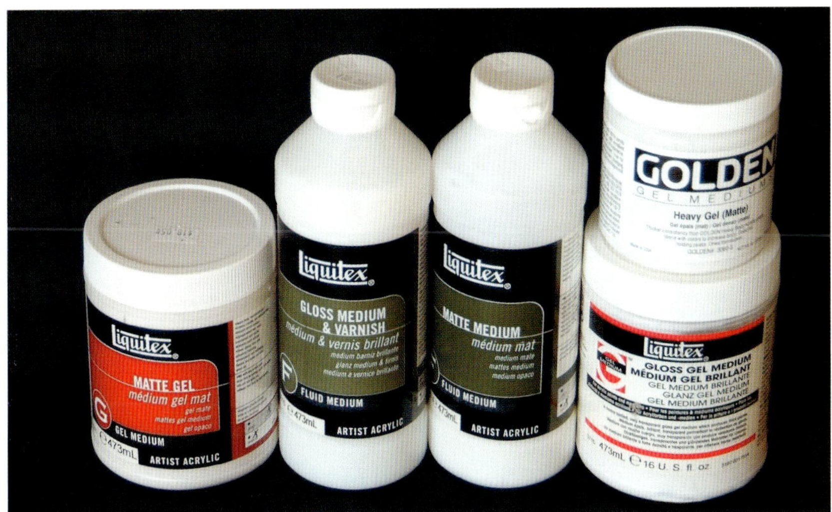

"If you are just interested in putting a nice gloss or satin finish, I would suggest getting the water based Premier Art ECO Print Shield. You can get the coating in gloss, satin or matte and I have found that the best satin is achieved by mixing half gloss and half satin to create a great eggshell finish," Duganne says. "Roll it on with a foam roller. The best rollers are the ones from a house painting supply store that sells packs of six. They have a roller bearing core which allows the coating to go on smoothly without the roller sticking and dragging on the print." To get the best result, "roll one coat one way and then, while it is still wet, keep rolling the other way and then back to the first direction and back and forth until the print seems fairly even and smooth," Duganne notes. "You don't have to worry about leaving ridges because they all dry out smoothly in that you are essentially just letting the weight of the roller itself be the only pressure on the piece as you roll."

He adds, "the coating also comes in a spray can if you wish to go that route."

If you want more than just a flat finish, that's where the painting comes in.

What follows are examples of the kinds of things you can do with acrylics.

You can choose any or all of them and in any combination. Don't be afraid to experiment. You'll eventually find the effects that you like best.

CLEAR BRUSH STROKES

One way to add texture to the printed canvas is to paint clear brush strokes.

Use gloss medium or matte medium, or a combination of the two.

Use plain medium for flat strokes and gel medium for tall strokes. Mix them together for strokes in between. Paint a combination of heights for variety.

Apply the medium with one of the previously mentioned tools or one that you find works well for you.

You can stop at this step if you like the result, or you can go to the next one. And by the way, you can use this step alone or in combination with any of the next steps as a basis for oil painting, covered in the next chapter.

TRANSLUCENT BRUSH STROKES

Add acrylic paint to medium and paint translucent strokes with a brush.

You can either paint colors where you see your highlights and shadows, or you can ignore the highlights and shadows and add brush strokes abstractly.

Or you can add a glaze, which is a coat of paint over an area of the painting or the whole thing.

OPAQUE BRUSH STROKES

Paint undiluted paint with a brush either as tones based on what's already on the canvas, or add strokes in a more abstract way, ignoring the canvas imagery.

First Coat

Mix gloss and matte gel and paint textured strokes on the background with a brush. Photo by Karen Sperling.

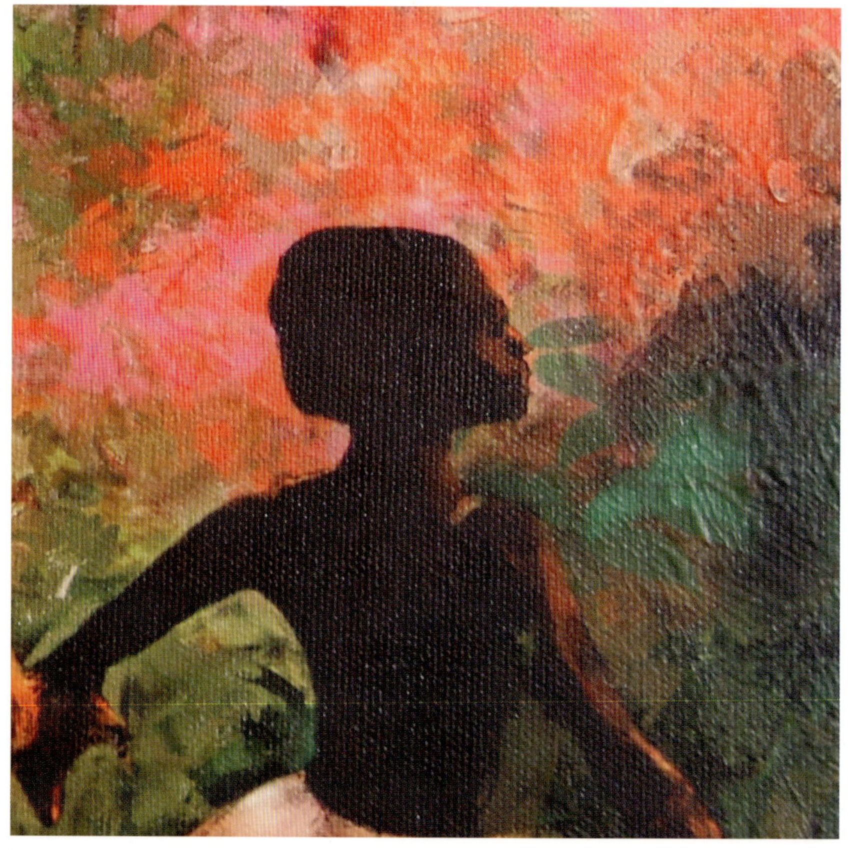

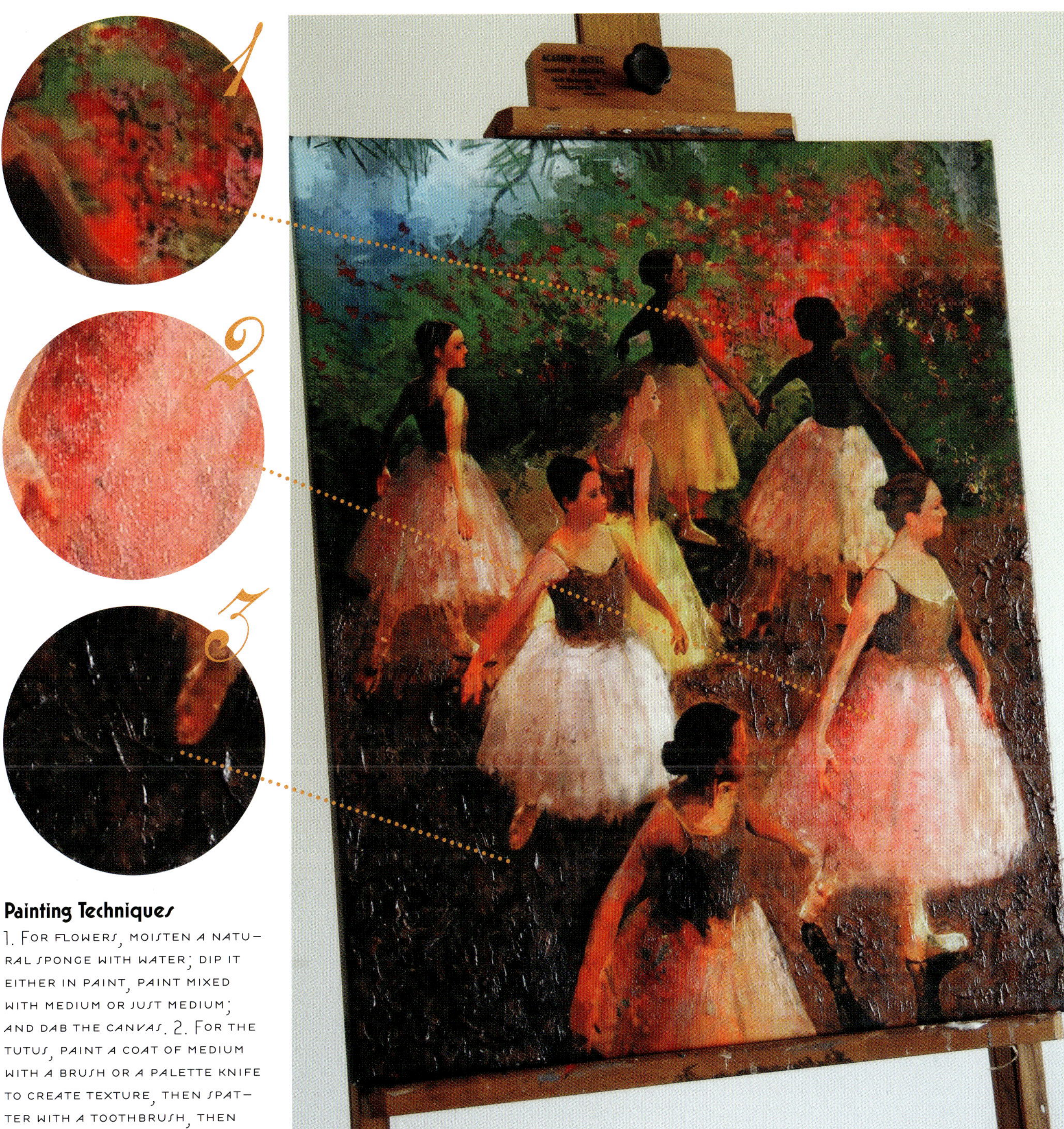

Painting Techniques
1. For flowers, moisten a natural sponge with water; dip it either in paint, paint mixed with medium or just medium; and dab the canvas. 2. For the tutus, paint a coat of medium with a brush or a palette knife to create texture, then spatter with a toothbrush, then dab on highlights with the sponge. Let each coat dry before doing the next one. 3. For the floor, paint a coat of gloss super heavy gel medium using swooshy strokes with a palette knife. After they dry, dab paint on with the sponge. Photo by Karen Sperling.

Accent Brush Strokes

An interesting accent and one of my favorites is spattered paint. Mix acrylics with water to make them watery, dip a toothbrush in the resulting "soup," hold the toothbrush next to the canvas, and run your finger along the toothbrush, spattering color on the canvas.

The best technique of all is to use all of the above and create a unique artwork.

These are just some examples of some of the things you can do with acrylics on your canvas.

The joy is to come up with your own ideas, effects and looks. Have fun!

PAINTING WITH OILS

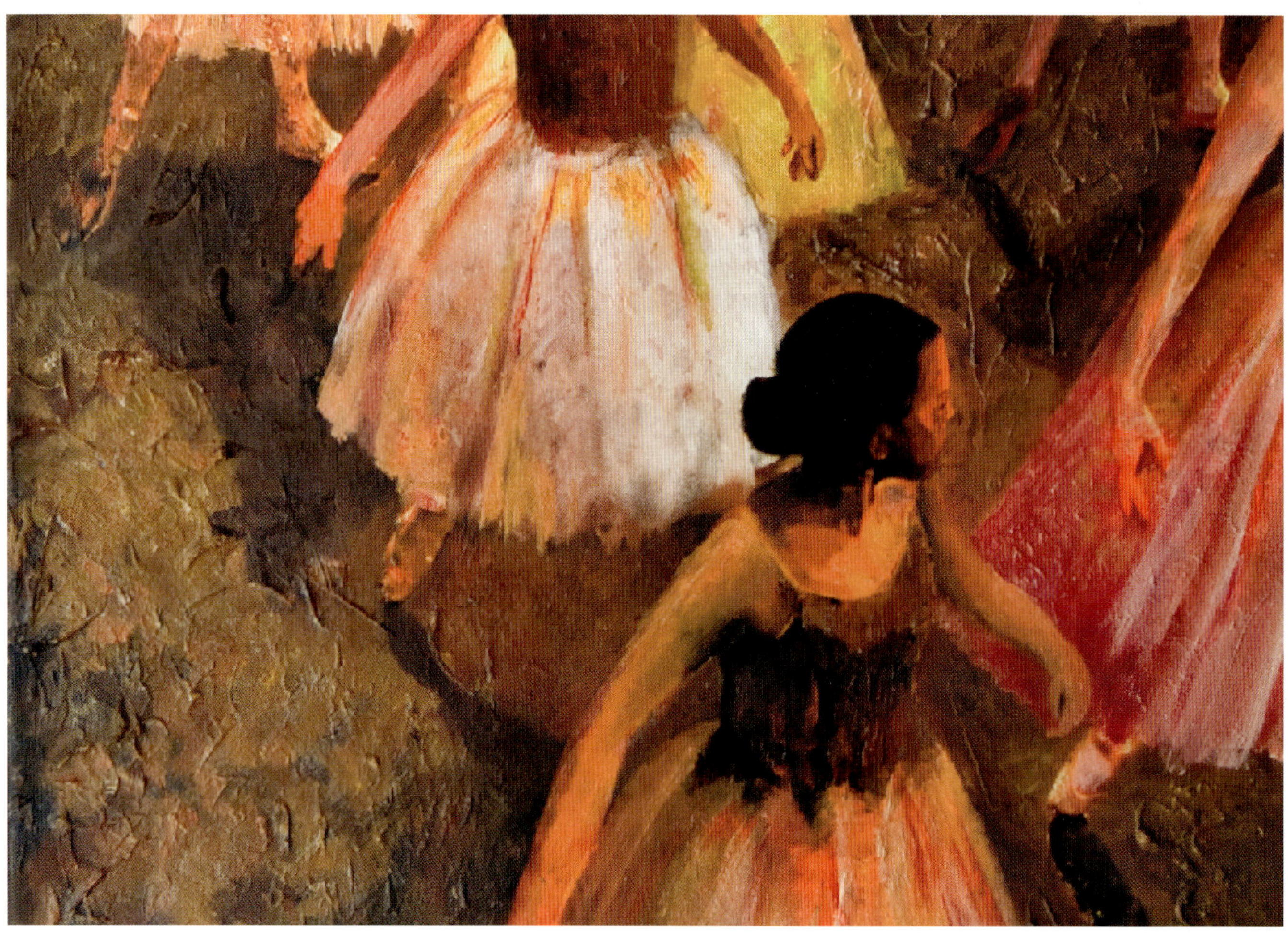

Oil Painting

Paint oils on acrylics, but don't paint acrylics on oils. Paint tones with the oils using the photo as your guide—compare the floor and tutus in this version with the one on page 123. The highlights and shadows have been enhanced in this version. Photo by Karen Sperling.

I painted with oils in the last century, and then didn't touch them again until last year, when I exhibited my art during Art Basel Miami—the gallery with whom I showed wanted my work to be done in oils.

As a result, I did a lot of research, and came up with a basic workflow.

Painting with oils is trickier than painting with acrylics because it's possible the oils on the canvas will eventually crack if you're not careful.

The guidelines in this chapter are what I found out during my research, and if you follow them, your paintings will be fine!

Before you paint on the print with oils, you need to apply several coats of paint to seal the print to prevent the ink from running and to avoid the oils bleeding into the canvas. This is normally a job for gesso, but you can use the coatings and acrylics discussed in the previous chapters as this base coat.

Be sure to have several coats, including the first one where you spray the canvas with a fixative, and allow plenty of time in between coats so that the acrylics are dry before you start painting with oils.

Depending on the thickness of the coats, a couple of days should be enough time.

You can't paint acrylics on top of oils, though, only oils on top of acrylics.

OK, so you have your canvas print with several coats of acrylics on it, and you're ready to paint with oils!

You need brushes and maybe palette

knives, if you enjoy them—I do!

You can use the soft brushes you got for acrylics for painting thin coats of oil paint. Get stiffer brushes like those made of hog hair to paint thicker coats of oil.

As for the oil paint, get artist grade, not student grade. Get the best brand your wallet will allow. The art store can guide you in your purchases, even if you order from online stores.

You'll also need a palette to mix colors—you can get a wooden one or you can get a pad of paper palette sheets.

And get metal cups at an art store, or use old cans, for cleaning brushes with turpenoid, a substance that has replaced turpentine nowadays.

Traditional artists like oils because of their slow drying time—several days and more—allowing for easier corrections because oils stay wet longer than acrylics, which dry quickly.

The down side is, oils are too slow for me—I like to see the results and move onto something else.

It's possible to speed up oils' drying times in a couple of ways.

The first is to use Winsor & Newton Griffin Alkyd fast-drying paint.

Another is to mix regular and fast-drying paint with a fast-drying medium called Liquin.

I have found that the quick-drying paint, and oils mixed with Liquin, dry in about 24 hours, while regular oils not mixed with anything take days to dry.

A traditional method for oil painting is to paint in layers.

To paint the painting on the opposite page, I did two coats.

I painted the first coat with oils mixed with turpenoid to thin them out. Mixing with turpenoid made the paint more fluid and easy to work with, but it didn't speed up drying time. It took several days for this first coat to dry. To check to see if the paint is dry, touch the canvas—it's dry when no paint comes off.

I painted the second coat with regular oils and fast-drying paint, both mixed with Liquin. This coat was thicker than the first coat, but dried more quickly.

For the first coat, squeeze out a little paint onto your palette. Pour a little turpenoid into a tin cup. Dip your brush in the cup, then dip your brush into your paint on your palette and paint.

Make sure you let this coat dry completely before you paint the next coat.

For the next coat, put some more paint on your palette with a little Liquin next to it, mix some paint and Liquin with your brush and add another coat.

Let this coat dry for about 24 hours, longer if you want to be sure it's dry.

You could add more coats of paint, but I painted just the two.

If you've read this book from the beginning through now, you have probably guessed that you're painting with the oils to emphasize the lights and darks in the painting.

I painted light and dark tones in the tutus, around the girls and in the floor.

I emphasized the light patterns in the floor, adding lighter paint to create the highlights and darker tones to enhance the shadows.

I also added colors and tones to the flowers in the back.

The first coat of oils established the tones better. The second coat also emphasized the tones, and additionally, added texture with thicker strokes.

See page 123 for the previous version.

Don't be afraid to paint with oils—they're very forgiving. You don't like a stroke that you painted? No problem—wipe it off with a rag and try again.

When done painting, rinse your brushes right away in turpenoid and then wash them with soap and water. Don't leave them lying around with paint in them because the paint will dry and ruin the brushes

Most important-have fun!

INDEX

INDEX

ABOUT THE AUTHOR

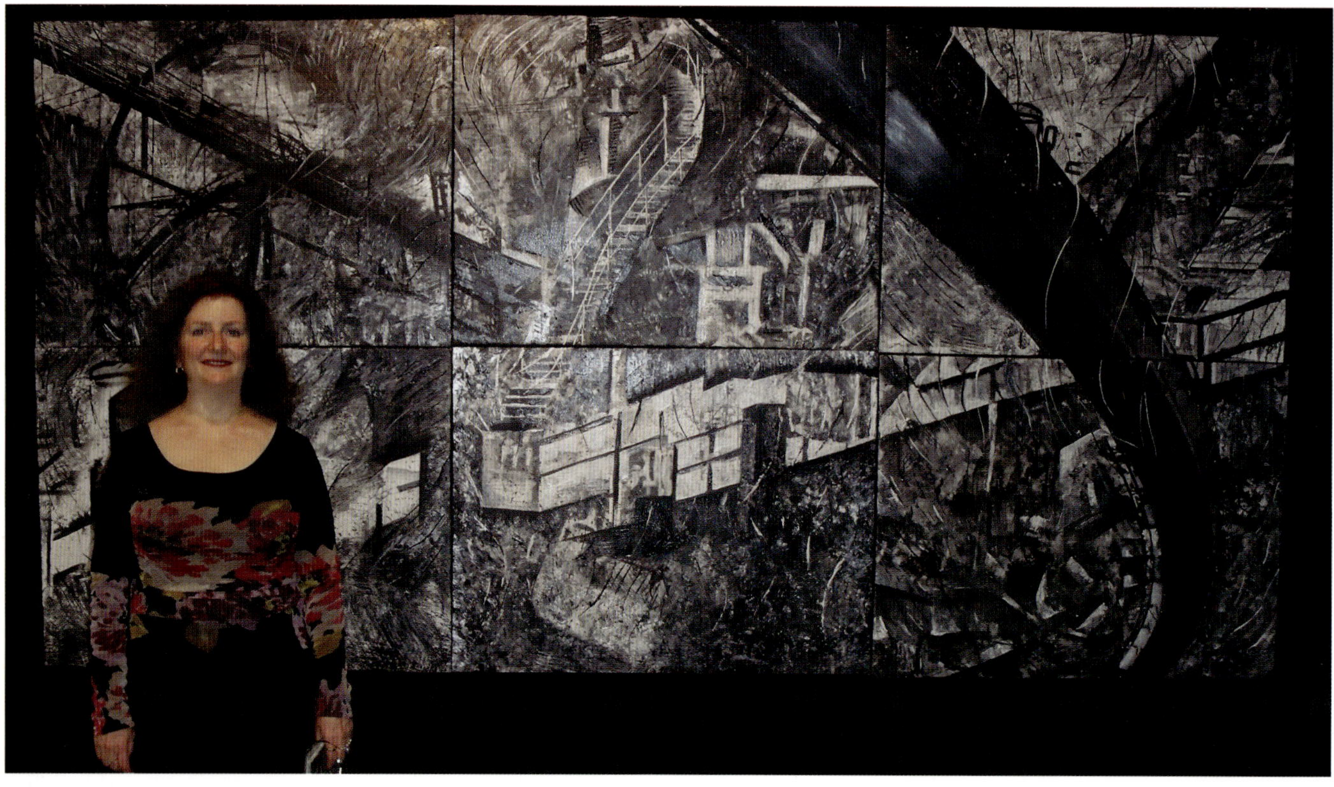

Magical Mystical Tours
Karen Sperling with her painting, Magical Mystical Tour #15, on display during Art Basel Miami.

Karen Sperling wrote the first Painter manual when the program debuted in 1991.

She went on to write the manuals for the next several versions of Painter and wrote several published Painter books.

Painting for Photographers is her fourth Painter book.

A graduate of Ithaca College, Karen has been a journalist for 30+ years, having worked freelance and on staff as a writer and as an editor for various magazines and newspapers.

Karen published the first printed Painter magazine, Artistry, and the first Painter e-zine, Artistry Tips and Tricks.

Karen's Painter tutorials have appeared in many publications including SBS Design, PEI magazine, Professional Photographers magazine and Rangefinder.

Karen has taught Painter for over 18 years all over the United States at companies such as Disney and American Greetings, and at institutions including the New School for Social Research in New York. She has given Painter talks and demonstrations at American Film Institute, Macworld, Seybold, SIGGRAPH, Professional Photographers of America and WPPI.

Karen creates abstract art both in Painter and with traditional media, and she has associations with galleries in Los Angeles, New York and London.

A photographer and an artist since childhood, Karen has exhibited her abstracts in New York's prestigious Chelsea section and during Art Basel Miami.

Her commissioned portraits and art are held in private collections internationally. Her fine art site is http://www.karensperling.com and her tutorials site is http://www.artistrymag.com/.